This collection of essays, by a distinguished international group of scholars, explores the world of Vienna and the development of opera buffa in the second half of the eighteenth century. Although today Mozart remains the best-known figure of the period, he was part of a lively operatic scene, involving not only composers, but librettists, patrons, impresarios, singers and, not least, audiences. The topics examined include the relationship of Viennese opera buffa to French theatre; Mozart and eighteenth-century comedy; gender, nature, and bourgeois society on Mozart's buffa stage; as well as close analyses of key works such as *Don Giovanni* and *Le nozze di Figaro*.

CAMBRIDGE STUDIES IN OPERA

Series editor: Arthur Groos

Volumes for *Cambridge Studies in Opera* explore the cultural, political, and social influences of the genre. As a cultural art form, opera is not produced in a vacuum. Rather, it is influenced, whether directly or in more subtle ways, by its social and political environment. In turn, opera leaves its mark on society and contributes to shaping the cultural climate. Studies to be included in the series will look at these various relationships including the politics and economics of opera, the operatic representation of women or the singers who portrayed them, the history of opera as theatre, and the evolution of the opera house.

Opera buffa in Mozart's Vienna

Edited by Mary Hunter and James Webster

CAMBRIDGE
UNIVERSITY PRESS

OF THE UNIVERSITY OF CAMBRIDGE

Cambridge, United Kingdom

CAMBRIDGE UNIVERSITY PRESS

The Edinburgh Building, Cambridge CB2 2RU, UK   http://www.cup.cam.ac.uk
40 West 20th Street, New York, NY 10011–4211, USA   http://www.cup.org
10 Stamford Road, Oakleigh, Melbourne 3166, Australia
Ruiz de Alarcón 13, 28014 Madrid, Spain

First published 1997
Reprinted 2000

Printed in the United Kingdom at the University Press, Cambridge

Typeset in Monotype Dante 10.75/14pt, in QuarkXPress™   [SE]

A catalogue record for this book is available from the British Library

Library of Congress Cataloguing in Publication data
Opera buffa in Mozart's Vienna / edited by Mary Hunter and James
  Webster.
      p.   cm. – (Cambridge studies in opera)
    Includes index.
    ISBN 0 521 57239 8 (hardback)
      1. Opera – Austria – Vienna – 18th century.   2. Mozart, Wolfgang
  Amadeus, 1756–1791.   I. Hunter, Mary.   II. Webster, James, 1942–
    III. Series.
  ML 1723.8.V6064   1997
  782.1´09436´1309033–dc21   96–50282   CIP MN

ISBN 0 521 57239 8 hardback

CONTENTS

ILLUSTRATIONS

Bruce Alan Brown is Associate Professor of Music History at the University of Southern California. He is the author of *Gluck and the French Theatre in Vienna* (Oxford University Press) and of *W. A. Mozart: "Così fan tutte"* (Cambridge University Press), as well of numerous articles on Gluck, Mozart, and eighteenth-century opera.

Marvin Carlson is Executive Officer of the PhD program in theater and Professor of Comparative Literature at the Graduate Center, City University of New York. He has written more than a dozen books, including *The Italian Stage from Goldoni to d'Annunzio* (McFarlane Press), *Theories of the Theatre* (Cornell University Press), and *Theatre Semiotics: Signs of Life* (Indiana University Press).

Tia DeNora is Lecturer in Sociology at the University of Exeter. She is the author of *Beethoven and the Construction of Genius* (University of California Press) and numerous articles on the social construction of genius, including "Musical Patronage and Social Change in Beethoven's Vienna" (*American Journal of Sociology*, 1991) and "Beethoven, the Viennese Canon, and the Sociology of Identity" (*Beethoven Forum 2*, 1992).

Sergio Durante is Professor of Music Philology at the University of Padua. His numerous articles include studies of Vivaldi, eighteenth-century singing technique, and Mozart's operas. He is the author of a monograph on *La clemenza di Tito* (forthcoming).

Paolo Gallarati is Professor of the History of Music and of Opera at the University of Turin. He is the author of *Gluck e Mozart* (Einaudi), *Musica e maschera: Il libretto italiano del settecento* (EDT/Musica), and *La forza delle parole: Mozart drammaturgo* (Einaudi).

Edmund J. Goehring is Assistant Professor in the Program of Liberal Studies at the University of Notre Dame and has been editor-in-chief of *Current Musicology*. His dissertation (Columbia University, 1993) is "The Comic Vision of *Così fan tutte*: Literary and Operatic Traditions," and he is the author of several articles on Mozart's operas.

Daniel Heartz is Professor of Music Emeritus at the University of

California, Berkeley. He is the author of *Pierre Attaingnant: Royal Printer of Music, Mozart's Operas* (both University of California Press), and *Haydn, Mozart, and the Viennese School, 1740–1780* (Norton).

Mary Hunter is Professor of Music at Bowdoin College. She is the author of numerous articles on Haydn's and Mozart's operas, opera buffa, and related topics and is a contributor to *The New Grove Dictionary of Opera*. Her book *The Poetics of Entertainment: Opera Buffa in Vienna 1770–1790* is forthcoming.

Marita P. McClymonds is Professor of Music at the University of Virginia. She is the author of *Niccolò Jommelli: The Last Years* (UMI Research Press) and many articles on eighteenth-century opera, especially opera seria, as well as co-editor of *Opera and the Enlightenment* (Cambridge University Press). She was an area editor of *The New Grove Dictionary of Opera*. Her forthcoming book is *Opera seria riconosciuta: The Reinterpretation of a Genre*.

John Platoff is Professor of Music at Trinity College. He is the author of numerous articles on Mozart and the Viennese opera buffa of the 1780s. His forthcoming book is *Mozart and the* Opera Buffa *in Vienna* (Oxford University Press).

Ronald J. Rabin's dissertation (Cornell University, 1996) is "Mozart and the Dramaturgy of *Opera Buffa*: Italian Comic Opera in Vienna 1783–1791." He is the co-author of "Arne, Handel, Walsh, and Music as Intellectual Property: Two Eighteenth-Century Lawsuits" (*JRMA* 120, 1995) and the author of 500 articles in *The New Harvard Dictionary of Musicians*.

Michael F. Robinson is Professor of Music Emeritus at the University of Wales, Cardiff. His many publications in this field include *Opera Before Mozart* (Hutchinson), *Naples and Neapolitan Opera* (Oxford University Press), and *A Thematic Catalogue of the Works of Giovanni Paisiello* (Pendragon).

Julian Rushton is West Riding Professor of Music at the University of Leeds. He is the author of *W. A. Mozart: "Don Giovanni," The Musical Language of Berlioz, W. A. Mozart: "Idomeneo," Hector Berlioz: "Roméo et Juliette"* (all Cambridge University Press), and *Classical Music: A Concise History* (Thames and Hudson).

Jessica Waldoff is Assistant Professor of Music at the College of the Holy Cross. Her dissertation (Cornell University, 1995) is "The Music of Recognition in Mozart's Operas." She is the author of "The Music of Recognition: Operatic Enlightenment in *The Magic Flute*" (*M&L* 75, 1994)

and co-author of "Operatic Plotting in *Le nozze di Figaro*" in Sadie,
Wolfgang Amadè Mozart.

James Webster is Goldwin Smith Professor of Music at Cornell University.
He is the author of *Haydn's "Farewell" Symphony and the Idea of Classical
Style: Through-Composition and Cyclic Integration in his Instrumental Music*
(Cambridge University Press) as well as numerous articles on the analysis
and interpretation of Mozart's operas, and co-editor of *Haydn Studies:
Proceedings of the International Haydn Conference, Washington D.C., 1975*
(Norton).

ACKNOWLEDGMENTS

This book began life as a conference at Cornell University in September 1994, funded by a generous grant from the National Endowment for the Humanities. We are grateful to the NEH and to Cornell University for material support of the conference itself and of the preparation of the typescript for publication. At Cornell, Don M. Randel, then the Harold Tanner Dean of the College of Arts and Sciences (now Provost), deserves particular thanks for his enthusiastic support; thanks as well to Dominick LaCapra, director of the Society for the Humanities. Unlike the book, the conference was graced by a spirited and evocative performance of parts of Sarti's *Fra i due litiganti il terzo gode*; we thank the Cornell staff (Edward Murray, Judith Kellock, Sonya Monosoff, James Cassaro) and students who contributed their talents to the occasion. The conference also included papers by Thomas Bauman, Caryl L. Clark, Silke Leopold, John A. Rice, and Gretchen A. Wheelock, which for various reasons could not appear in this volume. We are grateful to these scholars for their stimulating contributions. Jane Belonsoff and Estir Griffin rendered invaluable administrative help.

With respect to the book itself, we thank Ronald J. Rabin for his indefatigable checking of references, for preparing the music examples, and for technical and professional help; our task would have been much slower and less pleasant without his expertise. Thanks also to Victoria L. Cooper of Cambridge Press, and Arthur Groos, series editor, for their encouragement, enthusiasm, and critical skills, and to Jane Dieckmann for preparing the index. The major thanks with respect to the book must go to our contributors, who produced fine essays with exemplary promptness and with unalloyed good humor – a group disposition peculiarly appropriate to the subject-matter at hand.

Abbreviations

AMw   *Archiv für Musikwissenschaft*
AMZ   *Allgemeine Musikalische Zeitung*
AnM   *Analecta Musicologica*
CM   *Current Musicology*
CMS   *College Music Society Symposium*
COJ   *Cambridge Opera Journal*
EM   *Early Music*
JAMS   *Journal of the American Musicological Society*
JM   *Journal of Musicology*
JRMA   *Journal of the Royal Musical Association*
M&L   *Music and Letters*
MJb   *Mozart-Jahrbuch*
MQ   *Musical Quarterly*
MT   *Musical Times*
19CM   *Nineteenth-Century Music*
OQ   *Opera Quarterly*
PMLA   *Proceedings of the Modern Language Association*
PRMA   *Publications of the Royal Musical Association*

Short-titles

Allanbrook, *Rhythmic Gesture*	Wye J. Allanbrook, *Rhythmic Gesture in Mozart: Le nozze di Figaro and Don Giovanni* (Chicago: University of Chicago Press, 1983).
Goldoni	*Tutte le opere di Carlo Goldoni*, a cura di G. Ortolani, 14 vols. (Milan: Mondadori, 1952).
Heartz, *Mozart's Operas*	Daniel Heartz, *Mozart's Operas* (Berkeley and Los Angeles: University of California Press, 1990).
Kunze, *Don Giovanni*	Stefan Kunze, *Don Giovanni vor Mozart: Die Tradition der Don-Giovanni-Opern im italienischen Buffa-Theater des 18. Jahrhunderts* (Munich: Fink, 1972).

Michtner	Otto Michtner, *Das Alte Burgtheater als Opernbühne* (Vienna: Böhlaus, 1970).
Mozart, *Briefe*	*Mozart: Briefe und Aufzeichnungen. Gesamtausgabe*, collected and annotated by Wilhelm Bauer and Otto Erich Deutsch (Kassel: Bärenreiter, 1962–75).
Mozart, *Letters*	*The Letters of Mozart and his Family*, second edition, trans. and ed. Emily Anderson (London: Macmillan, 1966).
Muraro, *I vicini*	Maria Teresa Muraro and David Bryant, eds., *I vicini di Mozart: Il teatro musicale tra Sette e Ottocento*, 2 vols. (Florence: Olschki, 1989).
NMA	*Wolfgang Amadeus Mozart: Neue Ausgabe sämtlicher Werke* (Kassel: Bärenreiter, 1955–).
Sadie, *Wolfgang Amadè Mozart*	Stanley Sadie, ed., *Wolfgang Amadè Mozart: Essays on his Life and his Music* (Oxford: Clarendon Press, 1996).
Sartori	Claudio Sartori, *I libretti italiani a stampa dalle origini al 1800*. 7 vols. (Milan: Bertola and Locatelli, 1990–95).
Warburton	Ernest Warburton, ed., *The Librettos of Mozart's Operas*, 5 vols. (New York and London: Garland, 1991).
Webster, "Analysis"	James Webster, "The Analysis of Mozart's Arias," in *Mozart Studies*, ed. Cliff Eisen (Oxford: Clarendon Press, 1991).
Zechmeister	Gustav Zechmeister, *Die Wiener Theater nächst der Burg und nächst dem Kärntnerthor von 1747 bis 1776* (Vienna: Böhlaus, 1971).

Introduction

Mary Hunter and James Webster

Opera buffa was immensely popular in the second half of the eighteenth century. It was performed across Europe from Naples to St. Petersburg and London, in courts, court-sponsored theatres and public theatres, by great virtuosi and by traveling repertory companies. Vienna was no exception to the pan-European enthusiasm for this genre; between 1783 and 1792 some seventy-five *opere buffe* were produced there (of which twenty-two were written specifically for Vienna). Of this sizable repertory, however, the only operas now performed with any regularity are Mozart's three settings of librettos by Lorenzo Da Ponte: *Le nozze di Figaro, Don Giovanni*, and *Così fan tutte*. These canonic operas have typically been studied as isolated masterworks, with little or no reference to their original artistic and social contexts. It is becoming increasingly clear, however, that Mozart's operas responded directly to those contexts, and were, indeed, part of an elaborate artistic, cultural, and social "dialogue," involving not only composers, but civic and court authorities, impresarios, librettists, performers, and audiences as well. This book attempts to elucidate the nature of that dialogue more fully than has hitherto been the case.

The book does not, however, present Mozart simply as the sole surviving paradigmatic representative of one corner of this popular genre. Rather, despite its plainly declarative title, it raises a number of questions about the genre of opera buffa in Vienna and Mozart's relation to it. What, for example, does it mean, historically or methodologically, to locate (and thus partially to define) an entire genre by reference to the brief residence of a single composer in a given place? What might it mean to raise the same (primarily contextual) issues about Mozart's operas that we routinely raise about those of his contemporaries; conversely, what might it mean to ask the same questions of "the others" that have always been asked of Mozart? If composers and compositions are the focus of the book, as the title might suggest, where and how do librettists and singers, patrons and audiences, set-designers and prompters fit in? What are the historical, intellectual, and methodological implications of looking at opera buffa in terms of multiple structures – not only musical and textual, but also dramaturgical, scenographic, performative, and social? Although this book cannot fully answer any of these questions, it does address them all, whether explicitly or implicitly, in one essay or in several. The essays do not present a historical survey of opera buffa, but rather suggest a broad problematics of that genre as it flourished in late eighteenth-century Vienna, thus simultaneously evoking and moving beyond the particularities of our given place, time, and repertory.

THE PROBLEMATICS OF OPERA BUFFA

It has only recently become possible to think of opera buffa as having anything as sophisticated as a "problematics." One reason for this is that *opere buffe* were both peripatetic and mutable, frustrating even the most basic scholarly study. A given work could have as many as thirty or more productions, no two of which were exactly alike (indeed, it seems that significant changes were made even within production runs). New titles were often given to "old" works, minor characters were added and dropped, or major characters renamed as circumstances demanded, replacement singers received new arias in place of the originals (or substituted their own tried-and-true favorites), and pasticcio practices of various kinds were the norm. Although librettos from many of these productions survive – indeed, they form the chief record of the peregrinations of particular works – they often do not fully match the surviving scores. Moreover, the scores themselves often represent several layers of production and performance, which are virtually impossible to disentangle.[1]

These logistical problems have been immensely eased in recent years with the publication of reference sources like Sartori's *I libretti italiani a stampa dalle origini al 1800*,[2] *The New Grove Dictionary of Opera*,[3] and reprints of various local or regional library catalogues. These sources permit identification of the various versions of a given work, as well as its relation to other versions of the same work, other works on similar themes, other works in the same repertory, and so on. They also allow one to trace in some detail, if not with complete accuracy, the career of a given work, from autograph to revised production, to pasticcio-in-translation or "Favourite Songs." In addition to these recent comprehensive reference sources, in the last quarter-century there have been a number of groundbreaking studies of the genre,[4] discussions of particular aspects or repertories within

---

1 Of particular relevance to this volume is John Platoff's review-essay, "A New History for Martín's *Una cosa rara*," *JM* 12 (1994) 85–115. See also Dexter Edge, "The Original Performance Material and Score for Mozart's *Le nozze di Figaro*," paper presented at the 1995 meeting of the American Musicological Society.

2 Milan: Bertola and Locatelli, 1990–95, 7 vols.

3 London: Macmillan, 1992, 4 vols.

4 Among the most notable are Wolfgang Osthoff, "Die Opera Buffa," in *Gattungen der Musik in Einzeldarstellungen: Gedenkschrift Leo Schrade*, ed. Wulf Arlt, Ernst Lichtenhahn and Hans Oesch (Berne and Munich: Francke, 1973), vol. 1, pp. 678–743; Reinhard Strohm, *Die italienische Oper im 18. Jahrhundert* (Wilhelmshaven: Heinrichshofen, 1979); Charles R. Troy, *The Comic Intermezzo: A Study in the History of Eighteenth-Century Italian Opera* (Ann Arbor: UMI Research Press, 1980); Silke Leopold's contributions to Carl Dahlhaus, ed., *Die Musik des 18. Jahrhunderts* (Laaber: Laaber, 1985), pp. 73–84, 84–89, 89–99, 147–65, 180–87, 239–67; David Kimbell, *Italian Opera* (Cambridge: Cambridge University Press, 1991), Part IV: "The tradition of comedy." All of these recent studies pay some homage to the pioneering work of Andrea Della Corte, including *L'opera comica italiana nel Settecento: studi ed appunti* (Bari: Laterza, 1923); *Paisiello; con una tavola tematica* (Torino: Fratelli Bocca, 1922); and *Piccinni (settecento italiano): con frammenti musicali inediti e due ritratti* (Bari: Laterza, 1928); also to Hermann Abert, "Paisiellos Buffokunst und ihre Beziehungen zu Mozart," *AMw* 1 (1918–19), 402–21; repr. in Abert, *Gesammelte Schriften und Vorträge* (Halle: Niemeyer, 1929), pp. 365–96.

opera buffa,[5] studies of Mozart's contemporaries and predecessors,[6] and too many studies of individual composers to do
justice to here. Suffice it to say that among the composers here
discussed in any detail, several are the subjects of significant
recent work: Paisiello boasts an exhaustive thematic catalogue,[7]
Salieri is now the subject of three full-scale biographies,[8] and
Stephen Storace and Martín y Soler are both the subjects of
groundbreaking dissertations.[9] Much more research on particular
works, individual composers, and the genre more broadly considered will doubtless follow.

But beyond the fact that more and more of this material is
becoming available for musicological development, why should
this long-forgotten body of musical drama be of interest? What are
the virtues of opera buffa in Vienna as an object for scholarly study;
what does it have to say to us today? The essays in this book suggest
two large classes of answer to these questions. The first and
perhaps most obvious is indicated in the title, and is stated or
implied in every essay in the book. "Opera buffa in Mozart's
Vienna" is the repertory of works performed on the same stage, by
the same singers, and to the same audiences as Mozart's three great

5 Michael F. Robinson, *Naples and Neapolitan Opera* (Oxford: Clarendon Press,
   1972); Kunze, *Don Giovanni*; Muraro, *I vicini*, vol. 2, *La farsa musicale*, ed. David
   Bryant.
6 Most notable are: Muraro, *I vicini*; Abert, "Paisiellos Buffokunst"; Andrew
   Steptoe, *The Mozart-Da Ponte Operas: The Cultural and Musical Background*
   (Oxford: Clarendon Press, 1988).
7 Michael F. Robinson with the assistance of Ulrike Hofmann, *Giovanni Paisiello:
   A Thematic Catalogue of his Works*, 2 vols. (Stuyvesant, NY: Pendragon Press,
   1991–94).
8 Rudolph Angermüller, *Antonio Salieri: Sein Leben und seine weltlichen Werke unter
   besonderer Berücksichtigung seiner "großen" Opern*, (Munich: Katzbichler, 1971);
   Volkmar Braunbehrens, *Maligned Master: The Real Story of Antonio Salieri*, trans.
   Eveline L. Kanes (New York: Fromm, 1992); John A. Rice, *Salieri and Viennese
   Opera* (Chicago: University of Chicago Press, forthcoming).
9 Jane Catherine Girdham, "Stephen Storace and the English Opera Tradition of
   the Late Eighteenth Century" (PhD diss., University of Pennsylvania, 1988);
   Dorothea Link, "The Da Ponte Operas of Martín y Soler" (PhD diss., University
   of Toronto, 1991).

Da Ponte settings. Mozart is inevitably at the center of this book, even though he is not its subject. To study this repertory's conventions and circumstances with Mozart as an explicit and constant reference point is to ask of it the questions we are accustomed to asking of Mozart's operas; it implies that the analytical and critical methods applied to his masterpieces will both illuminate the works of his contemporaries and bring into relief the particularities of his genius.

But there is an opposite answer, equally though negatively focused on Mozart, which suggests that opera buffa is interesting precisely because it is *not* canonic, and does *not* bear the cultural burden of Mozart's masterworks. The genre can be seen without apology as embedded in its time and place, as governed by both social and aesthetic conventions, and can be interrogated in ways we are not accustomed to apply to Mozart. The methods and questions that emerge from studying an unfamiliar repertory with few claims to universality or transhistorical value may then, applied to Mozart, shed new light on his masterpieces. The complex relations between "positive" and "negative" Mozart-centricity are examined in the first section below.

A second sort of response sees the value of studying opera buffa, including Mozart, as part of the history of opera; as demonstrating larger historiographical and methodological problems in a special way, or with special clarity. For example, opera buffa was located squarely between "art" and "entertainment": it was devoted to contemporary topics and characters[10] and sensitive to a variety of contemporary aesthetic trends, yet equally rooted in the age-old traditions of improvisational comedy. As such, it provides a unique record of the *mentalité* of a given historical moment.[11] On the

10 Even its reworkings of Classical and other early myths and legends are made contemporary in various ways. The Bertati/Gazzaniga *L'isola di Alcina* (1772), for example, in which four contemporary gentlemen stumble out of a boat onto Alcina's enchanted island, commenting that they've arrived in a legend, is a particularly obvious example of self-conscious updating.

11 This is as true for venues like Vienna which used mainly "borrowed" repertory as for venues like Venice with a higher proportion of "native" pieces.

other hand, opera buffa's evident situatedness in its time and place also poses methodological problems. How accurately, and in what ways, does it represent the world it appears to imitate? How is it to be analysed or interpreted, particularly given that its verbal and musical texts (like those of improvisational comedy) only begin to suggest its meanings? Opera buffa seems to have marched inexorably towards respectability, necessitating not only an increasingly clear fixing of its text (verbal and musical), but also a rapprochement with the "opposed" genre of opera seria. Yet how, under these circumstances, are we to distinguish one genre of opera from another, especially when the *audible* signs of genre are less, or differently, marked than the distinctions of social class and of theoretical speculation to which they ostensibly correspond?

Although some essays clearly fall into one class of answer or the other – contextualizations of Mozart or methodological explorations – others respond in multiple ways to the question of why opera buffa is of interest. In what follows, we first discuss the "Mozart-centric" aspects of our authors' answers, moving from historical and cultural contexts to analytical or methodological ones. We then focus on more general methodological questions. That is to say, the organization of this introduction cuts across the thematic organization of the book; indeed, one of our purposes is to indicate both some underlying commonalities and some of the latent tensions among the essays.

MOZART IN CONTEXT

Historical and cultural issues

Although an understanding of Mozart's operatic context surely enriches our understanding of his masterpieces, the essays in this book suggest with startling clarity that this process of enrichment is multifaceted, and the results diverse and contentious. Indeed, even the apparently straightforward question of how to define Mozart's "context" has several possible answers, each with its own conceptual and methodological ramifications.

Let us begin with the historical or social context. For many historians, the abundance of information about theatrical and operatic life in Vienna in the 1770s and 1780s fuels the desire to paint a richly detailed picture of Mozart's immediate surroundings;[12] to understand (at least) the physical aspects of the theatre, Mozart's opinions of his contemporaries and theirs of him, and the politics of opera commissioning, production, and reception. This historicizing of Mozart's output (here brilliantly represented by Daniel Heartz and Bruce Alan Brown) implicitly valorizes that output; their interest in the detailed picture depends at least in part on the fact that it nourishes a fuller sense of familiar and much-loved works. The distinction between work and context in such studies is clear and strong; the way in which the contextual nourishment enhances appreciation of the works themselves is not – and need not be – specified.[13] This view permits the historical and the aesthetic imaginations to operate in different, even unrelated, realms; one is invited to exercise one's historical imagination in acts of homage to a set of essentially or potentially ahistorical aesthetic experiences. In an essay setting out a framework for cultural studies, Stephen Greenblatt notes that the "powerful and effective oscillation between the establishment of distinct discursive domains and the collapse of those domains into one another" is a defining attribute of cultural and intellectual life in our society.[14] These essays clearly represent the former pole of that oscillation.

In contrast to Brown and Heartz, Tia DeNora tends to "collapse" the domains, taking the new-historicist position that a work of art is

12 The most obvious and easily accessible sources include Zechmeister; Michtner; Rudolph Payer von Thurn, *Josef II als Theaterdirektor: Ungedruckte Briefe und Aktenstücke aus den Kinderjahren des Burgtheaters* (Vienna: Heidrich, 1920); Johann Pezzl, *Skizze von Wien* (Vienna 1786–90) partially translated in H. C. Robbins Landon, *Mozart and Vienna* (New York: Schirmer, 1991), and of course Mozart's letters.

13 Obvious exceptions to this involve instances where the work in question refers to or directly reflects an element of its context. A clear and relevant case in point is Daniel Heartz's "An Iconography of the Dances in the Ballroom Scene of *Don Giovanni*," in Heartz, *Mozart's Operas*, pp. 179–194.

14 Stephen Greenblatt, "Towards a Poetics of Culture," in H. Aram Veeser, ed., *The New Historicism Reader* (New York: Routledge, 1989), p. 8.

a "cultural workspace" or, in Greenblatt's terms, "the product of a negotiation between a creator or a class of creators, equipped with a complex, communally shared repertoire of conventions, and the institutions or practices of society."[15] In other words, context is not simply something that, as it were, surrounds a work and may affect it, but is in some crucial sense part of it. By linking Mozart's operas with the Viennese enthusiasm for botany and a newly sexualized notion of plant life, DeNora suggests that Mozart's *opere buffe* participated in the emergence of what Thomas Laqueur calls the "two-sex" conceptual model of sex and gender, in which male and female are seen as profoundly differentiated and essentially opposed, rather than as superficially differentiated versions of the same basic plan (the "one-sex model").[16] DeNora indicates Mozart's (and Da Ponte's) awareness of botany by pointing to flower-names for women, garden-settings, and a variety of botanical comments in the operas. One might add, continuing the fusion of text with context, that Mozart's Viennese operas model the emerging paradigm of binary sexual division in part by avoiding the sexually complicating figure of the castrato, by symmetrically opposing the soprano "pole" with a bass voice, and by focusing almost exclusively on matrimony. Neither these features nor the verbal ones mentioned by DeNora differentiate Mozart's *opere buffe* from those of his contemporaries, of course, nor are they meant to. She relies on the convenient appurtenances of canonicity accorded to Mozart – readily available editions, recordings, criticism, and so forth – but avoids the implication that Mozart's canonic status makes him an especially valuable or reliable representative of his time and place. Indeed, she implies that one will find similar versions of this cultural model in other *opere buffe* regardless of canonic status.

The essays by Paolo Gallarati, Jessica Waldoff, and Michael F. Robinson share with DeNora's the sense not only that text and

15 Ibid., p. 12.
16 Thomas Laqueur, *Making Sex* (Cambridge, MA: Harvard University Press, 1990). Laqueur insists, even while constructing the dichotomy between the one- and two-sex models, that each is embedded in the other.

context are embedded in each other, but also that the most pertinent contexts for Mozart are the broadest cultural and intellectual trends of his time, as long as they are grounded in verifiable historical connections.[17] They differ, however, in the ways they use Mozart's canonicity; whereas for DeNora the canonic status of Mozart's Da Ponte settings is in some sense a fortunate accident, Gallarati and Waldoff, and to a lesser extent Robinson, base their arguments on the particular genius of Mozart's Da Ponte settings. Gallarati is the most explicit regarding Mozart's "originality," and his essay serves as a salutary counter or challenge, both to the implicit political values of most of the other essays, which tend toward the egalitarian, and to their methodological values, which tend to emphasize historicizing over evaluating. Drawing on his earlier close analysis of Mozart's text-setting procedures,[18] and taking the ostensibly old-fashioned position that Mozart is simply superior both to the genre which spawned his comic masterpieces and to the run of composers who wrote in that genre, Gallarati rejects Mozart's contingent local context in favor of the pan-European one, and his well-documented competitive relations with other operatic composers writing for Vienna[19] in favor of a

---

17 In DeNora's case that connection is Mozart's familiarity with the von Jacquin family; in Gallarati's, it is Mozart's library and demonstrable theatrical interests.

18 In *La forza delle parole: Mozart drammaturgo* (Turin: Einaudi, 1993).

19 Daniel Heartz has documented the relation between *Le nozze di Figaro* and Paisiello's *Il barbiere di Siviglia* in "Constructing *Le nozze di Figaro*" (Heartz, *Mozart's Operas*, pp. 133–56). Dorothea Link has noted Mozart's reliance on Martín in "L'arbore di Diana: A Model for *Così fan tutte*," in Sadie, *Wolfgang Amadè Mozart*, pp. 362–73. Edmund J. Goehring's essay in the present volume also suggests a relationship between *Così fan tutte* and *Una cosa rara*. Several scholars have noted competitive dialogue between Mozart and Salieri: see especially Rice, "Rondò vocali di Salieri e Mozart per Adriana Ferrarese," in Muraro, *I vicini*, pp. 185–209), and the stunning discovery by Rice and Bruce Brown ("Salieri's *Così fan tutte*," COJ 8 [1996], 17–43) that Salieri started to set *Così fan tutte* before Mozart did. Mozart's dealings with other composers also hint at competition. His comic use of "Come un agnello" from Sarti's *Fra i due litiganti il terzo gode* in the second act finale to *Don Giovanni* is a case in point: the original aria describes a lamb going to the slaughter in an overblown metaphor for the singer's amorous miseries; Don Giovanni's inevitable fate turns this conceit – and the self-conscious naïveté of its music – inside out.

more speculative "progressive" alignment with Diderot and Lessing. In repudiating the value of opera buffa's frank manipulation of convention in favor of a rhetoric of originality and truth, then, Gallarati presents Mozart as a romantic genius, always already "universal" in his aims, and almost by definition at odds with any local or immediately generic conventions.

Although Waldoff and Robinson also place Mozart in a broad cultural context, they differ radically from Gallarati in their sense of Mozart's relation to conventions. Waldoff places Mozart in the canonic tradition of Aristotelian dramatic principles, but sees this tradition as a set of conventions, ripe for manipulation. Her point is that the particular genius of Mozart's and Da Ponte's version of *Don Giovanni* lies in the fact that the dramatic trajectory, having prepared the expected moment of peripeteia and recognition on the hero's part, diverges in such a way that everyone *but* the hero experiences this reversal. Mozart's and Da Ponte's rejection of the pervasive dramatic convention of heroic peripeteia does not render that convention irrelevant; rather, it is precisely their reinterpretation and manipulation of well-understood dramatic "rules" that engenders the enduring appeal of the work. The work's deepest meanings, then, emerge from its play with conventions.

Robinson also invokes the notion of peripeteia and concentrates on the ending of *Don Giovanni*, particularly insofar as it calls into question the generic conventions of comedy. This essay asks not only what it could mean to construct a context for a Mozart opera but, more generally, how scholars of canonical composers and works negotiate the competing claims of originality and adherence to convention. Robinson justifies his arguments about *Don Giovanni*'s contested generic affiliation – "black" comedy? comedy with a "tragic" ending? – by appealing to the local conventions of finale construction in the Viennese opera buffa repertory. He argues that it is justifiable to end the opera with Don Giovanni's cry as he is dragged down to hell, not only because some evidence suggests that Mozart may have considered or even sanctioned such an ending, but also because it would have conformed (if barely) to the tonal and dramatic conventions of Mozart's operatic milieu.

Ronald J. Rabin and Edmund J. Goehring go even further, in that they treat convention not as the consciously or unconsciously manipulated background to works of art, but as their very subject. Both essays are revisionist readings: Rabin's of an aria (Figaro's "Aprite un po'") and Goehring's of a historical / critical assumption. Rabin suggests that Mozart brilliantly *deploys* a conventional buffo aria to dramatize Figaro's vulnerability: having demonstrated his powers of rhetorical, dramatic, and psychological invention throughout the opera, Figaro now dramatizes his own exhaustion and near-defeat by resorting to an aria that precisely plays out all the expectations of its type. Mozart's dramatically timely and undisguised resort to convention thus suggests Figaro's psychological complexity. Psychological realism is often considered one of the hallmarks of Mozart's genius; it is also often considered a more general attribute of the Enlightened bourgeois aesthetic. Goehring suggests that the illusion of realism, as part and parcel of the mid-century sentimentalist movement, is also a convention, no less a deployable theatrical device than any other, particularly in opera. Mozart's comedies attain their richness by absorbing and reconfiguring in subtle and brilliant ways a variety of theatrical conventions, including the illusion of psychological realism.

In short, Mozart's historical context can be many things; from the most immediate, narrowly generic repertory (Viennese opera buffa) to the most comprehensive, broadly generic conventions (comedic happy endings, dramatic peripeteia); from the events and institutions bearing materially on his works (the cultural politics of the Habsburg court, for example) to a variety of more or less abstract intellectual and social structures (sentimentalism, or new notions of gender). Moreover, his connection to any of these contexts can be figured as conscious participation or rebellion, unconscious cultural embeddedness, or mere contemporaneity – or any combination of these. As with any major artist, the search for historical context is open-ended and does not lead to definitive answers.

Comparison and evaluation

Absent from the contributions discussed so far is any extended consideration of the value of Mozart's music in comparison to that of his contemporaries, and indeed of the larger question of how one might begin to consider questions of value. John Platoff's essay on the sextet from *Don Giovanni* proceeds from just such an evaluative issue: his feeling that the transition into the final section is both harmonically and dramatically unsatisfactory. He argues that this ensemble, particularly the V/vi–I progression between the end of the Andante and the beginning of the Molto allegro, is imbued with musical procedures more characteristic of instrumental music than of operatic music. He supports this observation by comparing this moment to structurally similar transitions between "movements" in opera buffa ensembles from the contemporary Viennese repertory, in which no equivalent harmonic move is found. Pointing out that most of Mozart's operatic contemporaries composed far more operas than instrumental pieces, he concludes that they employed effective if not original conventions of musico-dramatic organization, whereas Mozart, with his richer harmonic palette and more sophisticated control of "purely musical" form, could on the one hand produce musical drama of unparalleled insight, tension, and subtlety (as in the Andante section of the *Don Giovanni* sextet), but on the other, could also miscalculate.

Platoff's essay raises not only the contested question of the relation between operatic and instrumental music, but also the unresolvable issue of analytical methods and assumptions for Mozart in relation to "the others." As long as the focus of study remains Mozart's relations to contemporary musical or dramatic practice, the analytic procedures appropriate to and possible for his individual, canonical works, and those appropriate to and possible for "contemporary practice" (i.e. the dozens of operas by Paisiello, Salieri, Anfossi, Sarti, Righini, Guglielmi, Storace, Gazzaniga, and others) are likely to remain incompatible. To take just one example, what may count as a single "movement" in an ensemble by a contemporary (a section unified by tempo, meter and (sometimes) key), may count as two or more in Mozart, if subtleties of motivic organization, cadential structure, rhetoric, or accompanimental texture are taken into account, as they often are in analyses of individual masterworks, but tend not to be in studies of large or less-well-known repertories.

One answer to this inequality in analytical method is to abandon or sidestep the attempt to codify contemporary practice as if it were some sort of monolith, and to compare individual numbers (or entire works) of Mozart to those by other composers, thus acknowledging the possibility of differences within the repertory. Most of the numerous efforts in this direction have been dedicated to demonstrating Mozart's operatic origins or sources; they either implicitly assume or explicitly argue for Mozart's superiority.[20] Because they are essentially about Mozart and use methods rooted in Mozart criticism, such studies (insofar as they are analytical at all) ordinarily do not problematize their analytical methods.

James Webster's essay does exactly that. Applying to a Salieri aria (the Cavaliere Ripafratta's "Vo pensando" from *La locandiera*) the sorts of analytic techniques usually deemed unproblematically applicable to Mozart, he first demonstrates its musico-dramatic competence. However, he then explicitly refuses to make either of the usual next moves: to validate Salieri's aria on the basis of its adherence to procedures associated with Mozart's genius, or to compare Salieri and Mozart to the former's disadvantage. Webster's general point is that analysis alone cannot describe or confer value. Salieri's clever

20 Abert, "Paisiellos Buffokunst"; Kunze, *Don Giovanni*; Charles C. Russell, *The Don Juan Legend before Mozart: With a Collection of Eighteenth-Century Opera Librettos* (Ann Arbor: University of Michigan Press, 1993); Heartz, "Constructing *Le nozze di Figaro*"; Brown, "Beaumarchais, Mozart and the Vaudeville: Two Examples from *The Marriage of Figaro*," *MT* 127 (1986), 261–65; Daniela Goldin, "Mozart, Da Ponte e il linguaggio dell'opera buffa" and "In margine al catalogo di Leporello," in *La vera fenice* (Turin: Einaudi, 1985), pp. 77–163. Steptoe, *The Mozart-Da Ponte Operas*, describes some local influences on *Così fan tutte*, as does Edmund Goehring in "The Comic Vision of *Così fan tutte*: Literary and Operatic Origins" (PhD diss., Columbia University, 1993). See also Volker Mattern, *Das Dramma Giocoso: La Finta Giardiniera: Ein Vergleich der Vertonungen von Pasquale Anfossi und Wolfgang Amadeus Mozart* (Laaber: Laaber Verlag, 1989).

embodiment of the Cavaliere's indecision can best be discovered by Schenkerian analysis, but it is no more a guarantee of the value of "Vo pensando" that the fractured *Urlinie* has dramatic relevance than it is a guarantee of the value of "Porgi amor" that Schenkerian analysis reveals the progress of the Countess's self-understanding.

This point does not invalidate the question implied by Platoff's essay of how (or whether) we should level the analytic playing field when comparing a single canonical composer to his contextual repertory. But it does open new perspectives about the value of analysis, and the analysis of value, in opera. Neither Platoff's nor Webster's essay prescribes how to relate Mozart to his context, but in laying out so clearly the minefield of theoretical dichotomies – Mozart vs. "the others," Mozart vs. "an Other," operatic practices vs. instrumental practices (compositional and analytical), analysis vs. both interpretation and contextualization – both writers suggest a number of promising directions for future work.

METHODOLOGICAL ISSUES

If our control of the sources for opera buffa is rapidly improving, it does not follow that we should uncritically proceed to treat this genre in the same intellectual and historiographical framework that has guided most research about most music from the common practice period. Most questionable in the context of opera buffa is the traditional orientation towards the individual composer as sole author and the musical score as the primary authority for the work. Indeed the sources themselves suggest that these assumptions are misplaced – or at least inadequate – in this context. For example, although composers were regularly mentioned in contemporary accounts of opera-going,[21] and were indicated prominently in most

---

21 Zinzendorf, for example, whose diaries give us one of the most complete accounts of the Viennese operatic scene during the Mozart decade, almost always mentions the composer of the piece he is describing, especially the first time he sees it. Michtner is one of the best and most easily available sources for Zinzendorf's comments.

librettos as well as in scores, the performers attracted far more attention from almost every segment of the audience. In the vast majority of contemporary commentary on individual operas, the question of whether a performance was reproducing a text with sufficient fidelity was scarcely raised, and was never as prominent as discussion of the sensuous and performative qualities of the immediate event. One recent response to this situation has been an increase in scholarly attention to the careers and performing strengths of singers. Daniel Heartz's work has long been exemplary in this respect; his attention here to Baglioni, Carestini, and Carattoli continues that tradition. Patricia Lewy Gidwitz's research on Mozart's singers is perhaps the single most extensive project on the subject, complemented by John Rice's studies of Adriana Ferrarese and Maria Marchetti Fantozzi.[22]

Although this volume includes no full-scale studies of singers, the essays suggest a variety of ways of thinking about opera buffa as "performative." The most striking example is Julian Rushton's study of tessitura as an index of characterization. On one level an extension of the familiar notion that Mozart "tailored" his arias for particular voices, on another level it suggests that the notion of characterization was for Mozart inseparable from performance, and that it arose as much from the "grain" of a particular vocal tessitura as from the actions of the character or the musical *topoi* attached to those actions.[23] But several other authors transfer the notion of performance from the domain of the singer to that of the character (where it is seen as a component of dramatic action rather than a matter of sonority). Ronald J. Rabin's discussion of "Aprite un po'" strongly invokes the notion of the character as performer; in this reading, Figaro wilfully fails to come up with any-

22 Patricia Lewy Gidwitz, "Vocal Profiles of Four Mozart Sopranos" (PhD diss., University of California, Berkeley, 1991); "'Ich bin die erste Sängerin': Vocal Profiles of Two Mozart Sopranos," *EM* 19 (1991), 565–79; Rice, "Rondò vocali"; Rice, "Mozart and his Singers: The Case of Maria Marchetti Fantozzi, the first Vitellia," *OQ* 11 (1995), 31–52.

23 The reference is to Roland Barthes, "The Grain of the Voice," in *Image – Music – Text*, trans. Stephen Heath (New York: Hill and Wang, 1977), pp. 179–89.

thing more original than a misogynistic buffo aria. By contrast, when Salieri's Cavaliere (in Webster's interpretation) enacts his confusion by failing to perform a convincing structural descent, this failure is unwitting; its absence may be "performative," but its significance is compositional and dramatic.

These difficult distinctions – between singer and character, between the intentions of composers and those that appear to be the characters' own,[24] between performing and "performing"[25] – raise the larger methodological question of which domains we include in operatic analysis and how (or whether) they are defined or distinguished. Although the notion of "multivalence" – that opera's musical and dramatic meanings are often conveyed non-congruently in different domains – is accepted more or less without question by all the relevant writers in this collection,[26] the issue of the relation of non-texted elements to any theory of operatic meaning remains unresolved. The "performances" described by Rushton, Webster, and Rabin remain an aspect recoverable (at least within the framework of the analysis) from the various texts – words and notes – of opera buffa. But by all accounts the subtleties and vagaries of actual performance were crucially important in conveying opera buffa's meanings; the score is most often the merest shadow of the work's reality, which included not only the notes and words sounded but the intangible qualities of timbre, gesture, and inflection.

24 Edward T. Cone teases out some notions of operatic "voice" and "persona" most relevantly in "The World of Opera and its Inhabitants," in *Music: A View from Delft: Selected Essays* (Chicago: University of Chicago Press, 1989), but also in more general terms in *The Composer's Voice* (Berkeley: University of California Press, 1974). See also James Webster, "Cone's 'Personae' and the Analysis of Opera," *CMS* 29 (1989), 44–65.
25 Cone's writings on voice and persona in music have engendered an ongoing debate around the subject of composing and "composing," as they connect to performing and "performing." See Peter Kivy, "Opera Talk: A Philosophical 'Phantasie,'" *COJ* 3 (1991), 63–77; David Rosen, "Cone's and Kivy's 'World of Opera,'" *COJ* 4 (1992), 61–74; Ellen Rosand, "Operatic Ambiguities and the Power of Music," *COJ* 4 (1992), 75–80; Kivy, "Composers and 'Composers': A Response to David Rosen," *COJ* 4 (1992), 179–86.
26 This concept was adumbrated by Harold S. Powers in a 1984 study of Verdi's *Otello* (still unpublished); see Webster, "Analysis," pp. 103–04, 122–51.

In his ambitious attempt to connect European traditions of operatic hermeneutics with the analytical traditions of recent Anglo-American scholarship, Sergio Durante takes one aspect of opera buffa's performative dimension – the explicit and implicit stage directions – as a "domain" in its own right, which acts in consort or tension with the more usually considered domains of text and (written) music. This leads to a theoretical sketch of operatic drama (with particular attention to *Così fan tutte*) in terms of the semiotics of theatre, with its categories of "segmentation," "actants," and so forth. Admittedly, this does not add up to a theory of the infinitely various meanings conveyed by the vocal timbres, gestures, costumes, and bodies of actual performers in actual performances as they interact with the putatively more stable notated elements of the work (text and music); nevertheless, it represents an original and substantive contribution to the theory of operatic analysis.

Hunter's essay suggests that our constructions of multivalence, and thus our views of opera buffa's domains, will vary in relation to the question being asked. If, as for Durante, the question concerns the shape or coherence of an individual work, a study of the intersections of domains indicated more or less fully in the words and notes of the score and libretto may suffice. If, as for Webster, it is about the relations between analysis and the evaluative interpretation of particular works, not even an extension of analytical domains into the areas of gesture and staging can determine meaning in the areas of characterization and dramatic life; moreover, it is not clear that even the most extended domain-system imaginable could usefully address the question of value. If, as for Hunter, the guiding question has to do with the way opera buffa represents and embodies the social structures that give it life, a multivalent domain-theory of meaning is perfectly satisfactory; however, the relevant domains become, not "text, music, and drama," but texts (words and music), aesthetics (their signifying properties), and circumstances of production and consumption. Hunter suggests that just as with "text, music, and drama," the more broadly defined domains of texts, aesthetics, and production/consumption can work both congruently and non-congruently to locate works within a social nexus.

Although a number of other essays in this volume share Hunter's attention to representation, they exhibit important differences as well, which raise interesting questions about both the object and the manner of representation in opera buffa. DeNora and Marvin Carlson are the most concerned with its representation of larger social themes. DeNora's essay stresses the mutual embeddedness of social and artistic representation, locating opera's meaning as much in the interaction between audience and work as in "the work itself."[27] This methodological stance brackets the question of intention as surely as that of value. DeNora precisely does not suggest that Mozart and Da Ponte employed floral nomenclature and garden settings to make a point about sexual definition. Rather, she argues, the botanical aspects of these operas – hidden and unarticulated in exactly the ways that make them useful as clues to a larger ideology – became meaningful only insofar as they connected to what the audience might be likely to have brought to them. Hunter's arguments about the extent to which either the "enlightened bourgeois" narrative of Paisiello's *Le gare generose* or the atavistic pastoral message of Martín y Soler's *Una cosa rara* would have been taken as socially prescriptive relies similarly on the notion of unarticulated but well-understood codes – not only musical, but dramatic, social, and economic.

Although Carlson also takes the textual representation of social topics – here, class and gender – as his subject, he differs fundamentally from DeNora and Hunter in his attitude to intentionality. In reading Goldoni's libretto *Il re alla caccia* against earlier Spanish, English, and French versions of the same story (of which Goldoni certainly knew the last), Carlson argues that the later Goldoni was more interested in representing social tensions than other scholars

---

27 This stance is implicit in this essay, but explicit in DeNora, "The Musical Composition of Social Reality? Music, Action, and Reflexivity," *The Sociological Review* 43 (1995), 296–315.

have acknowledged. However, the sort of representation in which he is interested is less the incidental demonstration of social embeddedness than Goldoni's deliberate translation of social issues into dramatic terms. Carlson takes some of this to be more or less literally representational (or referential): for example, the King's speech about the socially leveling effect of being lost in the woods. But he is also interested in the indirect but still apparently intentional ways that Goldoni communicated social content, particularly his expansion of the female roles in this libretto as an expression of feminist consciousness.

Representation, however, is not simply a matter of the imitation of life (however complicated or attentuated). Many operas actually represent their own genre (or subgenre); they are "about" the genre as much as they are about life. This is one of Goehring's explicit themes; Rabin's treatment of "Aprite un po'" as a representation of a buffo aria (not merely an instance of one) also suggests the importance of intertextual or reflexive representation. Finally, Marita P. McClymonds raises the larger question of the extent to which genres can represent themselves. She suggests that despite both eighteenth-century and recent musicological rhetoric suggesting that opera seria and opera buffa were fundamentally opposed genres, they actually shared a number of musical (and musico-dramatic) types and gestures, particularly those signifying the "middle" from among the three social classes (high, middle, low) that dominated both social structures and their theatrical representations in this period. The self-representation of a genre, then, can be seen as both more superficial and more complex than has been recognized: on the one hand, if a work pronounces itself an opera seria it must be one, whereas on the other, a march or love song may not mean at all the same thing in a seria context as it does in buffa. McClymonds raises the fascinating question of the extent to which the "middle" is shared stylistic ground, accessible to both high and low genres and characters, and, conversely, the extent to which it can be used as contested territory, suggesting various shades of parody, disdain, ambition, and escape.

PROSPECTS

We have only begun to suggest the many ways in which this collection of essays opens out to larger questions of canon formation,
methodology, and representation. Although we have chosen not to
elaborate on the explicit topics of most of the essays, we do not
wish to conclude without noting two additional themes that are
pervasively, if often implicitly, present, in ways that suggest much
scope for further work.

One theme is the key role of Goldoni and his relation to later
opera buffa. Daniel Heartz notes that his historical connection to
opera buffa in Vienna is closer than has generally been acknowledged; a number of authors (Brown, Gallarati, Goehring, Hunter)
also refer to his dramatic innovations. One of these is the aesthetic
of dramatic naturalness propounded by Diderot and others: the
"fourth wall" that separated (or was supposed to separate) the dramatic action from the external behavior of the audience. Our contributors who emphasize this aspect of Goldoni's influence suggest
that, indirectly, at least, his plays had as much or more influence on
opera buffa as his librettos. By contrast, other authors (Hunter and
Carlson) distinguish between the libretti and the plays; Hunter in
particular works with Franco Fido's and Ted Emery's idea that they
use different means of signification. Altogether, the extent and
nature of Goldoni's influence on later opera buffa remains a rich
area for investigation.[28]

Gender is another important, if less pervasive, subtheme of this
book. Carlson and DeNora both address the straightforward representation of women. In addition, however, the related themes of
sentimentalism and naturalism in Gallarati's and Goehring's
papers raise the question whether the infusion of sentimental ele-

---

28 A promising examination of Goldoni's relation to later opera buffa is found in
Ronald J. Rabin, "Mozart, Da Ponte, and the Dramaturgy of Opera Buffa: Italian
Comic Opera in Vienna, 1783–1791" (PhD diss., Cornell University, 1996),
especially ch. 1, "The Poet as Dramatist: Goldoni and the post-Goldoni Libretto."

ments into opera buffa,[29] often associated with the process by which the genre became respectable in the last quarter of the century, also implied its "feminization." And the latter question inevitably raises the issue, addressed but not resolved by Carlson, of the extent to which the central role of female characters is coterminous with feminism in a more modern sense. What sort of power is embodied by women who are central, yet passive? What gendered message is conveyed by the haughty seria prima donna? In the "enlightened" Viennese context of the 1780s, what was the connection between opera buffa's "Italianness" and the pervasive sense of it as in some sense feminine?

We trust that readers of this volume will discover other fruitful connections, historical as well as thematic, among the essays collected here. We anticipate that it will not only stimulate further research on the questions raised in this introduction (and others), but will provide an initial context for developing answers to them. Most of all, we hope that our focus on the richness and open-endedness of opera buffa, on both the commonalities and the tensions among these studies, will induce or provoke enterprising performers to stage these works and thus to address – and perhaps even solve – some of the issues we have raised.

29 Cf. Della Corte's essays on *La buona figliuola* in *L'opera comica italiana* and *Piccinni*. See also Hunter, "'Pamela': The Offspring of Richardson's Heroine in Eighteenth-Century Opera," *Mosaic* 18 (1985), 61–76; "The Fusion and Juxtaposition of Genres in Opera Buffa 1770–1800: Anelli and Piccinni's *Griselda*," *M&L* 67 (1986), 363–80.

PART I

Historical and literary contexts

Goldoni, opera buffa, and Mozart's advent in Vienna
Daniel Heartz

Opera buffa sprang to life in Italy during the middle third of the eighteenth century. Its first phase played mainly on the stages of Naples and Rome, followed by those of Venice, where Carlo Goldoni put his indelible stamp on the process. Not long after Goldonian opera buffa began to flourish in Vienna in the early 1760s, Mozart joined the ferment. His initial visits to the imperial capital furnish material that rounds out this essay on the genre, the time, and the place of opera buffa in Mozart's Vienna.

Four operas by two Neapolitan composers formed the basis of a comic repertory that traveled throughout Italy and beyond in the 1740s and early 1750s: Gaetano Latilla's *La finta cameriera* and *Madama Ciana*, and Rinaldo di Capua's *La commedia in commedia* and *La libertà nociva*.[1] These full-length works in three acts constituted the first pan-Italian comic operas and they provided the models upon which Goldoni began creating Venetian opera buffa in 1748–49. The most widely performed of the four operas was the *commedia in musica* that began life as *Gismondo* by Gennaro Antonio Federico, poet of the famous intermezzo *La serva padrona* (1733). Latilla set *Gismondo* for the Teatro dei Fiorentini in Naples in the summer of 1737. During the following carnival season at the Teatro Valle in Rome it assumed the title *La finta cameriera*. With a great basso buffo, Francesco Baglioni, in the role of Don Calascione, the opera subsequently commenced its triumphant progress from theatre to theatre, often under the title of *Don Calascione*.

Venice welcomed *La finta cameriera* during the Ascension fair of 1743, when it was staged at the Teatro San Angelo. Competing with it for the applause of the public the same season was an opera seria,

---

1 Barbara Dobbs Mackenzie, "The Creation of a Genre: Comic Opera's Dissemination in Italy in the 1740s," PhD diss., University of Michigan, 1993.

Metastasio's *Ezio*, set by Lampugnani and staged at the Teatro Grimani di San Samuele. In his diary Giovanni Zanetti described the fortunes of these two operas in terms leaving no doubt that they vied with one another, also that they complemented each other.[2] On 23 May 1743 Zanetti noted that the singers in Latilla's comedy were all young, and that both operas pleased; in *Ezio*, he said, Carestini did himself great honor singing the contralto part. The following day Zanetti wrote that the comic opera began to please "excessively" and especially certain duets very smoothly set to music ("posti in musica molto politamente"), and then on 31 May he wrote, "Il musico che rappresenta il personaggio di don Calascione fa crepare la gente dalle risa" ("the singer who plays the part of Don Calascione makes people die laughing"). That singer was Francesco Baglioni; we can understand some of his comic appeal from a glance at the caricature made of him by Pierleone Ghezzi (Illustration 1.1).

The castrato Giovanni Carestini was around forty years of age in 1743 and in the third decade of a meteoric international career, first as a soprano, then as a contralto. *Ezio* drew in crowds and earned for Grimani a lot of money, says Zanetti. This should surprise no one – the public has always been willing to pay dearly to hear great voices sing solos. Angelo Mingotti, the impresario of *La finta cameriera*, also counted full houses and good revenues. With fine young singing actors, a score full of sprightly arias and ensembles, and above all with Baglioni in his prime, he could scarcely do otherwise. Two other excellent actor-singers who came north to Venice in the 1740s were the tenor Filippo Laschi and bass Francesco Carattoli.

Carlo Goldoni returned to his native Venice in 1748 after five years practicing law in Tuscany. He was no stranger to the Venetian theatres, where he had enjoyed successes as a playwright, and as a

2 Daniel Heartz, "Vis Comica: Goldoni, Galuppi and *L'arcadia in Brenta* (Venice, 1749)," in Maria Teresa Muraro, ed., *Venezia e il melodramma nel settecento*, vol. 2 (Florence: Olschki, 1981), pp. 70–71.

Illustration 1.1 Pierleone Ghezzi, caricature of Francesco Baglioni, from Giuseppe
Gherpelli, *L'opera nei teatri di Modena* (1988)

librettist for opera seria, comic intermezzi, and at least one three-act *commedia per musica, La contessina* (1743). In the case of his *opere serie* of 1740–41 he collaborated with his fellow Venetian Baldassare Galuppi. In 1748 he first worked with the composer Vincenzo Ciampi, the result being a *dramma giocoso* by Ciampi and others, *La scuola moderna*, a revision of an older Neapolitan libretto in which Goldoni rewrote the *parti buffe* but not the *parti serie*. In *Bertoldo, Bertoldino e Cacasenno*, a *dramma giocoso* for the carnival of 1749 composed by Ciampi, Goldoni made strides toward the buffo finale.[3] It probably helped that for the part of Bertoldino he had Carattoli. Then at Ascensiontide 1749 he had both Baglioni and Carattoli for *L'arcadia in Brenta*, and Galuppi as composer. Baglioni took the main role, Messer Fabrizio Fabroni di Fabriano, and Carattoli played his sidekick, Foresto. The commedia dell'arte play-within-a-play finale of the second act proved epochal as the first extended action finale, with Baglione as Pulcinella and Carattoli as Pantalone.[4]

Goldoni insisted repeatedly in his letters, prefaces, and finally in his memoirs how he wrote his stage works around the talents of the performers at his disposal. In lyric works of the 1750s he created particularly memorable roles for Baglioni, for example the gullible father figure of Buonafede in *Il mondo della luna*, the title role in *Arcifanfano*, the crafty Mengone in *Lo speziale*, and the rustic Nardo in *Il filosofo di campagna*, which brought Baglioni and Carattoli together again, as they had also been in *Lo speziale*. In fact Goldoni says in a preface that he wrote *Lo speziale* specifically to the demands of these two singers.[5] After *Il filosofo di campagna* of 1754, Galuppi's most successful comedy with Goldoni, the hour had struck for the repertory operas of the 1740s; they disappeared from the stage.

---

3 Daniel Heartz, "The Creation of the Buffo Finale in Italian Opera," *PRMA* 104 (1977–78), 68–78.
4 The music of the entire finale is printed in short score in Heartz, "Vis Comica," pp. 53–64.
5 Mackenzie, "The Creation of a Genre," p. 262, n. 82.

The importance of fine singing actors to the success of opera buffa is nowhere more evident than in the case of *La buona figliuola*, a libretto Goldoni derived from his play *Pamela* for his visit to Parma in 1756. In his *Mémoires* (1787) Goldoni says, "Duni wrote the music, and the opera gave much pleasure and would have given more had the execution been better, but too much delay led to engaging inferior performers" (vol. 1, p. 378). Duni's setting for Parma, still to be located, cannot have been the failure it is often made out to be, because it was given at Turin, Florence, and Modena in 1758–59, with Carattoli playing the Marchese, Baglioni playing the swashbuckler Tagliaferro, and the several daughters of Baglioni filling the soprano roles. In 1760 Piccinni made his setting of *La buona figliuola* for Rome; in it Carattoli took the plum part of Tagliaferro, which henceforth became his signature role. Goldoni wrote in his memoirs (ibid.) that "*La buona figliuola* was more happy in the hands of Piccinni, who preferred this old drama to all the new ones proposed to him."

Parma represented an important turning point in Goldoni's career. Here for the first time he witnessed the acting of French comedians, and he was astonished by their "naturalness." The peace treaty ending the War of the Austrian Succession in 1748 had taken the Duchy of Parma away from the Habsburg Empire and awarded it to a scion of the Spanish Bourbons, Don Philippe, Infante, who was married to no one less than the eldest daughter of Louis XV, Madame Louise Elizabeth. Goldoni's encounter with her at Parma presaged his move to Paris in 1762 and his eventual employment at the French court as teacher of Italian to her sister, Madame Adelaide.

During the 1750s, the Venetian editor Giuseppe Bettinelli brought out eleven volumes of *Commedie del Dottor Carlo Goldoni Avvocato Veneto fra gli Arcadi Polisenno Fregejo*. He preceded the first volume (1750) with an engraved portrait of the poet (Illustration 1.2). Goldoni derided the anonymous engraver for his work, and particularly the ape that appears at the bottom left intruding its

CAROLUS GOLDONI J.V.D.
ADVOCATUS VENETUS.

Illustration 1.2 Anonymous engraving from the Bettinelli edition of Goldoni's comedies

head into the oval frame.[6] Yet the ape was often used as a symbol of comedy, and despite Goldoni's protest, the poet's likeness was a good one, as can be seen by comparing it with other portraits of him. Moreover, the picture does project an undeniably comic verve.

By 1760 Goldonian opera buffa had spread far and wide, triumphing in many operatic centers, but not in Vienna. The Seven Years War from 1756 to 1763 severely strained government finances in Austria and it proved difficult for the theatre director, Count Giacomo Durazzo, to maintain the offerings of the two resident companies. The German troupe played mainly in the Kärntnertor-theater, but also in the Burgtheater, home of the French troupe. Thus the so-called *opéra-comique, Der neue krumme Teufel* by Joseph Kurz-Bernardon, with music by Joseph Haydn, was played in both theatres for six performances in late 1759.[7] Commedia dell'arte with a Viennese twist describes this typical offering of the German troupe, for which Haydn's substantial music has still not been located. What little Italian comic opera there was in Vienna at this time was confined mostly to intermezzos. *Neue krumme Teufel* itself was accompanied by an intermezzo, *Il vecchio ingannato*, for which Haydn did not write the music. What seemed like a promising collaboration for Haydn was cut short when Kurz-Bernardon, ever in disfavor with Empress Maria Theresa for allowing what she perceived as indecencies on the stage, left Vienna in 1760.

6 *La maschera e il volto di Carlo Goldoni: Due secoli di iconografia goldoniana*, ed. Gian Antonio Cibotto, Filippo Pedrocco, and Danilo Reato (Vicenza: Neri Pozza, 1993), p. 54. This large volume, issued to commemorate the bicentenary of Goldoni's death, is much more than a full iconography. It includes the poet's Italian memoirs from the prefaces to the Pasquali edition of his works, written between 1762 and 1772, and takes his life's story up to 1748. Cibotto's opening chapter argues (p. 47) that Goldoni saw into the hearts of women as did scarcely any other dramatist.

7 Daniel Heartz, "Haydn und Gluck im Burgtheater um 1760: Der neue krumme Teufel, Le Diable à quatre, und die Sinfonie 'Le Soir,'" in Christoph-Hellmut Mahling and Sigrid Wiesmann, eds., *Bericht über den Internationalen musikwissenschaftlichen Kongress Bayreuth 1981* (Kassel: Bärenreiter, 1983), pp. 120–35.

The imperial wedding of 1760 between Archduke Joseph, heir to the throne, and Isabella of Parma, the doubly royal young princess who was granddaughter to the reigning kings of both France and Spain, was celebrated in Italian operas composed by Hasse, Traetta, and Gluck, but these were weighty, allegorical works, as befitted such a grand event. To further celebrate the occasion, Martin van Meytens, imperial court painter, and his school, produced several enormous oil canvases that depicted various ceremonies and entertainments. One of these offered a fantasy view of Isabella's arrival at the Hofburg, accompanied by an immense throng of foot soldiers and parade of carriages (Illustration 1.3b). Noteworthy in the background is an overall view of the Hofburg as it appeared in 1760 from the inner city (if the inner city were vacated of all its buildings, which Van Meytens accomplished in order to give room for Isabella's procession). A sketch drawing has survived for this detail of the painting (Illustration 1.3a). These images depict from left to right: the palace of Prince Tarouca (home in later days to the Music Department and Albertina Graphic Collection of the Austrian National Library); the Augustinian monastery; the Augustinian church; the imperial library; the Redoutensaal (the facade of which was not then finished); the imperial Riding School; and lastly, dwarfed by its larger neighbor, the Burgtheater (the facade of which was finished). Across the front of what is now the Josephsplatz stretched an arcade that evidently connected the Augustinian church directly to the buildings on the other side of Fischer von Erlach's majestic imperial library. The Kärntnertor-theater, not shown on these images, was located further to the left, at the Carinthian or southern gate to the city. It was connected to the palace by a passageway through the ramparts. Josef Nagl's 1770 map of Vienna shows both theatres (Illustration 1.4).

Opera buffa came late to Vienna. Aside from the occasional visits of traveling companies the two Viennese theatres lacked the personnel to put on full-fledged opera buffa. This situation began to change only in 1762, when Durazzo engaged several Italian singers, among them the most renowned of Baglioni's daughters,

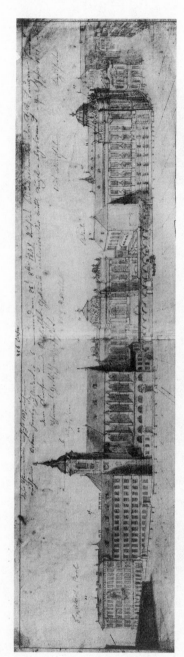

Illustration 1.3a The Hofburg in 1760: sketch, no longer extant, from Moriz Dreger, *Baugeschichte der k. und k. Hofburg* (1914)

Illustration 1.3b The Hofburg in 1760: detail from a painting by Martin van Meytens

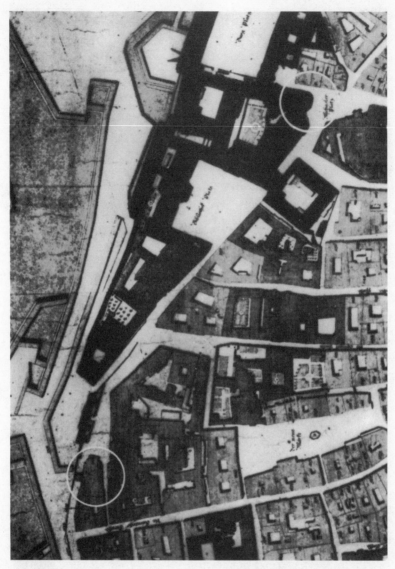

Illustration 1.4 Detail of Josef Nagl's map of Vienna, printed in 1770, showing the Hofburg, with the Burgtheater (above) and the Kärntnertortheater circled, from Zechmeister

Clementina, who had excelled in both opera seria and opera buffa. At some time impossible to specify, Vienna also became the residence of Giuseppe Scarlatti, an experienced composer in both genres who had made the first settings of at least three comic operas by Goldoni in Venice, in 1752, 1754, and 1757. For the 1763–64 season Durazzo engaged the buffa troupe of Giacomo Maso, enabling him to produce, among other works, Scarlatti's *La serva scaltra* as well as the first Viennese performances of Galuppi's *Il filosofo di campagna* and Piccinni's *La buona figliuola*, with Carattoli as Tagliaferro.[8]

Durazzo had high hopes of achieving for Viennese opera buffa the renown he had won with several other genres, notably *opéra-comique*, full-length pantomime ballet, and the radical reconstitution of lyric theatre represented by Gluck's *Orfeo ed Euridice* (1762). These hopes rested on the acquisition of a versatile Bohemian composer, Florian Gassmann, as composer of ballet to the imperial court in 1763 at age thirty-four. They rested also on the prospects of gaining the services of the famous poet who perfected opera buffa, none other than Carlo Goldoni, then, at age fifty-seven, residing in Paris. Gassmann had begun his career with successful carnival operas for Venice four years in a row, on opera seria librettos in 1757 and 1758, then in 1759 he made the first setting of Goldoni's *Gli uccellatori*, and in the following year the first setting of Goldoni's *Filosofia ed amore*. In 1764 Gassmann succeeded Gluck as *Theaterkapellmeister* of the imperial court.

Goldoni left Venice for Paris in the fall of 1762; he continued to write for the Venetian theatres, although he was never to return to his native city. What initially drew Goldoni to Paris was a lucrative two-year contact with the Théâtre Italien, where he hoped to further his reform of Italian spoken comedy by weaning the players away from their improvised routines and substituting his completely written-out comedy of character. The Italian players in Paris did not prove to be tractable, much to Goldoni's disappointment, which he expressed in numerous letters to his friends and

8 Zechmeister, pp. 252–64.

patrons in Italy, along with many other precious vignettes about life in general in the French capital, and about the theatrical life of the three royal theatres in particular.

News of Goldoni's disenchantment with the Théâtre Italien possibly reached Durazzo, and if so the likely conduit was the Count's Parisian agent, and Goldoni's close friend, the playwright Charles-Simon Favart, who was in charge of the *opéra-comique* wing of the Théâtre Italien. The first we hear about the project of securing Goldoni for Vienna comes from Favart's letter to Durazzo of 4 January 1764:

> I congratulate your excellency on your engagement of our divine Goldoni. He and I see each other very often. He belongs to a small society of men of letters, of which he is the ornament; he is an inexhaustible genius, who always produces something new. I dare assert that Vienna will be no less happy with his productions than Venice or Paris.[9]

There is no direct correspondence surviving between Goldoni and Vienna. Yet in some of Goldoni's letters that do survive from the first part of 1764, hints emerge as to what was afoot. For example, in a letter of 19 March the poet mentions that several new projects had been proposed to him, and in a letter of 28 May he specifies that Vienna was a place for which he was obliged to work, along with Lisbon, which had placed an order for Italian librettos.[10] It was probably not Durazzo's intention to bring Goldoni to Vienna, but rather to engage him as a long-distance collaborator for Gassmann, and perhaps for Gluck as well, these two composers standing the highest in the Count's favor. Dubious is the claim that "Goldoni's engagement for Vienna, had it actually come about, would probably have resulted in original plays in French, as well as Italian."[11] Vienna, unlike Paris, had no Italian players. Goldoni did

---

9 Charles-Simon Favart, *Mémoires et correspondances littéraires, dramatiques et anecdotiques*, ed. A.-P.-C. Favart, 3 vols. (Paris: Léopold Collin, 1808), vol. 2, p. 189.
10 Goldoni, vol. 1, pp. 314–15, 321–22.
11 Bruce Alan Brown, *Gluck and the French Theatre in Vienna* (Oxford: Clarendon Press, 1991), p. 81.

not venture an original play in French until 1771, when he wrote *Le Bourru bienfaisant* for the Comédie Française, that is to say after eight years of continual residence in France. This play, like so many others by the poet, eventually had Viennese consequences. Lorenzo Da Ponte turned it into a libretto for Martín y Soler, *Il burbero di buon cuore*, whose setting reached the stage of the Burgtheater in January 1786. Durazzo's plans for Goldoni in Vienna, whatever they were, came to nothing in 1764 because the Count himself was relieved of his post as theatre director and appointed ambassador to Venice instead.

Goldoni retained a keen interest in what was going on in the theatres of Venice after he moved to Paris; in fact his distance from them helped produce some of the most telling commentary on opera in his correspondence. In the fall of 1763, Goldoni wrote to his friend Gabriele Cornet in Venice asking for news about the outcome of a new *dramma serio-giocoso in musica* that had reopened the Teatro San Cassiano on 5 November 1763. This work was *La morte di Dimone, o sia L'innocenza vendicata* by Joseph Kurz-Bernardon. Giovanni Bertati put the libretto into Italian and Antonio Tozzi composed the music. Prompted by the idea of this semi-serious opera, Goldoni set forth his ideas on the possibilities and history of such a mixed genre.

> A *serio-giocoso divertimento* can please, if it is well written. Such were the operas in music of the past century and the beginning of our century. Kings, princes played the serious roles, and servants the buffo roles. Great pleasure was afforded by the old women, court jesters, chambermaids and go-betweens. With time the *parti buffe* were removed from operas and placed instead in intermezzi. Then came ballets, and they triumphed so completely that the pleasure of *musica buffa* was lost altogether. This has since been reborn as opera buffa. These works revenging themselves on the pretended superiority of the *opere serie*, admitted the noble parts into their company in order to make them hated. Little by little these works also became semi-buffo, and were banned entirely by some theaters. The lack of chiaroscuro is harmful; that which is entirely buffo and forever buffo cannot last. Thus you behold the case of novelty that can give pleasure, which is nothing other than the ancient form renewed.

The difference between this *divertimento serio-giocoso* and an ordinary opera buffa, is that in the latter the *buffi* constitute the principal parts, whereas in the former, the *serio-giocoso*, I believe the buffo parts will be accessory. However the case may be, a good book with good music can make everything come out well.[12]

As the most important Italian librettist of mid-eighteenth-century comic opera, Goldoni was uniquely qualified to make this summary of the genre's evolution.

According to Goldoni, buffo music existed before opera buffa, in the comic parts of older works from the seventeenth and early eighteenth centuries (before Zeno and Metastasio removed them from serious librettos). These buffo parts found refuge at first in comic intermezzi, but the vogue of ballets as entr'actes was so triumphant it suppressed buffo music, which was then reborn with the *opere buffe*. Clearly, only full-length works merited this name and thus Pergolesi's brilliant intermezzo *La serva padrona* was not an opera buffa, although it has often been called one, and even though it did project buffo music.

The mixing of seria and buffa parts such as Goldoni next describes applies to most of his own librettos from the late 1740s on. He speaks as a working dramatist when he says that the entirely

12 "Un divertimento serio-giocoso può far piacere, quando sia bene condotto. Così erano le opere per musica nel secolo passato e sul principio del nostro. I re, i principi facevano le parti serie, ed i servi le parti buffe. Facevano gran piacere le vecchie, i buffoni di corte, le cameriere, i mezzani. Col tempo hanno levato le parti buffe dalle opere, e ne hanno fatto degl'Intermezzi. Succedettero i Balli, e questi hanno talmente trionfato che si era intieramente perduto il piacere della musica buffa. Questa è poscia rinata colle Opere buffe le quali, vendicandosi della pretesa superiorità delle Opere serie, hanno ammesso in compagnia loro le parti nobili per farle odiare. A poco a poco sono divenute ancor queste semi-buffe, e da qualche teatro sono state intieramente bandite. La mancanza del chiaroscuro pregiudica, e il tutto buffo ed il sempre buffo non può durare. Ecco dunque il caso della novità che può dar piacere, cioè dell'antichità rinnovata; e la differenza che vi può essere da questo divertimento serio-giocoso ed un' opera buffa ordinaria, probabilmente sarà che in questa i buffi formano la parte principale dell'opera, e in quello credo che saranno accessori. Comunque sia la cosa, buon libro e buona musica ponno far trovar tutto bello *ecc.*" Goldoni, vol. 14, Letter CXI, to Gabriele Cornet (November 1763).

buffo work cannot endure because it is lacking in contrast. His final remarks suggest that he may have actually had Bertati's libretto for *La morte di Dimone* in hand when he wrote to Cornet. Perhaps the young poet – Bertati was twenty-eight in 1763 and this was his first libretto – sent it to Paris for approval by his famous predecessor. *La morte di Dimone* turned out to be an isolated experiment that had little success. That it was even attempted attests to the perceived need to keep reformulating opera in terms of how the buffa and seria strains are combined. Understood in these terms, mid-eighteenth-century attempts at amalgamation do indeed have traits in common with seventeenth-century norms.

Goldoni did not send any librettos to Vienna as far as is known. After Durazzo's fall, Gluck went on writing occasional works for the court in collaboration with Metastasio, or in the case of the none-too-happy adventure represented by *Telemaco* of January 1765, with Marco Coltellini. Gassmann set an old opera by Metastasio, *L'Olimpiade*, and the same poet's new *azione teatrale, Il trionfo d'amore*.

In August 1765 the court was at Innsbruck for the wedding of Archduke Leopold with the Infanta Maria Luisa. With it were the players, singers, and dancers of the Burgtheater, putting on a variety of spectacles besides the main wedding opera, *Romolo ed Ersilia* by Metastasio and Hasse. On the evening of 18 August, Emperor Francis Stephan attended the theatre where the entertainment consisted of Goldoni's play *Il tutore* and the tragic pantomime ballet *Iphigénie* by Angiolini and Gluck. Since the court had no Italian players, only Italian singers, presumably a troupe was brought from Italy to perform Goldoni's 1752 comedy, which was one of those with some parts in Venetian dialect. The choice of a play by Goldoni may indicate that he was one of the emperor's favorite authors. The court chronicler, Prince Khevenhüller, wrote that "the emperor sat through a serious [sic] play of Goldoni's, *Il tutore*, and the ballet of *Iphigénie*, as long as it is sad."[13] Returning to

13 Rudolf Graf Khevenhüller-Metsch and Dr. Hanns Schlitter, eds., *Aus der Zeit Maria Theresias: Tagebuch des Fürsten Johann Josef Khevenhüller-Metsch, kaiserlichen Obersthofmeisters 1742–1776*, 7 vols. (Vienna: Holzhausen, 1907–25), vol. 6, p. 198.

his rooms the emperor collapsed. He was attended by his eldest son Joseph, who got him to bed, but by the time a priest, a doctor, or Maria Theresa could arrive, Francis Stephan was dead. Everything changed in consequence. The empress, laid low by grief, named Joseph co-regent in place of her husband. She remained the ruler. Archduke Leopold and his new bride replaced his parents as Grand Duke and Duchess of Tuscany. The theatres were closed for a long period of mourning, and the first French troupe was given its outright release.

The German troupe was allowed to reopen the Kärntnertortheater first, during the post-Easter season of 1766. Not until the following November, according to Khevenhüller, was the Burgtheater reopened, with Gassmann's setting of Goldoni's 1757 libretto, *Il viaggiatore ridicolo*. Vienna now possessed an excellent troupe for opera buffa, including Clementina Baglioni, soprano, Teresa Eberardi, contralto, Giuseppe Pinetti, baritone, and the famous Francesco Carattoli, bass. For these forces, supplemented by tenor Giochino Caribaldi, Gassmann composed his most successful opera buffa, *L'amore artigiano*, for the spring season of 1767. Once again the libretto went back to a Goldoni original, first set for Venice by Latilla in 1761. With this work the first peak of specifically Viennese opera buffa was quickly reached.

Gassmann may have come of age in a musical sense when he was writing his early operas for Venice, but by the time of *L'amore artigiano* his music begins to sound more distinctively Viennese. He learned much from Gluck's fastidious orchestral palette. Woodwind color in particular interests him more and more. His harmonic richness also exceeds that of the average Italian composers of opera buffa in the 1760s. On occasion his combination of melodic and harmonic suavities seems to foretell Mozart. A good example of this is the big *aria d'affetto* in E flat for Caribaldi in the middle of the second act, "D'una parte Amore mi dice."[14]

Printed librettos show that Gassmann's *L'amore artigiano*

14 The opening of the aria is given in Daniel Heartz, *Haydn, Mozart and the Viennese School 1740–1780* (New York: Norton, 1995), p. 417.

enjoyed more than thirty different productions, many of them in Italy, between 1768 and 1793.[15] This number does not include the many productions of the German-language version, *Die Liebe unter den Handwerksleuten*. No other Viennese opera achieved such wide diffusion during these years. The next most widely diffused opera by Gassmann was *La contessina*, written on command from Emperor Joseph II as an entertainment given by the forces of the Burgtheater at the meeting in Moravia with King Frederick II of Prussia in the summer of 1770. For this Coltellini reverted to Goldoni's 1743 *commedia per musica* concerning the absurd pretentions to nobility of upwardly mobile commoners. Goldoni's original had to be greatly extended; it had only four characters and no finales. What sounds particularly Viennese in Gassmann's setting are the many ensembles aside from the finales. The first act begins, for instance, with two male-voice terzettos, separated by a short recitative. Gassmann stood high in the favor of Joseph II, if not of Maria Theresa. He became *Hofkapellmeister* in 1772, replacing Georg Reutter and set several more comedies for the Burgtheater, including Goldoni's *Le pescatrici*, before his early death in January 1774.

Mozart's first experience of a big city was not Vienna but Munich. During January 1762, father Leopold took his two children to the Bavarian court, where they were presented to the elector and performed for him on the harpsichord. Mozart turned six on 27 January 1762. His first real theatre (Salzburg had none at this time) must have been that jewel of Rococo architecture, the Cuvilliès-Theatre in the Residence, then quite new, and for which he later wrote *Idomeneo* (1781). The carnival opera there in early 1762 was Metastasio's *Temistocle* set by *Hofkapellmeister* Andrea Bernasconi, a production in which his stepdaughter Antonia, later one of Mozart's sopranos, made her debut.

The Mozarts first visited the imperial capital in the fall of 1762. Much is known about their stay because of Leopold's detailed descriptions in his letters written to Lorenz Hagenauer, his landlord in Salzburg. The musical feats of little Wolfgang created such

15 Sartori, vol. 1, s.v. *Amore artigiano*.

a sensation in Vienna that the Burgtheater was buzzing with conversation on the subject when Leopold went there for an evening's entertainment on 10 October 1762. There followed appearances before the court at Schönbrunn and before a very large number of the high nobility, who vied with each other to invite the *Wunderkinder*. On 23 November the four members of the Mozart family shared the box of Countess Lodron at the Burgtheater. Thanks to a recently recovered theatre chronicle we know what they witnessed on that evening, the main event of which was the fifteenth performance of Gluck's *Orfeo ed Euridice*. Not only did the child Mozart witness the most advanced opera of its day, he also saw the court theatre in the pristine beauty of its first state, as Nicolas Jadot had built it beginning in 1748.[16]

During the stay in Vienna, Leopold was already laying plans with the French ambassador and others for a grand tour that would take the Mozart family through southern Germany to Paris, London, and the Low Countries, and that would last from mid-1763 to late 1766. Mozart matured quickly as an astonishingly gifted composer, writing keyboard sonatas, symphonies, and also many arias, mostly on seria texts by Metastasio. Leopold was priming his son all the while for composing an opera, and clearly he was thinking ahead to an opera seria for one of the Habsburg courts, especially Milan (by way of which he first planned to return to Salzburg). He confided his plans to Friedrich Melchior von Grimm, who reported on Mozart's operatic ambitions in the *Correspondance littéraire* dated 15 July 1766.

Mozart was aware of Italian comedy, spoken and sung, before he went to Italy in 1769. Paris, London, and the south German courts offered buffo music in one form or another. So did Salzburg. One of the first pieces he wrote on his return was a big obbligato recitative and *Licenza* aria in D (K. 16), march-like and heroic in vein, for tenor and full orchestra with trumpets and timpani, to celebrate the anniversary of the Archbishop's consecration on 21 December 1766.

16 On the theatrical offering of 23 November 1762, see Heartz, *Haydn, Mozart and the Viennese School*, p. 495. On the architecture, see Heartz, "Nicolas Jadot and the Building of the Burgtheater," *MQ* 68 (1982), 1–31, especially p. 7.

This elaborate showpiece, which demonstrated his complete command of the seria style, capped an evening that had consisted of an itinerant Italian troupe performing Goldoni's comedy *Il cavaliere di spirito* followed by *Li tre gobbi rivali amanti di Madama Vezzosa*, a *farsa* for four voices by Goldoni and Ciampi (Venice, 1749). In May of 1767, Mozart wrote *Apollo et Hyacinthus* (K. 38), a musical intermedio to a Latin school drama, sung mainly by Salzburg cathedral choirboys. Its nine arias and ensembles gave him experience writing in a plain, non-seria style, also in making various tonal connections between recitative endings and set pieces.

The Mozarts left Salzburg again on 11 September 1767 for what was supposed to be a three-month stay in Vienna. In the event they did not return to Salzburg until January 1769. In early 1768 Leopold decided that the moment had come to impose his son on the Burgtheater as the composer of a full-length opera. He wrote to Hagenauer about the project at length on 30 January 1768:

> It is not an opera seria, for no operas of that kind are being given now, and moreover, people do not like them. It is an opera buffa, but not a short one, for it is to last about two hours and a half or three hours. There are no singers for opera seria here; even Gluck's opera of mourning [*trauerige opera*], *Alceste*, was performed entirely by opera buffa singers. Gluck himself is now writing an opera buffa, for there are excellent people here for an opera buffa.[17]

Leopold then names the Italian singers of the Burgtheater: messieurs Caribaldi, Carattoli, Poggi, Polini, and Laschi; mesdames Bernasconi, Eberardi and [Clementina] Baglioni. Was Gluck in fact contemplating an opera buffa? Or was this claim just a part of Leopold's propaganda?

Leopold maintained in the same letter to Hagenauer that Joseph II first suggested that Mozart compose an opera, which cannot be

17 Mozart, *Briefe*, vol. 1, p. 258; my translation. Mozart, *Letters* (pp. 82–83), translates "trauerige opera" as "serious opera," which is too free and too suggestive of "opera seria" (a species from which *Alceste* is far removed).

true because in his lengthy formal complaint to the emperor dated 21 September 1768, Leopold makes no such claim.[18] Rather, the suggestion was apparently made to Giuseppe Affligio, the impresario of the Burgtheater, by the Dutch ambassador, and by Carattoli. This veteran singer–actor served as de facto leader of Vienna's buffo troupe. He was a living witness to the whole evolution of the comic genre from the 1740s on and the active participant for whom Goldoni had created many roles. Presumably he was the one who chose the libretto for Mozart, Goldoni's *La finta semplice*, a witty comedy of manners set in imperial Lombardy, first composed by Salvator Perillo (Venice, 1764). The leading male role, that of the misogynist Cassandro, was to have been played by Carattoli himself. Since the libretto was relatively recent it required little revision by Coltellini, and even this much was regarded by Leopold as stalling. As spring turned into summer, by which time most of the work was composed and also revised to suit the demands of individual singers, it became apparent even to Leopold that Affligio was not going to stage it. Offering a number of excuses, then doubts about the work's effectiveness, Affligio refused to have the revised parts copied. Instead he put into rehearsal Goldoni's *La cascina*, as set for Venice in 1755 by Scolari and he followed this by rehearsing a new production of *La buona figliuola*.

Mozart's music for *La finta semplice* has twice the vitality of *Apollo et Hyacinthus*, for which a superior libretto is partly responsible, but also the stimulation of composing for first-class singing actors. All the music for the part of Rosina, presumably intended for Clementina Baglioni, is exceptionally fine. That the opera failed to be produced in Vienna can be blamed mostly on Leopold's clumsy manipulations. In his letter to Hagenauer of 30 July 1768 (*Letters*, p. 131; *Briefe*, vol. 1, p. 271), Leopold stated that had the work been an opera seria, he would have left at once and laid it at the feet of His Grace, the Archbishop of Salzburg. But, as it was an opera

---

18 The *Species facti*, as Leopold Mozart called it, is lacking in Mozart, *Letters*; it is translated in Otto Erich Deutsch, *Mozart: A Documentary Biography* (London: Black 1965), pp. 80–83, and in Heartz, *Haydn, Mozart, and the Viennese School*, Appendix 3.

buffa and, moreover, an opera that required certain types of "Persone buffe," he had no choice but to persist in Vienna.

The remark about "persone buffe" calls for comment. Salzburg had only church singers; perhaps they could sing the parts of an opera buffa but acting them was another matter. The editors of the *NMA* recently discovered in Paris a printed libretto of *La finta semplice* dated Salzburg, 1769. The regular Salzburg singers appear by name, but whether they actually performed the work is not known, and if they did, whether it was staged. In a letter to his son of 29 June 1778, Leopold Mozart ridiculed Giacomo Rust for adapting music from an opera buffa he had composed while setting Metastasio's serenata *Il parnasso confuso* (Salzburg, 1778), in which the buffo music did not suit the serious words at all.[19] As late as 1790, Lorenzo Da Ponte stressed the enormous difference between seria and buffa singing, also between seria and buffa acting.[20]

Failure of *La finta semplice* to gain the stage of the Burgtheater offers a marked contrast with the experience a year later of Antonio Salieri, a pupil of Gassmann who arrived in Vienna in 1766 at the age of sixteen. Giovanni Gastone Boccherini (brother of the famous composer) offered him his first libretto, *Le donne letterate*, newly written after Molière's *Les femmes savantes*. In the absence of Gassmann, who was in Rome with the emperor, but with the blessing of Calzabigi, Gluck, and Giuseppe Scarlatti, also of Affligio, young Salieri saw his first opera rehearsed and performed in the Burgtheater by the same forces for which Mozart had composed.

The rivalry between Mozart and Salieri must have begun at this time. Salieri's modest success with his first opera led to eleven more for Vienna between 1770 and 1776 in collaboration with various poets. The most successful was *La fiera di Venezia* on another libretto by G. G. Boccherini, a colorful work that includes Venetian dialect and owes much to Goldoni. This opera dates from 1772.

19 Mozart, *Briefe*, vol. 3, pp. 384–85 (this passage omitted in Mozart, *Letters*).
20 "Copia di Memoria da me presentata alla Direzione il mese di Xbre dell'anno 1790": "dell' enorme differenza che passa tra il canto, e l'azione buffa e seria"; cited from Michtner, p. 443.

When the Mozarts, father and son, returned to Vienna in the summer of 1773, Mozart did Salieri the hommage of writing keyboard variations (K. 180) on a minuet air in dialogue from Act II of *La fiera di Venezia*, "Mio caro Adone." Mozart's later variations on tunes by other composers, whether by Gluck, Paisiello, Sarti, or the Berlin cellist Duport, were all intended as gestures of friendship and flattery. By attempting to get into the good graces of Salieri in 1773, Mozart may have also been trying to obliterate Viennese memories of the *Finta semplice* fiasco.

When Gassmann died in 1774, Salieri succeeded him in the portion of his job that involved directing music in the theatre. Gluck was in Paris. Calzabigi and Coltellini had both left Vienna for good. There remained the lesser literary talents of poets Boccherini and Giovanni de Gamerra. Equally ominous was the decline in quality of the buffo singers. Few remained from the stellar group of Carattoli and company, and they were soon replaced with less expensive talents. The only singer added who would eventually make a name for herself was Caterina Cavalieri. As a whole, the buffo troupe pleased the public less than Hamon's French troupe, playing mainly the latest *opéras-comiques* from Paris, especially those by Grétry. The only outstandingly successful opera buffa in 1776 was Paisiello's *La frascatana* but not even this could rescue the Italian company. The impresario, by this time Count Koháry, suffered the disgrace of a written censure of the opera buffa from Khevenhüller, who underscored his point by giving up his box in the Burgtheater.

The situation with the Italian singers in 1776 needed to be taken in hand by a patient and generous ruler. Maria Theresa, who was such a ruler, had withdrawn from theatrical matters after the death of Francis Stephan. Joseph II was impulsive rather than patient, and bent upon making economies whatever the cultural costs. He allowed the remains of Viennese opera buffa, shunted to the Kärntnertortheater, to disintegrate. In the Burgtheater he installed the German troupe and pronounced it a "Nationaltheater." Two years later, in 1778, he added a Singspiel wing to the German troupe's regular offerings. Neither in spoken nor in lyric works did this theatre live up to expectations – much of its repertory in both was translated from the French. Some *opere buffe* continued on in Vienna in German translation. This was the case with Gassmann's *L'amore artigiano*. Paisiello's *I filosofi immaginari* of 1779, from which Mozart later took the theme of his keyboard variations (K. 398), was staged in the Burgtheater as *Die eingebildeten Philosophen*.

Paisiello in fact represented the best hope that the emperor would eventually reinstate opera buffa. Passing through Vienna on his way to St. Petersburg in the summer of 1776 the composer was acclaimed vociferously at one of the many performances of *La frascatana*. A reporter in the local press wrote a rapturous review of the event:

> A few days ago the famous maestro di cappella from Naples arrived here, and he was invited to the Burgtheater where his opera *La frascatana* was given – the favorite comedy with our public and the masterpiece in this genre. The nobility present received him with distinguished marks of great respect, and hardly did the loges and parterre lead off when a general wave of applause and vociferation expressed pleasure and gratitude for the delight this composer of genius has so often given every sentimental soul.[21]

The aged Metastasio, whom Paisiello visited, commented in a letter on "his most beautiful opera *La frascatana*; he attended a performance and at the end received long and loud applause from the entire audience."[22] The opinion of the venerable *poeta caesareo* still counted for a lot at the Viennese court. What mattered most, though, were the opinions of Joseph II.

In early 1780, Joseph II met with Empress Catherine II of Russia near Kiev. She brought with her Paisiello and his musicians, who

21 Jakob Bianchi in the *Realzeitung*; translated from the quotation in Hannelore Gericke, *Der Wiener Musikalienhandel von 1700 bis 1778* (Graz: Böhlau, 1960), pp. 89–90.
22 *Tutte le opere di Pietro Metastasio*, ed. Bruno Brunelli, 5 vols. (Milan: Mondadori, 1943–54), vol. 5: letter to Saverio Mattei of 23 September 1776.

staged *I filosofi immaginari* and another of his recent comic operas. Joseph was so delighted he ordered copies of the scores; moreover he placed a standing order for any future operas by Paisiello, but only in the comic genre. Thus was sown the seed that would lead to opera buffa's return to Vienna in 1783, with the Italian troupe led by Francesco Benucci, and to the hiring of Lorenzo Da Ponte as theatre poet. By an irony of fate, this troupe, destined to restore Vienna's operatic eminence, was recruited by the imperial ambassador to Venice, Count Durazzo.

Salieri remained in charge of music in the Burgtheater so it is not surprising that the new troupe's first offering was his *Scuola de' gelosi* composed to a libretto by Mazzolà for Venice in 1778. It was followed in quick succession by recent *opere buffe* by Cimarosa, Sarti, Anfossi, and Paisiello, whose setting of *Il barbiere di Siviglia*, composed for St. Petersburg in 1782, quickly became a great favorite with the Viennese public.

Mozart, settled in Vienna since the spring of 1781, was eager as ever to compose operas. Writing to his father on 5 February 1783, he mentioned choosing Goldoni's play *Il servitore di due padroni* for transformation into a German libretto, but this project, like several others, came to nothing. In a letter to his father of 7 May 1783, he wrote words that deserve our full attention: "Well, the Italian opera buffa has started again here and is very popular. The [basso] buffo is particularly good – his name is Benucci."[23] The future of opera buffa in Vienna was not secure even so when Benucci left Vienna in the fall of 1783 in order to honor a previous commitment to Rome. Joseph II declared that if Benucci did not return, all the other singers of the buffo troupe (and presumably Da Ponte as well) were to be dismissed. Benucci did return in the summer of 1784, and so did Paisiello, on his way back to Naples. Joseph took advantage of the composer's presence to commission *Il re Teodoro in Venezia*, on a new libretto by the poet Casti; Benucci created the role of the rich innkeeper Taddeo. Around Benucci's unsurpassed talents as a singer, and as an actor, Mozart and Da Ponte were inspired to bring to life their Figaro two years later. It took both Paisiello and Benucci – the true heir of Baglioni and Carattoli – to save the day for opera buffa in Vienna.

2 | *Lo specchio francese*: Viennese opera buffa and the legacy of French theatre
Bruce Alan Brown

From various statements in the *Memorie* of Lorenzo Da Ponte, it is clear that he was sensitive concerning the originality of his operatic texts, particularly as regards the question of French influence. With some irritation he reports Casti's grudging praise for his librettos for *Il burbero di buon cuore* and *Le nozze di Figaro*, in each case undercut by the remark "But, after all . . . it's only a translation . . .".[1] To Casti's charge that he had let a gallicism slip into his verses for *Burbero*, Da Ponte counters with accusations of similar transgressions in Casti's *Il re Teodoro*, and a justification of his own usage. And in describing a return visit to Vienna in 1792, following his ouster as theatre poet, Da Ponte scornfully notes his successor Bertati's reliance on a volume of French plays, among other literary aids.[2] This is all rather disingenuous, since it was with translations from the French that Da Ponte had begun his dramatic career, while still under Caterino Mazzolà's tutelage in Dresden.[3] Furthermore, French-derived pieces were conspicuous in the repertory of the Viennese opera buffa troupe throughout the whole of Da Ponte's tenure as theatre poet, as well as during his London sojourn.

For most of the eighteenth century, the French stage was a touchstone for other theatrical traditions in Europe: an elegant mirror of French manufacture, one might say, which revealed deformities in locally produced pieces, and helped guide the taste of playwrights and librettists. In Vienna, the legacy of French theatrical performances was crucial to the development of German spoken drama and opera, and not without significant impact on Italian musical theatre in the city. Yet French pieces were not the only models of excellence for original productions on Viennese

1 Da Ponte, *Memorie*, ed. Cesare Pagnini (Milan: Rizzoli, 1960), pp. 106, 118.
2 Ibid., p. 164   3 Ibid., pp. 74, 78.

stages; in 1763 the head of the court's theatres, Count Giacomo Durazzo, had declared that "the German theatre [was] embellished every day by the translation or imitation of . . . plays" by Goldoni.[4] The Venetian's influence was just as decisive for the development of Viennese opera buffa – though Da Ponte was loath to admit it.[5] The Habsburg capital was not unique in offering, at various times, German, French, and Italian spectacles to its citizens, but the degree to which these traditions interacted, and the excellence of original productions in all three languages, make it a particularly attractive focus of investigation. Though our focus here will be the specific ways in which French dramas or dramatic practices helped shape both the stagecraft of *opere buffe* produced for Vienna and spectators' habits of perception, we will also consider what this recourse to French sources reveals about deficiencies that the creators of Viennese opera buffa perceived in Italian and native theatrical traditions.

FRENCH CULTURE IN MARIA THERESA'S VIENNA

French language, literature, and theatre were well established among members of the Viennese nobility well before the so-called "Diplomatic Revolution" of 1756 cemented political relations between France and Austria. Caroline Pichler, *née* von Greiner (b. 1769), explained in her memoirs that in her youth "French was . . . the language of the higher classes, indeed of the educated world altogether . . . My mother had learned [it] beginning in her childhood as a sort of second mother tongue, indeed as her native language, and spoke and wrote it with equal fluency."[6] Even Emperor Joseph II, an avowed partisan of German letters, continued to use

---

4 Letter of 19 February 1763 to Charles-Simon Favart, in Favart, *Mémoires et correspondances littéraires, dramatiques et anecdotiques*, ed. A.-P.-C. Favart (Paris: Léopold Collin, 1808), vol. 2, p. 72.

5 See Heartz, *Mozart's Operas*, p. 134.

6 Caroline Pichler, *Denkwürdigkeiten aus meinem Leben*, ed. Emil Karl Blümml, 2 vols. (Munich: Georg Müller, 1914), vol. 1, p. 14.

French even decades later – in his correspondence with his theatre director Count Rosenberg, for instance. One reason for the persistence of French in Vienna (apart from its utility in a cosmopolitan capital) was the fact that the city's nobles, even its monarchs, spoke a decidedly common local dialect of German. So unaccustomed were they to employing *Hochdeutsch* in everyday conversation that it can be said to have existed in Vienna mainly as a written language.[7]

Performances by the capital's first professional French troupe, in existence between 1752 and 1765, were never as well attended as those of the German actors in the Kärntnertortheater,[8] where the repertory included – despite the empress's opposition – a large number of ribald, semi-improvised farces. But the French theatre provided an essential meeting place for the elites of Viennese society and resident foreigners, who together constituted the majority of its box-holders. Chancellor Wenzel Kaunitz, the architect of the *renversement des alliances*, emphasized this social role in arguing – unsuccessfully – for the French theatre's retention in 1765 (following the death of Maria Theresa's consort, Emperor Francis Stephen), noting that the German theatre provided no decent alternative:

> The German language not being as prevalent as the French or the Italian, and these, and the last especially, being in greater usage among the select society of Vienna, one would be depriving this society almost entirely of spectacle if one were to limit it to just the national [German] theatre . . . . There are no promenades here frequented as they are in London and Paris; those there are, are deserted during seven or eight months of the year. With the theatres closed, the hours dedicated to decent amusement are absolutely empty most of the time for persons of a certain

7 Ibid., p. 15.
8 Records of attendance are sparse for this period, but those of the second season following the 1752 reorganization of the court theatres, which do survive, show a marked disparity in box-office receipts, in favor of the German theatre; see Franz Hadamowsky, "Das Spieljahr 1753/4 des Theaters nächst dem Kärntnerthor und des Theaters nächst der K. K. Burg," *Jahrbuch der Gesellschaft für Wiener Theaterforschung* 11 (1959), 3–21. Zechmeister, p. 47, notes too that the German company performed nearly twice as often as did the French.

distinction. On this basis one will not easily be persuaded that in Vienna one should suppress the French theatre, already adopted in all of Europe as a school of morals and of politeness, and the Italian opera, which has been established among all enlightened nations as an assemblage of all the fine arts . . .[9]

The first French troupe had offered a full range of classic and more recent plays, as well as *opéras-comiques* by its music director Gluck and by Parisian composers. The German actors resented the favored treatment accorded their rivals, but had few scruples about dipping into the French repertory in order to supplement their stores of pieces. In the early 1760s opera buffa was also poised for a revival, fueled by the activities of local composers and itinerant troupes, and by Count Durazzo's temporary success in acquiring the services of Goldoni himself, who had recently abandoned his native Venice for Paris;[10] the arrangement must have ended with Durazzo's dismissal. It is not inconceivable that Goldoni's talents might have been used in more than just opera buffa, for which there was as yet no resident company. "Translation or imitation" of his pieces, already a regular practice in the Kärntnertortheater, was, for example, equally possible in the French theatre at court. The French comedy he eventually wrote for Paris (*Le Bourru bienfaisant*) was performed in three languages on Viennese stages.[11]

The demise of this first French troupe resulted from a coincidence of rising literary nationalism and official concern over the actors' high salaries. Kaunitz and like-minded nobles succeeded twice more in establishing French theatrical companies in Vienna. The first lasted until 1772, when it was disbanded on account of the

9 Wenzel Kaunitz, "Reflexions sur les spectacles de la Ville de Vienne 1765," quoted in Oscar Teuber, *Das k. k. Hofburgtheater seit seiner Begründung* (Vienna: Gesellschaft für vervielfältigende Kunst, 1896), p. 105, and in Bruce Alan Brown, *Gluck and the French Theatre in Vienna* (Oxford: Clarendon Press, 1991), p. 4.

10 See Favart's letter of 4 January 1764 (*Mémoires*, vol. 2, p. 189), in which he congratulates Durazzo on his "acquisition" of the playwright, quoted in Daniel Heartz's essay in this volume, p. 36.

11 For further information on Goldoni's dealings with Vienna, see Daniel Heartz's essay in this volume.

deficits it was causing. Another troupe of French actors performed briefly during 1775, concentrating on *opéra-comique*, and itinerant French players passed through Vienna even into the 1780s, taking advantage of Emperor Joseph's *Schauspielfreiheit*.[12] But even aside from these groups' performances, French pieces were a constant presence in Viennese theatrical life. The repertory of the "Nationalsingspiel" came to be dominated by translations of French *opéras-comiques*, due to the dearth of suitable original works. In the spoken theatre, adaptations of French plays figured prominently through the end of the century and beyond. Joseph von Sonnenfels included much discussion of foreign works in his *Briefe über die Wienerische Schaubühne*, thereby incurring the wrath of Berlin literary critics.[13] Indeed, he had begun his series of letters in the guise of a Frenchman, in order (like Montesquieu playing the Persian in his *Persian Letters*) better to criticize his countrymen's foibles. And the same Emperor Joseph who had founded a Nationaltheater in 1776 specifically instructed its director in 1782 to advertise for German translations of "French tragedies by the first-ranked and best authors, namely Corneille, Racine and Voltaire," even specifying German Alexandrine verses.[14] He probably welcomed recourse to French models in the opera buffa repertory as well.

Not only were French pieces continually before the Viennese public, but there were also important continuities, in terms of personnel and patronage, between the French and non-French periods and repertories of the city's theatrical life. Count Durazzo, the theatre director during the time of the first French troupe, and an author himself of both French comedies and Italian librettos, was

---

12 See, for example, the notice in the *Gazette de Vienne* for 15 January 1783, announcing the departure of a group of French actors.

13 See Roland Krebs, *L'Idée de «Théâtre National» dans l'Allemagne des Lumières: théorie et réalisations* (Wiesbaden: Harrassowitz, 1985), p. 466.

14 "Punkten für die Theatral-Direction," 8 February 1782, quoted in Rudolf Payer von Thurn, ed., *Joseph II. als Theaterdirektor: Ungedruckte Briefe und Aktenstücke aus den Kinderjahren des Burgtheaters* (Vienna and Leipzig: Verlag Leopold Heidrich, 1920), p. 28.

(as imperial ambassador to Venice) largely responsible for recruiting the opera buffa troupe that made its debut in 1783.[15] His secretary during his tenure in Vienna was Giuseppe Maria Varese, a fellow Genoan, who from 1772 was also an associate of the impresario Koháry;[16] he was evidently the same Varese whose collection of opera buffa librettos Da Ponte says he inspected on arriving in Vienna.[17]

No less significant was the continuity among spectators, whose memories tended to transcend boundaries of language or genre. There were partisans of the French theatre not only among older theatre-goers such as Kaunitz, but also among younger spectators, such as Baron Raimund Wetzlar, Da Ponte's great friend and sponsor and Mozart's landlord, who in 1775 was an *associé* of Hamon's *opéra-comique* troupe.[18] Our principal informant on the vicissitudes of Viennese theatrical life, through his 52-year diary, is Count Carl von Zinzendorf, who frequently compared what he saw on a given night to productions he had attended weeks, months, or years earlier. Thus he complained, for example, that the Singspiel *Diesmal hat der Mann den Willen* by Ordoñez, performed in 1778, pleased him less than the original setting by Monsigny, *Le Maître en droit*, which he had heard in 1763.[19] Zinzendorf's first reaction to opera buffa, also in 1763, was conditioned by his theatrical experiences in Vienna, which to that point had been mainly French. "The genre is peculiar," he wrote; "at the beginning I was bothered by all the trivialities that they sing at you emphatically, but in the end, the same thing happens in French *opéras-comiques*."[20]

15 See Michael Kelly, *Reminiscences of Michael Kelly, of the King's Theatre, and Theatre Royal Drury Lane, including a period of nearly half a century; with original anecdotes of many distinguished persons, political, literary, and musical*, 2 vols. (London: Henry Colburn, 1826), vol. 1, pp. 194–7. 16 Michtner, p. 20.

17 Da Ponte, *Memorie*, p. 95.

18 Zechmeister, p. 76. Wetzlar, like Da Ponte, was a converted Jew, a fact which probably helped facilitate their friendship.

19 See Michtner, p. 43.

20 "Journal du Comte Charles de Zinzendorf et Pottendorf" (Vienna, Staatsarchiv), entry for 15 May 1763. The piece in question was Goldoni's *Il mercato di Malmantile*, in a setting usually attributed to Fischietti.

When a work presented in Vienna was based on a French model, this was usually made known to the audience. The anonymous author of the pamphlet *Anti-da Ponte* faults the librettist for omitting Beaumarchais's name from the poster for *Axur*, but in most cases there was some public acknowledgment of the original author. The "Soggetto francese" of Da Ponte's *Il finto cieco* is boldly announced on the title page; this information is also noted in a review of the opera's performance.[21] In justifying liberties he had taken in producing his text for *Democrito corretto*, Gaetano Brunati states that "[t]he subject of the present drama can be unknown to few persons," in part on account of its "having been treated already by Monsieur REGNARD in his comedy entitled *Démocrite amoureux*."[22]

During the hegemony of French theatre in Vienna, the German theatre's players (and dancers) had frequently capitalized on the success of French plays or operas by imitating them on their stage, in the process also absorbing something of their competitors' polished performing skills. There is also some evidence of consciously planned presentation in the Burgtheater of a parody (musical or otherwise) in conjunction with its model.[23] Similarly, during the Josephinian era, the theatre direction seems consciously to have prepared the way for the Viennese premiere of Paisiello's *Il barbiere di Siviglia*, by scheduling a German-language performance of Beaumarchais's play eleven days beforehand, on 2 August 1783. In the case of *Il barbiere di Siviglia*, players and spectators alike benefited from the conjunction of original and imitation, for, as Emperor Joseph reported to Rosenberg, Francesco Benucci as Bartolo and Nancy Storace as Rosina had imitated to a tee in the opera the superb acting of Friedrich Ludwig Schröder and Mme. Adamberger (*née* Maria Anna Jaquet) in these roles in the spoken production.[24] Zinzendorf, in describing the premiere, drew on his

---

21 See Michtner, p. 201, quoting a review in the *Realzeitung* (1786, p. 204).
22 Libretto to *Democrito corretto* (Vienna: Franc. Antonio Kroyss, 1787), p. 6.
23 See Brown, *Gluck and the French Theatre*, pp. 100–04.
24 See his letter of 14 August 1783, quoted in Payer von Thurn, *Joseph II. als Theaterdirektor*, p. 35.

acquaintance with French theatre when noting that the emperor had demanded an encore of "the aria of the student" [Almaviva in disguise] "who comes in the guise of Tartuffe to wish 'gioa e pace' to the tutor."[25] The recognition of this archetype from Molière would have been a matter of course for a Viennese spectator of his experiences.

OPERA BUFFA "À LA FRANÇAISE"

By the later eighteenth century, recourse to French models in opera buffa texts – whether written for Italy or elsewhere – had become common. One attraction for librettists was the French theatre's respectability, compared to other national traditions. Opera buffa's reputation for low humor, improbable plots, and meager literary merit was a gross simplification, but it was a simplification perpetuated even by librettists themselves. In his preface to *Le pazzie d'Orlando* (London, 1771), for instance, Carlo Francesco Badini calls comic librettos "a continued blasphemy against common sense"; Da Ponte, in his memoirs, uniformly denigrates the productions of other opera buffa librettists.[26] Mozart shared this prevailing opinion of opera buffa, and of Italian comedies generally, on one occasion writing of a play by Gozzi that it was "only endurable if one remembers that it is an Italian play," with actions that were "really too indecent and unnatural."[27] Even so judicious a critic as

25 Entry for 13 August 1783: "l'air du Bachelier qui vient en Tartuffe souhaiter Gioja e pace au Tuteur." Zinzendorf also states that the action of the play, which he evidently knew, suffered from being set to music.
26 See Da Ponte, *Memorie*, pp. 78, 95. Da Ponte makes a grudging exception in the cases of Goldoni and Zeno, but only in a footnote in the English-language preliminary version, *An Extract from the Life of Lorenzo da Ponte* (New York, 1819), p. 4.
27 Letter to his sister of 15 December 1781; Mozart, *Letters*, p. 786; *Briefe*, vol. 3, p. 183 and vol. 6, p. 97. The reference here is to *Das öffentliche Geheimnis*, adapted by Friedrich Wilhelm Gotter after the play *Il pubblico segreto*. Zinzendorf too seems to have had low expectations of opera buffa librettos. Following a performance in German of Paisiello's *I filosofi immaginari*, he remarked "Pretty music by Paisiello and the text even passable" – although this may be in reference to the quality of the translation (entry for 10 November 1782).

Sonnenfels classed opera buffa among the "farcical" genres to be excluded from his proposed repertory of reform. He spares not even Goldoni, declaring that one "would be hard put to choose a single one of his sixty plays which could stand up to a rigorous critique, or be set alongside [Molière's] *Misanthrope*."[28] His example of a more tolerable "scherzhafte" (jocular) comedy, *Les Folies amoureuses*, is by Regnard.[29]

The anonymous author of the *Grundsätze zur Theaterkritik*, published in Vienna in 1790, found it self-evident that plots of *opere buffe* produced in Italy itself would be weak and confused, but stated that "[t]he Italian opera that has come into existence *in Germany* is a middling thing, in between good and bad" (my emphasis).[30] More often than in Italy, he implies, such works owed their success to more than just their music, also providing occupation for the minds of intelligent spectators, with well-developed plots, deft characterizations, and polished dialogue. These features were precisely what Viennese audiences had come to expect from comedies by the likes of Regnard, Destouches, and Marivaux.

Strong influences from Marivaux have been claimed for *Così fan tutte*,[31] but in several other *opere buffe* presented by Joseph's Burgtheater the modeling on works of French authors was rather more direct (see Table 2.1). The French originals included: two prose *comédies d'intrigue*, by Beaumarchais and Legrand; a verse

---

28 Sonnenfels, *Briefe über die Wienerische Schaubühne* (Vienna: Carl Konegan, 1884), "Zehntes Schreiben" (19 February 1768), p. 57.

29 Sonnenfels, *Briefe über die Wienerische Schaubühne*, pp. 139–41, cited in Krebs, *L'Idée de «Théâtre National»*, p. 488.

30 *Grundsätze zur Theaterkritik, über Einsicht[,] Sprache und Spiel in Menschenhaß und Reue*, (Vienna: Joseph Georg Oehler, 1790), pp. 36–37. It is possible that Oehler himself was the author. I thank John A. Rice for calling my attention to this source.

31 See Charles Rosen, *The Classical Style* (New York: Viking, 1971), p. 314; Andrew Steptoe, *The Mozart-Da Ponte Operas: The Cultural and Musical Background to "Le nozze di Figaro," "Don Giovanni," and "Così fan tutte"* (Oxford: Clarendon Press, 1988), p. 133; Heartz, *Mozart's Operas*, ch. 13; and Nicholas Till, *Mozart and the Enlightenment: Truth, Virtue and Beauty in Mozart's Operas* (London and Boston: Faber and Faber, 1991), pp. 235–36.

Table 2.1. *French-derived opere buffe performed in Vienna, 1783–90*

Model piece / genre	Author	Parisian premiere	Operatic version	Librettist	Composer	Viennese premiere
Le Barbier de Séville, ou La Précaution inutile (opéra-comique)/ comédie d'intrigue	Beaumarchais	1775	Il barbiere di Siviglia, ovvero La precauzione inutile	[Petrosellini?]	Paisiello	13 Aug. 1783
[episode in] Candide	Voltaire	1759	**Il re Teodoro in Venezia**	Casti	Paisiello	23 Aug. 1784
Le Bourru bienfaisant comédie (larmoyante)	Goldoni	1771	Il burbero di buon cuore	Da Ponte	Martín y Soler	4 Jan. 1786
L'Aveugle clairvoyant comédie d'intrigue	Legrand	1716	Il finto cieco	Da Ponte	Gazzaniga	20 Feb. 1786
La Folle journée, ou Le Mariage de Figaro comédie d'intrigue	Beaumarchais	1784	**Le nozze di Figaro**	Da Ponte	Mozart	1 May 1786
Démocrite amoureux comédie de caractère	Regnard	1700	**Democrito corretto**	Brunati	Ditters	24 Jan. 1787
Tarare opéra	Beaumarchais	1787	**Axur, re d'Ormus**	Da Ponte	Salieri	8 Jan. 1788
Nina, ou La Folle par amour opéra-comique	Marsolier	1786	Nina, ossia La pazza per amore	Lorenzi/ Da Ponte	Paisiello	13 April 1790

Note: Titles in bold indicate that the operatic version was written for Vienna.

comédie de caractère of Regnard from 1700; a *comédie larmoyante* of sorts by Goldoni; and a rather idiosyncratic operatic text by Beaumarchais. Despite the presence of two works from early in the century, the list is weighted towards recent pieces, by Beaumarchais in particular. Two of the sources had a whiff of scandal to them: *Figaro* on account of its political audacity, *Candide* because of its pervading ironic pessimism and implicit atheism. Given the Singspiel's reliance on *opéra-comique*, the absence of opera buffa adaptations of this genre (*Nina* apart) requires some explanation. Opera buffa already had a thriving tradition, whereas German comic opera was scarcely past its infancy and still sorely in need of models. Even then, the familiarity in Vienna of the original settings of *opéras-comiques* was problematic, as we have seen. It was mostly in places where the originals were less well known, as in London,[32] Eszterháza,[33] and Italy itself, that Italian translations or resettings of *opéras-comiques* were attempted. In addition, the ambitions of Da Ponte, and particularly of Casti, to attain the status of imperial poet, in succession to the late Metastasio, encouraged them to avoid "trivialities" of the sort that Zinzendorf found objectionable in both *opéra-comique* and opera buffa. For several reasons, then, the spoken genres of Paris's royally patented theatres were more attractive models for Italian librettists in Vienna.

A few words on the *drame* or *comédie larmoyante* are in order, for this species of entertainment enjoyed considerable success in Vienna. Zinzendorf, already aware that the genre was controversial, approved wholeheartedly of the first such piece he encountered, Nivelle de La Chaussée's *Mélanide*, performed in the Burgtheater in 1761: "There are many who disapprove of the *comédie larmoyante*, but they are wrong. That which is natural pleases. This play moved me to the point of shedding tears."[34] The genre was also championed by Sonnenfels because of the ease with

---

32 E.g. Da Ponte's *La bella Arsene*, after Favart/Monsigny and Mazzinghi, 1795; and *Zemira e Azor*, after Marmontel/Grétry, 1796.

33 E.g. Porta/Grétry, *Zemira ed Azor*, and Friebert/Haydn, *L'incontro improvviso*, 1775, after Dancourt/Gluck.   34 Zinzendorf, entry for 12 May 1761.

which audience members could identify with the characters.[35] Giovanni de Gamerra (dubbed the "poeta lagrimoso" by his contemporaries) introduced elements of the *comédie larmoyante* into his and Salieri's *La finta scema* in 1775; Bartolomeo Benincasa did likewise in Venice a decade later, with his *Il disertore*, after Mercier. These were by no means the first *opere buffe* in a sentimental vein; what is significant is that in their prefatory remarks the librettists specifically claim inspiration in the *comédie larmoyante*.

Goldoni's lacrimose comedy *Le Bourru bienfaisant* was first given in Vienna in January 1772, barely two months after the Parisian premiere. A translation by Stephanie the elder followed six months later, and was frequently revived. Da Ponte's operatic version for Martín y Soler held the stage for more than three years after its premiere in January 1786. Although something of the Venetian Pantalone is still recognizable in Goldoni's protagonist, Géronte,[36] the play successfully approximates the setting (Géronte's salon) and cast (a well-to-do household, complete with *laquais* and *gouvernante*) of an urbane French comedy, with an additional dose of sentimentality. Casti, thinking he was harming Da Ponte's chances of success with the piece, spread it about "that this was no subject for an opera buffa, and that it would not provoke laughter."[37] Recounting this to the emperor, Da Ponte quipped "all the better for me if it makes him cry."[38] He proudly reports that the spectators applauded even during the recitatives – implying that they listened to and understood them! Some of Goldoni's more memorable lines are rendered essentially verbatim in the recitatives. Da Ponte also reworked other poignant lines or speeches as aria texts. Madama Lucilla's anguished aria "Vado, ma dove?" (II. 5), which Mozart impressively reset, is equivalent in function to Mme.

35 Krebs, *L'Idée de «Théâtre National»*, p. 476.
36 And also, in the dialogue, some of the "ponderousness" and "mistrust of the spectator's powers of understanding" for which Sonnenfels had reproached Goldoni; see *Briefe über die Wienerische Schaubühne*, "Sieben und vierzigstes Schreiben," 21 November 1768, p. 283.
37 Da Ponte, *Memorie*, p. 105: ". . . che quello non era soggetto da opera buffa e che non farebbe ridere."   38 Ibid.: "meglio per me se lo farà piangere."

Dalancour's monologue as she realizes that she is the unwitting cause of her husband's ruin. The servant Castagna's aria about the remorse and generosity shown by his master Ferramondo (Géronte, in the play) after having injured him (II. 8) is also overtly sentimental (note the use of the word "lagrimar"), and no less indebted to Goldoni's text (in which he is named Picard, and the protagonist's maidservant is called Marton):

Goldoni, *Le Bourru bienfaisant* (III. I), Picard, Marton:

PICARD Oui, je boite un peu; mais cela n'est rien, j'ai eu plus de peur que de mal: cela ne méritoit pas l'argent qu'il m'a donné pour me faire panser.	PICARD Yes, I'm limping a little; but that's nothing, I was more afraid than hurt: it's not worth the money he gave me to have myself bandaged.
MARTON Allons, allons; à quelque chose malheur est bon.	MARTON Come, come: misfortune is good for something.
PICARD (*d'un air content*) Mon pauvre maître! ma foi, ce trait-là m'a touché jusqu'aux larmes; il m'auroit cassé la jambe que je lui aurois pardonné.	PICARD (*contentedly*) My poor master! upon my word, that gesture moved me to tears; I'd have pardoned him if he had broken my leg.

Da Ponte, *Il burbero di buon cuore* (II. 8), Castagna:

Questo è troppo, o padron mio; Voi mi fate lagrimar, Vostro servo alfin son io, Non vi state ad affannar.	This is too much, o master; You're making me weep, After all, I'm your servant, Don't worry yourself about me.
Vado vado, mio Signore (Quanto è mai dolce di core!) Se m'avesse rotto il collo, Glie l'avrei da perdonar.	I'm going, I'm going, sir (How goodhearted he is!); If he had broken my neck, I'd have to forgive him.

The operation of transferring the desirable features of the original piece to a new genre, with its own musical and dramatic requirements, was by no means foolproof. There being no action in Goldoni's play sufficient to provoke a *stretta* for the opera's first finale, Da Ponte invented a rather feeble excuse for one: Angelica's lover Valerio enters, having mistaken one door for another. Considerable rearrangement and invention of scenes was necessary in order gradually during the finale to bring all the characters on stage, and there were important structural changes also in the next act. A particularly unfortunate accretion was the duet (II. 13) in which Giocondo, ruined by debt and afraid to approach his surly uncle for aid, asks his friend Dorval "How could I suffer that terrible voice, that fierce regard?" – to which Dorval answers "Stop up your ears, don't look him in the eye . . . and pretend to sleep."[39] Such inanities stood out glaringly in the otherwise genteel dialogue of French-derived pieces, and were precisely the sort of thing critics of opera buffa found objectionable. Even more flawed was Brunati's *Democrito corretto*, whose libretto was so insipid that Emperor Joseph is supposed to have banned his works henceforth from the stage of the Burgtheater.[40] The libretto develops very differently from the play, with such extraneous additions as an onstage battle and a prison scene. Only a single speech – the burlesque definition of love by Democrito's gluttonous follower Strabon (I.5) – remained intact to give some indication of the tone of Regnard's ribald and witty comedy:

Regnard, *Démocrite amoureux* (I. 5), Strabon:

L'amour, ne vous déplaise, est un je ne sais quoi,	Love, if you please, is a certain something,
Qui vous prend, je ne sais ni par où, ni pourquoi;	That takes you, I know not by where, or why;
Qui va je ne sais où; qui fait naître en notre âme	That goes I know not where; that makes rise in one's soul
Je ne sais quelle ardeur que l'on sent pour la femme:	A certain ardor that one feels for a woman:
Et ce je ne sais quoi, qui paraît si charmant,	And this certain something, which seems so charming,
Sort enfin de nos cœurs et je ne sais comment.	Finally leaves our hearts I know not how.

39 Turatevi gli orecchi,
  Non lo guardate in faccia:
  Se grida, se minaccia,
  Pensate di dormir.

40 Da Ponte, *Memorie*, pp. 126–27.

Brunati, *Democrito corretto* (II. 3), Strabone:

E' l'amor un non so che	Love is a certain something,
Ch' entra in noi, per dove non so	That enters us, I know not by where,
Scende poi, ma dove va	That descends, but where it goes
Io veduto mai non l' ho[.]	I have not seen.
Questo tale non so che	This certain something
Ha in se stesso tal virtù	Has in itself such power
Che l' uom trae, nè so perchè	That it attracts a man, I know not why,
Colla donna a tu per tu[;]	Into a tête-à-tête with a woman;
Alla fin dal cor si parte	In the end it leaves the heart
E ci toglie ogni bruccior[,]	And takes with it every smart,
Ma non so poi per qual parte	But I do not know by what part
Il briccon se n' esca fuor[.] . . .	The rascal makes his escape . . .

Another cautionary example, in some respects, was the mercilessly literal translation of *Le Barbier de Séville* for the francophile court of St. Petersburg. As Daniela Goldin has observed, the librettist (usually said to be Petrosellini), working from instructions and at a distance, clumsily despoiled the play of much of its wit in trying to pare it to the dimensions demanded by the court, and to maximize the use of cognates for the benefit of an audience ignorant of Italian.[41] In the process, the libretto became little more than a reminder of Beaumarchais's text. Both poet and composer issued exculpatory statements in the libretto, Paisiello referring to his opera as an "extract" of the play. Da Ponte too uses this term in his preface to the libretto of *Le nozze di Figaro*, and mentions the same constraints of brevity and operatic convention. But Da Ponte ends by claiming to have created, along with his collaborator, "a quasi-novel genre of spectacle," worthy of "a public of such refined taste and such just understanding."[42] The greater length and complexity

41 See Daniela Goldin, *La vera fenice: Librettisti e libretti tra Sette e Ottocento* (Turin: Einaudi, 1985), ch. 5, "Il *Barbiere di Siviglia* da Beaumarchais all'opera buffa."
42 Quoted and translated in Heartz, *Mozart's Operas* pp. 120–21.

of his model account for this in large part, but Da Ponte, unlike Paisiello's collaborator, did not hesitate to put sophisticated language into his recitatives and set pieces. There were certainly some members of the Viennese audience who lacked Italian, but many spectators' comprehension was very good. Just prior to the debut of the new buffo troupe, for instance, Zinzendorf remarks on a casual discussion over dinner of Italian poets, and mentions appearances by the poetic *improvvisatore* Angelo Talassi.[43] One of his friends and fellow theatre-goers, Count János Fekete de Galántha, is known to have translated several cantos of Ariosto's *Orlando furioso*. Even if such spectators were in the minority, they represent the level of competence towards which Da Ponte and Casti were aiming.

One technical feature of *Le Barbier de Séville* that was translated quite mechanically in the opera was Beaumarchais's repeated use of the subtitle, "La Précaution inutile," within the body of the piece, as a device to draw spectators into complicity with the author. These references (albeit fictional) to a play outside the frame of the drama made for a sense of *double entendre* not unlike that provided in an *opéra-comique* by *vaudevilles*: pre-existent tunes, often employed repeatedly, whose titles, or *timbres*, conjured up the tunes' original texts and a wealth of connotations. The allusions to Bartholo's "Précaution inutile" were somewhat blunted in the operatic version, since the librettist's retrenchments had eliminated even the line in which Bartholo explains this phrase's significance.[44] But the same technique appears prominently in *Così fan tutte*, now applied to the main title. This time, both librettist and composer were careful to integrate the strategy into the entire fabric of the piece, starting already in the overture, before the curtain even went up.[45]

---

43 Entries for 16 December 1782, 12 December 1782, and 7 February 1783, respectively.   44 See Goldin, *La vera fenice*, p. 171.

45 See Bruce Alan Brown, "Beaumarchais, Paisiello, and the Genesis of *Così fan tutte*," in Sadie, *Wolfgang Amadè Mozart*, pp. 312–38.

LESSONS IN FRENCH MUSIC

We turn now to some specifically musical contributions from French sources to Viennese opera buffa. Some of these were borrowings of styles or forms – the *vaudeville final*, for example, as in the first-act finale of Salieri's *La locandiera*. Other contributions were the result of librettists reacting to interesting situations or characterizations in French originals, and of composers in turn reacting to the resulting texts in ways that took them outside the usual opera buffa conventions. Beaumarchais's Figaro plays gave rise to both sorts of interaction.

Le Barbier de Séville had originally been conceived as an *opéra-comique*, and even as revised for the Comédie Française in 1775 it still retained many realistic opportunities for onstage music. (There was also an impressive orchestral storm as an entr'acte, inspired by the *tempête* in Monsigny's *opéra-comique Le Roi et le fermier*.)[46] Figaro's song-composing air at the beginning of the opera (I. 2), Almaviva's serenade (I. 6), Rosine's music lesson (III. 4) and the simple *séguedille* with which Bartholo answers it (III. 4–5) – all had close analogues in Paisiello's score, where they were interrupted, commented upon, or accompanied by pantomime. (The *ariette* that Rosine sings as her music tutor Bartholo slumbers was reset by Mozart in 1789 as "Schon lacht der holde Frühling" [K. 580] for insertion into a German-language production of Paisiello's opera.) And because the St. Petersburg translation was so tenaciously literal, several other set pieces emerge from the recitative with striking naturalness, whatever the sacrifice in wit. Bartolo, as he confronts Rosina with evidence that she has written to her lover "Lindoro," is so perfectly insinuating that one scarcely notices that his music has moved from recitative into aria (see Example 2.1). In addition, the short phrases with which Beaumarchais's Bartholo begins his speech – "Certes, j'ai tort; se brûler le doigt, le tremper dans l'encre . . ." – seem already to suggest a sing-song melody such as Paisiello composed.[47] In the same spirit was the aforementioned duet that

46 Marvin Carlson's essay in this volume discusses the libretto of this opera.

47 "Certainly I'm wrong; burning one's finger, dipping it in ink . . .". As early as 1786 critics were noticing the latent musicality of Beaumarchais's prose in *Le Barbier de Séville*; see Goldin, *La vera fenice*, p. 165.

Example 2.1 Paisiello, *Il barbiere di Siviglia*, No. 9

Example 2.1 *(cont.)*

cer - to ch'es - ser può:

Bartolo: I'm truly mistaken, for sure; when one burns one's finger, it can be cured with ink, that's certain.

Emperor Joseph so admired, with the disguised Almaviva's unctu-
ous, reiterated greeting (III. 1; see Example 2.2). In calling for this,
of all pieces, to be repeated, Joseph encouraged his fellow spectators to value caricature and situation – of the sort featured in the
best modern French comedies – over the more purely musical
attractions of the showpieces that were more usually encored.

The transformation of *Le Mariage de Figaro* into *Le nozze di Figaro*
has been described in detail by Daniel Heartz and others.[48] Here we
shall simply note the degree to which French musical conventions
still color certain numbers of Mozart's score. In Act II, scene 4 of
the play, Chérubin sings a song to the Countess in which he gradually reveals his infatuation with her. Though set to a popular tune
("Malbroug s'en va-t-en guerre"), in other respects Chérubin's song
displays the usual features of the operatic *romance*, then very much
in vogue: an amorous subject, and an antique tinge to both words
and melody, which make their effect only gradually, across several
strophes.[49] (The form was familiar enough in Vienna for Gluck to
compose a convincing example in *Orfeo*; Salieri's *Axur* likewise con-

48 See Heartz, *Mozart's Operas*, ch. 6; Goldin, *La vera fenice*, ch. 5.
49 See Bruce Alan Brown, "Beaumarchais, Mozart and the Vaudeville: Two
   Examples from 'The Marriage of Figaro,'" *MT* 127 (1986), 261–5.

Example 2.2 Paisiello, *Il barbiere di Siviglia*, No. 12

Almaviva: May joy and peace be with us.

tains one.) In Habsburg Vienna it was not possible to depict the amorous tension between the page and his godmother as explicitly as in Paris, but Da Ponte followed Beaumarchais in providing eight short strophes (counting the reprise of the first stanza), and provided referentiality of a sort (substituting for that of Beaumarchais's *timbre*) by modeling his text on a duet in *Il re Teodoro in Venezia*.[50] Mozart's setting goes far beyond the simple strophic form provided him, as Wye Allanbrook has demonstrated, but is sufficiently reminiscent of it to remain convincing as a stage song.[51]

Even more reliant on French convention is the so-called letter duet, in which the Countess and Susanna concoct an invitation for the Count to an assignation in the park. The equivalent passage in the play (IV. 3) is a song-writing scene like that in *Le Barbier de Séville*, but now using French *vaudeville* technique. The Countess dictates: "Chanson nouvelle, sur l'air . . ." ("A new song, to the tune of . . .") and, after a moment's hesitation, gives the *timbre*, or name of the tune: "Qu'il fera beau ce soir sous les grands marronniers." This much is sufficient, they agree, for the message to

50 I. 4: "O giovinette / Innamorate, / Deh mi spiegate, / Che cos'è amor . . .".
51 See Allanbrook, *Rhythmic Gesture*, pp. 104–11.

get across. Da Ponte's version of this text is quite literal, apart from his substitution of "pines" for "chestnuts." But many translators have been confused by the heading "Canzonetta sull'aria," rendering it as "Song to the Zephyr" rather than "Song, to the tune of . . .". Indeed, Da Ponte's inclusion of the word "zeffiretto" in his made-up *timbre* encourages ambiguous interpretations, as if he were purposely accommodating spectators both with and without knowledge of *vaudeville* practice. Mozart sets the *vaudeville*'s caption apart, after the recitative cadence, and provides an eighth-note figure in 6/8 which depicts equally well Susanna's writing and the breezes of which the women sing (see Example 2.3).

Among the more progressive features of this opera is the prominence of action numbers, quite apart from the finales: Susanna's aria as she dresses Cherubino, their duet as he prepares to leap from the balcony, and the *vaudeville*-writing duet, among others. These are conspicuous also in *Il burbero di buon cuore*, Da Ponte having taken his cue from several striking scenes in Goldoni's French original. The back-and-forth of the timid Angélique and her forbidding uncle Géronte became, in Da Ponte's hands, a close prototype for an ensemble in *Così fan tutte*, which shares the earlier number's poetic meter and vocabulary:

Goldoni, *Le Bourru bienfaisant* (I. 8), Géronte, Angélique:

GÉRONTE Approchez.	GÉRONTE Come here.
ANGÉLIQUE (*avec timidité, ne faisant qu'un pas*) Monsieur . . .	ANGÉLIQUE (*timidly, taking just one step*) Sir . . .
GÉRONTE (*un peu vivement*) Comment voulez-vous que je vous entende, si vous êtes à une lieue de moi?	GÉRONTE (*a little sharply*) How am I supposed to hear you, if you're a league away from me?
ANGÉLIQUE (*s'avance en tremblant*) Excusez, monsieur.	ANGÉLIQUE (*comes forward, trembling*) Excuse me, sir.
GÉRONTE (*avec douceur*) Qu'avez-vous à me dire?	GÉRONTE (*gently*) What do you have to say to me?
ANGÉLIQUE Marton ne vous a-t-elle pas dit quelque chose?	ANGÉLIQUE Hasn't Marton said something to you?

Example 2.3 Mozart, *Le nozze di Figaro*, end of recitative (III:9)

Countess: Write. Susanna: Me, write? But madam... Countess: Write, I tell you;
I'll take all the blame myself. (*dictating*) Song to the tune of...
Susanna (*writing*) : To the tune of... Countess (*dictating*) What a gentle breeze...

GÉRONTE (*il commence avec tranquillité et s'échauffe peu-à-peu*) Oui; elle m'a parlé de vous; elle m'a parlé de votre frère, de cet insensé, de cet extravagant qui se laisse mener par une femme imprudente, qui s'est ruiné, qui s'est perdu, et qui me manque encore de respect!

GÉRONTE (*he begins calmly and becomes gradually agitated*) Yes: she has spoken to me of you; she has talked to me about your brother, about that senseless, extravagant man who allows himself to be led around by his imprudent wife, who has ruined himself, who's been undone, and who is also lacking in respect towards me!

(*Angélique veut s'en aller.*)

(*Angélique tries to leave.*)

GÉRONTE (*vivement*) Où allez-vous?

GÉRONTE (*sharply*) Where are you going?

ANGÉLIQUE (*en tremblant*) Monsieur, vous êtes en colère . . .

ANGÉLIQUE (*trembling*) Sir, you are angry . . .

Da Ponte, *Il burbero di buon cuore* (I. 7), Ferramondo, Angelica:

FERRAMONDO Venite fanciulla;
  Movetevi un pò;
  Se posso far nulla,
  Son quì, lo farò.
ANGELICA Signore, scusate . . .
  (*fa un altro passo*)
FERRAMONDO Se non v'accostate,
  (*un po' più vivamente*)
  Udirvi, capirvi

  Affè non potrò . . .

FERRAMONDO Come, girl,
  Move yourself a bit;
  If I can do anything for you,
  I'm here, I'll do it.
ANGELICA Sir, excuse me . . .
  (*takes another step*)
FERRAMONDO If you don't come
  closer, (*a bit more sharply*)
  I won't be able to hear or
    understand
  You at all . . .

Da Ponte, *Così fan tutte* (II. 4), Alfonso:

La mano a me date (*prende per mano Dorabella*)
  Movetevi un po. (*Despina prende Fiordiligi etc.*)
  Se voi non parlate
  Per voi parlerò . . .

Give me your hand (*takes Dorabella by the hand*)
  Move yourself a bit. (*Despina takes Fiordiligi*)
  If you don't speak,
  I'll speak for you . . .

In the next scene of *Il burbero di buon cuore*, after a meditative aria for Angelica, there comes another action aria, again modeled directly on Goldoni's prose. Here Ferramondo (played by Benucci) takes both sides in a game of chess, in an imaginary rematch with his friend Dorval (see Example 2.4). Ferramondo's progression from a tentative beginning to a triumphant checkmate was just the sort of crescendo that Benucci had performed so effectively in Basilio's "Calunnia" aria in *Il barbiere di Siviglia*.

One further aspect of French musical style in opera buffa – frivolous but not insignificant – is caricature. More than in cities without experience of French theatre, in Vienna there was a ready appreciation of comedies mocking Parisian *petits-maîtres* (fops) or *viaggiatori ridicoli*. There was a long tradition of such pieces in the city's French and German theatres, and even its Italian opera (e.g. Metastasio's *Le cinesi*, as revised in 1753). The European vogue for such pieces had crested by about 1770, but the repertory of Joseph's opera buffa company still included works in this vein, such as Cimarosa's *Il pittore parigino* (performed 1785), and Anfossi's *Le gelosie fortunate* (given in 1788). Naturally, the clichés of French music – trills, appoggiaturas, and dotted rhythms – were duly trotted out. Mozart, no admirer of French music himself,[52] parodies a French cadence with trill in *Così fan tutte*, as Despina alludes to the success in France of Mesmer's magnetic stone. Theatre audiences were also treated to snatches of French text, or fake-French, as in Example 2.5. Da Ponte demonstrates a lighter touch, with Marcellina's knowing comment "L'argent fait tout" ("Money cures all") in the recitative before her insult duet with Susanna, and Despina's advice to treat love "en bagatelle."

---

52 His distaste is expressed at its strongest, perhaps, in his letter of 5 April 1778. After remarking that the French were by now at least capable of listening to good music, he notes "But to expect them to realise that their own music is bad or at least to notice the difference – Heaven preserve us! And their singing! Good Lord! Let me never hear a French-woman singing Italian arias. I can forgive her if she screeches out her French trash, but not if she ruins good music! It's simply unbearable." Mozart, *Letters*, p. 522; *Briefe*, vol. 2, p. 332.

Example 2.4 Martín y Soler, *Il burbero di buon cuore*, No. 6

Andante maestoso

Ferramondo

Example 2.4 *(cont.)*

Example 2.4 *(cont.)*

Ferramondo: Quietly now, let's take a look: *(starts to place the pieces [on the board])* This is his situation, and this is mine; it's my turn: the king castles; and the castle goes over here.

In the broadest sense, French contributions to Viennese opera buffa were institutional in nature. Only because of the ability of theatre director Durazzo "to assemble on a single stage the dancers, musicians, and decorations of both theatres" had it been possible, in the reform operas of the 1760s, to bring to the stage of the Burgtheater the same conspicuous use of chorus, spectacle, and ballet as in French *tragédie lyrique* – a genre of which few Viennese spectators had any direct experience.[53] Even after this reformer's departure, the taste for integrated entertainments still made itself felt, in various genres. In 1779, long before the battle over the third-act fandango in *Figaro*, the Singspiel troupe managed to persuade Emperor Joseph of the necessity of hiring dancers, by pointedly choosing to perform Grétry's *Zémire et Azor*, in which ballet was an integral element.[54] After attending the premiere of Salieri's *Il ricco d'un giorno* in 1784, Zinzendorf commented, "beautiful decorations" and "many choruses," singling out resources not often

53 Letter to Favart of 20 December 1759; Favart, *Mémoires*, vol.1, pp. 3–4.
54 See Michtner, p. 75; and Da Ponte, *Memorie*, pp. 116–17.

Example 2.5 Anfossi, *Le gelosie fortunate*, No. 5

Example 2.5 (*cont.*)

Example 2.5 (*cont.*)

Madama Giuditta: Really, no compliments *(aping him with a bow)*, oh no,
I'm much obliged; I have no desire at present to dance the minuet.
Monsieur Girò: Ah, upon my word how handsome he is! The little dear is
ridiculous! My dear friend, are you the buffoon of the house?

exploited in opera buffa.[55] Da Ponte's attribution of the failure of
this, his first opera, to Salieri's "completely French music," composed in the shadow of *Les Danaïdes*,[56] is itself an indication of the
close connections between Parisian and Viennese spectacles, for
Salieri's warm reception in Paris had been prepared by the earlier
success of his mentor Gluck, a success facilitated in large part by
the personal intervention of the former Habsburg Archduchess
Marie Antoinette. Indeed there are echoes of Gluck in *Il ricco d'un
giorno*, in such pieces as Strettonio's "Già tutto intesi, o cara," with
its initial five-measure phrase (see Example 2.6). Salieri's debt to
Gluck is even more explicit in his and Da Ponte's *Axur*, after
Beaumarchais. The opera constituted a full-scale reimportation to
Vienna of Gluckian reform opera, with minimal coloratura,

55 Zinzendorf, entry for 6 December 1784; quoted in Michtner, p. 394, n. 38. A
contemporary librettist, Bartolomeo Benincasa, had pointed specifically to
French models a few years earlier, in advocating a more balanced use of
resources in opera buffa, and an end to "la negligenza della proprietà nelle
decorazioni . . .". (Benincasa, preface to *Il disertore*, [Venice, Carnival 1785], p. 6).
Benincasa styled his work a "dramma serio," after the model *drame* by Mercier.
56 Da Ponte, *Memorie*, p. 100. This contradicts his previous statement (p. 97) that
Salieri had completed the music before departing for Paris.

Example 2.6 Salieri, *Il ricco d'un giorno*, No. 11

Strettonio: I've understood everything already, my dear, I already know that you adore me.

numerous choruses, and orchestrally accompanied recitative throughout. And yet *Axur* was performed by the buffo troupe, and at many points speaks the same language as Mozart's Italian comic operas. Mozart's own reminiscences of works by Gluck for Vienna's French theatre, in *Die Entführung*, *Le nozze di Figaro*, and *Don Giovanni*, are further reminders that a single generation of spectators saw the language of the Burgtheater's musical offerings change from Italian (Metastasian opera seria) to French (*opéra-comique*) to Italian (opera buffa during the 1760s and 70s), to German (Joseph's *Nationalsingspiel*), and back again to Italian (Joseph's opera buffa troupe).

Experiments with French sources and practices in Viennese opera buffa were diverse in approach, of widely varying success, and do not lend themselves to generalization. In tracing some of these here we have concentrated on explicit instances of modeling and translation, but no less important are the more fleeting, indirect influences from French sources, which cumulatively bear greatly on the crucial matter of taste. Sonnenfels himself had demonstrated a path from a monolithic, French-oriented view of drama to a more critical, eclectic one, in first assuming and then dropping the mask of a Frenchman in his *Briefe über die Wienerische Schaubühne*. Through this stratagem he sought to show that French pieces and taste could be just as bad as those from elsewhere, and then to demonstrate how one might still profit from them. Austria's loss of its empire, and consequently its cosmopolitan outlook, has helped obscure (in the recording of its spectacles' history) the fact that the creators of opera buffa in the Josephine decade generally heeded Sonnenfels's advice, helping reveal in the genre a potential for gallic wit, urbanity, and naturalness – features Sonnenfels had looked for in vain in earlier examples in that repertory.

Il re alla caccia and *Le Roi et le fermier:* **Italian and French treatments of class and gender**
Marvin Carlson

In his thoughtful and illuminating book on Goldoni as a librettist for the *dramma giocoso*, Ted Emery understandably but unfortunately ends his analysis with Goldoni's departure from Venice in 1762, arguing that this date marks "the end of his most productive years as a playwright" and therefore the end of the period that should concern a study which examines the librettos "largely for what they suggest about the comedies."[1] One can certainly forgive Emery for acknowledging that most readers are likely to consider Goldoni's comedies of more interest than his librettos and therefore look more favorably upon a study that considers the latter primarily in view of the light they shed upon the former. However, it is worth considering Goldoni's contribution to the development of the libretto as of equal importance to his contribution to modern comedy. It is perhaps even more important to consider whether a deference to the cultural superiority of the comedies might not ultimately misrepresent the librettos, their role in Goldoni's career, and their place in the cultural and musical world of the late eighteenth century.

This problem becomes particularly clear in the context of defining Goldoni's career. While it can be argued that his most productive years as a playwright ended with his departure from Venice, this is by no means true of his activity as a librettist, since during his exile in Paris he continued to produce major librettos for theatres all over Europe, including, of course, those in Venice. Ignoring these later works may lead to serious misjudgments about his career. Emery, for example, argues that the most important link between Goldoni's plays and librettos is the reflection in each of the

1 Ted Emery, *Goldoni as Librettist: Theatrical Reform and the "Drammi giocosi per musica"* (New York: Peter Lang, 1991), p. xvi.

same political trajectory – beginning in his formative years with a traditional deployment of established themes and situations, then in mid-century using carnivalesque, reverse-world, and Arcadian themes to explore gender and political issues, and finally, from the mid 1750s, turning to a darker, more pessimistic, conservative, and paternalistic view. This brings us to the brink of Goldoni's departure from Venice and, according to Emery, the depressing end of his ideological trajectory, especially in the librettos. The stronger voice and role given to women in the mid-century plays and librettos are replaced by "a conservative and even misogynistic voice" that "underscores the frailty of Goldoni's feminism."[2] After 1760, Emery concludes, "Goldoni's critical sense of his society largely disappears from the operas, which henceforth seem to lack an ideological voice," and after his departure from Venice "the ideological content of his libretti shrinks nearly to insignificance."[3]

Had Emery examined the post-Venetian librettos with the same care that he extended to the earlier ones, he would have discovered that these conclusions were quite incorrect – that Goldoni, far from abandoning his mid-century ideological concerns involving class relationships and the position of women, explores them even more fully in some of these later librettos than he had in the earlier works. To illustrate this, I will look closely at one of the first post-Venetian works, *Il re alla caccia*, written in Paris but premiered with considerable success at San Samuele in the autumn of 1763. Here Goldoni both takes up the social implications of his mid-century "Arcadian" librettos and emphasizes the rights and interests of the female characters.

In both of these respects *Il re alla caccia* marks an advance not only over Goldoni's own "progressive" mid-century works, but also over Sedaine's and Monsigny's popular *opéra-comique*, *Le Roi et le fermier*, which Goldoni saw premiered in Paris in 1762 and which served as the immediate model for his own work. In his *Mémoires* Goldoni judges that Sedaine's work had "more action, greater live-

---

2 Emery, *Goldoni as Librettist*, p. 220.   3 Ibid., p. 207.

liness [*gaîeté*]" than its competitors, qualities that the Paris public gradually came to recognize: "I was extremely pleased with it, and I was grieved to see it on the brink of failure, but it recovered little by little and received its just due. It was presented an infinite number of times, and can still be seen with pleasure." Goldoni characterized Monsigny's music as "expressive, harmonious, pleasant."[4]

Goldoni also took this occasion to point out that his libretto and Sedaine's, along with Charles Collé's popular *La Partie de chasse de Henri IV* (1771), not an opera at all but a play with songs, have all been considered as derived from an English play, *The King and the Miller of Mansfield*, presented in London in 1737.[5] Goldoni also notes that behind the English play was a still earlier source, Lope de Vega's *Alcade de Zalamea*, and he briefly summarizes what he sees as the characteristics and qualities of each. The Spanish play contains "much intrigue – a daughter ravished, a father avenged, an officer strangled, and the Alcade serves as judge, party to the action, and executioner all in one." In the English version one finds "philosophy, politics, criticism, but too much simplicity and too little action". Goldoni found Collé's dramatic version "extremely clever and interesting" with a good king precisely calculated to appeal to current French interests.[6]

Goldoni tactfully avoids any direct comparison between his own work and Sedaine's, the closest to it, but he does significantly remark that in the opinion of some, "Italian comic operas are only farces unworthy to be placed in comparison with the poems of that name in France." Nevertheless, he continues, "Let those who understand the Italian language take the trouble to look over the six volumes which include my works in this genre and they will perhaps see that neither the ideas nor the style are so despicable [*méprisables*]."[7] Indeed in the case at hand, Goldoni's libretto is certainly equal or superior to Sedaine's on both these counts.

4 Goldoni, vol. 1, p. 496.
5 Actually Goldoni is a bit confused on this reference, speaking of "le Roi et le
   Meunier, Comédie Angloise de Mansfield" ("The King and the Miller, an English
   comedy by Mansfield"). The play was in fact by Robert Dodsley, Mansfield the
   location of the mill.   6 Goldoni, vol. 1, p. 496.
7 Goldoni, vol. 1, p.497.

Despite considerable variation in detail, each of these dramatic works is built around a situation widely found in European literature from the Renaissance onward and particularly closely associated with the pastoral tradition. An aristocrat, usually a knight, is attracted to a peasant and carries her off, overcoming her resistance by force or by false promises of love. Sometimes he has his way with her; more often the seduction is thwarted by her own resistance or by the interference of a higher authority, and she returns to her proper and socially appropriate lover. Probably the best-known example of this dramatic trope in the standard operatic repertoire is the subplot in *Don Giovanni* concerning Zerlina and Masetto, but it can be found as early as Adam de la Halle's thirteenth-century *Jeu de Robin et Marion*. Francesco Bianchi's *La villanella rapita* (libretto by Bertati), performed in Vienna in 1785, and for which Mozart wrote two substitute ensembles, represents a particularly "pure" version of the trope.[8] In a common variation, the peasant girl is importuned but not actually abducted, as in *Le nozze di Figaro* or in Da Ponte's and Martín y Soler's *Una cosa rara*.

Clearly class and gender tensions are central to the operations of this basic pastoral plot, but the extent to which they are developed has naturally depended on each dramatist's cultural context and particular concerns. Lope's *Alcade de Zalamea* weaves a complicated web of power relationships among members of various levels of society, but male/female relationships interest him only slightly, and Isabella, the suffering daughter of Crespo (the mayor), is little more than a useful object in the plot, saying next to nothing about her condition or fate. Her abductor is an army captain, which gives rise to arguments over whether the civil or military authority should prevail when the mayor arrests the Captain for raping his daughter. The King appears as a *deus ex machina* to resolve the dispute, making Crespo, who has ordered the Captain executed, perpetual mayor, while the dishonored daughter is hustled off to a convent, her own reactions to all of this cloaked in silence.

8 See Maria Grazia Accorsi, "Teoria e pratica della 'variatio' nel dramma giocoso: a proposito della 'Villanella Rapita' di Giovanni Bertati," in Muraro, *I vicini*, vol. I, pp. 139–63.

When Dodsley reworked this story two centuries later in England as *The King and the Miller of Mansfield* he made a number of striking changes that would have a profound impact on later musical versions of this story. First, the setting is changed, from the bustling town of Zalamea to a remote woods, Sherwood Forest to be precise.[9] The country, the domain of rustics and fools for an earlier generation of playwrights, was represented by the new generation as the dwelling place of simple but honest and good-hearted folk. The old Robin Hood tradition contributed strongly to this of course, but surely equally important was Shakespeare, and especially the Forest of Arden in *As You Like It*.[10]

The replacement in England of the Stuart kings with the more bourgeois House of Orange encouraged a more familiar treatment of royalty (though here too Shakespeare provided a model, most notably with the much loved Prince Hal). King Henry in Dodsley's play is as far from the remote and aloof King in Lope's play as Sherwood Forest is from Zalamea. Dodsley makes him a major character, and the opening scenes show him separated from his hunting party and delivering an emotional monologue, the burden of which is that a King lost in the woods is no different from any other man – a democratic, emotional, and personal note quite alien to the monarchs in Lope's plays, but regularly repeated in the subsequent French and Italian versions of this story. As night falls and foul weather threatens, the King is found by one of his gamekeepers, a miller, who takes him for a courtier, and invites him for dinner at his cottage. There the King in disguise joins in a song celebrating

9 This shift in setting had profound social and cultural implications for a British audience of the early eighteenth century. The opening years of the century had seen a striking shift in theatrical taste from the urbane brilliance of the Restoration drama, the last great example being Congreve's *The Way of the World* in 1700, to the gentler world of sentimental comedy and drama.

10 Early in *As You Like It* Charles informs Oliver of the old Duke's banishment to the forest, specifically relating the idyllic existence there to the Robin Hood legends: "They say he is already in the forest of Arden, and many merry men with him; and there they live like the old Robin Hood of England. They say many young gentlemen flock to him every day, and fleet the time carelessly, as they did in the golden world." (I. I).

democracy, listens to stories of corruption in London told by the miller's son, Dick, and hears how Lurewell, a courtier, attempted to seduce Dick's fiancée Peggy by making her believe scandalous falsehoods about Dick. Lurewell and others in the hunting party arrive at the cottage and reveal the King's identity. Lurewell is accused as a villain and condemned by the King. Dick and Peggy plan to marry and the King makes Dick's honest father a knight. Almost all of the action in Dodsley's drama is carried out by the male characters, but Peggy, unlike Lope's Isabella, is at least able to contribute her testimony to the investigation of Lurewell. She also assures the financial stability of her future by requesting from the King a pension for her husband-to-be.

The almost simultaneous French and Italian reworkings of this story twenty-five years later by Sedaine and Goldoni derive much of their basic plot from Dodsley's play, but with striking and often very different elaborations. Both versions follow Dodsley in being set in a forest during a royal hunt, and in and around the cottage / mill of the gamekeeper who provides shelter for king and courtiers. These versions also use the motif of the lost king who learns a lesson about humanity, but both move it to the beginning of the second act, after the romantic exposition. This later placement allows time for an emotional build-up to the scene; in addition, Sedaine and Goldoni both made the most not only of the political implications of the lost king but also of the powerful emotional, musical, and scenic possibilities in the depiction of a frightened and helpless individual lost in a dark wood with a storm brewing.

Both authors devote the first act to a rather elaborate exposition of the love interest, with much more attention to the emotional states of the young lovers than Dodsley. In addition Goldoni adds a number of new details, re-focusing the drama on class and gender tensions. His most striking addition is Milady Marignon, an aristocratic widow in love with Milord the seducer of the peasant girl (Giannina, or Jenny, in the Sedaine). This not only adds to the complexity of the emotional relationships, but provides a major new female voice, since Milady, though not particularly sympathetic, demands and receives attention for her strong opinions concerning her rights and her treatment.

In terms of generic convention, the addition of this character completes the pair of noble lovers (the *parti serie*) who join the *parti buffe* (servants, peasants, and others) in most of Goldoni's mature *opere buffe*.[11] As a bridge between the two Goldoni created the *mezzo carattere*, represented in *Il re alla caccia* both by King Henry and by the conciliatory courtier Riccardo, a breeches role. On the other hand, Goldoni's addition of Milady goes far beyond the simple structural matter of providing a female seria part to balance Milord. In the matter of gender representation she offers a bold new direction scarcely suggested in earlier versions, seeking no male champion but speaking out to demand a righting of her wrongs. Yet, important as this gender representation may be, in matters involving the aristocracy Goldoni's interest in class prejudice takes precedence over that of gender. Even while condemning the inconstancy of men in general, Milady seeks no common cause with other wronged women; she gives no hint that the "vulgar woman" Milord is pursuing might be as much his victim as Milady herself.

Goldoni's representation of Milady as more bound to her class than to her gender relates her to other snobbish noble ladies in the buffa tradition, such as Marchesa Lucinda in Goldoni's own *La buona figliuola* (1756) or Arminda in Anfossi's and Mozart's settings of *La finta giardiniera* (librettist(s) unknown, 1774 and 1775). Even so, I would argue that because Goldoni is exploring both class and gender tensions, Milady plays a more complex role than either Lucinda or Arminda. Daniel Heartz, citing Goldoni's strong comment that *opere buffe* admitted noble roles "in order to make them hated,"[12] argues that this suggests how to interpret a character like the haughty Marchesa Lucinda, an aristocrat so passionately attached to the privileges of her class that she is not merely

---

11 See Goldoni, vol. 14, p. 302, letter to Gabriele Cornet, on the function of the *parti serie* in opera buffa. See also Heartz, *Mozart's Operas*, ch. 11.

12 Letter to Gabriele Cornet. See Daniel Heartz's article elsewhere in this volume.

unpleasant, but even, if we take her creator at his own words, detestable. Milady is more ambiguous, since even if she refuses to see herself and Giannina both as victims of Milord, the audience may be aware of their common persecution; thus, Milady is ambiguously situated in a double role as both champion of class privilege and wronged woman.

Like Dodsley but unlike Sedaine, Goldoni begins his version with his aristocratic characters, and instead of the rather sentimental lover's complaint that opens Sedaine's play (Richard bewails the abduction of Jenny by Lurewell, and is consoled by various other characters), Goldoni begins with the less common device of an opening chorus by the King's hunters describing the pleasures of the hunt.[13] His first scene parallels Sedaine's, showing two men discussing the abduction of the miller's daughter; instead of the suffering lover, however, we find the ravisher himself, boasting of his deed to a fellow courtier, Riccardo, who warns him that Milady has come to the forest to complain to the King that Milord has scorned her despite his promise to marry her. Milord's response indicates clearly that gender and class will dominate the negotiations of power in this play. The King will never force him to marry Milady, he asserts, since "Elle è vedova alfine, e non zitella" ("after all she is a widow, and not a spinster," 1. 1. 169), while the gentle Giannina, whose favors he is attempting to buy, is beautiful and virtuous, but unworthy of more serious attention since she is not noble.[14]

The King appears on the scene with other courtiers, shortly followed by Milady, whom the King agrees, with some reluctance, to

13 *Una cosa rara* (Martín y Soler and Da Ponte) is another of the relatively few *opere buffe* with this sort of opening, and it too has a chorus of hunters.

14 These feelings are elaborated in an aria "Se di sangue e di bellezza / Io misuro il pregio" ("If I measure the value of blood and of beauty") which calls nobility "un ricco fregio" ("a rich adornment"), since it is so widely esteemed in the world, but that it is beauty, "D'un bel ciglio il dolce incanto" ("the soft magic of a lovely eye") that alone constrains love (1. 2. 169). All *Il re alla caccia* quotations are from Goldoni, vol. 12, pp. 161–219. An extra note of piquancy was probably added to this scene's discussion of male / female relationships by the fact that the *mezzo carattere* Riccardo was actually a breeches role, played by Cammilla Pasi.

hear. In keeping with her greater identification with her rank than with her gender, Milady's complaint focuses less on Milord's betrayal of her affection that upon the fact that she has been replaced by a rival of inferior social status, a "femmina vil" ("vulgar woman," 1. 3. 170). This emotion is repeated later in an aria in which she expresses anger at both the unworthiness and the stubbornness of her rival ("Se il terren resiste ingrato," 1. 5. 172).

Having thus established his themes in the aristocratic sphere, Goldoni shifts his scene to the cottage. While Sedaine and Dodsley both give more of a voice to the threatened maiden than Lope, she remains in both these versions little more than a plot device, with her suffering lover providing most of the commentary about her situation and the emotions it arouses. Goldoni, having already given Milady an opportunity to articulate her concerns, now gives the peasants Giannina and her sister Lisetta a parallel opportunity. When Giorgio hears how Giannina escaped, his love for her is rekindled, but she condemns his lack of trust. A series of discussions and songs follow on the theme of trust in love, a theme already introduced by Milady, and one of the dominant themes throughout the opera buffa tradition. The act closes with a quartet for the four lovers: "Amor può serenare / Le cose più funeste, / Amor fra le tempeste / Può rallegrare il cor" ("Love overcomes the worst matters, Love shelters the heart from the storm," 1. 14. 184).

Goldoni's second act includes all the action in Sedaine's last two acts; we will see that his third act expands on some of the political and ideological themes suggested in the first two. Table 3.1 shows the correspondences.

The two second acts begin similarly, with a duet of comic confusion in the darkening woods soon followed by the scene of the lost and frightened king singing a solo with essentially the same message: Sedaine: "Quelle nuit! quelle obscurité! . . . Hélas! dans cette inquiétude / Que me servent la Royauté, / Et le Trône & la Majesté?" ("What night! What darkness! Alas, in this disturbing state, what use is royalty, throne, or majesty to me?" 11. 2)[15]

---

15 All quotations from *Le Roi et le fermier* are taken from the Paris 1762 libretto.

Table 3.1. *Correspondences between Goldoni's Act II and Sedaine's Acts II and III*

Sedaine, Act II	Goldoni, Act II, scenes 1–9
	Opening scene – confused duet by foresters
	The King lost in the woods
	The King rescued and invited to dinner at the mill
Lurewell boasts of his conquest	Milady bemoans her fate
	Milady confronts Milord
	Arrest of courtiers by the foresters
Sedaine, Act III	**Goldoni, scenes 10 onward**
	Songs of the women at the mill
	The King's interaction with the mill family
	Supper at the mill
	Arrival of the foresters and the lord
	The seducer condemned, young lovers united

Goldoni: "Quando è solo in un bosco, agli altri è eguale" ("When one is alone in the woods, he is equal to the others." II. 187) The King is then found by the young hero, who takes him for a courtier and invites him to shelter and supper. Here the plots diverge slightly, even though each dramatist focuses on the errant lord. Sedaine provides a scene in which Lurewell boasts to a colleague of his conquest, after which they are arrested by the two forest guards. Goldoni, as before, devotes more attention to Milord's female victims than to his own boasts, and Milady bewails her fate, confronts her faithless lover, is arrested with him, and concludes this section with a sentimental aria, "Fra l'orror di queste selve" (II. 9. 194).

Two scenes in particular offered both Goldoni and Sedaine a strong combination of emotional strength and political import. The first is the King lost in the woods, with its democratic message of the disappearance of social distinctions in common human situations of fear and danger. The second is the supper in the cottage, which engages in direct social critique by arguing the superiority of the simple rustic meal over the artificial and corrupt life in the city and at court.

Those familiar with Goldoni's mid-century work will recognize a close parallel between the ideological content of the supper scene and of the "Arcadian" operas,[16] depicting a freer and more innocent agrarian world in contrast to a corrupt court. The actual preparation and serving of the supper is given much more attention in Goldoni and Sedaine than in Dodsley, perhaps due to the theatrical interest of seeing the King enjoying this humble fare, but also reflecting the growing interest in the theatre (as in the painting) of this period in realistic depictions of domestic situations.

This orientation also has implications for the depiction of women, since the shift to a domestic sphere provides greater opportunity to depict women engaged both in action and song. Sedaine here as before provides more of a voice for the women than Dodsley, but distinctly less than Goldoni. In both Sedaine and Goldoni the women serve while the King and the hero eat, but in Sedaine the women's subsidiary role is more pronounced. Although they sing several airs and converse among themselves, their invariable subject is the men and their activities. After serving the two men, they retire to the next room, where they become a kind of surrogate audience, watching the two men eat and speculating in a trio about the elegant guest Richard has brought home. Sedaine's use of these two spaces reinforces the distribution and the content of the songs. Although the entire stage may be said to represent the domestic sphere, there remains a distinction between the public dining area, associated with the men, and the private kitchen area, the domain of the women. And although the songs in the act are more or less evenly divided between men and women, no woman sings in the men's area, and the women's songs in their own area all concern the men.[17]

Goldoni's scene is set in the courtyard of the mill, a somewhat

16 Emery's term. *Goldoni as Librettist*, pp. 124–41.

17 Cf., for example, the trio for Jenny, Betsy, and the mother, "Ah! Ma tante" / "Hé oui contente" (III. 5. 45). And even when Richard pursues Jenny into the kitchen for a romantic interlude and a love duet might be expected, the duet they in fact sing is focused not on themselves but on the waiting guest in the other room, to whom Richard is bringing a bottle of wine ("Un instant" / "Il m'attend," (III. 9. 50).

less domestically encoded place, where the men and women of the action meet on more equal footing. Giannina's opening aria in this setting, "Bella cosa è il vedere un mulino" ("Lovely the sight of the mill," II. 10. 195), like the songs of Sedaine's women, is really about the men. She engages in some criticism, however, comparing the demands of Giorgio and Milord to two grindstones. Giorgio announces that his guest has promised that the King will give them justice, but Giannina is more cynical. Only three keys open doors at the court, she says: "L'oro, l'adulazione e la bellezza" ("gold, flattery, and beauty," II. II. 197). On being informed that the presumed courtier is tired, she tells him she does not understand how intelligent men can waste their energy on something so detestable as the hunt, following horse and hound and deserting their wives. The King, far from being offended, praises her spirit, which "equals her beauty." The situation has distinct echoes of a scene in *Bertoldo, Bertoldini, e Cacasenna* (1748), one of the first of Goldoni's "Arcadian" operas, in which the outspoken Bertoldo extols the virtues of a rustic life over the hollow values of the court and is subsequently praised by the King for his frankness. Significantly, Sedaine follows Goldoni's earlier practice by assigning this key air on the relative values of court and country to a male lead, Richard, while Goldoni departs both from his own earlier model and from Sedaine in giving it to Giannina rather than to Giorgio.[18]

After Giorgio and the King share a simple meal, Giorgio offers a toast to the presumably absent monarch and in his enthusiasm smashes his glass. Giannina complains about this waste and the King offers to pay, but Giorgio, a bit tipsy, haughtily refuses with a song mocking the misplaced generosity of courtiers. When he leaves, the King, in a scene parallel to that in Sedaine, offers a purse to Giannina and Lisette. Giannina, like Giorgio, refuses, but Lisette accepts. The situation is similar to the gold coin sequence in Sedaine and both suggest a common character configuration in

---

18 In so doing, he reinforces the growing eighteenth-century association between women and "the natural," discussed in Tia DeNora's paper elsewhere in this volume.

opera buffa, where the secondary female characters from the lower class are more mercenary, more crassly practical, and more broadly comic than the more idealistic and sentimental primary characters.[19] Goldoni somewhat softens the traditional hard-nosed practicality of his secondary female character by giving her a charming song explaining her action and arguing that as a gift to her dowry this offering can be considered both honest and innocent. Once again the King is impressed by the candor and sensitivity of his hosts, and once again it is the arguments of a woman that stimulate his comments.

After the supper, other guards arrive with the aristocratic would-be seducer as prisoner and he reveals the King's identity to his astonished hosts. Both Sedaine and Goldoni now move rapidly to the solution to the problem of the young lovers and the evil courtier. In both plays the seducer claims that the girl actually sought his protection, but she denies this and the King orders his arrest. In both plays the King knights the young hero and in Sedaine promises a dowry to Jenny as well. A general chorus in both plays celebrates this judgement and vindication of innocence and honor.

Sedaine ends his play here, following the pattern of Dodsley and Lope, but Goldoni has only reached the conclusion of his second act (see Table 3.1). The most obvious loose end is the fate of the spurned Milady. According to the conventions of comedy, Goldoni could have brought her to the cottage with Milord, where her problem could be included in the general wrapping up of the action. The plot's obligatory scene is the confrontation between Milord and the young lovers, with the King as the agent of resolution. A standard comedy would at this point move quickly to its conclusion (as Sedaine's and Dodsley's versions do), with all characters on stage for the tying up of loose ends and the pairing of the lovers.

19 This tradition carries on into nineteenth-century melodrama, which inherits much of the buffa tradition. Here again we find sentimental lower class heroines pursued by aristocratic villains along with secondary, rougher, and more comic male and female allies of the primary characters.

Goldoni, however, uses the unfinished plot line of Milady to extend his story into a further act, albeit as a pretext to expand his commentary on class relations. The setting is significantly not at the court, even though the King will be taking care of "official" business, but rather in the more "natural" setting of a shady bower, where the King with his attendants establishes a temporary court and tribunal. This setting reinforces the concerns with the "private," "natural" and thus (as Tia DeNora points out) "feminine" concerns of "feeling, warmth, individuated love" and, of course, the celebration of marriage as the focus of these concerns. Milord has already been placed under arrest. Milady soon arrives, also arrested in the woods by Giorgio's friend, Pascale, but there is much comic delay and confusion before this fact is known, since Pascale is so overwhelmed by being in the presence of the King that he must spend some time in expressing his servility and deference in words and in song before the King can get a report from him. Far from being irritated, however, the King is much amused by this singular character, unlike anyone at court, and while the situation hardly causes him to reflect seriously upon Giannina's claim that the country is superior to the court, it does provide him with fresh evidence, as did his experience at the mill, that there are interesting and amusing parts of his domain of which he was unaware while he remained in his limited and confined (and male-oriented) public world. Milord and Milady present their cases in a duet to the King, Milord repeating his earlier argument that as a widow Milady has no claim upon him, and adding that in any case both would suffer if he were forced to marry where he has no affection. Milady, undeterred, says, in anticipation of the rejected ladies of Gilbert and Sullivan, that whether she gets his heart or not she will be satisfied with his hand. The King, noting that Milord has twice offended in love, grants the lady's request.

The action now shifts to Giorgio and Giannina, and from gender tension to class tension. Now that Giorgio has been knighted, Giannina becomes much more concerned with the trappings of social position. Members of the nobility seem happy, she sings, but that is only because of the goods and power they possess. Rather than taking this as a lesson to be content with less, she presses Giorgio to find out just what his knighthood is worth. Can they now have pages and a coach, as befits a knight and lady? A new problem arises when Lisette announces her desire to wed Pascale. Now that her social class has risen, Giannina has become as intolerant of members of the lower classes as Milady had been earlier and she becomes as ruthlessly pragmatic as any secondary comic character. Now that she is a lady, she cannot allow her sister to make so humble a match. The King sings an aria "Se rallentate il freno / All'appetito umano" ("If you slow the brakes on human appetites" iii. 9. 215–16) wryly noting the infinity of human desire; as a *mezzo carattere* this is the closest he comes to comic commentary.[20] Nevertheless he makes Pascale a Captain of Infantry so that the marriage can take place. His generous action naturally delights all of the young lovers, but Giorgio and Giannina also reflect on his words and sing a love duet expressing their more "natural" realization that true happiness lies in a tempering of ambitions.

A final scene offers a combined song and dance in the open country in which all three united couples hail the just and generous king and the god of love, even Milord promising at last to give hand AND heart to Milady. The tensions of class and gender that have fueled much of the action in Goldoni's script dissolve, as is proper to comedy, in a traditional marriage celebration and dance. Yet the resolution is very much imposed and manipulated by the benevolent King, who has the means and inclination to resolve gender conflict by fiat and class conflict by ennobling everyone who asks. Goldoni provides a much more extensive exploration of the tensions aroused by this story than either Dodsley or Sedaine, and looks more deeply into them than even in his innovative librettos of

---

20 One may be reminded of the King in Hugo's *Hernani*, who also comments wryly on the passionate search for hollow honors by his courtiers while remaining quite unaware of the similarity to his own striving to become Holy Roman Emperor.

a decade and more before. Nevertheless, he concludes, not surprisingly, according to the expectations of the genre, with a reinscription of the traditional social order and of its ongoing class and gender relationships, its stability and its justice assured by a powerful and enlightened controlling monarch.

4 | Mozart and eighteenth-century comedy
Paolo Gallarati

Opera buffa undoubtedly contributed to the development of Mozart's theatre by offering him specific and detailed linguistic and formal models. Without the *dramma giocoso* as it developed in the second half of the century, with large ensembles, arias in a variety of forms, and a stylistic multiplicity that broadened his available materials, Mozart would not have had at his disposal the tools to compose *Le nozze di Figaro* and *Don Giovanni*. But we cannot understand the deep historical and aesthetic bases for these masterworks without considering the fundamental fact that from about 1780 on, opera buffa did not satisfy Mozart anymore. As he himself noted, his completely new dramaturgical project required that opera buffa's repertory of theatrical, vocal, and instrumental forms be reformulated. I am convinced that the context of opera buffa is too limited to provide a proper understanding of Mozartean drama and the aesthetic ideas from which it sprang; it is thus necessary to look at other sorts of eighteenth-century theatre for the impetus that permitted him to transform the *dramma giocoso* into true musical comedy founded on the representation of life. That wider context is the subject of this essay.

On 17 May 1783 Mozart wrote to his father from Vienna:

> Well, the Italian *opera buffa* has started again here and is very popular. The buffo is particularly good – his name is Benucci. I have looked through at least a hundred libretti and more but I have hardly found a single one with which I am satisfied; that is to say, so many alterations would have to be made here and there, that even if a poet would undertake to make them, it would be easier for him to write a completely new text – which indeed it is always best to do.[1]

---

1 Mozart, *Letters*, p. 847; *Briefe*, vol. 3, p. 268.

Harsh words, indeed: they imply scarcely less than unequivocal rejection of a genre which Mozart had not practiced since *La finta giardiniera* of 1775, and which he tried to revive in 1783 (the year of the letter) with *L'oca del Cairo* and *Lo sposo deluso*, projects begun but soon left unfinished. Why? After the composition of *Idomeneo* and *Die Entführung aus dem Serail*, Mozart had come round to the idea of a new kind of musical theatre oriented towards a representation of life and based on the dynamic force of individual psychology. Italian comic opera, in contrast to this aesthetic, had never aspired to an accurate representation of reality, but aimed at presenting a conventionally stylized abstraction of life in the manner of a rationalistic game. Carlo Goldoni was well aware of this. Although he had revitalized opera buffa and provided a model comparable in diffusion and normative force to the Metastasian model in opera seria, he despised the genre, considering it a purely escapist form of entertainment whose music made it incapable of representing the moral, sentimental, and psychological complexity of life by means of a rigorous coherence of behavior, characters, and plot.[2] This was exactly what Mozart was hoping to achieve by opening up new perspectives for the musical theatre.

But in order to bring about this revolution Mozart first sought a subject more refined and complex than those supplied by the vast repertoire of contemporary opera. His choice fell, that same year, 1783, on Goldoni's comedy *Il servitore di due padroni*, which he decided to set to music for his own enjoyment:

> I am now writing a German opera for myself. I have chosen Goldoni's comedy "Il servitore di due padroni," and the whole of the first act has already been translated. Baron Binder is the translator. But we are keeping it a secret until it is quite finished.[3]

2 See the prefaces to the librettos *I portentosi effetti della madre natura* (Goldoni, vol. 10, pp. 1157–58) and *De gustibus non est disputandum* (Goldoni, vol. 11, pp. 103–04).

3 Mozart's letter of 5 February 1783, to his father from Vienna; Mozart, *Letters*, p. 751; *Briefe*, vol. 3, p. 255. The tenor aria "Müßt' ich auch durch tausend Drachen," K. 435 (416b), and the bass aria *Männer suchen stets zu naschen*, K. 433 (416c), probably formed part of the project of this opera.

But it was not merely the search for a subject that had driven him to explore the world of theatrical comedy; it was a whole complex of dramatic problems which the spoken theatre had solved during those years in various parts of Europe, producing, in the works of Lessing, Diderot, and Goldoni (in Germany, France, and Italy, respectively) a new and more faithful representation of reality.

Mozart was a passionate theatre-goer, and had attended regularly from the very first months of his residence in Vienna. "My sole entertainment is the theatre. How I wish that you could see a tragedy here!" he wrote to his sister on 4 July 1781, on which date the tragedy most recently staged at the Burgtheater had been none other than *King Lear*.[4] A connoisseur of *Hamlet* since the time of *Idomeneo*, Mozart was immersed in a thoroughly Shakespearian milieu; his friend Schikaneder and his brother-in-law Joseph Lange, Aloysia Weber's husband, were great actors specializing in Shakespeare, whose rediscovery in the eighteenth-century had, as I have described elsewhere,[5] led to an extraordinary proliferation of performances. During Mozart's ten years in Vienna there were stagings of *Hamlet* (every year), *King Lear* (1781, 1782, 1784, 1788, 1789, 1790, 1791), *Romeo and Juliet* (1781, 1782, 1787, 1788, 1789), *Othello* in the translation by Wieland (1785, 1787, 1790), *Henry IV* (1782), and *Coriolanus* (1789). But it was not only Shakespeare whom Mozart could admire in the Viennese theatres; the works of all the best contemporary playwrights, from Gozzi to Marivaux, from Voltaire to Marmontel, and from Schiller to Goethe, were also performed there.

In the realm of comedy Goldoni's influence was particularly important.[6] In addition to a large number of librettos, several of his

4 Performed 19 July. Mozart, *Letters*, p. 751; *Briefe*, vol. 3, p. 138. Information on theatrical performances in Vienna is taken from Franz Hadamowsky, *Die Wiener Hoftheater (Staatstheater) 1776–1966: Verzeichnis der aufgeführten Stücke mit Bestandnachweis und täglichem Spielplan*, 2 vols. (Vienna: Prachner, 1966).

5 Paolo Gallarati, *La forza delle parole: Mozart drammaturgo* (Turin: Einaudi, 1993), pp. 30ff.

6 Cf. also the essays by Bruce Alan Brown and Daniel Heartz elsewhere in this volume. (Eds.)

plays were performed in German translations or adaptations: *Il servitore di due padroni* (1788), *I due gemelli veneziani* (1778–1790), *Un curioso accidente* (every year except 1789), *Il burbero benefico* (1781, 1783, 1785, 1786, 1787, 1791), *Il padre di famiglia* (1780), *Il bugiardo* (1781, 1782, 1784, 1786, 1790, 1791). Also represented was that other champion of avant-garde comedy, Denis Diderot. His *Le Père de famille* was staged in 1781, 1783, 1784, 1785, 1788, 1789, 1790, and 1791. The triad of great masters of the new European drama was completed by Lessing, whose major theatrical works – *Emilia Galotti, Minna von Barnhelm, Miss Sara Sampson, Philotas*, and *Nathan der Weise* – enjoyed unprecedented success on the German stages of the period; several were in the regular repertory of Schikaneder's troupe.[7] There is no doubt that Mozart knew them, and it is likely that he had also read Lessing's *Hamburgische Dramaturgie*, for, in the famous letter of 26 September 1781, he describes his aesthetic of expressive naturalness with the same words as Lessing and in a manner very similar to that of the German playwright:

[Lessing:] Neither our eyes nor our ears should be offended [*weder unsere Augen noch unsere Ohren beleidiget werden*] and only when everything is avoided in the expression of violent passions [*heftige Leidenschaften*] that can be unpleasant to these, can acting possess that smoothness and polish which Hamlet demands from it even under these circumstances, if it is to make the deepest impression and to rouse the conscience of stiffnecked sinners out of its sleep.[8]

[Mozart:] The passage "Drum beim Barte des Propheten" is indeed in the same tempo, but with quick notes; and as Osmin's rage gradually increases, there comes (just when the aria seems to be at an end) the Allegro assai, which is in a totally different meter and in a different key; this is bound to be very effective. For just as a man in such a towering rage oversteps all the bounds of order, moderation, and propriety and

---

7 Schikaneder's repertory included *Minna von Barnhelm, Emilia Galotti*, and *Die Juden*. See Kurt Honolka, *Papageno: Emanuel Schikaneder, Man of the Theater in Mozart's Time*, trans. Jane Mary Wilde (Portland, OR: Amadeus, 1990), pp. 45, 53.

8 G. E. Lessing, *Hamburgische Dramaturgie*, ed. Otto Mann (Stuttgart: Kröner, 1963), p. 25 (15 May 1767); translation by Helen Zimmern from *Selected Prose Works of G. E. Lessing* (London: G. Bell, 1913), p. 247 (slightly altered).

completely forgets himself, so must the music too forget itself. But since passions, whether violent or not [*die leidenschaften, heftig oder nicht*] must never be expressed to the point of exciting disgust, and as music, even in the most terrible situations, must never offend the ear [*das Ohr niemal beleidigen*], but must please the listener, or in other words must never cease to be music, so I have not chosen a key foreign to F (in which the aria is written) but one related to it – not the nearest, D minor, but the more remote A minor.   [Mozart, *Letters*, p. 769; *Briefe*, vol. 3, p. 162]

In view of his exposure to current European drama and also to Molière, whose comedies Mozart possessed in the three-volume translation of Friedrich Samuel Bierling (Hamburg, 1752),[9] it is natural that he should have been increasingly drawn towards the idea of a theatre profoundly different from that presented by the Italian comic opera; a realistic theatre which aimed, as in Lessing's plays, at a minute analysis of the human heart, where the tragic, the pathetic and the comic – comic, that is, in the realistic-everyday sense – germinate reciprocally from one another, and laughter, casting aside the mask of sarcasm, is lit up by a "Mozartean" affection for humankind. The aesthetic problem which Mozart was to solve in *Le nozze di Figaro* had, in short, a close affinity with that posed by Lessing in his *Theatralische Bibliothek* (Berlin, 1754), where he wrote:

> farce seeks only to provoke laughter, and lacrimose comedy seeks only to move; true comedy seeks to attain both aims[10]

– by recourse, we might add, to that "middle tone" in which the voice of the bourgeoisie was identified as the humanized incarnation of nature.[11] To make this voice ring out in music was precisely the task that Mozart had set himself in some passages of *Idomeneo*

9 Cf. the letter of 24 March 1778 to his father, from Paris. Mozart, *Letters*, p. 518; *Briefe*, vol. 2, p. 328.

10 "Gotthold Ephraim Lessings Theatralische Bibliothek; Lustspiel-Abhandlungen," in Karl Eibl, ed., *Gotthold Ephraim Lessing Werke* vol. 4, *Dramaturgische Schriften* (Munich: Carl Hanser Verlag, 1973), p. 56.

11 See P. Chiarini, *Introduzione* to G. E. Lessing, *Drammaturgia d'Amburgo*, (Rome: Bulzoni, 1975), p. xxxiv.

and, more extensively, in *Die Entführung aus dem Serail*, but which he did not fully accomplish until he crossed over into the field of theatrical comedy by taking on the subject of *Le Mariage de Figaro*, which Da Ponte transformed, under his supervision, into a libretto entirely free of those binding conventions which rendered the fixed and schematic dramaturgy of the *dramma giocoso* so intolerable to Goldoni.

In his librettos for Mozart, Da Ponte substituted for the disjointed drama of his rival Giambattista Casti and others like him a drama of organic development, suitable for a musical comedy of action; he splinters the dialogue of the ensembles into extremely short segments to accentuate the realism of musical conversation; he refines the dialogic aria to an extraordinary degree, and abolishes every rhetorical and dramaturgical interruption in the transitions between recitatives and arias and ensembles.[12] Of course Da Ponte's librettos also contain elements typical of opera buffa; Susanna's pastoral "Deh vieni non tardar," and Figaro's buffo aria "Aprite un po'" in the fourth act of *Le nozze di Figaro* are significant examples. But Mozart assumes a fundamentally new position in relation to such "stereotypes"; for him the conventional forms are no longer pre-constituted templates used mechanically to shape the music; they are, rather, a repertory of theatrical and musical elements to deploy according to new rules (those of Classic sonata procedures) in organisms that express the individuality of a character or situation. Thus Susanna's pastorale, while maintaining certain traditional stylistic features, becomes the most personal expression of erotic lyricism and loses all expressive reference to the rigidity of Arcadian convention. And the buffa aria in which Figaro turns directly to the audience becomes a typically Mozartean marvel of semiotic complexity; while on the one hand it momentarily alludes to the theatrical game by shattering the fourth

12 Cf. Gallarati, *Musica e maschera: Il libretto italiano del Settecento* (Turin: EDT, 1984) pp. 162–98. A revised and condensed English translation has been published as "Music and Masks in Lorenzo Da Ponte's Mozartian Librettos," *COJ* 1 (1989), 225–47.

wall, consciously using the conventionality of the buffa aria as an element of comic alienation, on the other hand it offers a psychological portrait of the character, who, instead of being absorbed into the description of the object – the infidelity of women – shows all his tormented interiority.[13] Neither *Le nozze di Figaro* nor *Don Giovanni* have much in common with Italian opera buffa; their characters are not, like the fixed types of the earlier opera, defined *a priori*, but are individuals capable of encountering situations that may be serious or comic or somewhere in between, and of changing in response to the events and vicissitudes of real life. Mozart thus achieves a result analogous to that achieved in spoken comedy by Goldoni, who had progressively freed comedy from the fixed conventions of the theatre of masks – preserving its scenic rhythm, its mimetic aspects, and its speed of dramatic action, but replacing the largely improvised plots of commedia dell'arte with a fully-written script presenting characters and unmasked faces drawn from the direct observation of reality.

All the great European comedy of the second half of the century arises from a polemical reaction to the theatre of masks and fixed types, whether farcical or *larmoyante*. In his celebrated treatise *De la Poésie dramatique* (1758) Diderot proposed the renewal of comedy as a representation of reality, and he puts his program into practice in *Le Père de famille*, which ran at the Burgtheater for eight seasons between 1781 and 1791, providing the theatrical culture of Vienna with a concrete model of a drama where the representation of life – understood as a dynamic encounter between various tendencies and individuals – aimed at achieving truth and naturalness. "Truth and naturalness" are recurring expressions in Mozart's letters and a norm of aesthetic judgement.[14]

Diderot distinguished between "farce," "merry comedy," "serious comedy," and "tragedy," advocating the development of an intermediate genre as the ideal medium for a faithful representa-

13 For another reading of the conventionality of this aria see the essay by Ronald J. Rabin elsewhere in this volume. (Eds.)
14 See Gallarati, *La forza delle parole*, pp. 27–29.

tion of reality.[15] This enables us to define precisely the aesthetic space between opera seria and opera buffa, and between *tragédie lyrique* and the Viennese Singspiel, which Mozart's great musical comedies occupied. By dissolving all rigid distinctions, this intermediate space makes *Le nozze di Figaro* – even though it is technically a "merry comedy" – not the caricature of human vices characteristic of that subgenre, but a representation of the duties of man, which, according to Diderot, "are as rich a source for the dramatic poet as are man's ridiculous aspects and vices."[16] *Don Giovanni*, on the other hand, is a "serious comedy" bordering on tragedy; it represents the pain which any of us might feel in the face of treachery, or moral or physical violence, or the murder of our dear ones. Thus Mozart's two operas, breaking free of all the sung theatre's rigid conventions, find a far more precise aesthetic reference in the spoken theatre than can be detected, external appearances apart, in the work of Paisiello, Cimarosa, Sarti, Anfossi, Gluck, or Piccinni, not to mention the more modest Singspiel repertory.

Our suspicion that spoken comedy constituted a direct model for Mozart's musical theatre can also be confirmed in other ways. For example, both the new comedy and Mozart's Da Ponte settings implied a transformation in the habits and tastes of the public. Goldoni was well aware of the need for such a transformation, for in the comedy *Il teatro comico* (1759) he put the following into the mouth of Orazio:

> once people went to see comedies only in order to laugh, and did not
> wish to see anything but masks on the stage; and if the serious characters
> carried on a dialogue of any length, they immediately grew bored; now
> they are getting used to listening to serious parts; they enjoy the words
> and delight in the events; they appreciate the morality and they laugh at
> the jokes and witticisms which are made to flow from the serious
> itself (ii. 10).[17]

15 Denis Diderot, *De la Poésie dramatique* in *Oeuvres esthétiques* (Paris: Garnier, 1988), p. 202.   16 Diderot, *De la Poésie dramatique*, vol. i, p 192.
17 Goldoni, vol. 2. Published in English translation as *The Comic Theater*, trans. John W. Miller (Lincoln: University of Nebraska Press, 1969).

Mozart and Da Ponte were similarly aware of the striking novelty of their work, where the serious and the comic are closely intertwined; for in the preface to the libretto of *Le nozze di Figaro* they speak of proffering to an audience "of such refined taste and such judicious understanding" a "kind of performance" which they describe, with studied understatement, as "almost new." And on 10 February 1784, during the planning of *L'oca del Cairo*, the composer proudly reassured his father about the originality of his work:

> I guarantee that in all the operas which are to be performed until mine is finished, not a single idea will resemble one of mine.[18]

"Expression and novelty," those fundamental principles of Romantic aesthetics, were from the time of *Idomeneo* onwards the qualities on which he most prided himself. Behind the experimental boldness of language and style of this great serious opera lay a new concept of theatre which gradually took shape and found its true path when Mozart met the comic-everyday subject, especially in Italian opera.

Thus Goldoni, Lessing, Diderot, and Mozart shared a sense of novelty and originality; it arose from their awareness that they were radically shaking up an outdated mode of theatre, breaking free from the schematism of eighteenth-century rationalism and moving towards a more faithful representation of reality.

In this type of theatre, based on the specific attributes of individuals, the performer came to assume enormous importance in determining not only technical elements (as he had done throughout the eighteenth century), but also stylistic-expressive ones, and indeed the very personality of the character he played. "I like an aria to fit the singer as perfectly as a well-made suit of clothes," the composer declared in a letter of 28 February 1778, and in the letter of July 30 the same year he recommended to Aloysia Weber that she go to the actor Marchand for lessons in recitation – something he considered essential to the formation of the personality of a

18 Mozart, *Letters*, p. 867; *Briefe*, vol. 3, p. 300.

singer.[19] This, in addition to many places in the letters about *Idomeneo*, shows that Mozart modeled his characters as much on the dramatic gifts of his singers as on their purely vocal abilities. There developed a close relationship between singer and *dramatis personae*; singers like Anton Raaff, Dorothea Wendling, the tenor Adamberger, the bass Fischer, Francesco Benucci, and Nancy Storace, to name but a few, were decisively important in shaping the characters of their respective parts, whose music Mozart moulded to harmonize with the characteristics of the actor-singers. This process, which continued in the work of leading musician-dramatists of the next century, including Verdi and Wagner, parallels exactly the practice of contemporary dramatists, especially Goldoni, who declared that he always took his inspiration from the personality of the individual actors, the "raw material" from which he sculpted the personalities of his characters.

On the linguistic level the radical novelty of the transition from a theatre of masks and fixed types to a dramaturgy aiming at the representation of real life leads to a new richness of vocabulary. We find this in Goldoni, who renders the particularity and variety of the situations in which the characters become involved, and in Mozart, who, with the organic unity of the classical style, fuses the most diverse musical forms and vocabularies – opera buffa, opera seria, instrumental style, sacred style, Lied, etc. – into new forms modeled according to the individual case and the expressive demands of the theatrical situation.

To illustrate this variety of form would require an examination of every aria in its distinct structural originality; such an examination is clearly not possible here. However it is important to note the relation of that variety to another demand which was felt much more strongly in spoken comedy than in contemporary comic opera, namely the tension of the dramatic rhythm. This tension, which, as I have shown elsewhere,[20] constitutes the supreme law of

19 Mozart, *Letters*, p. 496; *Briefe*, vol. 2, p. 304 (letter of 28 February); *Letters*, p. 582; *Briefe*, vol. 2, p. 421 (letter of 30 July).
20 Gallarati, *La forza delle parole*, pp. 39, 179, and *passim*.

Mozart's drama from *Idomeneo* onwards, is clearly illustrated by
Diderot, who urges that performance be rich and various; that the
spectator, satisfied with that which is present, should ardently wish
for that which is to follow; that one character should create a desire
for another; that one event should drive towards the next one, to
which it is linked; that the scenes should be rapid; and that they
should contain only facts essential to the action. From 1781, when
Mozart developed the conviction that opera should no longer be
understood as a series of arias, recitatives and ensembles placed one
after another according to the criterion of decorative variety, but as
an organic whole, permeated by a dramatic flow affirmed in a progressive continuity of tension, he worked towards the goals set out
by Diderot. His treatment of the act as a single indissoluble organ-
ism, then, accords with Diderot's vision of reality as an organic
flow which the theatre must represent.

An aesthetic of this kind, while it has no parallel in eighteenth-
century opera, and of which indeed it is the antithesis, closely links
Mozart's new opera to spoken comedy. As in bourgeois drama, the
action in Mozart's opera is enclosed within a self-sufficient semiotic
circuit, defined by what has been described as the "fourth wall." For
Diderot it is a fundamental principle that realistic drama takes place
within the confines of the stage, excluding the audience as direct
interlocutors:

> Whether you are writing or acting, give no more thought to the spec-
> tator than you would if he did not exist. Imagine on the edge of the
> stage, a great wall that separates you from the auditorium; act as if the
> curtain had not risen.[21]

Mozart felt this need so strongly that he imposed on Da Ponte a
rhetorical style of libretto quite different from the one he employed
in his texts for other composers. The arias and ensembles of *Le
nozze di Figaro*, *Don Giovanni*, and *Così fan tutte* systematically
abolish the declarative rhetoric common in earlier opera, where
the characters describe their states of mind through syllogisms,

21 Diderot, *De la Poésie dramatique*, p. 231.

similes, external images, and moral aphorisms more or less implicitly addressed to the audience. Mozart's characters, by contrast, directly express the *cri de la passion*, as Diderot demanded, revealing their states of mind directly to themselves or to other interlocutors present on the stage. In this way Mozart erects a fourth wall between the stage and the audience, only occasionally amusing himself by breaching it, when, for example, Figaro or Guglielmo addresses the public ("Aprite un po' quegli occhi." "Donne mie la fate a tanti"), with a very powerful effect of comic alienation. But this sudden breaking of the fourth wall to achieve comic alienation had already been contemplated in the theories of Diderot, who asserts that when Molière breaks the fourth wall by making a character address the audience, "the license taken by a man of genius proves nothing against common sense."[22] The same may be said of these Mozart arias, for their effect of sudden comic alienation – significantly absent in *Don Giovanni* – serves only to emphasize the power of the fourth wall to enclose the drama within the autonomous representation of truth and naturalness – this last a concept on which Mozart insists repeatedly in his letters, and which illustrates how his theatre originates from a rejection of every form of artificial conventionality and spontaneously allies itself with the aesthetic of Diderot. "What naturalness! what truth!" wrote the *philosophe*, commenting on the plan for a play on the death of Socrates, where laughter and tears are indissolubly intertwined.[23]

This emphasis on truth and naturalness gives rise to another fundamental feature of bourgeois comedy, namely the abandonment of classical satire in favor of Romantic irony. Hermann Abert makes some illuminating comments on this characteristic of Mozart's comedy, whose provocative novelty comes boldly to the fore in *Le nozze di Figaro*. Here composer and librettist faithfully translate Beaumarchais's aesthetic program, expressed in the *préface fondamentale* to *Le Mariage de Figaro*, where he discusses the problems of characterizing the roles as individuals:

22 Ibid., p. 232.
23 Ibid., p. 199.

One can only correct men by showing them as they really are. Useful, truthful comedy is not a lying eulogy, a vain academic speech. But let us beware of confusing this general criticism, one of the most noble aims of art, with odious personal satire; the advantage of the former is that it corrects without wounding.[24]

The fidelity with which Mozart follows this program in rejecting the satire which had played such a prominent part in Italian opera buffa is too obvious to require discussion. More interesting in this context would be a detailed comparative analysis of the expressive and dramaturgical problems raised by Beaumarchais's preface, by the text of his play, and by Da Ponte's libretto version, to see how skillfully and with what independence of method Mozart and his librettist achieved in music that wonderful fusion between comedy of intrigue and comedy of character which constitutes the true novelty of Beaumarchais's masterpiece and which, through Mozart's music, reaches a level of aesthetic and expressive profundity far superior to that of its theatrical model. The importance of Da Ponte's made-to-measure libretto to this enterprise is clearly explained by Leopold in his letter to Nannerl of 11 November 1785:

> God grant that the text may be a success. I have no doubt about the music. But there will be a lot of running about and discussions before he gets the libretto so adjusted as to suit his purpose exactly.[25]

Both the aesthetic conception and the technical execution of *Le nozze di Figaro* and *Don Giovanni* – and in some respects also of *Così fan tutte* – become especially clear when set in relation to the problems raised by Shakespeare, Molière, Goldoni, Diderot, Lessing, and Beaumarchais. To set Mozart in context in this way may help us to define more precisely the revolutionary historical significance of Mozart's operas, and especially their European dimensions, represented by the intersections of the Germans' psychological profundity and receptiveness to the Romantic and *Sturm und Drang*

---

24 Jean Meyer, ed., *Le Mariage de Figaro ou la Folle Journée de Beaumarchais* (Paris: Editions du Seuil, 1953), pp. 18–19.
25 Mozart, *Letters*, p. 893; *Briefe*, vol. 3, pp. 443–44.

metaphysics, with the scenic and gestural vivacity of the Italians, and with the French interest in that middle aesthetic space between tragedy and comedy. Of course, this field of research is one that still remains to be developed; my intention here has simply been to draw attention to some potentially fruitful themes and areas of research, in order to place Mozart's theatre in its correct historical and aesthetic context – a context which goes beyond the restricted confines of Italian comic opera and embraces the history of European theatre in its totality.

PART II

Social and generic meanings

5 | The sentimental muse of opera buffa

Edmund J. Goehring

Comedy was created to correct vice and ridicule bad habits, and when the comedies of the ancients were written in this manner, the entire populace opted for them because, seeing the copy of a character on stage, each found the original either in himself or in someone else. But when comedies became merely ridiculous, no one paid attention any more, because with the pretense of making people laugh, they admitted the highest, loudest blunders. Now that we have returned to fish for comedies in nature's *Mare magnum*, however, men feel their hearts touched again (II. 1).[1]

These words, delivered by a character in Carlo Goldoni's *Il teatro comico* (1750), may be taken to speak for the author himself, and they signal a manifesto for one of the most important developments on the eighteenth-century stage: the reform of comedy. There is little doubt about the popularity and influence of Goldoni's reformed works; their success in reconciling aims with achievement is less clear, as is their effect on the world of comic opera. The difficulty in assessing Goldoni's reform is in part a function of his eclecticism as a playwright. Not all of his comedies obediently line up under one definition of comedy, nor is there an ineluctable chronological movement toward reform. Even a work like *Il servitore di due padroni* (1745), sometimes heralded as the "crowning glory" of the very commedia dell'arte that Goldoni later repudiated, has an ethos arguably more characteristic of the later reform comedies than of the commedia dell'arte.[2] At the same time, works written during and after the reform do not always

1 Goldoni, vol. 2, pp. 1066–67.
2 For *Il servitore di due padroni* as the "crowning glory" of the commedia dell'arte, see Heinz Riedt, *Carlo Goldoni*, trans. Ursule Molinaro (New York: Ungar, 1974), p. 19. Elizabeth Blood, however, argues convincingly that the influence of the *Théâtre italien* significantly altered the character of *Il servitore*. See "From *canevas* to *commedia*: Innovation in Goldoni's *Il servitore di due padroni*," *Annali d'italianistica* 11 (1993), 111–19.

embrace the aims Goldoni articulated so forcefully in *Il teatro comico*.[3]

Reception and differences in regional taste further complicate the picture. The following account from a German periodical of 1768 shows a public caring little for poetics, far more for amusement:

> This part of the public – by far the largest, and that which values Goldoni
> not for his service in reforming the stage but rather for the comic
> elements of his works – brought in the most money, a fact no director of
> a German theatre overlooks. Indeed, *Un curioso accidente*, his most rule-
> bound [*regelmäßigste*] comedy, had the poorest attendance; *Il servitore di
> due padroni* pleased more than *L'adulatore*.[4]

An essential aspect of Goldoni's reform was his intention to create a more natural representation, once again "fishing for comedy in Nature's great sea." "Natural" means many things in the eighteenth century; in this context, it indicates a rejection of Aristotelian poetics, which holds that comedy depicts men as worse than they are in real life, in favor of something truer to life. For Goldoni, the abandonment of the ridiculous in comic representation was the precondition of a theatre that not only permitted but positively encouraged the audience's emulation of the behavior on stage. The idea of comedy as a moral agent was an old (if not always convincing) way of defending the genre from its detractors. What was new with Goldoni was the desire to instruct by positive example.

This aspiration enjoyed support from many quarters. Here, for example, is an excerpt from the entry on comedy in Sulzer's *Allgemeine Theorie der schönen Künste*:

3 Ted Emery, in particular, identifies categories, like "arcadian" or "satire-fantasy,"
  that either modify or stray significantly from the aims of the reform. *Goldoni as
  Librettist: Theatrical Reform and the "Drammi giocosi per musica"* (New York: Lang,
  1991). He also addresses (as do others) the question of genre and its relation to
  the reform, pointing out that opera and its librettos have different aims and
  audiences than spoken plays.

4 *Deutsche Bibliothek der schönen Wissenschaften Halle* 2 (1768), 449. Cited in Arnold
  E. Maurer, *Carlo Goldoni: seine Komödien und ihre Verbreitung im deutschen
  Sprachraum des 18. Jahrhunderts* (Bonn: Herbert Grundmann, 1982), p. 165.

It can be exceedingly useful to show us the absurdities of men in their true light. Should it, however, be less useful to touch us through examples of sensible [*vernünftigem*] conduct, of noble disposition, of honesty, of every necessary virtue in daily life in such a way that we receive lasting impressions from them? . . . One therefore acknowledges the value of mocking and laughing comedy, yet also keeps the stage open for that which entertains without laughter, through noble portraits – for all that shows us human nature in its beautiful and charming sides.[5]

This theory differs from Goldoni's only in its tolerance of Aristotelian poetics. In most other respects, it coincides nicely with the aims expressed by Goldoni in, for example, his comments on an early reform play, *La putta onorata* (1749): "I offered my audience a model for imitation. Provided that one inspires honesty, is it not better to win over hearts with the attractions of virtue than with the ugliness of vice?"[6]

The success of this enterprise hinges on the presence of such realist devices as a preference for plausible explanations, a distaste for language laced with metaphors and other rhetorical devices, and a desire to use the theatre to reinforce general social truths. Without them, the spectator would find neither himself nor his neighbor on the stage, and comedy would lose the chief source of its moral didactic power: the pleasure of recognition.[7] But some interpretations take a different view of Goldoni's realism, concentrating less on its promotion of virtue than on the society it represents on stage. Bartolo Anglani makes one of the most forceful arguments of this kind; he views Goldoni's comedy as a theatre of failed bourgeois social therapy, ultimately unable to eradicate the

---

5 Johann Georg Sulzer, *Allgemeine Theorie der schönen Künste*, 2nd edn. (Leipzig, 1792; reprint, Hildesheim: Olms, 1994), vol. 1, p. 488.
6 *Mémoires de M. Goldoni*, in Goldoni, vol. 1, p. 256.
7 Mario Baratto has a compelling formulation of the didactic functions of Goldoni's reformed comedies: "At the end of the spectacle we are sent back to ourselves more enlightened and full of wonder; disposed, through an intellectual pleasure, to know, and thus with an increased capacity for change." *Tre studi sul teatro (Ruzante–Aretino–Goldoni)* (Venice: Neri Pozza, 1964), p. 216.

original social disorder it diagnoses and portrays.[8] Although Anglani sometimes gives more weight to bourgeois matters than Goldoni's intentions or the evidence of the comedies will bear,[9] his readings have been highly influential. Ted Emery, for example, bases much of his study of the intermezzos on Anglani's ideological foundations, in ways that strictly oppose theatrical and realistic impulses. For Emery, the conventional devices of comic theatre – or, to use Goldoni's oft-cited metaphor, *Il teatro* rather than *Il mondo* – only stand in the way of a fully developed realistic, social theatre.[10]

But for Goldoni it was not enough just to represent virtue on the stage – its presence had to be attractive. The realization of this aim required not a separation of the theatre from the world, but rather a fusion of the two. Such a union was achieved under the guiding hand of sentimentalism, a concept using realism for theatrical and aesthetic effect. Sentimentalism was a potent force in numerous areas of eighteenth-century thought, and following its migrations from novel into play and then into libretto can illuminate the aims and achievement of some of the most important and successful *opere buffe* of Mozart's Vienna.

OF SINCERITY AND ARTIFICE: RICHARDSON'S "PAMELA"

Like taste, reason, and nature, sentimentalism (and its cognate, sensibility) eludes most efforts to capture its meaning. One reason for this is etymological. Derived from the Latin *sentire*, sentimentalism in its many and varied uses embraced two opposing meanings of the root, a rational one (to perceive in the mind) and a

---

8 Bartolo Anglani, *Goldoni: il mercato, la scena, l'utopia* (Naples: Liguori, 1983), see especially pp. 79–82.

9 This is especially so in *Il teatro comico*, where the financial concerns of a number of parties are arguably sideshows to the main business of the play. Anglani, however, moves these monetary matters to center stage.

10 Emery, *Goldoni as Librettist*, pp. 5–6.

sensual one (to feel through the senses); in the eighteenth century the meaning drifted away from the intellectual toward the passionate.[11] Another complication comes from the breadth of the concept. Far more than a bourgeois phenomenon or a specific sub-genre of comedy like the *comédie larmoyante*, sentimentalism is a central issue in disciplines ranging from moral philosophy and aesthetics to medicine and psychology.[12] Yet the word first brings to mind the literature of the eighteenth century, and here its presence was so strong that "Age of Sensibility" has been proposed as a banner around which to marshal works written roughly from the 1740s to the 1790s.[13] Although a single work obviously cannot speak for the entire corpus, Samuel Richardson's *Pamela* (1740) ranks among its most significant representatives, and its popularity and influence on Goldoni make it a good exemplum of the aims and devices of sentimental literature.

One of Richardson's most effective strategies in *Pamela* was to set it as a series of letters coming directly from Pamela herself. In one place only (Pamela's abduction) can the reader detect Richardson's presence, and there it is as an editor rather than an author. The rest of the book proceeds from the fiction that *Pamela* is

11 Jean H. Hagstrum, *Sex and Sensibility: Ideal and Erotic Love from Milton to Mozart* (Chicago: University of Chicago Press, 1980), p. 161. See also E. Erämetsä, "A Study of the Word 'Sentimental' and of Other Linguistic Characteristics of Eighteenth-Century Sentimentalism in England," Thesis, University of Helsinki, 1951.

12 In his introduction to a volume of essays entitled *Poets of Sensibility and the Sublime* (New York: Chelsea House Publishers, 1986), Harold Bloom rejects limiting the term to a "Victorian exaltation of middle-class morality [or] a modern celebration of proletarian, natural simplicity" (p. 8).

13 Northrop Frye, "Towards Defining an Age of Sensibility," anthologized in Bloom, *Poets of Sensibility and the Sublime*, p. 11. For an argument against Frye's application of the term, see Howard D. Weinbrot, "Northrop Frye and the Literature of Process Reconsidered," *Eighteenth-Century Studies* 24 (1990–91), 173–95. Frye's effort to find a satisfying designation for the literature of the time addresses the same kind of historiographical issues raised by Daniel Heartz concerning the music from 1730 to 1770 in "Opera and the Periodization of Eighteenth-Century Music," in International Musicological Society, *Report of the Tenth Congress, Ljubljana 1967* (Kassel: Bärenreiter, 1970), pp. 160–68.

less Richardson's creation than his discovery. This use of the epistolary mode collapses the distinction between the fictional characters
and real reader, an effect Richardson exploited by having all of the
major characters (and some of the minor ones, too) read Pamela's
letters. This leaves the physical reader of the tale with the impression that he is only one of several observers of these events.

The use of the epistolary mode has other consequences for the
structure and character of the tale, especially with regard to plot.
Because it pretends to lack a conspicuous authorial voice that
governs and arranges events, *Pamela* appears to take place in the
present tense only, with a future as yet unimagined. Northrop Frye,
in an influential essay, calls this "literature as process over
product."[14] Samuel Johnson puts it less delicately: "Why, Sir, if you
were to read Richardson for the story, your impatience would be so
much fretted that you would hang yourself."[15] Following this
Richardsonian model, works like Sterne's *Sentimental Journey* (1768)
and Mackenzie's *Man of Feeling* (1771) show characters chancing
from incident to incident, with much less weight given to rationally
ordered events, and much more to the feelings these episodes evoke.
Again, Johnson: "You must read [Richardson] for the sentiment, and
consider the story as only giving occasion to the sentiment."[16]

The fragmented sentimental plot is intimately connected to the
nature of its protagonist and can even be considered a kind of
extension of the protagonist's psyche. The sentimental character
practices a curious kind of heroism: he or she is not an active doer
of deeds but is instead passive, a victim of a cruel society or
world.[17] But if the external world is malevolent and flawed, the pro-

14 Frye, "Towards Defining an Age of Sensibility," pp. 12–13.
15 George Birkbeck Hill, ed., *Boswell's Life of Johnson* (Oxford: Clarendon Press, 1887), vol. 2, p. 175.
16 Ibid., p. 175. The relationship between plot and character is also discussed by Ann Jessie Van Sant, *Eighteenth-Century Sensibility and the Novel: The Senses in Social Context* (Cambridge: Cambridge University Press, 1993), pp. 117–19.
17 Janet M. Todd, *Sensibility: An Introduction* (London: Methuen, 1986), p. 3. The relationship of sensibility to sex is a topic for a different paper. In literature and on the spoken stage, sentimentalism was often seen as a means of civilizing the male, as it is in *Pamela*. Most sentimental types on the operatic stage, however, were female.

tagonist's internal, moral one approaches the heroic, revealing an almost unbounded optimism in the human capacity for altruism: "Sentimentality is a state of mind based on the assumption that one's own character is perfect, or as near perfection as necessary, or if certain grave faults seem to emerge, they must not be regarded as inherent."[18] As much in her swift and complete forgiveness of her wrongdoers as in her lengthy resistance to their assaults on her virtue, Pamela speaks nicely for this optimistic reading of human nature.

The sympathetic portrayal of the deeply feeling protagonist forces a reconception and refashioning of virtually every component of literary representation; this is as true of language as it is of plot and character. Like plot, language normally indicates rational activity. And, again like the sentimental plot, sentimental language abjures coherent speech to dramatize the emotional intensity of the protagonist, who is generally more interested in feeling for its own sake than for the object that inspires it. "Teach me, dear sir," Pamela says as she kisses Mr. B.'s hand, "teach me some other language, if there be any, that abounds with more grateful terms, that I may not thus be choked with meanings, for which I can find no utterance."[19] This is a wonderfully representative passage – the heroine's keen emotional sensitivity paralyzes the mind, and almost the body, too; to suggest that madness is the ideal expression of sentimental passion barely overstates the issue.

At the same time, this moment in *Pamela* and others like it only *appear* to be devoid of artifice. The repetition of Pamela's command "teach me" calls to mind the rhetorical figure *conduplicatio* – a device using repetition of a phrase for emotional effect – and its use here reveals the fine line sentimentalism holds between realism and artifice. A realistic depiction of lower-class figures like Pamela required a simple style, and Richardson's success can be seen, ironically, in the criticism he received for the baseness of the novel's

18 Paul E. Parnell, "The Sentimental Mask," *PMLA* 78 (1963), 535.
19 *Pamela; or, Virtue Rewarded*, ed. Peter Sabor (New York: Penguin, 1980), pp. 390–91.

language. But verisimilitude in language was not enough for sentimentalism, whose aims were not just to instruct, but to persuade.
(In *Pamela*, Richardson solves this problem by creating the fiction of
Pamela's education under the guidance of her mistress. In a literally realistic depiction, Pamela would not have been able to read at
all.)

One obvious function of this treatment of plot, character, and
language is to conceal the artifice of the novel. The epistolary mode
dissolves the boundaries between reader and author; the representation of lower classes and the reliance on unaffected language
makes the protagonist's heroism more convincing. But these nods
toward the verisimilar are also highly theatrical, and, what is more,
self-consciously so. Clearly, Pamela is conscious of being a theatrical object; indeed, she deftly wields the spectacle of her life as a
weapon in the defense of her virtue.[20] Nor does Richardson shy
away from exposing the artifice of the work, otherwise he would
have excised remarks like this, from Mrs. Davers: "Pr'ythee, child,
walk before me to that glass: survey thyself, and come back to me,
that I may see how finely thou canst act the theatrical part given
thee."[21] Paradoxically, Richardson uses the artifice of *Pamela* precisely to break down the boundaries separating fictional character
from reader. In this way, the book attempts to realize the quintessentially sentimental aim of using the devices of realism to awaken
sympathy in the reader.

Sentimentalism's confounding of the world with the theatre
has much in common with the pastoral mode, which seems to
issue from the same impulse. Richardson's appropriation of the
pastoral encompasses both ends of the mode, the nostalgic and
the cynical. The nostalgic version is evident in the equation of
virtue with the simplicity of the lower orders of society, yet this
view is itself founded upon a cynical dissatisfaction with the
higher strata of society. And the novel is as aware of its own pas-

20 Mary Hunter, "Rousseau, the Countess, and the Female Domain," in Cliff Eisen,
    ed., *Mozart Studies*, 2 (Oxford University Press, forthcoming 1997).
21 *Pamela*, p. 410.

toral nostalgia as it is of its theatricality, most notably in a long speech delivered by Mr. B. on the sixth day after his marriage to Pamela. Only one from Pamela's class will do as a wife, he argues, because wealth has spoiled all those from his own.[22] In other words, "the lower in social order you go, the more admirable mankind appears to be."[23] The point is less to give an accurate depiction of rural life than to open up a path for readers and their emotions to enter into the work.

The inherent theatricality of sentimental works left them open for ridicule and parody. Fielding's *Shamela* (1741) turns Pamela into a brazen opportunist; in another anti-sentimental work, Goethe's *Der Triumph der Empfindsamkeit* (1787), the protagonist discovers he has been in love not with a woman but with a dummy stuffed with sentimental novels. Mixed in with the chaff (Häckerling) at the bottom of this sack he finds, among other things, *La Nouvelle Héloïse* and *Die Leiden des jungen Werthers*. Still, to see sentimental works only as acts of authorial bad faith overlooks a fundamental epistemological question with which their authors wrestled: Was it possible to feel another's emotions? Not according to Adam Smith, who argued in his *Theory of Moral Sentiments* that the only possibility for creating an empathetic or sympathetic experience was for the beholder, using external signs as a guide, to recreate the emotional experience of the object.[24] This makes sympathy an imaginative experience, and therefore also an aesthetic one: "Our sympathy, like the work of art that moves us, takes place within the realm of fiction, mimesis, representation, and reproduction. If the success of a novel, play, or painting depends on acts of

22 Ibid., pp. 463–66.
23 R. F. Brissenden, *Virtue in Distress: Studies in the Novel of Sentiment from Richardson to Sade* (New York: Barnes and Noble, 1974), pp. 5–6. Michael Fried observes a similar process of breaking down the distance between object and beholder in pastoral painting, which creates the "fiction of the beholder's physical presence within the painting, by virtue of an almost magical recreation of the effect of nature itself." *Absorption and Theatricality: Painting and Beholder in the Age of Diderot* (Berkeley: University of California Press, 1979), p. 132.
24 Adam Smith, *The Theory of Moral Sentiments* (London, 1759; reprint, New York: Garland, 1971), p. 2.

sympathy, our experience of sympathy depends on an aesthetic experience."[25]

But if the sentimental character cannot help but be an actor, a question still remains: What kind? In an essay relating sensibility to the theatre, Earl Wasserman identifies two reigning eighteenth-century theories. The naturalistic school takes its motto from the Horatian "Si vis me flere," and insists that the actor can create a convincing representation only if he shares the feelings of his character.[26] This theory invokes a Cartesian metaphor: the successful actor, rather than having a strong personality, is malleable, much like soft wax.[27] Diderot represents the other position, which holds that the actor "must render exactly the external signs of ideal feeling, but must himself be a disinterested onlooker having intellectual penetration but no sensibility."[28] In its insistence on the actor's detachment and coldness, Diderot's theory seems diametrically opposed to the Horatian. Yet neither suggests that acting is anything but an illusion, and each theory leads to the annihilation of personality: the one through the actor's getting lost in a part, the other through a chameleon-like behavior that arises from changing roles. Whatever the theory, realism is not an issue: even the "sincere" variety cannot be equated with realism, for "the sympathetic imagination . . . permits the actor to enter, not into the distinctive, but into the ideal forms of reality."[29] Acting is mimesis, reality filtered through the lens of the theatre.

The thespian dimensions of the sentimental protagonist set into relief a paradox of this character-type. On the one hand, a distinguishing trait of characters like Pamela is an almost maudlin hypersensitivity. A famous instance in Richardson is the episode at the pond with Mrs Jewkes, where Pamela throws back a carp she

25 David Marshall, *The Surprising Effects of Sympathy: Marivaux, Diderot, Rousseau, and Mary Shelley* (Chicago: University of Chicago Press, 1988), p. 21.
26 Earl R. Wasserman, "The Sympathetic Imagination in Eighteenth-Century Theories of Acting," *Journal of English and Germanic Philology* 46 (1947), 264–72. See also Carl Dahlhaus, "'Si vis me flere,'" *Die Musikforschung* 25 (1972), 51–52.
27 Wasserman, "The Sympathetic Imagination," p. 268.
28 Ibid., p. 272.   29 Ibid., p. 271.

caught because she could not separate her own misfortune from that of the fish. This is a sentimental move through and through, where the subject's feeling is disproportionate to the object that inspires it.[30] But the sentimental protagonist also has another side, often remarkably cold. Perhaps the best eighteenth-century representation of this double nature is Suzanne, the heroine of Diderot's *La Religieuse*, who moves from intensely passionate, even erotic, behavior to a stony distance. In *Pamela*, the heroine's coldness wears a slightly different guise, as "pertness" or "sauciness," terms given to Pamela by her adversaries. This particular manifestation of the double nature has comic potential, which will sometimes be exploited in the move from sentimental novel to sentimental opera.[31] Indeed, Pamela's quick, "saucy" retorts to challenges to her virtue set her in the tradition of the finest comic servants.

This overview of the aims and techniques of sentimentalism as exemplified in Richardson provides a foundation for understanding the nature of Goldoni's reform. By way of preface, it is important to note that sentimentalism's theatrical mask does not completely conceal realism in Goldoni's plays, but it does alter its significance. Like *Il mondo* and *Il teatro*, realism is a metaphor describing a theatrical experience that unites the verisimilar with the artificial. The intimate connection of the two is no less important in Goldoni than in Richardson, and it reveals the extent to which mimesis, rightly understood, still held a vital place in eighteenth-century

---

30 Many have observed the moral problem created by sensibility when imitation becomes an occasion solely for raising feelings. See, for example, Van Sant, *Eighteenth-Century Sensibility and the Novel*, p. 123. Another danger of sentimentalism is its clouding of the distinction between real and theatrical distress, between life and representation. For a discussion of this issue in relationship to Rousseau's antitheatrical prejudice, see Marshall, *The Surprising Effects of Sympathy*, ch. 5, "Rousseau and the State of Theater."
31 A stimulating discussion of this sentimental double nature in Mirandolina from Goldoni's *La locandiera* is found in Gerhard Regn, "Jenseits der 'commedia borghese': Komödienspiel, Karnevalisierung und moralische Lizenz in Goldonis 'Locandiera,'" *Germanisch-Romanische Monatsschrift*, n.s., vol. 44 (1994), pp. 324–44.

aesthetics. Imitation is nature beautified, which is another way of saying that the author has freedom to exercise imagination and genius in his depiction of the world.

FROM NOVEL TO PLAY: "PAMELA NUBILE"

Pamela nubile (1750) was not Goldoni's first reformed comedy,[32] but its proximity to Richardson's novel makes it a logical place to examine the transformation of the sentimental impulse from novel to play. Only the epistolary format was too unwieldy to make the move to the new genre, and the play makes but an occasional nod to Pamela's letter-writing. Most of the other traits of the sentimental novel, however, are present and conspicuous. Milord Bonfil, for example, is transformed from a brute into a paragon of sentimental sensitivity; furthermore, the fundamental passivity of the couple is emphasized in the resolution of the play, which is possible only by the lucky discovery of Pamela's noble lineage.[33] Also like Richardson, Goldoni spares no theatrical device in casting Pamela's virtue in the most heroic and flattering light, as in her speech in Act I, scene 6. Part rebuke against libertinism, part defense of honor, part plea for social egalitarianism ("Noble blood is an accident of fate; true greatness comes from noble actions"), the resulting soliloquy, among the longest in the play, is so effective that Bonfil is left literally dumbfounded, speech being returned to him only in the next scene.

Like Richardson's *Pamela*, Goldoni's reformed comedies are

---

32 Emery argues that *Pamela nubile* is not even a reform work at all; rather, it represents an Arcadian phase of Goldoni's output that runs against the reforming impulse. *Goldoni as Librettist*, pp. 124, 212.

33 This is a clumsy solution from the standpoint of realism, but necessary for a satisfying psychological conclusion. Emery, however, takes an opposing view of the denouement of *Pamela nubile*, arguing that "we can hardly call love the victor here, for passion triumphs in *Pamela* only by default: love is possible in the end only because reason allows it to be so" ("Goldoni's *Pamela* from Play to Libretto," *Italica* 64 [1987], 576). I would argue that love is indeed the victor here, that a conclusion *not* allowing the fulfillment of the couple's passion would be still more unsatisfactory.

beholden to the pastoral world in their nostalgic portrayal of the lower classes, and this means a change in the style of language. His oft-stated distaste for the elevated style stems in part from a desire to create a more natural representation of the simple heroism of gardeners, villagers, and foundlings. This is the reason he gives for using Venetian dialect to portray the gondoliers in *La putta onorata*. But Goldoni also rightly understood that elevated language was a central part of comic hyperbole. Indeed, this was an important tool in the commedia dell'arte, especially for the part of the lovers (*innamorati*), whose *zibaldoni*, or commonplace-books, provided a repository of *concetti* and rhetorical devices.[34] Goldoni did not object to the language of the commedia dell'arte because it was too low (with the obvious exception of vulgarity) but because it was too high, associated with an aristocratic conceit.[35]

In *Pamela nubile* the presence of sentimentality leads to a remaking of comedy, which is why it and similar plays should be numbered among reform works.[36] Not only did Goldoni relegate ridiculous characters to the side,[37] he even took the rather desperate measure of trying to improve the behavior of the comic actors of the spoken and musical stage. This is an important issue in *Il teatro comico*, and it shows Goldoni's affinity for the Horatian theory of acting: both actor and character should be held to the same high standards of morality. In any case, Goldoni was keenly aware of the extent of his reform, so much so that he proposed a different generic label for the *Pamela nubile*: "Following the definition of the French, the comedy *Pamela* is a *drame*."[38] What he means by *drame* and the French definition of it is explained earlier in the *Mémoires*, in his discussion of *La putta onorata*:

---

34 K. M. Lea, *Italian Popular Comedy: A Study in the Commedia dell'arte, 1560–1620, with Special Reference to the English Stage* (New York: Russell & Russell, 1962), vol. 1, pp. 104–5.

35 Regn, "Jenseits der 'commedia borghese,'" p. 334, equates Mirandolina's coquetry with aristocratic behavior.   36 See note 32, above.

37 He calls Ernold the character who "infinitely cheers the seriousnesss of the work." Goldoni, vol. 1, pp. 279–80.   38 Ibid., p. 280.

When I speak of virtue, I do not mean that heroic virtue, touching through its misfortunes and tearful in its delivery. These works, which in French are given the title *Drames*, certainly have their merit; they are a type of theatrical representation between comedy and tragedy. This is an entertainment made more for tender hearts [*coeurs sensibles*] – the misfortunes of heroic tragedies interest us from a distance, but those of our kind ought to move us even more.

Comedy, which is nothing other than an imitation of nature, does not deny itself virtuous and pathetic sentiments, provided that it's not stripped of those significant and amusing actions that form the fundamental core of its existence.[39]

It is hard to overemphasize the theatrical importance of this mixing of styles. Goldoni sought to make tragedy more effective and more touching; and he made this possible by attaching nobility of feeling and behavior to character-types who, unlike the heroes of tragedy, were close to the audience in status and experience.

OPERA BUFFA IN THE SENTIMENTAL MODE

Goldoni's sentimental comedies provided a widely imitated model for opera buffa librettos. The success of a work like *La Cecchina; ossia La buona figliuola*, set to music by Piccinni (1760), is measured not only in the number of productions generated but especially in the number of works that follow in this tradition: *La finta giardiniera* (Mozart/Petrosellini[?], 1775), *La vera costanza* (Haydn/Puttini, 1779), *La pastorella nobile* (Guglielmi/Zini, 1788), *La cifra* (Salieri/Da Ponte, 1789), *Nina, o sia La pazza per amore* (Paisiello/Lorenzi, 1789), and so on. Another sentimental opera, *Il disertore* (Bianchi/Benincasa, 1785), contains a preface with dramaturgical aims virtually identical to those articulated by Goldoni decades earlier. Like Goldoni, Benincasa draws inspiration for his conception of drama from France: "There it's called simply *Drame* and is indicated with the term *Pièces larmoyantes*. It aims to excite tender or terrifying affects with ordinary actions and characters

39 Ibid., p. 256.

who are not heroic but instead common."[40] But the opera most permeated with sentimentalism is Martín y Soler's and Da Ponte's *Una cosa rara* (1786), among the most successful operas of the Josephine decade.

Opera is inherently disposed to convincing representations of sentimental passion: music, a pre-verbal medium, persuasively conveys the emotional intensity central to its psychology, and opera, often a singer's rather than a composer's art, tends to conceal the author behind the work. But sentimental opera also highlighted its heroines with a specific subtype of aria, the "breathless" cavatina. "Ah pietade, mercede," the number marking Lilla's initial entry, is an exemplary musical expression of virtue in distress (Example 5.1). Its text displays the keenness of Lilla's sensibility through a collapse of language itself. She literally lacks the words to convey adequately the intensity of her emotion. Her grief is incoherent, of course (otherwise it would not be grief), but its pointedly physical manifestation, where it leads to a shutdown even of breathing, is typical of the physiology of sensibility.

This loss for words has a parallel in musical representation. But whereas Richardson needs hundreds of pages to sustain this emotional intensity, music takes the road of brevity. The absence of an introductory ritornello, the avoidance of periodic closure (the only perfect authentic cadence falls in the antepenultimate measure), the reliance on a single affect, and the ever-present eighth-note string figures generate emotional urgency and immediacy. These cavatinas seem designed to surprise, even astonish, their listeners by their compactness. This is music as "process over product," in other words; it abandons clearly articulated formal patterns that create a rationally ordered presence comprehending past, present, and future. In Martín as in Richardson, the sentimental type knows only the present.

"Ah pietade, mercede" may be exemplary in its portrayal of the sentimental heroine's distressed virtue, but it is not unique. It belongs, rather, to a subtype used to depict sentimental heroines

40 Preface to *Il disertore* (Venice, 1785), p. 8.

Example 5.1 Lilla, "Ah pietade, mercede" (No. 3) from *Una cosa rara*

Example 5.1 (*cont.*)

Lilla: Ah pity, mercy, help. I am so weary from fear, torment, and running
that I am out of breath and scarcely have the energy to speak.

from Violante in *La finta giardiniera* to Rosina in *La vera costanza*
(Example 5.2). In some of these other sentimental operas, so high-
pitched is the protagonists' emotional sensitivity that they occasionally go mad, as does Violante in *La finta giardiniera* or Nina in
Paisiello's opera; the latter – in a fine display of sentimental philan-
thropy – gives presents to the poor villagers who take care of her
during her amnesia. To be sure, distress is not the only characteristic of operatic heroines of feeling: like Pamela, they, too, can
reveal a double nature that has its "saucy" sides. In *Una cosa rara*, for
example, Lilla accuses Ghita of plotting against her out of jealousy
at Lilla's superior beauty: "From the day that they said I was more
beautiful, you always looked upon me with spite" (I. 13). But even
these comic episodes ultimately serve a serious purpose, as a yard-
stick by which to measure the virtue of the heroine. As with
Goldoni in *Pamela nubile*, Martín and Da Ponte dedicate the devices
of the theatre to portraying the most heroic sides of the sentimental protagonist. In *Una cosa rara*, the ethos of reformed comedy is
evident in this melding of a common type (a villager) with heroic
constancy and virtue. Although Ghita may be mocking Lilla when
she calls her the phoenix of her sex (II. 3), the voice of the opera
means this seriously, naming her "una cosa rara."

If "breathless" cavatinas like "Ah pietade" are reserved for special

Example 5.2a Barbarina, "Soccorretemi, Sorelle," from *La forza delle donne*
(Anfossi/Bertati)

Example 5.2a (*cont.*)

Barbarina: Help me, sisters. Quickly, quickly, for heaven's sake.

Example 5.2b Rosina, "Dove fuggo" (No. 12b) from *La vera costanza* (Haydn/Puttini)

[Presto]

Rosina: Where do I flee, where do I hide without help and without escort?

Example 5.2c Violante, "Crudeli, fermate" (No. 21) from *La finta giardiniera*

Allegro agitato

Example 5.2c (*cont.*)

- ma - te,

p

Violante: Stop, cruel ones, oh God.

characters in special situations, the simplicity of their vocal and instrumental style has a much wider range in the repertory. In an essay appearing in this collection, Mary Hunter gives a persuasive account of the appeal of song style in *Una cosa rara*.[41] I would add that this style – not so much a middle point between the elevated and ridiculous as a typically Goldonian union of simple language with noble bearing – emanates from a sentimental and pastoral impulse. As in Richardson, all of the operatic sentimental types are or seem to be from the lower orders of society. Violante in *La finta giardiniera* is a slight exception, as she is aware of her aristocratic lineage from the start. Yet even her and Belfiore's madness in the second act takes the form of a dialogue reenacted between two pastoral types, Thyrsis and Cloris (Example 5.3). The duet typifies the wonderful complexity arising out of sentimentalism's union of nature and artifice, of the world and the theatre: though mad, and though acting out a scene, Violante is in some sense at her truest here, expressing in the bucolic idiom the thoroughly pastoral desire to escape from society to a place offering an uncomplicated life with her beloved.

41 The designation "song style" is from Dorothea Link, "The Da Ponte Operas of Martín y Soler" (PhD diss., University of Toronto, 1991).

Example 5.3 *La finta giardiniera* (II.17)

Sandrina: My Thyrsis, hear the sweet Sirens. With soothing enchantment they unloose their song.

This episode has the following setting: "A deserted and wild region of ancient, partly ruined aqueducts, among which there is an accessible dark cave."[42] These are all emblems of the sublime mode. At first glance, the tenderness and the civilizing character of sentimentalism seem to have little in common with the majesty of the sublime, but in its focus on the transcendental, its abandonment of reason for passion, and especially in its heroic aspirations, sensibility enjoys a "complex fusion" with the sublime mode.[43] It is important to recognize sentimentalism's relation to the sublime because it discourages facile equations of musical simplicity with sincerity and artifice with deceit. Opera has its own stylistic and linguistic idioms, and these do not always work well in a spoken setting. Witness, for example, Benincasa's dismay at having to include wretched language in the libretto to *Il disertore*: "I myself protest against certain words that please in music but that in writing are displeasing to good taste, and against the repetitions of so many other words that make up the impoverished, dilapidated dictionary of grand arias."[44] Here, opera buffa departs somewhat from Goldoni's reforms, since it can make allowance for the sympathetic portrayal of virtue in an elevated language.[45]

The appeal of works like *Una cosa rara* gives a measure of the

---

42 For a discussion of stage settings in opera buffa, see Mary Hunter, "Landscapes, Gardens, and Gothic Settings in the *Opere Buffe* of Mozart and his Italian Contemporaries," *CM* 51 (1993), 94–104.

43 Bloom, *Poets of Sensibility and the Sublime*, p. 8.

44 Preface, p. 10.

45 See Mary Hunter, "Some Representations of *Opera Seria* in *Opera Buffa*," *COJ* 3 (1991), 107, both for the importance of context and for the observation that the presence of opera seria within opera buffa is not an *a priori* cause for ridicule. An example of elevated musical language used to portray sentimental virtue is Eurilla's "Sola e mesta fra tormenti" from Salieri's *La cifra*. Of this aria and its introductory recitative, Salieri remarked that they were "pieces of great seriousness, but suitable for the character who sings them and the situation in which they are found, and above all because they were composed for a celebrated virtuoso who knew how to execute them with perfect sentiment and who had the greatest applause." Cited in Rudolph Angermüller, *Antonio Salieri: Sein Leben und seine weltlichen Werke unter besonderer Berücksichtigung seiner "großen" Opern*, Part III: Dokumente (Munich: Katzbichler, 1971), p. 54.

vitality of the sentimental tradition on the musical stage. It is both instructive and amusing to refer to an anecdote to illustrate the effect this kind of opera had upon its audiences. In the first run of Paisiello's *Nina* in Naples in 1789, it was reported that during Nina's romanza "Il mio ben quando verrà" men in the audience were weeping and cried out to Coltellini, "Rest assured, your lover will return!"[46] The opera had achieved its aims of moving the audience to the point of collapsing the wall separating the audience and the stage. In any case, the offspring of Goldoni's reform flourished, and so great was their success that some have argued that sentimental comedy eradicated more artificial traditions, like the commedia dell'arte, during the second half of the century.[47] Yet it is important to recall that artificial forms of comedy indeed survived alongside sentimental ones,[48] and the clearest image of the boundaries and limitations of operatic sentimentalism can be detected in Mozart's handling of the phenomenon.

"COSÌ FAN TUTTE LE COSE RARE": ANTI-SENTIMENTALISM IN THE MOZART-DA PONTE OPERAS

Mozart made a contribution to the sentimental opera, but not in a Da Ponte work: as suggested above, rather, in *La finta giardiniera*. In

46 Cited in Andrea Della Corte, *Paisiello* (Turin, 1922), p. 175. The literary example par excellence of this sentimental breaking down of the wall between the novel and reader is Diderot's *La Religieuse*, which started out as a practical joke.

47 Piero Weiss, "Carlo Goldoni, Librettist: The Early Years" (PhD diss., Columbia University, 1970), p. 100. See also Allardyce Nicoll, *The World of Harlequin: A Critical Study of the Commedia dell'arte* (Cambridge: Cambridge University Press, 1963), p. 189; and David Kimbell, *Italian Opera* (Cambridge: Cambridge University Press, 1991), p. 291.

48 In his *The Rakish Stage: Studies in English Drama, 1660–1800* (Carbondale: Southern Illinois University Press, 1983), Robert D. Hume cautions against the idea of a comedy of laughter struggling to reassert itself against a dominant tearful strain. Tracing this fallacy in part to Goldsmith's attack on sentimental comedy, Hume argues that Goldsmith's argument refers to, at best, a trend during a single season (p. 313 *passim*).

Violante one finds the defining gestures of the sentimental type: refinement of feeling that leads even to madness, a union of the pastoral and the elevated in her disguise as a gardener, even the "breathless" aria (see Example 5.2). The Da Ponte operas, however, all depart from this model, and in the forefront is *Così fan tutte*. This work offers a rebuttal not just of sentimentalism in general but of *Una cosa rara* in particular, which in fact was in the repertory during the 1789–90 season, having performances on 3 and 23 November 1789 and 2 and 24 January 1790, the last of these only two days before the premiere of *Così fan tutte*. Even the two titles vie with each other, offering competing claims about the proper nature of comedy: if Goldonian sentimental opera aims to champion the exceptional – "una cosa rara" – as an object worthy of imitation, comedy generally takes a more leveling view – "così fan tutte."[49] But the most conspicuous parody in Mozart's opera is Don Alfonso's cavatina "Vorrei dir" (Example 5.4). Virtually a direct quotation of Lilla's "Ah pietade, mercede" (see Example 5.1), it is, if anything, a more eloquent statement of sentimental distress, with its dismay at the cruelty of the world ("barbaro fato") and depiction of a passion so overwhelming that words become impossible: "Balbettando il labbro va; / Fuor la voce uscir non può." Musically, Mozart's parody shows stronger formal organization (mm. 9 and 14 have perfect-authentic cadences, and there is a double return at measure 20). Nonetheless, by beginning in *media res* and eliding its phrases, "Vorrei dir" creates the immediacy required of the portrayal of sentimental affliction.

Don Alfonso's cavatina destroys the naturalist, sentimental

---

49 Alan Tyson has suggested that *Così fan tutte* was Mozart's own title for *La scola degli amanti*, and that it was chosen at a very late stage in the genesis of the opera; see "On the Composition of Mozart's *Così fan tutte*," in *Mozart: Studies of the Autograph Scores* (Cambridge, MA: Harvard University Press, 1987), pp. 190, 197. More recently it has become clear that the libretto was originally to be set by Salieri; see Bruce Alan Brown and John A. Rice, "Salieri's *Così fan tutte*," *COJ* 8 (1996), 17–43. Perhaps the recent performances of *Una cosa rara* were one of the inspirations behind the last-minute change.

Example 5.4 "Vorrei dir" (No. 5) from *Così fan tutte*

Allegro agitato

theory of the Horatian school of acting. "Vorrei dir" seems to say that one need not feel emotion in order to touch; it is enough to mimic the gestures that represent feeling. Don Alfonso admits as much several scenes later, following the nostalgic "Soave sia il vento": "Non son cattivo comico," he says, and by "comico" he must mean not just comedian, or even actor, but creator.

Example 5.4 (*cont.*)

Countering the sentimental strategy of effacing the author to give the characters the appearance of autonomy and spontaneity, Don Alfonso exposes the theatricality of this illusion by wresting control of the stage. This is the reason for *Così fan tutte*'s artifice, for the symmetry of its organization: we are seeing everything through the contrivance of Don Alfonso. Were *Così fan tutte* a film,

Example 5.4 (cont.)

Alfonso: I would like to tell you, but I don't have the heart. My lips are
stuttering, I can't get the words out, they are stuck in my throat. What
will you do? What will I do? O, what a great catastrophe. There could be
nothing worse.

then Don Alfonso would be controlling the lens that presents the
spectacle to us.[50]

To be sure, Don Alfonso's direction is often subtle and under-
stated. *Così fan tutte* typically does not resort to the farce of an "Ah
chi mi dice mai," for example, where the composer, through the
agency of Don Giovanni and Leporello, surrounds Donna Elvira's
oath of vengeance with ironic marginalia. The irony of "Come
scoglio," on the other hand, resides less in its musical language (big
vocal leaps and ornamentation by themselves are not necessarily
tokens of ridicule) than in the context in which this style appears.[51]
Unlike in *Pamela nubile*, where Milord is left stunned by the persuasiveness of Pamela's words, Fiordiligi is denied the exit her aria

50 This argument suggests that Don Alfonso's authority is not successfully usurped
    in the opera, indeed, that the voice of the opera and that of Don Alfonso are
    virtually identical. Although this is not a common view of the opera, a couple of
    readings have looked more favorably upon Don Alfonso. See, in particular,
    Cornelia Kritsch and Herbert Zeman, "Das Rätsel eines genialen Opernentwurfs
    – Da Pontes Libretto zu *Così fan tutte* und das literarische Umfeld des 18.
    Jahrhunderts," in *Die österreichische Literatur: ihr Profil an der Wende vom 18. zum 19.
    Jahrhundert (1750–1830)*, Part I (Graz: Akademische Druck- und Verlagsanstalt,
    1979), pp. 359–60; and Bruce Alan Brown, *W. A. Mozart: "Così fan tutte"*
    (Cambridge: Cambridge University Press, 1995), pp. 82–85.
51 See Sergio Durante's essay elsewhere in the volume.

demands, and this fatally undermines her authority. The same procedure of placing passion at a distance – of moving the private into the public – also informs the climactic duet "Fra gli amplessi." In a different context, this seduction duet could be an unambiguously stirring moment for the audience. But the audience is not exactly watching a seduction duet: it is watching Don Alfonso and an enraged Guglielmo watch a seduction duet. Don Alfonso raises questions about the sentimental vision merely by holding it up for inspection, and he weakens the fourth wall of the theatre simply by showing us that it is there, by calling to the spectator's attention the theatricality of the dramatic activity.[52]

For this reason, *Così fan tutte* has been called an inhumane work, and Don Alfonso a heartless or diabolical scientist.[53] But the last vestige of sentimentalism to fall away from *Così fan tutte* is the *amanti*'s overblown confidence in the perfectibility of human nature, where everyone aspires to be a phoenix or at least a Penelope. Don Alfonso is the one, after all, who urges the soldiers to avoid the test of fidelity in the first place: "O pazzo desire! / Cercando scoprire / quel mal che trovato / meschini ci fa" (O mad desire, seeking to uncover that evil, which, when found, makes us wretched ["La mia Dorabella," I. I]), a statement bringing *Così fan tutte* into the orbit of works like Ariosto's *Orlando furioso*, several cantos of which place blame not on those who fail tests of fidelity, but on those who make them in the first place.[54] The soldiers figure this out, eventually, when they take back the sisters with these words: "Te lo credo, gioia bella, / Ma la prova io far non vo" (I believe it of you, my joy, but I do not want to make a test of it

---

52 This makes Don Alfonso a quintessentially comic protagonist along the lines of Baudelaire's "double man," in whom "there is not one single phenomenon of his double nature of which he is ignorant." "On the Essence of Laughter," p. 465.

53 Donald Mitchell calls him (along with Despina) "rather disagreeable" and "a little sly" ("The Truth about 'Così,'" in *A Tribute to Benjamin Britten on his Fiftieth Birthday*, ed. Anthony Gishford [London: Faber and Faber, 1963], p. 97). Intimations of a wicked, diabolical side come from, among others, Wolfgang Hildesheimer, *Mozart*; trans. Marion Faber (New York: Farrar, Straus, Giroux, 1981), pp. 289, 294.

54 On the relations of *Così fan tutte* to Ariosto, see Brown, *Così fan tutte*, pp. 60–70.

[11.18]). This admission signals the downfall of the *amanti*'s senti-mental/heroic vision. Don Alfonso's view, eschewing the rigid extremes of rationalism and sentimentalism, is intended to be rea-sonable and humane, first gently exposing then accepting human frailty. It is this recognition of human contingency that motivates *Così fan tutte*'s refutation of the sentimental tradition.

To say that *Così fan tutte*'s intentional artifice turns it away from realism, to say that the work cautions its audience about sympa-thetic responses at the same time that it encourages them, is to venture a definition of comedy itself.[55] And a look at the comic in *Così fan tutte* might reshape the understanding of the earlier Da Ponte operas. One appealing assessment of them is that they liber-ated comic opera from convention and fixed types, creating in their place a psychological realism hitherto unseen on the operatic stage.[56] But artifice, whether in the portrayal of the impossibly successful and impossibly damned libertine or in the sudden dis-covery that an adversary turns out to be one's long-lost and beloved mother, was positively inspirational for Mozart. Realistic readings, whether psychological or social, are in their own way sentimental, accepting the pretense of realism without acknowledging the theatrical devices used to create it. They are of limited utility even for truly sentimental works, and still less so for those that, like the Mozart-Da Ponte operas, move moments of private passion (upon which so much of the success of sentimental education hinges) into a public light.

A compelling illustration of the distance between Goldoni and Mozart-Da Ponte can be found in a comparison between their respective treatments of the Don Juan legend. Mozart and Da Ponte restore many of the improbabilities of the sub-literary tradi-tions that Goldoni tried to eradicate. They also restored the ele-vated language that Goldoni rejected, for, as Stefan Kunze has

---

55 For these dimensions of comedy, see Christopher Herbert, *Trollope and Comic Pleasure* (Chicago: University of Chicago Press, 1987), pp. 23–26.
56 Cf. Paolo Gallarati's essay elsewhere in this volume.

persuasively argued, the incorporation of *seria* elements paradoxically increased the potential for farce and ridicule.[57] The Da Ponte operas take the range of tone afforded by Goldoni's reform, but jettison the moralizing dimension.

This is not to argue that comedy is not true, or that one does not find on stage some element of society. But, to paraphrase Don Alfonso in one of his many metatheatrical moments, comedy undeceives through deceiving, and the mirror it holds up to society, like those in a carnival, distorts for amusement and pleasure (and instruction), granting to the imagination a release from the quotidian. In his reform of comedy Goldoni proposed an ambitious program: to find in comedy a means for the sympathetic portrayal of passion. That the Mozart-Da Ponte operas treat passion with considerable ambiguity and irony reminds one of their distance from sentimentalism.

57 Kunze, *Don Giovanni*, p. 55.

6 | The biology lessons of opera buffa: gender, nature, and bourgeois society on Mozart's buffa stage[1]

Tia DeNora

Now would I have a book where I might see all characters and planets of the heavens, that I might know their motives and dispositions . . . nay, let me have one book more, and then I have done, wherein I might see all plants, herbs and trees, that grow upon the earth.

Goethe, *Faust*

Opera buffa in Mozart's Vienna has typically not been considered in the context of its participation in a wider intellectual and creative milieu. Even musicologists with overt interests in context typically leave unexamined the ways in which opera interacted with endeavors in culture-producing fields beyond the most obvious. Yet disciplinary boundaries in the late eighteenth century were permeable, and exponents from a variety of intellectual and creative enterprises met regularly to exchange ideas. Circa 1789 it was possible to believe that the world's knowledge could be contained encyclopedically, and well-educated amateur could still reasonably expect to keep abreast of developments in both science and art. Indeed, in his youth, even Da Ponte dabbled in the study of "human nature" by writing a Rousseau-inspired essay entitled, "Whether man is happier in an organized society or in a simple state of nature."[2] Given this lively cross-fertilization of cultural practice, interdisciplinary perspectives would seem to be indispensable to the study of opera. That these perspectives have so far been underrepresented is perhaps due to the fact that musicologists rarely employ the notion of

1 I would like to thank Miss Sylvia Fitzgerald, Chief Librarian and Archivist at The Royal Botanic Gardens, Kew, for help with locating works by and about the von Jacquin family. Thanks to Bruce Alan Brown, Frankie Peroni, Ronald J. Rabin, John A. Rice, Douglas Tudhope, and Robert Witkin for "fruitful" discussions.
2 Nicholas Till, *Mozart and the Enlightenment* (London: Faber and Faber, 1992), p. 240.

intellectual and artistic "worlds"[3] – networks of interdependent actors who import and export aesthetic materials and ideas from one field to another in the course of carrying out their cultural work.

What, then, was the nature of the cultural field that opera buffa inhabited? And how can an awareness of opera buffa's location in a wider cultural terrain enrich our understanding of the social and cultural role of musical theatre? In the eighteenth century, opera was the most elaborate kinesthetic form available for the depiction and discussion of social life. In its shift away from stories of gods, kings, and mythological topics, opera buffa was expressly oriented to the representation of "ordinary" life. To what extent, then, is it possible to observe ideas and images from other cultural enterprises – science and social philosophy for example – being acted out, elaborated, transposed, and clothed in the form of human situations on the buffa stage? This essay attempts to address these questions by considering some of the links between opera buffa and a crucial and, even controversial, science in late eighteenth century Vienna – botany. I suggest that opera buffa was a "cultural workspace" wherein new lessons concerning, among other things, social and sexual relations could be registered imaginatively through sight and sound.

"AGOG WITH THE VEGETABLE KINGDOM AGAIN" – BOTANY IN EARLY MODERN EUROPE

In *The Order of Things*, Michel Foucault outlined the eighteenth-century emergence of a particular mode of thought or *episteme* which he dubbed "Classical," contrasting it with an earlier "Renaissance" mode. With the notion of *episteme* Foucault attempted to map out a history of epistemology, to convey a sense in which the form and style of knowledge production has varied

---

3 See Howard S. Becker, *Art Worlds* (Berkeley: University of California Press, 1982) and Pierre Bourdieu, "Intellectual Field and Creative Project," *Social Science Information* 8.2 (1969), 89–119.

over time and place. His contrast between the "Renaissance" and emerging "Classical" episteme is intended to highlight a shift – away from knowledge characterized by analogy and interpretation and toward a concern with classification and taxonomy.[4] Foucault characterizes the pursuit of knowledge in eighteenth century Europe as increasingly concerned with delineating, describing, and ranking the contents of the natural world. The ambitious scholarly projects of this time – such as the *Encyclopédie* and Johnson's Dictionary – exemplified this concern, as did, perhaps most strikingly, the development of a taxonomy and nomenclature for the so-called "three kingdoms of nature" ("Animal, Vegetable, and Mineral") in Carolus Linnaeus's *Systema naturae*.

Linnaeus's work initially appeared in 1735 as a modest folio of twelve pages. By 1766, in its twelfth edition (the last one to be revised by Linnaeus himself), it had swelled to a 2,400-page, three-volume set.[5] By the late 1770s, his reputation and system were secured within the natural science worlds in Paris, London, Vienna, and Berlin. Thus, in the heyday of opera buffa, Linnaean classification provided the working basis for (in Thomas Kuhn's terms) the "normal sciences" of zoology, mineralogy, and botany.

Of these, botany was perhaps the most socially salient. It was linked, on the one hand, to foreign exploration and colonial expansion; on the other, its proliferation gave rise to botanical gardens where rare and exotic plants were brought "home" and exhibited to the public.[6] That the pleasure garden emerged at this time in the British Isles and on the continent (Viennese examples include the Prater and the Augarten) attests to the eighteenth-century fascination with nature – albeit the socially arranged nature of the garden or pleasure ground. Among aristocratic ladies, botanical science became a fashionable pastime, particularly in England, while on the

4 Michel Foucault, *The Order of Things* (New York: Pantheon, 1970), pp. 46–77.
5 Londa Schiebinger, "Why Mammals Are Called Mammals: Gender Politics in Eighteenth-Century Natural History." *American Historical Review* 98.2 (April 1993), 383.
6 Lucile H. Brockway, *Science and Colonial Expansion: The Role of the British Royal Botanic Gardens* (New York: Academic Press, 1979).

continent it was pursued by leading literary and political figures. "I am agog," wrote Goethe to his intimate friend Frau von Stein in 1786, "with the vegetable kingdom again . . . the enormous realm is simplifying itself out in my soul, so that I will soon be able to see through the most difficult problems straight away."[7]

At this time, Vienna was in the forefront of botanical practice, enjoying what has subsequently been referred to as the "golden age" of Austrian botany.[8] Its chief exponents were Nikolaus Joseph Baron von Jacquin (1727–1817) and his eldest son, Joseph Franz (1766–1839). The elder Jacquin was born in Leyden, the son of a cloth merchant of French origin. He became a protégé of Gerhard van Swieten, Maria Theresa's personal physician (and father of Mozart's and Haydn's patron Gottfried van Swieten). He studied in Antwerp, Louvain, Leyden, and Vienna. He went to Paris in 1750 and returned to Vienna in 1752, whence he embarked on a scientific expedition to the Antilles, from 1755 to 1759. He spent most of the 1760s in Schemnit. He returned again to Vienna in 1769 as professor of botany and chemistry at the University of Vienna, where he remained until he was succeeded in his post by his son. He designed both the Rennweg Botanical Gardens and the Schönbrunn park, and published seventeen books between the years 1760 and 1811 (he made his reputation as a taxonomist with *Selectarium stripium americanaum* in 1763). He was ennobled in 1806.

Nikolaus Jacquin was known as the "Austrian Linnaeus"; he became one of the staunchest supporters of the so-called Linnaean "reform." In return he received the following accolade from Linneaus after one of his collecting expeditions: "We [that is all naturalists and scientists] receive and honor you as the ambassador of Flora itself, bringing us the treasures from foreign worlds, so far neither heard of nor seen."[9]

7 Nicholas Boyle, *Goethe: The Poet and the Age*: vol. 1: *The Poetry of Desire (1749–1790)*, (Oxford: Clarendon Press, 1992), p. 386.
8 Frans A. Stafleu, *Linnaeus and the Linnaeans: The Spreading of their Ideas in Systematic Botany 1735–89*. (Utrecht: A. Oosthoek's Uitgeversmaatschappij N.V. for the International Association for Plant Taxonomy, 1971), p. 185.
9 Ibid.

The career of Joseph Franz was perhaps less illustrious than his father's, though it demonstrates the international character of botany during the late eighteenth century. Joseph Franz published five works between 1784 and 1825 and is perhaps best known for his tour of European botanical centers, begun in 1788. He traveled to Prague, Karlsbad, and Dresden, where he was much taken with the gardens of the Elector (Kurfürst) whom he viewed as a "passionate botanist."[10] He then moved on to Leipzig, Halle, Berlin, Göttingen, and Leyden, arriving in London (which he considered to be the leading European center for botany) at the end of the year. He was invited to become an associate of the recently formed Linnean Society, and his father was simultaneously invited to hold the post of honorary president of the botanical side of the same organization.

The Jacquins were active in Vienna's social and cultural scene. Their home was the setting for a group of artists and scholars who met weekly for discussion, music making, and light entertainment. Among those who attended regularly was Mozart, who became acquainted with the Jacquins in 1783 (he dedicated the Notturnos K. 436–9 to his close friend Gottfried Jacquin, the younger brother of Joseph).[11]

The extent to which this group directed their attention to the latest developments in botany will probably never be resolved. That these meetings occurred at the Jacquin household would suggest, however, that botanical matters were aired at least occasionally,

10 A. B. Rendle, "Letters of J. F. von Jacquin (1788–90)," *The Journal of Botany* 61 (1923), p. 288.

11 Would Da Ponte also have been part of this group? It does not seem implausible, given that Mozart and Da Ponte met at the house of Baron Wetzlar (a member of the so-called "second society" of ennobled professionals and merchants) and that the Jacquin salon was an upper-middle-class (professional) salon. We know that Mozart's young friend Gottfried Jacquin took an interest in his success since Mozart wrote to him twice from Prague to describe how his works were faring abroad. We also know that Wetzlar volunteered to underwrite *Le nozze di Figaro* if the emperor would not sponsor it; (Wetzlar would have arranged to have it produced in France or London – see Lorenzo Da Ponte, *Memoirs of Lorenzo Da Ponte, Mozart's Librettist*, trans. L. A. Sheppard (Boston and New York: Houghton Mifflin, 1929), p. 129.

especially given the social status of the science. For example, the elder Jacquin's course of lectures was published in German in 1785 (*Anleitung zur Pflanzenkenntniss nach Linnés Methode* [*Lessons on Botany according to Linnaeus's Method*]). This was the only one of his seventeen publications to appear in German rather than Latin, then as now the official scientific language of botany. That this work was published in the vernacular suggests it was intended to be quasi-popular, a precursor of modern popularizations of science.[12] One can speculate that it might at least have been mentioned within a circle devoted to the discussion of intellectual and social matters of the day, particularly as it had been written by a hosting member.[13] What then, did this book contain that would have held the interest of non-scientists and, more to the point, opera librettists and composers? What was it about botany in the 1780s that held its observers, practitioners, and non-practitioners, so "agog"?

THE "MANLY" AND THE "WOMANLY" IN PLANTS

"Plants," as the elder Jacquin's course of instruction tells us, "feel nothing...[they] have no heart, no lungs...no mind, no stomach, no urinary tract, no anus."[14] Astonishingly, however, plants do possess,

12 It was reissued in 1792 and 1798. The second edition appeared in 1800, with a preface signed by Joseph Jacquin, who made some corrections. The third edition was published in 1840.

13 Joseph Franz Jacquin's entry in Mozart's autograph album refers obliquely to matters botanical. He wrote (in Latin), "To thee who canst 'gently move the attentive oaks with thy melodious strings'. In token of friendship. Joseph Franz Jacquin, Vienna, 24 April 1787." Otto Erich Deutsch, *Mozart: A Documentary Biography* trans. Eric Blom, Peter Branscombe, and Jeremy Noble (Stanford: Stanford University Press, 1965) p. 29. The quote is from Horace.) We know that Mozart took at least some interest in natural history as the list of books owned by him contains two works (written for children) on nature, F. Osterwald's *Historical Description of the Earth for the Benefit of the Young* (published in Strasburg in 1777) and Johann Jakob Ebert's *Natural Science for the Young* (published in Leipzig, 3 vols., 1776–78). See Deutsch, *Mozart: A Documentary Biography*, pp. 601–02.

14 Nikolaus Jacquin, *Anleitung zur Pflanzenkenntniss nach Linnés Methode: Zum Gebrauche seiner theoretischen Vorlesungen* (Vienna: Christian Friedrich Wappler 1785), pp. 5–6.

like humans, sexual organs (*"Fortpflanzungsorgane"*). In a section entitled "The sexuality of plants," Jacquin observes that "the Ritter von Linnaeus called his system of plant classification a sexual system [*Geschlechtssystem*] . . . in plants the male and female genders are represented, and fertility [*Fruchtbarkeit*] is created between them."[15]

Linnaeus was originally introduced to the idea of plant sexuality in 1727 by a fellow scientist, Johann Rothman. At the time this idea was little known and not widely accepted,[16] but Linnaeus employed it from the start of his publishing career in *Systema naturae*. According to his system, plants were categorized first into *classes* and then into the subcategory of *orders*. Classes, the higher category, were derived according to the relative proportions and positions of the *male* parts of flowers, the stamens. Orders, which were subdivisions of the various classes, were based on the proportion and position of the flower's *female* parts, the pistils. (A flower could thus possess both male and female parts in various proportions.) Thus, the female attributes of plants were classified in relation to male attributes and the female properties of plants were rendered subordinate to the male. Further distinctions – genera, species, and variety – were in turn based upon differences between the gender-neutral calyx, flower, fruit, leaves, and a variety of other characteristics.

As Londa Schiebinger has observed in "The Private Life of Plants," Linnaeus's so-called "scienticization" of botany during the eighteenth century "coincided with an ardent 'sexualization' of plants."[17] Thus, in taking up and helping to elaborate Linnaeus's *systema sexuale*, Nikolaus Jacquin was simultaneously involved in a larger, pan-European, project of sexualizing nature. Sex, in Mozart's Vienna, had been introduced as the very essence of vegetable life.[18]

15 Jacquin, *Anleitung*, p. 164.
16 Tore Frängsmyr, ed., *Linnaeus: the Man and his Work* (Berkeley: University of California Press, 1983), p. 64.
17 Londa Schiebinger, "The Private Life of Plants: Sexual Politics in Carol Linnaeus and Erasmus Darwin," in Marina Benjamin, ed., *Science and Sensibility: Gender and Scientific Inquiry 1780–1945* (Oxford: Blackwell, 1991), p. 123.
18 Stafleu, *Linnaeus and the Linnaeans*, p. 55.

But sex of what kind? Or rather, according to what conventions did flowers conduct their amorous affairs? Crucial to the project of botany in the 1780s and 1790s were debates about the shape and conduct of plant sexuality, and the metaphors employed in describing the "nature" of this conduct represented rival attempts to inscribe plant life with human values. According to Linnaeus, the proper location for vegetable love was in the "lawful marriage" of plants or "plant nuptials." Schiebinger recounts how, in describing the sexual relations of plants, Linnaeus did not use the terms "stamen" and "pistil," but employed instead the Greek terms *andria* and *gynia* – husband and wife. Trees and shrubs donned floral "wedding gowns," while the anatomy of flowers burgeoned with sexual metaphor. The calyx, or "nuptial bed," was compared to human *labia majora* and foreskin; the corolla, or "bridal curtains," to *labia minora*. All were described as conspiring with the verdant bridegroom, preparing him "to embrace his beloved bride and offer her his gifts."[19]

The rigidly binary character of sexual difference that Linnaeus imposed upon plants thus paved the way for the heightened notions of sexual difference in human beings. Different however was the degree to which plants, but not humans, were understood as engaging in the legitimate pursuit of a variety of reproductive modes. Unlike the "lawful marriages" of humans, only one order of plants, the "one-husband" or *monoandria* class – the *monoandrian-monogynias* – practiced monogamy. Other plant classes and genera possessed flowers containing two or more "husbands" (stamens) and two or more "wives" (pistils). In other words, plants reproduced in a variety of polygynous and polyandrous relations, one bride with several bridegrooms or vice versa, or indeed, several of each.

To some observers and scientific commentators such as William Smellie, chief compiler of the first edition of the *Encyclopaedia Britannica*, Linnaean botany went "beyond all decent limits,"[20] while to others, it did not go far enough. In *The Loves of Plants*, pub-

---

19 Linnaeus, quoted in Schiebinger, "Private," p. 127.
20 Schiebinger, "Private," p. 130.

lished in 1789 and again in 1791 along with *The Economy of Vegetation* (the two were collectively entitled *The Botanic Garden*), Erasmus Darwin popularized Linnaeus's ideas in passages that advocated the "free" expression of plant/human sexuality in a plethora of forms. Darwin – who viewed sex as "the cordial drop in the otherwise vapid cup of life" – poeticized the "wanton" nature of plant conduct in a way that invited human parallels to be both drawn and acted upon. His project, as he described it in an advertisement for *The Botanic Garden*, was to "inlist Imagination under the banner of Science."[21]

While Darwin is by no means the only creative artist to be so explicit about the project of popularizing or imaginatively re-clothing science, it is relatively rare for developments in science or technology to be so directly employed, and in so didactic a manner, as the basis for artistic work. As a number of cultural historians and science studies scholars have documented,[22] the interrelationship between the arts and sciences is typically complex and hard to trace. This is certainly the case with opera buffa and the late eighteenth-century biological sciences. Nevertheless, it is possible to view opera buffa as partaking of a culture in which vegetation and the metaphors of plant life were socially salient, sexually charged, and controversial. What, then, was the relationship between opera buffa and botanical imagery?

"HAN PIÙ FOGLIE CHE FRUTTI"? – WOMEN AND MEN IN THE BUFFA GARDEN

Come, lovely joy, do not delay. Come where love calls you to delight . . .
Flowers smile, the grass smells fresh; everything quickens the pleasures

21 Quoted in Maureen McNeil, *Under the Banner of Science: Erasmus Darwin and his Age* (Manchester: Manchester University Press, 1987), p. 184.
22 See Svetlana Alpers, *The Art of Describing: Dutch Art in the Seventeenth Century*, (Chicago: University of Chicago Press, 1983); Gordon Fyfe and John Law, eds., *Picturing Power: Visual Depiction and Social Relations*, (London: Routledge, 1988); Robert W. Witkin, *Art and Social Structure* (Cambridge: Polity Press, 1995).

of love. Come, my beloved, through these dark trees. I long to crown
your brow with roses.

Le nozze di Figaro, IV.10 (trans. Mann, p. 431)

In Act II of *Le nozze di Figaro*, Cherubino leaps from a balcony
outside the Countess's boudoir and lands in the garden below. We
are meant to hear the sound of breaking glass – a cloche or cold
frame perhaps, for a non-indigenous planting sheltered by the
castle wall?[23] We learn later that it was a pot of carnations. Antonio
– Head Gardener at Aguasfrescas – presents it indignantly to his
employers. People are always flinging things out of the windows,
he complains, but this is the first time a human being has been jetti-
soned.

As others have observed,[24] the garden provides a frequent
setting for opera buffa. It is perhaps fitting that Cherubino – or
Cherubin d'amore as he is called on one occasion by Basilio – makes
his escape to the garden, since gardens in Mozart have scenic
specificity; they are nearly always erotically charged. For example,
Susanna (the gardener's niece) arranges to meet Almaviva in the
shadowy evening garden, "beneath the pines of the grove" as she
and the Countess put it in the letter they compose together. Later,
in the crepuscular atmosphere of the evening garden, she describes
how nature "conspires with the secrets of love": the flowers smile,
the grass smells fresh. "Come, my beloved," she sings, ostensibly to
Almaviva but in truth to Figaro, "through these dark trees. I long to
crown your brow with roses."

As Wye Allanbrook has observed,[25] the pastoral features prominently in Mozart's operas. Both musically and poetically, it provides
a natural-historical backdrop for love in all its guises. More
specifically, she has suggested that the pastoral is a *topos* associated
with the feminine and feminine sexuality (and the grace of sexual

23 Beaumarchais mentions melons.
24 Wye J. Allanbrook, "Human Nature in the Unnatural Garden: *Figaro* as Pastoral,"
   CM 51 (1993), 82–93; *Rhythmic Gesture*; Mary Hunter, "Landscapes, Gardens, and
   Gothic Settings in the *Opere Buffe* of Mozart and his Italian Contemporaries,"
   CM 51 (1993), 94–104.   25 Allanbrook, *Rhythmic Gesture*.

expression within the bonds of love). It is also associated with feminine inconstancy.

Opera buffa was by no means the only cultural form to be preoccupied with women, love, and sex. During Mozart's adult lifetime blurred genres abounded; for example, social-scientific "lessons" concerning sexual, reproductive, and familial relations were often presented through the media of fiction (e.g. Rousseau, Bernardin de Saint-Pierre) and painting (e.g. Greuze, one of Diderot's favorite painters).[26] As Ludmilla Jordanova has observed, natural history cast its net widely during the eighteenth century. The specific interest in reproduction within the natural sciences spiralled back into the growing preoccupation with human sexuality as an object of scientific study. The result blended biology and eroticism.[27] At one level, then, opera provided yet another cultural "workspace" in which questions concerning nature and human nature could be debated and dramatized. At another level, opera could depict particular configurations of the erotic, as these arose from and could be justified by "scientific" knowledge. Of special interest, however, is that in company with a number of other cultural enterprises – anatomy, physiology, fiction, and social theory – the natural history lessons of opera buffa were drawn from an interrogation not of *human*kind, but specifically of *women*.

As a number of cultural historians have observed, woman increasingly came to be associated with "the natural" – with being less rational and less physically disciplined – during the eighteenth century. "Man is more solid; woman is softer. Man is straighter; woman is more supple. Man walks with a firm step; woman with a soft and light one. Man contemplates and observes; woman looks and feels" – these, according to Lavater in 1775–78, were the differences between the sexes.[28] In his *Dictionnaire de la conservation de l'homme*, L. C. H. Macquart suggested that women were more sen-

---

26 L. J. Jordanova, "Naturalizing the Family: Literature and the Bio-Medical Sciences in the Late Eighteenth Century," in L. J. Jordanova, ed., *Languages of Nature: Critical Essays on Science and Literature* (New Brunswick, NJ: Rutgers University Press, 1986), p. 90.   27 Jordanova, *Naturalizing*, p. 87.
28 Quoted in Jordanova, *Naturalizing*, p. 92.

sible (sensitive or sensitized) than men – in fact they were like children in this regard – and also more passionate because of "the great mobility of their fibres, especially those in the uterus; hence their irritability, and suffering from vapours."[29] According to Linnaeus, woman's ability to lactate placed her closer than man ("homosapiens" [sic]) to other mammalian creatures.[30] In choosing the breast as the key distinguishing feature of mammals and in rejecting earlier distinctions, such as the one based on a creature's number of legs, Linnaeus's system reflected his current preoccupation with the breast and breast-feeding, and his involvement in anti-wet-nurse campaigns.[31] Moreover, as with his system of plant classification, Linnaeus introduced sexual difference as a salient feature of life itself.

In examining the cultural history of the breast, we can follow ideas about gender being imported and exported in a convoluted journey from social campaign to scientific classification and back again to social campaign, as a range of writers (as, for example, Rousseau) were quick to capitalize on the idea of the breast as "nature's sign" and the essential basis of woman's nurturant social role. Through such mutual referencing and borrowing between different branches of the social and natural sciences, cascades of biological inscriptions accrued in ways that eventually came to locate women (of all classes)[32] both within their naturally "rightful" place within the private sphere of the family[33] and within the

---

29 Ludmilla Jordanova, *Sexual Visions: Images of Gender in Science and Medicine between the Eighteenth and Twentieth Centuries* (Madison: University of Wisconsin Press, 1989), p. 28.   30 Schiebinger, "Mammals," pp. 393–94.

31 Ibid.

32 The "bourgeois" family ideal articulated by thinkers such as Rousseau applied to aristocrats as well. For example, Linnaeus suggested that baby farming, namely lower-class milk, could corrupt upper-class babies (Schiebinger, "Mammals," p. 407.)

33 The word family (*Familie*) was virtually unknown in the German-speaking world until around the second half of the eighteenth century. Ute Frevert, *Women in German History: From Bourgeois Emancipation to Sexual Liberation*, trans. Stuart McKinnon-Evans (Oxford: Berg, 1989), p. 14, has described how it is first listed in Krünitz's *Oeconomische Encyklopädie* in 1788 ("married couples and their children").

purview of the emerging "clinical gaze" of the newly mobilizing profession of medicine.[34] "By around 1800," Thomas Laqueur has observed, "writers of all sorts were determined to base what they insisted were fundamental differences between the male and female sexes, and thus between man and woman, on discoverable biological distinctions . . .".[35]

Thus, in a range of eighteenth century texts woman's anatomy and physiology made her more "natural" than man;[36] her bodily parts, her cycles, indeed, her very fibers rendered her less predictable and hence more subject to nature's laws. Woman was posited as natural and beautiful, but also as wild, dark, and dangerous. In short, woman was a potential bundle of troubles, emotionally and sexually unstable, medically problematic, and in need of scientific scrutiny. What better way of underscoring the instability of woman-as-nature than by associating her with that highly eroticized and sexually variegated entity – the flower?

"FIOR DI DIAVOLO" – OR, WHAT KIND OF FLOWER IS WOMAN?

> You are the flowers of life . . . You civilize the human race . . . You are the Queens of our beliefs and of our moral order.
>
> (*Bernardin de Saint-Pierre, from the 1806 preface to* Paul et Virginie)[37]

34 See Anne Witz, *Professions and Patriarchy* (London: Routledge, 1991); Jean Donnison, *Midwives and Medical Men: A History of the Struggle for the Control of Childbirth* (2nd edn.), (London: Historical Publications, 1988), especially ch. 3, "The Ascendancy of Men" pp. 53–71; Barbara Ehrenreich and Deirdre English, *Witches, Midwives and Nurses: A History of Women Healers* (Old Westbury, NY: Feminist Press, 1973); William Ray Arney, *Power and the Profession of Obstetrics* (Chicago: University of Chicago Press, 1982); Ann Oakley, *The Captured Womb: A History of the Medical Care of Pregnant Women* (New York: Blackwell, 1984).

35 Thomas Laqueur, *Making Sex: Body and Gender from the Greeks to Freud* (Cambridge 1973, MA: Harvard University Press, 1990), p. 5.

36 Jordanova, *Sexual Visions*, ch. 2, *passim*.

37 Ibid., p. 34.

The association between women and flowers was hardly new to the late eighteenth century; indeed, its origins were pre-Linnaean.[38] New, however, was the overtly sexualized character of flowers. Given the social salience of botany in the 1780s, it seems reasonable to suggest that aristocratic and upper-middle-class audiences would have been at least vaguely aware of this new, anthropomorphic and overtly sexualized addition to flower imagery. If so, they would no doubt have appreciated its uses in opera.

The woman-flower comparison is frequently employed by Mozart and Da Ponte. For example, in Act I of *Le nozze di Figaro*, a chorus of flower-bearing country people describes how the Count's magnanimity in rescinding the *droit de Seigneur* has preserved for them "the divine innocence of an even lovelier flower." As Allanbrook has observed, the most musically "florid" part of the text they sing begins with the word *fiore*.[39] Later, a chorus of peasant girls presents flowers to the Countess – it is perhaps no accident that Beaumarchais named her Rosina; nor perhaps that nearly half the female characters in Mozart's buffa works have flower names.[40] In the Beaumarchais version, Figaro's famous monologue was a diatribe about politics. In the Da Ponte version political satire is removed. Instead, in Act IV, Figaro turns his attention to women ("Aprite un po' quegl'occhi, uomini incauti e sciocchi" – "Open your eyes a little, you incautious, silly men"). Angered and exasperated, Figaro compares women to a range of natural and supernatural entities: witches, sirens, owls, comets, vixens, she-bears, and malign doves. He also compares them to "thorned roses."

What kind of flower, then, was woman? And how was she to be

---

38 We can see it in Shakespeare, for example, in *The Winter's Tale*, where Perdita ushers in summer wreathed in flowers: "Here's flow'rs for you / Hot lavender, mints, savory, marjoram, / The marigold, that goes to bed wi' th' sun / And with him rises weeping; these are flow'rs / Of middle summer and I think they are given / To men of middle age" (IV. 4). The garden is also featured in this play as the setting for a woman's trial.

39 Allanbrook, *Rhythmic Gesture*, p. 92.

40 Rosina in *Le nozze di Figaro*; Rosina in *La finta semplice*; Violante in *La finta giardiniera* (and also the Count "Bel Fiore"); Fiordiligi in *Così fan tutte*; Giacinta in *La finta semplice*.

classified? Women, as Bernardin de Saint-Pierre put it in the 1806 preface to *Paul et Virginie*, may be the "flowers of life," but like all natural objects, they are subject to laws that lie outside human convention. On the one hand woman / nature could bestow grace upon men, and shelter them from the exigencies of mundane life. We see this point clearly illustrated in the finale of *Le nozze di Figaro*. When all the confusion is sorted out, properly individuated love is protected by the efforts of women and is secured within the "lawful" institution of bourgeois companionate marriage.[41] On the other hand, love (and woman) are morally vulnerable and both can be "led astray" by an excess of desire. Woman was paradoxically configured as moral garantor on the one hand and temptress on the other. Within this paradox, nature and culture (social convention) could come into conflict when woman's sensual vulnerability led to the transgression of convention and the traduction of men (as Figaro observes in the conclusion of his Act IV monologue). Woman therefore required study – she could be controlled through understanding of the laws governing her behavior. "What kind of animal," asks Don Alfonso in Act I of *Così fan tutte*, "are these beauties of yours?" ("Che razza d'animali son queste vostre belle?"). As we have seen, this concern with taxonomy was characteristic of eighteenth-century thought; it should therefore not seem surprising that buffa plots abound with interrogations of woman's nature, and, within this enquiry, convey an almost obsessive interest in woman's sexual weakness.

One of these interrogative modes was the seduction plot, a creature of the late eighteenth century (e.g. Laclos, *Les Liaisons dangereuses*, 1781).[42] It consisted of a contrived or *man*-made environment in which the controlled or quasi-experimental proce-

41 We know this was a preoccupation of Mozart himself. As he wrote to Gottfried Jacquin on 4 November 1787, "Surely the pleasure of a transient, capricious infatuation is as far removed as heaven from earth from the blessed happiness of a deep and true affection?" *Letters*, p. 913; *Briefe*, vol. 4, p. 59.
42 Nineteenth-century commentators found it repugnant. H. C. Robbins Landon, *Mozart: The Golden Years* (New York: Schirmer, 1989), p. 177.

dure of testing women could be carried out in clinical detail.[43] The proving ground for man's observation of woman was, perhaps not surprisingly, often the garden – nature's laboratory. Mozart's and Da Ponte's *Così fan tutte* is a prime example of a seduction plot. Here, two gardens ("a garden by the seashore"/"a pretty little garden") provide the backdrop for women's temptation, resistance and eventual seduction. Dorabella and Fiordiligi ("lily-flower" – Da Ponte doled out flower symbolism with a heavy hand [lily=purity] for this more resistant sister) are described by Despina as "poor fools ... wandering in the garden" ("Le povere buffone / stanno nel giardinetto" [1.12]). In Act II, scene 3, Don Alfonso calls the sisters to come at once to the garden where, in scene 4, Ferrando and Guglielmo arrive by boat, distributing garlands of flowers. Their servants distribute further flowers. The disguised lovers and the sisters then pair off and stroll in the garden. Later, when the men reconvene to discuss the sisters' behavior (Dorabella has succumbed to Guglielmo's advances), Ferrando, who has remained unsuccessful in his attempts to seduce Fiordiligi, tells his friend that she is "chaste as a lily" ("pura como columba" [literally, any plant from the arum family, such as jack-in-the-pulpit or calla lily]). When Fiordiligi objects to Dorabella that she doesn't understand how the heart can change in only one day, her sister replies, "Now you're being ridiculous! We're women!" ("Che domanda ridicola! Siam donne!"). Later still, after Fiordiligi has finally responded to Ferrando's wooing, Guglielmo refers to her as "flower of the devil" ("fior di diavolo").

This investigative attitude toward women (and the trial of women in gardens) is by no means unique to Mozart's operas. It is also featured in Da Ponte's and Martín y Soler's reworking of the plot of *L'arbore di Diana* (first produced in 1787; it was the work Da Ponte himself considered to be his best). As Mary Hunter has

43 Andrew Steptoe, *The Mozart-Da Ponte Operas: The Cultural and Musical Background to Le nozze di Figaro, Don Giovanni and Così fan tutte* (Oxford: Clarendon Press, 1988), p. 123.

observed,[44] the text was reworked from a 1721 *festa teatrale* by Metastasio. A magic tree in Diana's garden lights up and plays music when pure nymphs walk beneath it, but its fruit blacken and pelt impure nymphs who pass under it. After Cupid's three youthful helpers have seduced all of Diana's nymphs, and eventually even the Goddess of Chastity herself, the garden is transformed into a palace of love. In Da Ponte's reworking of the story, the obstacle to the union of Diana and Endimione is no longer his inexperience, but Diana's commitment to virginity which, of course, is then duly tried and eventually vanquished in the course of the opera, underscoring once again the emerging modern notion of woman's paradoxical character as both virtuous and vulnerable to temptation.

Of course, not all women are so weak. In the Da Ponte–Martín y Soler *Una cosa rara* (performed first in the autumn of 1786), a beautiful "girl of the mountains" loves a mountaineer but is pursued by an infatuated Infante of Spain. She resists the Infante's advances (both before and after her marriage) and for this (apparently astonishing) "virtuous" female conduct, she is awarded the appelation "*cosa rara*" or "rare thing," following, as Da Ponte tells it, the famous line of the satirist, "*Rara est concordia formae atque pudicitiae*" – "rare is it that beauty and virtue go together." She could perhaps just as easily have been referred to as a "flower of grace and virtue" ("Fior di grazie, e di virtu") – Rusticone's words in the 1789 Da Ponte–Salieri work, *La cifra*.[45]

To what extent are the "biology lessons" of opera buffa conveyed, not only through plot and librettos, but also through musical characterization? In recent years this important question has been addressed by several pioneering scholars. Of these, Gretchen Wheelock's analysis of the gendered distribution of musical material in Mozart's operas is highly compelling. Wheelock has

---

44 Mary Hunter, "Some Representations of *Opera Seria* in *Opera Buffa*," *COJ* 3 (1991), 101–05.

45 John Platoff, "The Buffa Aria in Mozart's Vienna," *COJ* 2 (1990), 99–120. According to Da Ponte, *Una cosa rara* was a particular favorite of the ladies. Lorenzo Da Ponte, *Memoirs*, p. 149.

described how the social force of Mozart's female characters is musically undermined by the use of the so-called weak and unstable realm of the minor mode – a predominantly feminine musical medium. Wheelock's work speaks clearly to sociologists and others who are interested in the non-cognitive means through which social classifications are achieved and reinforced.[46]

Charles Ford has suggested that musical femininity in Mozart is achieved through fluid, aperiodic and functionless musical material which demarcates the feminine as a "sub-style," removed from the more musically purposive "public discourse" of diatonic musical masculinity. According to Ford, the chromatic color and nuance characteristic of Mozart's female vocal lines inscribes the feminine as, musically, a private world of feeling and sensibility; this is, of course, as Ford points out, a *male* representation of feminine sensibility.[47] The musical unpredictability of so much of Mozart's feminine musical material, particularly when women are undergoing seduction, Ford suggests, renders woman as "an empty but plenitudinous space," one in which the Enlightenment, in the form of its many projects and spokesmen, can project its classifications and "scientific" claims.

These specifically musicological explorations, which attempt to document musical constructions of gender differences, illuminate music as a crucial medium in the articulation of modern gender imagery. It should therefore come as no surprise that the biology lessons of the Enlightenment era were echoed and given further substance through the text and tones of opera buffa.

Woman as natural, as unstable, as in need of surveillance, as belonging in the realm of the private sphere – woman in this set of representations was deprived of participation in the then emerging realm of public life. At the same time the household or "private

---

46 "*Schwarze Gredel* and the Engendered Minor Mode in Mozart's Operas," in Ruth A. Solie, ed., *Musicology and Difference: Gender and Sexuality in Music Scholarship*, (Berkeley and London: University of California Press, 1993), pp. 201–21.

47 *Così? Sexual Politics in Mozart's Operas* (Manchester: Manchester University Press, 1991), p. 138.

sphere" was being transformed. Not only a locus of reproduction and physical maintenance, it increasingly came to be viewed as a feminine haven of feeling, warmth, and individuated love. Thus, the eighteenth-century obsession with woman, worked out in a range of media, provided a means for articulating and publicizing the bourgeois notion of marriage and its various antagonisms. To be sure, these views did not pass uncontested. Mary Wollstonecraft's *Vindication of the Rights of Woman* (1792) is perhaps the best-known work today to object to the gender bias of Enlightenment thought – its implicit pairing of woman with the private, and man with the public, sphere.

During the 1780s, dicta concerning the nature of woman and the social shape of love were being reinforced in a variety of cultural media. Opera buffa provided yet another "workspace" for the imaginative elaboration of gender difference as it was initially articulated in its modern, bourgeois form.[48] Of course, opera is impoverished if it is reduced to a mere venue for the rehearsal and mobilization of social imagery and sexual politics. But restoring opera's links to the social, scientific, and cultural contexts in which it was produced and consumed can also empower opera studies. Opera buffa gave dramatic, scenic, and musical flesh to the peculiarly Enlightened obsession with woman and her nature. Conversely, when nature and social convention are depicted as poised in harmony (through the medium of woman's constancy), as at the end of *Le nozze di Figaro*, opera buffa served as a crucial medium for the celebration (and modern articulation) of the fragile but glorious joys of love.

48 Perhaps because of its highly sensuous nature (dramatic action, music, scenery, costume, sound effects and props, poetry) opera is one of the most persuasive media. To look at how twentieth-century music scholars themselves have not been immune to opera's seductive and sometimes insidious "biology lessons" would no doubt be instructive. For example, whatever could William Mann (whose writing on Mozart's operas is often delightful) have been thinking when he wrote, ". . . it would be beneficial to [Donna Anna's] personal growing-up if she had been pleasantly raped by Don Juan"? Mann, *The Operas of Mozart* (New York: Oxford University Press, 1977), p. 468. (This passage is also quoted in Ford, *Così?*, p. 185.)

This paper has two primary aims. One – largely historical – is to suggest that non-Mozartean opera buffa in Vienna in the 1780s was more engaged with and embedded in the emergence of bourgeois social structures and cultural values than has hitherto been acknowledged.[1] The other – largely methodological – is to examine *how* an emergent bourgeois *mentalité* might manifest itself in this genre of opera.[2] But what is an "emergent bourgeois *mentalité*"? What domains of experience does it encompass? What does "bourgeois" mean in this context? Elsewhere in this volume Paolo Gallarati suggests that Mozart's Da Ponte settings embody with particular clarity and strength the "enlightened bourgeois" values of representational truth and expressive naturalness championed by such Enlightenment figures as Diderot and Lessing. For Gallarati (as for many others) "bourgeois" in this context is an aesthetic rather than a sociological term, indicating a naturalistic style emphasizing individual subjectivity, capable of extraordinary expressive and rhetorical immediacy, and located between the artifices of high-flown language and the clockwork mechanics of buffoonish comedy.[3] Contemporary expressions of this bourgeois aesthetic of naturalness also include a social dimension, often manifest in the requirement that artworks involve "ordi-

---

1 Cf. the paper by Paolo Gallarati in this volume for a different view of this subject.
2 This aspect of my essay connects in various ways to the essay by Edmund J. Goehring. It is also comparable to recent work on opera seria by Martha Feldman, especially her "Magic Mirrors and the *Seria* Stage: Thoughts toward a Ritual View," *JAMS* 48 (1995), 423–84.
3 The standard statement on this subject is still Leo Balet and E. Gerhard, *Die Verbürgerlichung der deutschen Kunst, Literatur und Musik im 18. Jahrhundert* (Strasbourg: Heitz & Co, 1936).

nary" characters, settings, or events. Bartolomeo Benincasa's preface to his libretto *Il disertore* (Venice, 1785)[4] is no exception, echoing in the operatic realm Diderot's and Lessing's calls for a "bourgeois" or "intermediate" dramatic genre whose most important features are an elevatedly natural style and recognizable characters:

> Why should there not be an . . . attempt at a Dramma in Musica which stands between grand heroic opera and comic operetta? The distance between these two extremes should not be equal; this genre should be considerably more distant from the latter than the former [i.e. closer to heroic opera]. Let us explain in more detail. One imagines an action – probable, even ordinary, and above all interesting. This action takes place among characters of a condition not as far from us in time or in kind as Alexander the Great or Dido. This action should be serious and important, its language no longer lyrical, but noble, full of sentiment, of truth, and should concern itself more with ideas than with everyday objects.[5]

Although Benincasa's preface ostensibly concerns dramatic aesthetics, its theme of a middle way and its tone of high seriousness connect with the contemporaneous writings of Josephinian apologist Johann Pezzl, and especially with his quasi-sociological *Skizze von Wien* (1786–90):

> For me an enlightened man is one with a properly developed moral instinct, one who can derive satisfaction from an occupation which chance or the laws has given him, who acts correctly from conviction, who likes his work . . . who shows a love of order in his domestic and public life, who is moderate in his eating and drinking and looks after his health . . . who is never tempted to live beyond his means, who strives constantly to improve those talents necessary to his destiny in society; who knows and practices the duties of a citizen, friend, husband and father; who realizes that in bourgeois society it is necessary, for the

4 Goehring's essay elsewhere in this collection also refers to this preface.
5 Bartolomeo Benincasa, preface to his libretto *Il disertore* (Venice, 1785). This libretto was itself based on *Le Déserteur* (1770), a play by Louis-Sébastien Mercier, based in turn on a libretto by Michel-Jean Sedaine (1769).

maintenance of the whole, to bear individual burdens and sacrifice private advantages . . .[6]

A cavalier of ancient lineage and no merits may ride in a coach and six, give banquets, occupy the best boxes in the theatre, keep a great house; no-one minds about this, but if because of it all he thinks himself a great man and demands respect he won't get it. Nowadays a ne'er do well and dissolute scion of princely or baronial lineage is accorded no respect by the genuine aristocracy . . . [The genuine aristocracy] appreciate a bourgeois scholar, artist and businessman much more than a useless nobleman.[7]

The most striking shared feature of these passages is their sense of the interdependence of old and new ways of thinking, of aristocratic and bourgeois values, and of the new fluidity of social and aesthetic boundaries. Benincasa, for example, combines his demand for new, "ordinary" subject matter with a strong sense that the prevailing tone or mode of expression should derive from aesthetic categories (nobility and seriousness) associated with the well-worn genre of opera seria. Pezzl, in his turn, suggests that aristocrats should embrace the bourgeois values of thrift and civic responsibility. Indeed, he praises the ennoblement of bourgeois who amassed money "through commerce, supplying the army, and entering into all kinds of other important transactions."[8] Conversely, he commends the imperial court for living in a prudent and economical manner, representing bourgeois values while living on essentially feudal income.

Perhaps more important than Benincasa's and Pezzl's shared interest simply in combining old and new is their shared sense of the different ways in which old and new phenomena convey meaning. In the social realm Pezzl suggests that while bourgeois values carry moral weight, they need the social clout of approval and absorption by the "genuine aristocracy" to gain currency and validity. Benincasa's dramatic analogy to this is his suggestion that "ordinary" plot material must be validated by the social and

6 Johann Pezzl, *Skizze von Wien*, Part III, 1787. Translated in H. C. Robbins Landon, *Mozart and Vienna* (New York: Macmillan, 1991), p. 129.

7 Ibid., Part I (1786) in Landon, *Mozart and Vienna*, p. 71.

8 Ibid., Part II (1786) in Landon, *Mozart and Vienna*, p. 105.

intellectual weight of aesthetic standards drawn from opera seria. This notion of different, often non-congruent, but always inter-dependent layers of meaning, whether in art or in life, is funda-mental to a serious examination of opera buffa's cultural place in Josephine Vienna, and it is perhaps most usefully examined via the semiotic distinction between reference and signification. "Reference" here indicates a more or less direct relation between a representation and the real life object, person, or situation it imi-tates. "Signification" is more oblique, and can involve matters of tone (irony, satire, sentimentalism) as well as the relations between semantic systems (music, text(s), performance style, marketing strategies, etc.).[9] Thus Benincasa's middle genre *refers to* ordinary settings and characters, but *signifies* nobility in the way it treats the material.

In what follows, then, I want to suggest that while in any attempt to understand the social implications of opera buffa in 1780s Vienna it is important to consider what the works represent (or refer to), it is equally important to consider what they signify. Opera buffa's "signifieds" result not only from its treatment of its representa-tional material, but also, as the excerpts from Pezzl and Benincasa imply, from the ways its various domains – textual, aesthetic, and circumstantial – intersect. I use the word "domain" here in counter-point to Sergio Durante's use of the term to indicate the different textual areas of analytical/interpretative investigation in individ-ual works.[10] I would argue that to consider opera in relation to social issues like class requires an expansion of "the work" (and thus of its "domains") to include not only its words, notes, and printed stage-directions, but also the acts of performing, producing and consuming it. A broader and more fluid conception of the work

9 Umberto Eco illustrates the difference between reference and signification in language with the example of the word "unicorn," which signifies by virtue of a web of intertextual and symbolic systems, but which cannot refer, since there is no such thing as an actual unicorn. See Franco Fido, *Guida a Goldoni* (Turin: Einaudi, 1977), p. 72.

10 See his "Analysis and Dramaturgy: Reflections towards a Theory of Opera," in this volume.

and its domains allows a broader and more flexible range of connections between an opera and the society in which it played; this flexibility is particularly important when that society is – as Josephine Vienna was – in flux, and when the genre has – as opera buffa did – only the most oblique referential connection to that flux. Indeed, it is often in the tensions or contradictions within and between these broad domains of text, aesthetics, and circumstances, that opera buffa's connection to the complex and contradictory processes of emergent bourgeois *mentalités* is most evident. The "domains" I have indicated as relevant to this essay, then (textual, aesthetic, circumstantial), are intended not to correct or replace Durante's more analytically oriented domains, but to suggest that different questions about meaning and the resultant different conceptions of the nature of the work will inevitably produce different understandings of that "work's" constituent parts.

The majority of this essay involves a discussion of how social meaning arises from the tensions among the domains in two operas – Palomba's and Paisiello's *Le gare generose*,[11] and Da Ponte's and Martín's *Una cosa rara*.[12] However, the entire repertory of opera buffa in Josephine Vienna played in a field of irresolvable tensions, and thus participated in the fluid and sometimes contradictory relations between old and new, aristocrat and bourgeois, feudalism and capitalism, described by both Benincasa and Pezzl. Despite being performed for an audience consisting largely of aristocrats and high officials, for example, it featured ridiculous or corrupt nobles opposite sympathetic peasants and servants.[13] Despite being derided in the press as empty entertainment for the aristocrats, it

---

11 Naples, 1786; Vienna, 1786; probably derived from Calzabigi's libretto *Amiti e Ontario* (1772).   12 Vienna, 1786.

13 Otto G. Schindler, "Das Publikum des Burgtheaters in der Josephinischen Ära: Versuch einer Strukturbestimmung," in Margret Dietrich, ed., *Das Burgtheater und sein Publikum* (Vienna: Verlag der Österreichischen Akademie der Wissenschaften, 1976), p. 92. John A. Rice, "Vienna under Joseph II and Leopold II," in Neal Zaslaw, ed., *Man and his Music: The Classical Era* (Englewood Cliffs, NJ: Prentice Hall, 1989), p. 128, points out that even the cheapest seats in the Burgtheater in the 1770s were worth a full day's wages for a mason.

played to (at least putatively) the same subscribers as the self-consciously "bourgeois" and didactic offerings of Joseph II's Nationaltheater. And despite being considered "mere entertainment" it was underwritten and supported by an emperor whose thrift, simplicity, hard work, and despotism embodied the contradictions of the Enlightenment in Vienna perhaps better than any other single person or circumstance. These contradictions in this repertory's broad circumstances both surround and pervade individual works.

"LE GARE GENEROSE": BOURGEOIS SENTIMENTALITY AND AESTHETIC DISTANCE

Before the action of *Le gare generose* begins, the Neapolitan couple Gelinda and Bastiano Ammazzagatte have tried to elope to Halifax under the assumed names Dianina and Bronton, but their ship is taken by pirates. Destitute and in debt, they are bought as slaves by the Boston merchant Mr. Dull. The opera opens with the couple already in Mr. Dull's house. Mr. Dull inevitably falls in love with Dianina, and his niece Miss Meri does the same with Bronton. Miss Meri, however, is supposedly engaged to Mr. Dull's protégé, Don Berlicco, who has been sent abroad (to Naples among other places) to make his fortune. Berlicco returns, having failed to invest the money that Mr. Dull gave him, and consequently deeply in debt. He has a warrant for the arrest of two escaped Neapolitans, on whose heads there is now a bounty, and he is jealous of his fiancée's interest in Bastiano / Bronton. He thus has both financial and emotional interest in exposing the identity of the slaves. In fact in the end, Gelinda confesses her identity and situation to Mr. Dull, and throws herself on his mercy. He (of course) relents and relinquishes his own interest in her and promises to have Don Berlicco arrested for debt. Gelinda in turn pleads for mercy for Berlicco, and underwrites his debt.

On the level of reference, this work embodies the bourgeois / enlightened values praised by Pezzl. In fact, just as solvency and prudence form the foundation of Pezzl's hierarchy of values, financial dealings pervade and support the plot of *Le gare generose*. The unusually long *argomento* in the Neapolitan libretto of the premiere details with unusual care the various exchanges of money both before and during the opera (these passages are underlined below).

Gelinda Cucciardi, orphan of a rich French merchant established in Naples, annoyed by the hardships imposed upon her by her guardian, who administered her property, resolves to flee to America, and persuades a Neapolitan of gentle birth [*di civile condizione*] called Bastiano Ammazzagatte, to go with her. He, head over heels in love with her, determines, not without difficulty, to emigrate. She leaves orders to have most of her possessions sent to Cadiz, and takes with her only silver, jewels, and a bit of ready cash. Once in Cadiz, she marries Bastiano, and, fearing the persecution of the guardian still in Naples, they resolve to change names [Gelinda to Dianina, Bastiano to Bronton]. From the bank of Alonzo Perez, Dianina takes out promissory notes on [*sopra*] the firm Buble of Halifax. They set sail for America, but on the way their vessel is set upon and taken by pirates. However, shortly afterwards, a Bostonian frigate attacks the pirates and in the battle, their wooden boat [*corsaro*] burns, along with the little box containing Gelinda's jewels, cash and promissory notes. The pirates are taken to Boston and all hanged according to the law. Bastiano and Gelinda almost suffer the same fate, but since they swear that they are not pirates themselves but rather their prisoners, and although their story is regarded with suspicion, by virtue of the pleas of Mr. Dull, principal citizen of Boston, their punishment is commuted to perpetual slavery. The said Mr. Dull buys them as his servants, paying the price to the soldiers of the Bostonian frigate.

Meanwhile, the first promissory notes drawn on the Buble firm of Halifax are returned in protest because the funds were not transferred from Naples to Cadiz, due to the impediments created by Gelinda's relatives. But, recognizing the injustice they were doing her, they ceased their opposition, furnished the funds to Cadiz and then on new orders from the banker Perez, the Halifax banker accepted the second promissory notes. What dangers the two unfortunates would endure during their stay in Boston because of this non-acceptance of the promissory notes, how they would come to be discovered, with what generosity the Bostonian Dull would treat them, and what generosity Gelinda would return to him, as well as to him who revealed her identity, and how they would come to recover their freedom and peace of mind, will be seen in the course of the drama.

Throughout the opera, financial competence and honesty are the hallmarks of virtue; Don Berlicco is portrayed as a villain of sorts for squandering the fortune he was supposed to invest; his malicious interest in turning in Gelinda and Bastiano for the 200 guineas reward money is also clearly condemned. When Gelinda confesses her identity to Mr. Dull, his first question is whether she is guilty of fraudulent contracts, and his second concerns her debts; not until he is satisfied with her contractual probity does he ask about Bastiano's status. Once she has satisfied him that she is honest in every respect (and sung a touching *rondò* to boot), he is moved to pity and decides to let the couple escape:

> I feel in my heart the stirrings of pity for her. I'm thinking of letting them escape; ah, if generosity triumphs over misery, love gives way.
> [Sento che intorno al core un senso di pietà per lei s'aggira[.] Penso farli fuggir, ah si trionfi dei miseria favore la generosità[,] ceda l'amore[.]]]

Gelinda's final generosity to Don Berlicco is explicitly financial – she underwrites his debts.

The sheer quantity of reference to money matters in this opera is unusual in this repertory. *Opere buffe* played in Vienna in the 1780s fairly often include references to money, but such references are rarely continuous enough to constitute a significant theme. (The bet between Don Alfonso and the lovers in *Così fan tutte*, Act I, scene 1, and the byplay between Don Alfonso and Despina in Act I, scene 10 for example, is much more typical of the repertory than the pervasive references to money in *Le nozze di Figaro*.) *Le gare generose* is additionally unusual in its positive attitude to trade and investment. This libretto in some ways resembles what many critics have described as the optimistic mercantilism of Goldoni's spoken plays. In *Il cavaliere e la dama* (1749) for example, the merchant Anselmo retorts to an insolent *cavaliere*:

Mercantile activity is useful to the world, necessary to the commerce of nations and those who exercise it honorably, as I do, should not be addressed as plebean.[14]

In contrast to the attitude in this play and in *Le gare generose*, money in this repertory of opera buffa is more often used to display vice or corruption than to present an exercise of virtue. Avarice, ambition, and the capacity to corrupt or hold sway over innocent victims are more frequently found than monetary generosity; and greedy, miserly, and cynical bourgeois are far more common than generous ones. In this sense, many *opere buffe* set in bourgeois circumstances do not seem to regard the economic underpinnings of bourgeois life with much sympathy. Indeed, the only truly admirable merchants in the repertory I have looked at are Mr. Dull and the Dutch merchant Sumers in Petrosellini's and Cimarosa's *L'italiana in Londra*, who renounces his amorous interest in the heroine and pays surety to keep her out of jail.

It is probably not coincidental that both these generous merchants are foreign and shown in British (or British-influenced) settings. However, the elaborately Bostonian setting of *Le gare generose* has, I think, three functions beyond feeding (albeit in a rather backhanded way) continental Anglomania. The first and most superficial is a sort of exoticism; one stage setting calls for rows of "American plants and fruits," and at one point in Bastiano's series of scrapes he is seen in jail chained to an African. The second is a utopian strain made palatable by its distance from Europe; Mr. Dull makes a number of pronouncements about the rights and obligations of *Bostonensi*, including that it is a crime not to dispense mercy when possible ("Ai Bostonensi il non usar pietà divien delitto" [1. 6]). The third, connected to this utopian strain, is that Mr. Dull, the Boston citizen, is *by virtue of his riches* in a position to dispense the sort of mercy and generosity normally arrogated to Pashas and other monarchs. Tito comes to mind here; indeed, Ivan Nagel has pointed out how "enfeebled" and "domesticated" the notion of

14 Quoted in Ted Emery, "Carlo Goldoni as Librettist," PhD diss., Brown University, 1985, pp. 151–52.

mercy had become even by the time of Metastasio's *La clemenza di Tito*;[15] Palomba's libretto takes this notion one step farther, so to speak, and literally domesticates and bourgeoisifes the dispensation of generosity. Dull's act of self-sacrifice is not epic in scope, to be sure, but neither is it the "clapped-on" or merely celebratory ending of much opera buffa.[16] Unlike the grudging concessions of most of opera buffa's old men to the laws of nature and the effects of trickery, Dull's dispensation comes after some struggle; at one point in the second act finale he says as an aside that Gelinda and Bastiano will never know how much his principles have cost him.

Gelinda's competing generosity at the end lends her moral weight as well; she explicitly asserts in the second act finale that her authority to be generous is the same as Mr. Dull's: "se generoso / Meco fosti, anch'io tal sono" ("if [since] you were generous to me, I will act likewise"). This moral authority comes at the expense of a certain material loss, however, since she is (of course) not employed, and has not evidently invested her money. The public celebration of woman's exchange of temporal or material independence for moral authority is integral to Enlightenment doctrine on the "woman question";[17] it is probably not coincidental that the most striking displays of female generosity, both financial and emotional, in the late eighteenth-century Viennese buffa repertory are

15 Ivan Nagel, *Autonomy and Mercy: Reflections on Mozart's Operas*, trans. Marion Faber and Ivan Nagel (Cambridge, MA and London: Harvard University Press, 1991), p. 10: "It is precisely as a private person that the disabled ruler seeks refuge in ceremony: in the theatrical device of clemenza, which no longer functions to establish the absolute state, but instead every night, with laudatory fanfares and choruses in a sumptuously torchlit finale, bears the state to its grave."

16 The term "clapped-on" comes from Wye J. Allanbrook, "Mozart's Happy Endings: A New Look at the 'Convention' of the 'lieto fine,'" *MJb*, 1984/85, pp. 1–5.

17 See, for example, John Adams's letters to Abigail Adams (31 March, 14 April, 7 May 1776) in Charles Francis Adams, *Familiar Letters of John Adams and His Wife Abigail Adams During the Revolution* (New York: Hurd and Houghton, 1876), on temporal vs. emotional power. Erica Rand, "Depoliticizing Women: Female Ager y, the French Revolution, and the Art of Boucher and David," *Genders* 7 (1990), 47–68, discusses this phenomenon in relation to both rococo and neoclassical French art.

by married women.[18] Contained by the institution of marriage and freed from the overriding need to find a mate, they are uniquely positioned to be morally authoritative exemplars without threatening the social and civil order.[19]

The high moral tone of the end of Palomba's libretto, and the assimilation of noble mercy into non-aristocratic surroundings surely connect in some way to the above-mentioned Enlightened demands for an "intermediate genre" of drama between high-flown tragedy and frivolous comedy, and for action on a moral scale fit for nobles but set in recognizably middle-class and contemporary venues. Is *Le gare generose* then the paradigm of that intermediate genre? Does it respond fully to Diderot's, Goldoni's, Benincasa's, and others' demands for moral seriousness? Well, no. For much of the libretto, the characters and the action seem to follow the commedia dell'arte-derived plot archetype of the *innamorati* escaping the clutches of the lustful guardian. Until the end the characters are quite conventional; Bastiano is, for example, a rough Neapolitan sort[20] and is resolutely stupid about Gelinda's various schemes for evading recognition, and even Gelinda until the end exhibits a more or less unmediated combination of clever minxhood and victimized sentimentality. At its best the music comments ironically on the vicissitudes of the situation and illustrates the mechanical aspects of the comedy rather than developing the moral or emotional aspects of the characters.

To illustrate this point one might compare the moment where Mr. Dull decides to be generous, which is set as a brief moment of secco recitative not even dignified by a final cadence (Example 7.1),

18 Some obvious examples include not only Gelinda's financial generosity, but also the Countess's dispensation of mercy in *Le nozze di Figaro*, Griselda's endless self-sacrifice in Piccinni's 1793 setting of that story, and even the Queen's various dispensations and kindnesses in *Una cosa rara*.

19 Even Lilla in *Una cosa rara*, safely married and supported by the Queen, displays a certain generosity in forgiving the Prince and swearing allegiance to him (Act II finale).

20 In the surviving Viennese score Bastiano's part is written in Neapolitan dialect, but the 1786 Viennese libretto translates this into the standard Tuscan of the rest of the libretto.

Example 7.1 Palomba-Paisiello, *Le gare generose* (US-Wcm M1500 P23 G3, Sukowaty copy), II.13. Mr. Dull's conversion to generosity

Dull: I feel in my heart the stirrings of pity for her. I'm thinking of letting them escape. Ah yes; were generosity towards the poor creatures to triumph, love would give way.

with the wonderful moment in the first act finale where Bastiano and Berlicco both try to tell Mr. Dull their plans regarding Gelinda. Berlicco wants to marry her to spite Mr. Dull's niece, to whom he is officially engaged; Bastiano wants to assert a claim on her simply to thwart Berlicco. Mr. Dull, who still has designs on Gelinda, pedantically and overbearingly interrupts their sentences, announces his own intentions, and leaves the two rivals high and dry, united in subjection to Mr. Dull, and so bewildered that all they can do is repeat his boring tune (Example 7.2). Unlike Mr. Dull's moment of

Example 7.2 Palomba-Paisiello, *Le gare generose*, Act I finale, beginning

conversion, which is a dramatically and psychologically crucial event downplayed by the music, this moment in the finale is of relatively little psychological or dramatic importance, but the music wonderfully illustrates the comic realities of power in that house-

Example 7.2 (*cont.*)

hold at that moment. The wonderful wit of the music has, however, no bearing on the enlightened or aesthetically bourgeois aspects of the plot. The mechanistic alternation of declamatory and singing styles, and the raw scalar material of Mr. Dull's tune positively discourage sympathetic identification with any of the

Example 7.2 (*cont.*)

three characters, and focus attention on the imbroglio itself rather than on the men's inner lives or feelings.

In the second act finale, there are moments where the music plays up the solemnity of Mr. Dull's generosity and the new relationship of respect between him and his former slaves, but these are

Example 7.2 (*cont.*)

undercut or shied away from as they go along. For example, where he and Gelinda and Bastiano say goodbye to each other, the music moves from G Minor to E flat (the finale as a whole is in C) and within E flat from a stealthy unison to two almost hymn-like moments of benediction, intensified by the pedal in the bass.

Example 7.2 (*cont.*)

However, the second of these phrases ("or si spande per il cielo") is allowed no repose; its cadence dissolves into the clockwork rhythms of the typical buffa cadential figure, made even more mechanical by the hocket between the tenor and bass as they plan their escape (Example 7.3).

In short, although *Le gare generose* is set in bourgeois surround-

Example 7.2 (*cont.*)

Berl: Sirs... Bast: Ladies and Gentlemen... Berl: I have to tell you... Bast: I need to say.
Dull: Quickly, quickly, act like brothers. Berl. and Bast: Yes, we'll be as quick as we ca
Berl: That woman... Bast: That slave... Dull: ...is modest, beautiful, and clever.
Berl: And so... Bast: And so, I... Dull: ...and so I've also been figuring...
Bast: But you're mocking... Berl: Interrupting... Bast: It seems you're joking.
Berl: And tricking us. Dull: Quickly, quickly, act like brothers.

Example 7.3 Palomba-Paisiello, *Le gare generose*, Act II finale

Example 7.3 (*cont.*)

Example 7.3 (*cont.*)

Gelinda, Bastiano, Dull: Friendly shadows, now spread a thick veil
over the sky; [let's] escape for heaven's sake.

ings, extols the enlightened virtues of solvency and generosity, and
bestows nobility and moral authority on characters of non-aristocratic status, it maintains a certain aesthetic distance from these
enlightened values. To the extent that it fails to make Mr. Dull a
fully or richly sympathetic figure, and does not include music that
draws the audience toward the felt experience of his conversion, it
refers to but does not *signify* or embody those values. This "failure"
is not, however, due to any lack of aesthetic capacity on Paisiello's
or Palomba's parts; it is, rather, a symptom of the tentativeness
with which opera buffa introduced sympathetic and fully realized
portraits of the economic bourgeoisie. Even in *Le nozze di Figaro*, in
which the lower-class characters are as fully realized as one might
desire, the most sympathetic non-aristocratic characters are the
servants, whose freedom of action is still constrained by feudal
obligation to their master.[21]

---

21 Cf. Nicholas Till, *Mozart and the Enlightenment: Truth, Beauty and Virtue in
Mozart's Operas* (London: Faber and Faber, 1992), p. 145.

THE PASTORAL: "UNA COSA RARA" AND THE POWER OF SIGNIFICATION

Le gare generose is one of the relatively few clear examples of the post-Goldonian urban comedy in the Viennese repertory in the 1780s. Not only urban settings, but concrete references, topicality, and the exploration of larger social issues (in this case financial probity) are characteristic of this generic strand. It is typical of this sort of opera to defuse its social tensions not only by means of the happy ending and other devices common to all comedy, but also by an essentially mechanistic aesthetic, where intrigue takes precedence over character development, and the interest in imbroglio prevents a sentimentally effective presentation of the moral message.

The other generic strand evident in this repertory is the pastoral, whether fully developed, or implicit. (I call both pastoral and post-Goldonian urban comedy "generic strands" rather than subgenres, because I mean not only – sometimes not even – the distinction between country and city settings, but also the choice of a fantastic or realistic aesthetic stance, the use of more or less blurred class distinctions, or the projection of a sweeter or more acerbic overall tone. Many operas (like *Le nozze di Figaro*) blend the two strands.) Wye Allanbrook has persuasively analyzed *Le nozze di Figaro* as pervaded by pastoral elements which provide aesthetic and psychological space for the exploration of love and friendship unconstrained by social division.[22] One could extend her argument to the way the opera's pastoral substrate affects its social and political meanings, and argue that the relocation of cross-class friendship to the pastoral realm defuses the dangers of literal reference to such potentially subversive intimacy. Arguably, however, the use of the garden as a place for the dissolution of social boundaries also signifies (perhaps more powerfully than a more mundane representation) an ideal to which people of all ranks might aspire. In other words, the pastoral is inherently unstable as a social signifier.

22 Allanbrook, *Rhythmic Gesture*.

The power of the pastoral element in *Le nozze di Figaro*, and, for that matter, in *Così fan tutte*, is largely musical.[23] It is the power of music to refer by means of well-understood *topoi* to a realm other than that represented onstage or in the text, and thus to allow text and music together to signify something not apparent from either alone. Mozart's use of the pastoral mode in works which are not on the face of it pastorals is particularly virtuosic, but his interest in the pastoral *topos* runs parallel to the way opera buffa in Vienna developed over the course of the 1780s, with increasing emphasis on frankly pastoral themes and settings.[24] In addition, the way in which multilayered and sometimes ambiguous social meanings emerge from Mozart's use of the pastoral is also not without parallel elsewhere in the repertory.

Lorenzo Da Ponte's and Vicenzo Martín y Soler's *Una cosa rara* is one of the Viennese repertory's clearest examples of a pastoral.[25] Set in the Spanish countryside, it describes the resistance of the shepherdess Lilla to the importunings of both the Prince and his courtier Corrado, her constancy to her country lover Lubino, and the power of the highest royalty to keep society in order. When Lilla's lover and her brother discover the gifts that the Prince gave Lilla's sister to pass on to Lilla as yet another token of his "affection," they decide to take the matter to the Queen, who, smitten with the sweetness and honesty of country life, and of these young women in particular, banishes the courtier, who becomes the scapegoat for the Prince. The Prince himself remains undiscovered and unpunished. The simple life of the peasants, disturbed only by the occasional trivial quarrel, is throughout compared to the corruption of the court, and the honesty of pure rural life is compared to the wiles of the city. The frame of the royal hunt (the opera

23 Goehring, "Despina, Cupid, and the Pastoral Mode of *Così fan tutte*," *COJ* 7 (1995), 107–34.
24 Goehring, "Despina, Cupid," p. 112, comments on the late 1780s vogue for bucolic settings in opera buffa.
25 Dorothea Link, "The Da Ponte Operas of Martín y Soler," PhD diss., University of Toronto, 1991, pp. 175–84, describes in some detail the pastoral aspects of Martín's compositions.

opens with a chorus of huntsmen and ends with the Queen returning to the hunt) serves further to separate the action from "real
life." Insofar as the plot of this opera conveys social meanings in a
referential manner, they are that female fidelity is a virtue, that the
preordained social strata should remain separate, that benevolent
royalty is an unadulterated good, and that the peccadilloes of
princes can be pasted over by means of scapegoats. Unlike *Le gare
generose*, where the distant setting is primarily a vehicle to make
political or social points, and only secondarily an occasion for decorative exoticism, *Una cosa rara* uses its foreign location in baldly pic-
turesque ways. The second act finale, for example, includes a
"seghidilla" and other touches of local colour, purely and literally
as entertainment, and the buffo bumpkin Titta complains at his
girlfriend Ghita in a comic mixture of Spanish and Italian when she
hits him, a mixture that emphasizes both his foreignness and his
inarticulateness.

This is not a work that *refers to* bourgeois or enlightened social
conditions any more obviously than *Le nozze di Figaro* refers to the
pastoral. However, several aspects of Martín's opera *signify* what
we might call aesthetic bourgeoisification. The first aspect is his
pervasive use of what Dorothea Link has appositely called "song
style": apparently artless melodies set more or less syllabically in a
medium tessitura.[26] This style has two connections to values at
the intersection of "enlightenment" and "bourgeois"; one has to
do with the nature of the style and the other with the characters
who use it. As Link points out, contemporary commentary on
Martín's music typically focused on the "sweet," "tender," "graceful," and even "naïve" qualities of his melodies; in other words,
the expressive, or affective (or sentimental) qualities of the music,
rather than either its evident craft or the way it displayed the performer.[27]

This style exemplifies the virtues praised by many reformist and
Enlightened theorists of opera. For example, Antonio Planelli's

26 Ibid., ch. 5, *passim.*   27 Ibid., pp. 155–57.

"three laws of theatre music" read as though they could have been Martín's stylistic guidelines:[28]

1. Theatre music requires few notes. The reason is that music padded with notes, whether simultaneous or successive, is incapable of producing pathos . . .
2. This style abhors tones that are too high and too low. Pathos consists of a just medium.
3. Theatrical style prefers songs that are performed in a parlante rather than an ornamented style.

The qualities of this style also correspond to those described as German rather than Italian in Joseph Richter's skit "Ein Beytrag zum Patriotismus und Theatergeschmack der Wiener" in *Der Zuschauer in Wien* (1790).[29]

HERR V. Z: And I can assure you that I have seen several German sopranos, who sang with the appropriate expression and true feeling, and combined correct acting with singing; while on the other hand I can hardly remember an Italian prima donna who showed in the least that she understood and felt what she sang.

MUSIKKENNER: Why so much fuss over feeling and action? The throat of a German is not as well suited to high notes as that of the Italian singers
. . .

HERR V. Z: You don't mean trills and warbling?
. . .

MUSIKKENNER: Warbling! Warbling! Excuse me, Mr. Z., but you are incompetent to judge music. As you told me just yesterday, you don't know a note of it.

HERR V. Z: That's true, but I thought there was in us a certain feeling capable of judging the agreement of music with the passions it was supposed to express; a feeling that resonates with our own inner passions and that a man of taste at least cannot mistake.

28 From *Dell'opera in musica* (Naples, 1772), quoted in Enrico Fubini, *Music and Culture in Eighteenth Century Europe*, trans. Bonnie J. Blackburn (Oxford: Oxford University Press, 1994), pp. 248–50.
29 Joseph Richter, from *Der Zuschauer in Wien, oder Gerade so sind die Wiener und Wienerinnen*, 3rd edn., in 6 vols. (Vienna: Hochenleitter, 1790), vol. 5, pp. 13–22, "Ein Beytrag zum Patriotismus und Theatergeschmack der Wiener."

What Herr von Z. likes is music that does not draw attention to the technique of performance, but rather to the sentiment of the dramatic moment – not to the singer, but to the character. This performative "transparency" is one aspect of the all-absorbing illusion of reality promoted by enlightenment writers on theatre; it is part of the "fourth wall" which encloses the stage and admits the audience only as spectators (however morally or aesthetically engaged), rather than as audible, visible, or dramatically acknowledged participants in the theatrical artifice.[30] Sonnenfels's theory of "Täuschungsvertrag" or the willing suspension of disbelief[31] is a Viennese example of this idea, which corresponds to Goldoni's statement in *Il teatro comico*, that "when an actor's alone on the stage he must suppose that he is neither heard nor seen. Addressing the audience is an insufferable habit and should never be permitted."[32] Song style as it is used in *Una cosa rara* reinforces this illusion; not only do none of the pieces in song style literally address the audience (most of them in fact address an onstage character),[33] but the style itself draws little attention to the act of performance; it seems utterly "natural."

This style, which exists between the high-flown displays of seria utterances and the comic extravagances of buffa music, is to be found in all sorts of opera buffa, of course,[34] but it is particularly prevalent in *Una cosa rara*, and marks the work as a whole in quite exceptional ways. As Dorothea Link points out, both the aristo-

30 See Paolo Gallarati's and Goehring's essays in this volume for further discussion of the fourth wall and the theatrical illusion of realism.

31 According to Hilde Haider-Pregler's *Nachwort* to Sonnenfels's *Briefe über die Wienerische Schaubühne* this theory is most fully explained in Sonnenfels's *Mann ohne Vorurtheil* (*Gesammelte Schriften*, vol. 3 [Vienna 1783], p. 167ff.). Sonnenfels, *Briefe*, ed. Hilde Haider-Pregler (Graz: Akademische Druck- und Verlagsanstalt, [1988]), p. 370.

32 *The Comic Theatre: A Comedy in Three Acts by Carlo Goldoni*, III. 2, trans. John W. Miller (Lincoln: University of Nebraska Press, 1969), 61; Goldoni, vol. 2, p. 1089.

33 Titta has two arias, "In quegli anni in cui solea" and "Ah mal aya," and Ghita has one, "Colla flemma," in which the characteristically comic turn to the audience is made. All three of these are in buffa style.

34 And not only in opera buffa, as Marita P. McClymonds points out in her essay in this volume.

cratic pair (Queen and Prince) and the sentimental shepherd couple
(Lilla and Lubino) sing solos in song style, which then functions as
the musical marker of a pastoral space where class distinctions
blur.[35] This is nowhere more true than in the central canonic
section of the duet and trio complex in the first act, where the
Queen comes in on Lilla and Ghita's quarrel and resolves it
(Example 7.4). Here the notion of song style as the common property of rustics and royalty is literally enacted, as the two shepherd-
esses and the Queen sing the same tune. This common language
forms a counterpoint to the otherwise rigid class distinctions in the
plot. Whether in relation to the feudal social structure, the exot-
icized setting, and the conservative plot one reads this counter-
point as subversive, sentimental, or politically irrelevant, will
depend in part on production decisions.

In any case, however "enlightened" or "reformist" this style and
even its development may be, it does not outweigh or obliterate the
more escapist and conservative elements of the work any more
than the emphasis on mechanistic comedy in *Le gare generose* out-
weighs or obliterates its more than usually sympathetic picture of
bourgeois morality.[36] Both operas project a tension between their
referential and their signifying levels; a tension that mirrors the
strains inherent in Pezzl's explanations of enlightenment, and that
is also congruent with (if not as rich as) Mozart's complex deploy-
ments of the pastoral mode in *Le nozze di Figaro* and *Così fan tutte*.

The tensions between conservative or escapist and reformist or
"engaged" elements in *Una cosa rara* are complicated and enriched
by its extraordinary contemporary success, not only on the stage
but also in the marketplace. Artaria published altogether 18 out of
31 numbers – all, as Link points out, in eminently performable and

35 Link, "The Da Ponte Operas," pp. 183–84.
36 Durante (rightly, I think) suggests that operatic analysis requires a hierarchical
    arrangement of domains, even if the particular ranking changes within a number
    or section or varies from one analytical question to another. I am less sure that the
    evaluation of social meaning requires the ranking of domains. That is probably a
    topic for another paper.

Example 7.4 Da Ponte-Martín y Soler, *Una cosa rara*, no. 12

Example 7.4 (*cont.*)

Lilla and Ghita: For pity's sake don't be disdainful; please listen. This lament about the torment of my heart will move you.
Queen: Their lament moves me.

domesticatable song style.[37] These publications happened within three months of the premiere, and were thus at least potentially available while the show was still running. There is thus a sense in which any performance of *Una cosa rara* functioned in part as a parade of items for sale, as part of the bourgeois marketplace. Obviously this opera was not unique in this respect – Mingone's aria "Come un agnello" from Sarti's *Fra i due litiganti*, which is also

37 Link, "The Da Ponte Operas," p. 202.

in song style, was extremely popular in Vienna (as Mozart's quotation of it in the second act finale to *Don Giovanni* attests), as were excerpts from Paisiello's *Il barbiere di Siviglia*, and numerous other comparable pieces. Martín's even more thoroughly songful *L'arbore di Diana* was also a big item on the domestic market. Even so, the intensity of the craze for *Una cosa rara* seems to have been unusual. RISM lists no fewer than 90 items from *Una cosa rara*, the vast majority of them being obviously for domestic consumption – the overture arranged for two flutes, endless piano reductions of the arias, etc. This compares to 36 items for *L'arbore di Diana*, and only 20 for *Le gare generose*. My point is less that *Una cosa rara* is unique than that the values projected within a work may interact in complicated ways with its function as an object for sale in the public marketplace; that if one takes "the work" to include its commercial life as well as its texts and performances, its connections to social and political circumstances emerge as richer and truer to the complications of changing tastes and values.

CONCLUSION

Opera buffa in Vienna in the 1780s was not literally instrumental in bringing about the social or political changes of the period. Nor was it considered so by contemporary writers. As a foreign genre it could not participate in the nation-building aims of Joseph II's *Nationaltheater*. As a genre whose content was considered trivial at best – Italian nonsense, improbable, in bad taste, not funny, and incompetent[38] – it could not exert the moral authority proper to entertainment in an Enlightened polity. Indeed, in contrast to the amount of contemporary journalistic comment on the spoken theatre, which included numerous descriptions and evaluations of individual plays, there was next to no public comment in Vienna on

---

38 The last four epithets are from Joseph Sonnenfels's *Briefe*. The first one ("Italian nonsense") is from Richter's *Der Zuschauer*.

individual *opere buffe*, though there was some discussion of the way certain singers performed particular roles. Indeed, the small amount of commentary in the theatrical almanacs and other publications between the late 1760s and the 1790s quite often contrasts the stupidity of the genre with the skill of the singers. Mozart's operas got no more notice in these sources than Paisiello's or Martín's; those works that we may now perceive as the embodiment of the ideals to which Pezzl, Joseph II himself, and many others subscribed were not evidently so perceived by Mozart's Enlightened (and politically engaged) contemporaries. Indeed, the famous comment about Mozart's setting of Beaumarchais's scandalous sequel to *Le Barbier de Séville* – "what may not be spoken may be sung"[39] – testifies to the way music was (at least by some) thought politically to neutralize its subject, or to function in a separate conceptual arena from the tendentious referentiality of verbal texts.

The notion that the music of opera buffa could "inoculate" its texts was used less often about the political content of libretti than about their sheer vacuousness. The conceptual separation between the genre's words and sounds was stated in perhaps its most extreme form as early as 1768 by Joseph von Sonnenfels. In his twelfth letter on the Viennese stage he asked, "should not . . .music bestow its protection on [the singers of opera buffa]; and the pleasure of the ear [thus] mitigate the dissatisfactions of reason, or at least allow us not to notice [the unreasonableness of the plot]?"[40] Fifteen years later Mozart himself noted in his letter of 21 June 1783: "[Varesco's] libretto will certainly not go down if the music is no good. For in the opera the chief thing is the music."[41] Both the critic and the composer were indicating (in ways that wonderfully reflect their different occupations) that the meaning and value of an opera buffa's music had no simple relation to the meaning and value of its

39 From the *Wiener Realzeitung*, 1 May 1786. Quoted in Michtner, p. 208.
40 Sonnenfels, *Briefe*, p. 63.
41 *Letters*, p. 853; *Briefe*, vol. 3, p. 275.

text. I have argued above that both *Le gare generose* and *Una cosa rara* demonstrate the semantic non-congruence among domains that Mozart and Sonnenfels both (for different reasons) describe. However, rather than concluding, with contemporary opinion, that opera buffa therefore has no relation to the social and political realm, I would suggest that it is precisely in the "mismatches" between the narrative and the musical tone, or between the plot content and the market value of a particular musical style, that these works signify full engagement with (if not exactly incitement of) the lengthy and complex emergence of bourgeois *mentalités* in Vienna and elsewhere.

8 | Opera seria? Opera buffa? Genre and style as sign
Marita P. McClymonds

Ever since the "Arcadian" reforms of the 1690s established serious and comic musical theatre as separate genres, an unbridgeable chasm has seemed to divide opera seria from opera buffa. Certainly this has been the dominant tradition in musicological writings. The former genre, we read, deals with idealized characters drawn from Classical history and occasionally from mythology; the latter, with characters, settings, and situations that (however stylized or exaggerated) were recognizably based on contemporary life. Because of these differences in plot, setting, singer–actors, and much else, music historians have tended to assume that the two genres were also mutually exclusive in style – that genre functioned as a sign of style and style as a sign of genre.

This widespread notion cannot be sustained. Once Goldoni and Galuppi had introduced serious and semiserious characters into their sophisticated courtly comedies of the 1750s – characters whose passions required musical gestures proper to opera seria – most *drammi giocosi*, as such "mixed" works were often called, exploited the full spectrum of musical styles. Indeed we have long been aware of Mozart's use of seria style in his later comic operas, for example in the arias of the Queen of the Night in *Die Zauberflöte*, Fiordiligi's "Come scoglio" in *Così fan tutte*, or the seria-derived two-tempo *rondò*.[1] However, the pervasiveness of seria style in opera buffa generally has hardly been noticed.[2] Moreover, this relationship operated in the other direction as

---

1 On the seria origins of the *rondò*, see Marita P. McClymonds, "Aria," in *The New Grove Dictionary of Opera*, vol. 1, pp. 174–75; Don Neville, "Rondò," ibid., vol. 4, p. 37.
2 A notable exception is Mary Hunter, "Some Representations of *Opera Seria* in *Opera Buffa*," *COJ* 3 (1991), 89–108.

well: many types of number that we take as characteristic of buffa have counterparts in opera seria. Marches, tender love arias like Zerlina's in *Don Giovanni*, and light-hearted arias such as Despina's in *Così fan tutte* are all found in opera seria, as we shall see.

Admittedly, these relations are complex and not easily sorted out. In the first place, one must distinguish between individual set pieces and entire operas. Many numbers in comic operas unmistakably use seria style without compromising their buffa status; this is especially characteristic of arias for high-class or pretentious characters. As we shall see, the converse is also true: many numbers in opera seria use "buffa" characteristics without violating the genre. A second distinction is that between stylistic traits or number-types that are *borrowed*, and those that are *shared*. In the former case, a trait or number-type proper to one genre is "cross-referenced" in the other; such cross-referencing can be a straightforward sign of character, an intertextual reference, or parodistic. In the latter case, a trait, character, or number-type is legitimately at home in both genres; examples include the march, the *aria d'affetto*, and the soubrette-aria. Finally, one must distinguish (insofar as eighteenth-century style permits) between factors that were specifically generic, whether to seria or buffa, and those which formed part of the larger musical signifying system of the time, related to the world at large: *topoi*, the "rhythmic gestures," and, especially important for our purposes, the threefold division into "high," "middle," and "low" musical style.

Eighteenth-century writers like Johann Adolf Scheibe and Ernst Ludwig Gerber observed three stylistic levels in music, roughly equivalent to the three levels of society: high (clergy and nobility), middle (bourgeois), and low (peasant). They assigned to the high style "all great, exalted, dreadful feelings and violent passions" (Gerber), such as magnanimity, majesty, power, magnificence, pride, astonishment, anger, fear, madness, revenge, and doubt (Scheibe); to the middle style "softer, milder feelings, such as love, calmness, satisfaction, cheerfulness, and joy" (Gerber), expressed in music that is "ingenious, pleasant, and flowing, designed to please rather than excite or to induce reflection" (Scheibe); and to the low style "what is more popular and obvious than genteel, more trifling and merry than clever, and particularly everything that pertains to caricature and comedy" (Gerber), avoiding all clever elaborations, permitting no extensions, and representative of nature in its simplest form (Scheibe).[3]

The point is not so much this threefold division as such, as the fact that the "middle" style could function as a kind of common ground, easily conjoined to either high or low style. Leonard Ratner concludes that "the opposite ends of the spectrum – high and low – represent the clearest definitions of musical status and the sharpest mutual contrasts, those of the serious and the comic. The middle was flexible and could be oriented to either style."[4] Indeed, in the operatic context the middle style was shared between seria and buffa, at home in both; hence (and this is the crucial point) it did not function as a sign of either genre. An aria *di mezzo carattere*, other things equal, could fit equally well in an opera seria and an opera buffa, particularly during the first half of the century, when arias in both genres were short and in da capo form. Take, for example, two contemporary arias by Johann Adolph Hasse: from the intermezzo *La serva scaltra* (1729), the maid Dorilla's "Per te mio dolce ardore" (1. 1; Example 8.1), and from the opera seria *Cleofide* (1731), the prima donna's "Se mai turbo il tuo

---

3 Gerber, "Etwas über den sogenannten musikalischen Styl," *Allgemeine musikalische Zeitung* 2. 19 (Feb. 6, 1799), cols. 295–96: "Zu der hohen, wären dann alle grossen, erhabenen, auch schrecklichen Empfindungen und heftigern Leidenschaften zu rechnen. Unter die gemässigtere und mittlere Musikart, rechnete man das, was die sanften and mildern Empfindungen der Liebe, Ruhe und Zufriedenheit, Heiterkeit und Freude angeht. Und zur niedern, was mehr populär und fasslich als edel, mehr lustig und tändelnd als geistreich, und überhaupt alles was zum Komischen und zur Karrikatur gehört." Compare Johann Adolph Scheibe, *Der critische Musikus*, 2nd edn. (Leipzig, 1745; facs. reprint Hildesheim: Olms, 1970), pp. 126–30.

4 Leonard Ratner, *Classical Music: Expression, Form, and Style* (New York: Schirmer, 1980), pp. 7, 364–96; here, p. 364.

Example 8.1 Hasse, *La serva scaltra*, Dorilla, "Per te mio dolce ardore"

Andante un poco sostenuto

Dorilla: Because of you, my darling, my heart is full of torment.

riposo" (1. 8; Example 8.2).[5] Both are graceful, sophisticated, and charming love songs, which fit Gerber's and Scheibe's description of the middle style perfectly: short-phrased melodies decorated with appoggiaturas, slides, and other tasteful ornaments; short, graceful coloraturas bringing each section to cadence; brief passages in an untroubled minor mode in the B section. These two

5 *Cleofide*: no published score available, manuscript scores of the first production (Dresden, 1731) in D-B, D-Mbs, and F-Pn (I am grateful to the Music Library, University of California, Berkeley, for permission to quote from their microfilm of the MS in D-B); recording by Cappella Coloniensis, cond. William Christie (Capriccio 10 193/196). *La serva scaltra*, ed. Luciano Bettarini, *Collezione Settecentesca Bettarini*, vol. 16 (Milan: Nazionalmusica, 1985); recording by Gruppo srumentale dell'Orchestra Sinfonica di Sassari, cond. Gabriele Catalucci (Bongiovanni GB 2101-2).

Example 8.2 Hasse, *Cleofide* (Dresden, 1731), Cleofide, "Se mai turbo il tuo riposo"

Cleofide: Should I ever disturb your tranquillity, should another flame
set me afire, then let my heart never know peace.

arias occupy stylistically neutral ground: they signal neither the
class of the character singing nor the genre of the work.

By contrast, arias in high and low styles functioned as signs of both
class and genre. Early eighteenth-century writers agreed that opera
seria should contain a mixture of high and middle style but nothing
in low style; comic opera, low and middle style but nothing in high
style. In his *Commedie* (1761) and his later *Mémoires* (1787) Goldoni
transmits somewhat different accounts of advice he received early in
his career from Count Prata, a theatrical director in Milan, regarding
the construction of an opera seria libretto. According to the later
version, the librettist must furnish the composer with shades of
chiaroscuro, by carefully distributing the bravura arias, the action
arias, the arias *di mezzo carattere*, and the minuets and *rondòs*, making
sure that two pathetic arias did not succeed one another. He must
also consider rank; for example, impassioned arias, bravura arias, or
rondòs should not be given to the secondary roles;[6] their middle style

---

6 "L'Auteur des paroles doit fournir au Musicien les différentes nuances qui forment
le *clair-obscur* de la musique, et prendre garde que deux airs pathétiques ne se
succèdent pas; il faut partager, avec la même précaution, les airs de bravoure, les
airs d'action, les airs de *demi-caractères*, et les *menuets*, et les *rondeaux*. Sur-tout, il
faut bien prendre garde de ne pas donner d'airs passionnés, ni d'airs de bravoure,
ni des rondeaux aux seconds rôles." Goldoni, vol. 1, p. 129.

should throw the high style of the principal characters into relief. However, this did not mean that high ranking characters would never sing arias *di mezzo carattere*. According to Goldoni's *Commedie*, Prata specified that the leading lady and the leading tenor would expect an *aria patetica*, an *aria di bravura*, an *aria parlante*, an *aria di mezzo carattere*, and an *aria brillante*.[7]

Writing in 1789, John Brown cited yet a slightly different list of arias then in vogue in opera seria, along with their affects: *aria cantabile* (tenderness), *aria di portamento* (dignity), *aria di mezzo carattere* (serious yet pleasing), *aria parlante* (agitation or passion), *aria di bravura* (vocal display).[8] The neutral aria *di mezzo carattere* figures in all three lists. Similarly, as if in reaction to the introduction of serious characters into comic opera, Sulzer in 1774 identified three levels of comedy, in a hierarchy that was virtually indistinguishable from earlier categorizations of style in general: low (farcical and absurd), middle (genteel; that which pleases and delights), and high (approaching tragedy in content and mood, and engaging powerful and serious passions).[9]

With the introduction of high style into opera buffa, it became increasingly difficult for genre to function as a sure guide to style, or the style of a given set piece as a sign of genre (except that opera seria still avoided arias in low buffo style). In Jommelli's *La schiava liberata* (1768), an *opera seria-comica*, much of the music in high and middle style gives no clue that it belongs to a comic opera rather than his contemporaneous *opere serie* such as *Vologeso* (1766) or *Demofoonte* (1764–65). *Chiaroscuro* was achieved in opera buffa by contrasting the gentility of the middle style with the low style's buffoonery. Elements of high style were employed as well; they could be parodistic, but could also be a "straight" sign of high rank;

---

7 Carlo Goldoni, *Commedie* (Venice: Pasquale, 1761), vol. 11, pp. 5–6; as paraphrased in Michael F. Robinson, *Naples and Neapolitan Opera* (Oxford: Clarendon Press, 1972), p. 88.

8 Brown, *Letters upon the Poetry and Music of the Italian Opera* (Edinburgh: Bell and Bradfute, 1789), pp. 36–40.

9 Johann Georg Sulzer, *Allgemeine Theorie der schönen Künste*, 2 vols. (Leipzig: Weidmann, 1771–74), vol. 1, pp. 212–13; as translated in Ratner, *Classic Music*, p. 386.

for example, in Haydn's *Lo speziale* (after Goldoni), Volpino's rage aria "Amore nel mio petto" marks him as a young patrician.

Even the proportions of high to middle style may not reliably signal one genre or the other. A letter of Mozart's to Leopold of 16 June 1781 (during the composition of *Die Entführung aus dem Serail*) implies that Leopold had admonished him to compose his *opere serie* in a lighter style, perhaps to ensure their success. Wolfgang retorted:

> Do you think then that I should write a comic opera like a serious one? –
> However little playfulness there should be in an opera seria, and however
> much of the learned and reasonable, just so little of the learned must
> there be in an opera buffa, and so much more of the playful and comic
> . . . I can't help it if in an opera seria people wish to have comic music
> as well.[10]

Mozart's very protestations suggest the perceived need for balance between seriousness (high style) and lightness (middle style) in both genres. Daniel Heartz discusses one such "lapse" into playfulness, in the love duet near the beginning of act three of *Idomeneo*.[11] In fact, as we shall see, even elements of low comic style can be found in opera seria.

In short, despite the contrasting plots and conventions of serious and comic opera, the style of individual numbers was determined not so much by genre as such, as by a complex web of dramatic and musical factors: rank, class, affect of the text, characterization, situation, and the need for variety and contrast or *chiaroscuro*. Hence many arias and other numbers in both genres were composed within the large neutral area of the *stile di mezzo carattere*. Among these are marches, the pastoral, the soubrette aria, the "middle" style love aria and duet, and non-parodistic numbers for serious characters in *opere buffe*. In addition, many musical numbers exhibit *mixed* styles, beginning in one style, but later moving to another, often in response to textual cues. Such stylistic mixture

---

10 Mozart, *Letters*, p. 467 (*Briefe*, vol. 3, p. 132); this translation from Heartz, *Mozart's Operas*, p. 73. 11 Heartz, *Mozart's Operas*, pp. 47–52.

may occur briefly within a given section, or dominate a separate, contrasting section. The overture, which in many respects relates to the symphony of the period, falls into this category almost by definition.

Although genre was not a sign of style nor style a sign of genre, genre did influence how a given topic or stylistic trait could convey meaning. For example, three famous Mozart rage arias, all in "high" style, evoke very different interpretations: Elettra's "D'Oreste, d'Ajace," in *Idomeneo* (opera seria; "genuine" emotion); The Queen of the Night's "Der Hölle Rache," in *Die Zauberflöte* (Singspiel; feigned [?] emotion for Pamina's benefit); and "Come scoglio" (opera buffa; exaggerated [parodistic?] reaction). That is, the strongest influences of the sort ordinarily attributed to "style" are actually located in the subgeneric areas of rank or class, text, context, and topic. These, after all, were the principal means by which the librettist communicated to the composer, as he distributed arias of contrasting affects among the characters, controlled the *chiaroscuro*, and achieved balance in the work as a whole.

Given the traditional musicological association of "middle" style with opera buffa, my thesis that it functioned as a common ground between buffa and seria depends upon identifying instances of its use in the latter genre. I have selected examples from Haydn's *Armida* (Eszterháza, 1784; libretto by Porta); Cimarosa's *Gli Orazi e i Curiazi* (Venice, 1796; Sografi); and Mozart's *La clemenza di Tito* (Prague, 1791; Mazzolà's adaptation of Metastasio).[12] The relatively late date of these works (motivated primarily by their ready availability) does not imply that the middle style entered into opera seria only in the 1780s; as is clear from the preceding discussion, it was part of the genre from its beginnings.

Although it is obviously not possible to establish a definitive list of characteristics common to a given style, a summary of tendencies may be useful. The "great, exalted, dreadful feelings and

12 *Armida: Joseph Haydn: Werke* xxv / 12; *La clemenza di Tito: NMA* v /20; *Gli Orazi e i Curiazi* (Paris: Imbault, 1802): facs. in *Monumenti musicali italiani*, ix /2 (Milan: Zerboni, 1985).

violent passions" of the high style tend to require full orchestra and extremes of range, dynamics, and rhythm. Melodies tend to have long phrases and extensive coloratura passages; crescendo, *fp* accents, coloratura, and accelerating rhythmic motion combine to build intense climaxes. Developmental transitions, because of their intensity and passion, tend to be perceived as high style (serious) in whatever genre or number type they appear. In opera buffa, coloratura (vocalises) are an even more consistent sign of high class than vocal difficulty.[13]

For the "softer, milder feelings" and the "sophistication and charm" of the middle style, composers cultivated a "light" affect, in order "to please rather than to excite." The affect of charm is often expressed by triple or compound meter (minuet and pastorale); phrases are short, articulated with brief interjections by the violins or winds and lightly decorated with graces, Lombard rhythms, slides, and appoggiaturas. The lively, more robust march often employs dotted rhythms; the winds, often prominent in the middle style, connote love, ease, and happiness. Finally, for the trifling and merry low style, composers turned to patter-singing, quick dialogue, short, repetitive vocal phrases in a narrow range, and lively, detached orchestral motives. Peasant dance rhythms, "folk" song, or drones may suggest a rustic quality or the pastoral. However, the boundary between seria and buffa remains porous; the short phrases and repetitive parlando of Poro's rage aria in *Cleofide*, "Dov'è? si afretti" (II. 9; Example 8.3) call attention to the role of context in shaping our perception of stylistic meaning.

Six types of musical number in later eighteenth-century opera seria tend to share stylistic similarities with opera buffa: (1) the overture (mixed styles); (2) the march (middle style); (3) the aria for the *seconda donna* (playful middle style, comparable to the buffa soubrette); (4) the love aria or duet (serious middle style); (5) the aria in contrasting styles (mixed); and (6) the ensemble (mixed). In addition (as happens in every operatic genre), the musical style

---

13 Robinson, *Neapolitan Opera*, pp. 225–26. As with many others, this stylistic feature is thus a sign, not of genre, but of a subgeneric attribute (rank).

Example 8.3 Hasse, *Cleofide*, Poro, "Dov'è? si affretti"

Poro: O barbarous fate, why do you betray me, unfaithful spouse.

often seems to work at cross purposes with the text, action, or generic context, often generating new meanings or implications on the meta-level of the work or number. (This is the case especially in *Gli Orazi e i Curiazi* and *La clemenza di Tito*, as we will see.)

The generic ambiguity of mixed style often becomes apparent at the very beginning of the opera: in the overture, which, in comic and serious operas alike, presents a variety of textures, moods, and themes. In Cimarosa's *Gli Orazi e i Curiazi*, the brutal plot (like that of *Romeo and Juliet*) centers on two lovers, one from each of two warring families. When Orazia finds her fiancé among the dead, she steadfastly denounces her brother, who, goaded to anger, kills her and throws her body down the stairs. However, this horrifying ending is not the main topic of the overture, which, instead, presents a succession of short contrasting ideas. Solemn octave unisons in high style soon give way to a series of sections in high, middle, and even low style (see the short, repetitious figures in Example 8.4, mm. 16–19), in turn overcome by an outburst in high style (mm. 20–21), immediately followed by lyrical wind duos over a drone in middle style (mm. 22–26). This pairing of contrasting ideas continues throughout the overture. In particular the march topic functions in a rondo-like manner, returning twice after transitional sections in dramatically intense high style. Cimarosa's overture

Example 8.4 Cimarosa, *Gli Orazi e i Curiazi*, Overture

thus both foreshadows the action – the joyous prenuptial scenes, the glorious march into battle, the military skirmishes – and maintains the character of a buffa overture, in the brief motivic gestures, strong repeated notes, and abrupt shifts in topic. No aspect of style unequivocally signals that the opera will be serious rather than comic.

Haydn's overture to *Armida* also presents strong contrasts in a mixture of high and middle styles. An imperious opening unison (high style) gives way to quiet lyrical ideas enlivened with short motives, turns, and staccato (middle style). The second idea begins as a sprightly staccato march in middle style for the winds (Example 8.5a); as in Cimarosa's overture, the strings pass through high-style dramatics on the way to a cadence back in middle style. The middle section is a minuet in middle style (Example 8.5b); the solo oboe and arpeggiated triplet accompaniment suggest pastoral tranquillity. While the stormy sections that separate these ideas might seem to hint that the plot will be serious, similar contrasts in mood are found in buffa overtures as well, such as Haydn's *La fedeltà premiata* and *La vera costanza* and Cimarosa's *Il matrimonio segreto*.

Mozart's overture to *La clemenza di Tito*, like the overture to *Gli Orazi e i Curiazi*, utilizes all three styles. After an imperious unison (high), the principal theme encompasses two contrasting ideas, which will dominate the overture (Example 8.6a); quiet, playful staccatos (middle or low style), then *forte* chords, turns, syncopations, and dotted rhythms (high style). (Continuity is assured by the repeated notes in the bass.) As the overture progresses, these juxtapositions create a sense of ambiguity, perhaps even conflict. A long crescendo serves as a transition (high style) to the second subject, comprising a march for the oboes with dotted rhythms, turns, and staccatos, then a lyrical consequent for the bassoons (middle style). The end of the exposition returns to the contrasting ideas of the principal theme, but the chords are now diminished sevenths shrieking at the top of the winds' range. These soon give way to a fugato (Example 8.6b) based on the staccato idea, whose style is elevated by this sophisticated treatment. The contrasting

Example 8.5a Haydn, *Armida*, Overture

Example 8.5b Haydn, *Armida*, Overture

Example 8.6a Mozart, *La clemenza di Tito*, Overture

Example 8.6b Mozart, *La clemenza di Tito*, Overture

emotions and ambiguity of style expressed here foreshadow the conflicting emotions of the opera: Tito's nobility, the flirtatious and ruthless Vitellia, Sesto's terrible dilemma and the horror of betrayal. And yet it is arguably no more conflicted than the overture to *Don Giovanni* (a *dramma giocoso*), with its brooding introduction and its frequent turns to minor even in the D-major Allegro.

The second category of number common to both seria and buffa is the march, which is a topic in its own right. Marches share many features in all contexts, and hence cannot reliably act as a sign of either genre. In particular, instrumental marches are quick, with upbeat rhythms, even jovial, not only in buffa, but often in seria as well. As adumbrated by their overtures, all three operas under consideration here include such marches. These fall squarely into

Example 8.7 Haydn, *Armida*, Zelmira, "Se tu seguir me, vuoi"

[Allegretto]

Zelmira: Have faith, and then leave all other cares to me.

the middle style: they are too light-hearted to be high, but their consistently periodic phrase structure and chordally reinforced beats are too stately and predictable for low style.

The third category of number common to both genres comprises the playful, charming, or lovely arias often sung by the soubrette role in opera buffa or giocosa: Zerlina, Despina, or even Susanna. These arias are neither parodistic nor frankly comical, but delightful and sophisticated pieces in middle style, which are also found in opera seria, often sung by the *seconda donna*. In *Armida*, such arias characterize the Egyptian princess Zelmira, whose role is to persuade, to lure. Her first aria, "Se tu seguir me vuoi" (Example 8.7), has the short, detached phrases punctuated by brief instrumental interjections, ornamented vocal line, quick pairs of

Example 8.8 Haydn, *Armida*, Zelmira, "Torna pure al caro bene"

Zelmira: ...but return as a lover to console her pain.

slurred notes, contrasting slow and quick motion, and solo winds characteristic of this style. Even her exasperated second aria, "Tu me sprezzi," has the same short-breathed phrases, quick dotted notes, slurred eighths, detached style, and wind commentary.

Zelmira's third aria, "Torna pure al caro bene" (Example 8.8), illustrates the fourth category of musical number common to both genres: the love song. Brown defined it as "serious yet pleasing," and indeed this type is more serious and less playful than many other numbers in middle style. "Torna pure" is a beguiling attempt to dissuade Rinaldo from his mission to destroy Armida's magical powers. Its minuet topic recalls the overture (Example 8.5b), while its rocking triplet accompaniment and the seductive winds again suggest the pastoral, as in the letter duet "Sull'aria" in *Le nozze di Figaro* or Susanna's ravishing "Deh vieni, non tardar."[14]

Armida includes two other arias in middle style for secondary characters. Clotarco's "Ah si plachi il fiero Nume," about how to achieve peace, is sandwiched between Zelmira's "Tu mi sprezzi" and Idreno's "Teco lo guida al campo," primarily in high style with sizable sections in middle style. Together they establish a relatively light-hearted and optimistic tone at the beginning of Act II, which extends until Rinaldo's resolve to leave Armida. The second aria in

14 On the pastoral aspect of these numbers, see Allanbrook, *Rhythmic Gesture*, pp. 145–49, 174–77.

middle style, Ubaldo's "Prence amato," about friendship and valor, uses both the serious middle style of the love song and the light middle style of the march; it provides relief between Armida's rage aria "Odio, furor, dispetto" and the high style of the trio finale to the act.

Haydn depicts Rinaldo's internal conflicts with arias in mixed styles. The three quatrains of his big three-part aria "Cara, è ver, io son tiranno" in the middle of Act II move dramatically from beautiful love music in serious middle style, through declamatory high style as he agonizes over his decision to leave Armida, to exclamations of anguish in brilliant high style. Similarly, in his "Dei pietosi, in tal cimento" the beautiful, serious middle-style music of Rinaldo's continued love – his weakness where Armida is concerned – conflicts with his sense of duty, as he takes courage in high style. Their duet at the end of Act I and their trio with Ubaldo at the end of Act II are also in a mixture of styles. The duet eventually resolves their conflicts in middle style and even playfully refers to a low-style folk tune in the concluding section. The trio vacillates between high-style anguish at parting and middle-style expressions of love.

Rinaldo's and Armida's complex relationship further manifests itself in the obbligato recitative and cavatinas at the beginning of Act III, where the middle-style enchantment of her forest gives way to high-style confrontation as he destroys the source of her magical powers. Even the joyous march of the final chorus is punctuated with Armida's rage and Rinaldo's love. Overall, Haydn's distribution of marches, middle-style arias for the secondary characters, and mixed numbers and recitatives for the principals maintains a balance of *chiaroscuro* against what might otherwise have been an excess of high style. Even the long stretches of predominantly serious music at the beginning of Act I and the end of Act II are broken up, by a march and Ubaldo's aria of friendship, respectively.

Gli Orazi e i Curiazi takes a slightly different approach to *chiaroscuro*, although Cimarosa is careful to provide relief even when the plot is

at its darkest. Like Haydn, he achieves this by consistently composing both obbligato recitatives and set pieces in mixed style. Most
numbers include internal contrast; for example, the serious arias
move to middle style at thoughts of love. Also, again as in *Armida*,
the seria style of many numbers send such strongly "high" signals
that they could transfer into an opera buffa only in the *parti serie*.

The detached dotted rhythms and wind color of the many
marches are the most consistently light-hearted aspect of the
opera. Many lighter passages in serious numbers derive from
march rhythms; for example, the middle section of the love duet for
Orazia and Curiazio at the beginning of Act II. Most of the
numbers in middle style occur near the beginning, when there is a
brief hope that the union of the Alban Curiazio and the Roman
Orazia will bring peace to troubled Alba. In her first aria, Sabina, an
Alban married to a Roman, expresses her hopes for a truce between
the two nations in a charming aria in middle style, "Un raggio
sereno" (1. 2). It is full of Lombardic rhythms, trills, and appoggiaturas with rocking, broken-chord accompaniments, orchestral dia-
loguing, and lively comments in the ritornellos. Curiazio's "Quelle
pupille tenere" (1. 4; Example 8.9) is a love aria in light middle style;
its coloratura would imply high rank if it were in an opera buffa.
The graceful vocal line is ornamented with slides and appoggiaturas, while orchestral strings and winds exchange short motives in
the ritornellos. A call to arms in the text occasions an abrupt
modulation, as octave unisons and sforzando accents punctuate the
repeated-note accompaniment; but this dark moment quickly
passes. Scene 7 opens with a lovely *duettino* for Orazia and Curiazio,
whose light middle style recalls similar duettinos in *La clemenza
di Tito*.

As the plot develops, the set pieces (except for the marches) tend
to be mixed. Most are predominantly serious in high style, with
either lighter sections in middle or even low style, or contrasting
orchestral, accompaniments. Orazia's high-style aria "Nacqui, è
ver" (1. 8), for example, has a B section in a lighter middle style; in
the repeat of this shift (Example 8.10), the oboe joins her in a lovely

Example 8.9 Cimarosa, *Gli Orazi e i Curiazi*, Curiazio, "Quelle pupille tenere"

Curiazio: ...those tender eyes that shine with love.

duo, cadencing with Lombardic rhythms. At the end, on the words "la sua compita felicità," a pedal or drone accompaniment suggests the pastoral.

Not surprisingly, low style in seria works tends to occur in internal ensembles and arias with chorus, both relatively new elements of the genre. In ensembles the rapid exchanges of vocal dialogue tend to evoke the buffa finale. This tendency is also exemplified in *Gli Orazi e i Curiazi*. In scene 3 a lively chorus with soloists leads to a joyful trio predominantly in middle style, "Oh dolce, e caro istante"; the trio also contains passages that approximate both high style (the transitions) and low style (some of the lyrical sections). It begins slowly, in a lovely choir, with winds in the ritornellos

Example 8.10 Cimarosa, *Gli Orazi e i Curiazi*, "Nacqui, è ver"

[Allegro]

Orazia: I am your daughter, your sister, even if [I live] by the Tiber,
a Roman woman...

Example 8.11a Cimarosa, *Gli Orazi e i Curiazi*, "Oh dolce, e caro istante"

Orazia, Curiazio, M. Orazio: My heart is full...

(middle style). Quick parlando follows (Example 8.11a), with a clarinet accompaniment of repeated motives, turns, and staccatos (low style). A crescendo (high style) builds to a separate ensemble (middle style). A sprightly violin obbligato accompanies a solo by Marco Orazio (middle style), and a duo follows with syncopated accompaniment and quick comments in the ritornellos (middle style). Another transition in high style leads to a parlando dialogue in detached style between the duo and the soloist (low or middle style; Examples 8.11b and 8.11c), which alternates with high/middle style to close the ensemble.

Similar contrasts are found in Marco Orazio's aria with chorus, "Se alla patria ognor donai" (1. 5), where he revels in the glory to be gained from the coming battle. The dotted march rhythms, scurrying repeated notes, and short rising motives impart a middle-style sense of joy to the otherwise serious high style; his detached, repetitive exchanges with the chorus resemble the language of the buffa finale (Example 8.12). Similarly, in the Act I finale march rhythms produce a lively effect, and staccato approaches to cadences, snatches of lyricism, and the dotted-rhythmed stretta recall the buffa finale.

In Act II, Orazia's role provides most of the middle-style

Example 8.11b Cimarosa, *Gli Orazi e i Curiazi*, "Oh dolce, e caro istante"

Orazia, Curiazio, M. Orazio: I am [full of] love and friendship.

Example 8.11c Cimarosa, *Gli Orazi e i Curiazi*, "Oh dolce, e caro istante"

Orazia, Curiazio, M. Orazio: ...of love, and of friendship.

Example 8.12 Cimarosa, *Gli Orazi e i Curiazi*, Marco Orazio, Chorus, "Se alla patria ognor donai"

Orazio: But is it true? **Coro:** Do not doubt it.

numbers. She begins with a *scena* and love duet with her beloved Curiazio, "Se torni vincitor" (II. 1), in serious middle style.[15] In scene 3, fearing for her husband's life, she attempts to calm the heated passions of the competing partisans with the charming and beautiful aria "Se pietà nel cor" (II. 3), also in middle style. Finally, in the penultimate scene, Orazia sings a duet with her proud and

15 Placing a love duet of this magnitude at the beginning of Act II, the traditional position of the throwaway "sorbet aria" for a minor character, shows how far opera seria had moved from traditional conventions by the mid-1790s.

murderous brother Marco Orazio, who was responsible for Curiazio's death. This duet ("Svenami ormai"; II. 6) is a masterpiece of irony. As in the ballroom scene in *Don Giovanni*, the charming dance music and light accompaniment set off Orazia's loathing and heartbreak and Marco's rage and contempt, counterpointing the fatal passions that will soon lead to her death at his hands.

Cimarosa's *chiaroscuro* in individual numbers and constant shifting among styles in recitatives and scene complexes produce a consistent balance of high and middle style throughout the opera. The dark moments soon lighten; the music does not convey the deepening horror and brutality of the tragic plot, but rather shields the audience from this potentially wrenching emotional experience. For all its innovative dramaturgy, *Gli Orazi e i Curiazi* still observes the traditional rule that good taste enjoins restraint.

Mozart's approach to *chiaroscuro* in *La clemenza di Tito* differs from that in the other two operas. Part of the difference stems from Metastasio's libretto, part from Mazzolà's reworking of it into two acts rather than three.[16] But a large part can be attributed to Mozart's music, in its enhancement or disregard of the text. As in *Gli Orazi e i Curiazi*, the music in *La clemenza di Tito* begins in a lighthearted middle style, but becomes increasingly serious as the plot darkens to violence and betrayal during the course of Act I. Even Vitellia, the daughter of the deposed emperor who thirsts for revenge, at first uses the middle style to persuade Sesto to assist her in her treasonous plot. Her first aria, "Deh se piacer mi vuoi," assumes a coquettish seductiveness. The vocal line is graced with appoggiaturas, sixteenth-note ornaments, and Lombardic rhythms (Example 8.13); weak cadences are approached with lower appoggiaturas; the accompaniment is light and syncopated, and the winds comment decoratively. In the second couplet, a drone and repetitive broken chords evoke pastoral images. At the beginning of

16 On the relations between Metastasio's and Mazzolà's *Tito* librettos (germane throughout the following discussion), see John A. Rice, *W. A. Mozart: "La clemenza di Tito"* (Cambridge: Cambridge University Press, 1991), ch. 3.

Example 8.13 Mozart, *La clemenza di Tito*, Vitellia, "Deh se piacer mi vuoi"

[Larghetto]

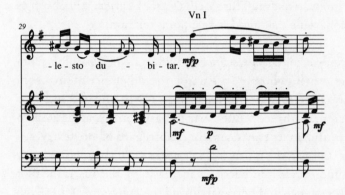

Vitellia: Do not fatigue me with these tiresome doubts.

the Allegro B section, she momentarily forgets herself, returning to her characteristic overbearing manner; however, she soon regains control and becomes even more seductive than before.

Although the treasonous undercurrents are gaining momentum, they do not surface until late in Act I. Most of the first act depicts an ideal court blessed by Tito's virtue and unsuspecting faith. Much of the music is ravishingly beautiful, at times decorated with playful instrumental gestures in caesuras and ritornellos. The charming duettinos, "Deh prendi un dolce amplesso" for Sesto and

Example 8.14 Mozart, *La clemenza di Tito*, Sesto, Annio, "Deh prendi un dolce amplesso"

Sesto, Annio: Come let me embrace you, my faithful friend.

Annio in pastoral 6/8 meter (Example 8.14), and "Ah perdona al primo affetto," for Annio and his beloved Servilia (Example 8.15) would serve equally well in an opera buffa; the same is true of the lively march that introduces scene 4. The great beauty of Tito's first aria, "Del più sublime soglio" (Example 8.16), takes on a light-hearted aspect with the staccato accompaniments and commentary of the violins. In the introduction to his next aria, "Ah, se fosse intorno al trono ogni cor," the bassoons' oscillating staccatos and oboes' jolly interjections would not be out of place in a buffa aria; at the same time the melody remains dignified, both here and in the vocal sections (Example 8.17), except for Tito's brief reference to military style on "un vasto impero."

Only when Sesto finally agrees to assist Vitellia in her treason does the music become serious. His aria of capitulation, "Parto, ma tu, ben mio," begins with beautiful, serious love music in middle style, but as the tempo quickens with his thoughts of vengeance, the music moves into high style, where it remains. During the rest of Act I the horror mounts, as the terrible consequences of Vitellia's intrigue result in Sesto's betrayal of Tito, the burning of Rome, and Tito's apparent death. (Metastasio had placed the insurrection in the middle of the second act, followed by arias of reaction, the last two for Sesto and Vitellia. Mazzolà extended his first act so that the insurrection, still in the middle of the work, could become an action finale.)

At the beginning of Act II of *La clemenza di Tito*, as in *Armida*, the

Example 8.15 Mozart, *La clemenza di Tito*, Annio, Servilia, "Ah perdona al primo affetto"

Servilia, Annio: When one soul is united with another, what joy a heart feels.

middle-style arias of the secondary characters set off and thus prepare the later arias of the principals. In fact, the entire act, which begins at a point equivalent to Metastasio's Act III, accentuates the middle style. Together with Sesto, we learn immediately that Tito is not dead. But his relief at learning that Tito is alive and will espouse Vitellia is soon replaced with terrible feelings of guilt, fear of discovery, and eventually a firm resolve to face the consequences. In Mazzolà's libretto and in Mozart's response, Tito's great generosity of spirit becomes the overriding affect; it determined what would be cut, what would be kept, and what would be rewritten. It also, we may infer, determined the emphasis on the middle style in both text and music.

Several moments of high emotional intensity and conflict occur in ensembles. The trio "Se a volto mai ti senti" springs from Sesto's meeting with Vitellia (originally at the end of Metastasio's second act). It is a masterpiece of individual characterization through con-

Example 8.16 Mozart, *La clemenza di Tito*, Tito, "Del più sublime soglio"

Tito: ... [the rest] is all torment and servitude.

trasting styles: Sesto expresses his unwavering love for Vitellia in a light, middle style; Vitellia expresses her remorse, horror and fear in high style; Publio, who has come to arrest Sesto, mediates between them. The second trio, "Quello di Tito è il volto" (Example 8.18), is an expression of unspoken thoughts, as Sesto appears in all of his guilt before Tito and Publio. It is similar to "Vengo! Aspettate!" in the first act, where Annio and Publio comment on Vitellia's almost hysterical state (Example 8.19); in

Example 8.17 Mozart, *La clemenza di Tito*, Tito, "Ah se fosse intorno al trono ogni cor"

Tito: Ah, if every heart were so sincere when by the throne,
a vast empire would be not a torment but a delight.

Example 8.18 Mozart, *La clemenza di Tito*, Sesto, Tito, Publio, "Quello di Tito è il volto"

Sesto: ...could not suffer more.
Tito, Publio: The traitor trembles, and dares not raise his eyes.

both, as in Cimarosa's trio and aria with chorus, the duetting pair speak in buffa parlando to differentiate them from the soloist. The effect is not funny, but the "buffo" texture requires strongly "serious" signs for the remaining, chief character.

Besides the ensembles in Act II, there remain two arias for Annio and one each for the rest of the characters. Here Mazzolà's and Mozart's choices give the middle style the edge, tempering Metastasio's emotionally charged libretto. Annio's aria in soubrette style, "Torna di Tito a lato" (II. 1), which urges Sesto to return to Tito, replaced Metastasio's aria of mixed emotions for Sesto "Fra stupido e penoso" (II. 7); Tito's angry aria "Tu, infedel, non hai difese" (II. 11), disappeared as well. Next, Publio sings an aria from the beginning of Metastasio's Act III, "Tardi s'avvede d'un tradimento," observing how slow Tito is to believe ill of anyone. Mozart set this text in a fast, middle-style minuet. The remaining arias for

Example 8.19 Mozart, *La clemenza di Tito*, Vitellia, Annio, Publio, "Vengo! Aspettate!"

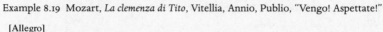

Vitellia: Oh my insane fury, what anguish, what torment.
Annio, Publio: Oh how great happiness can confound the heart.

the secondary characters use a mixture of styles, with middle style still predominant. Metastasio's impassioned text for Annio, in which he pleads for clemency for Sesto, "Pietà, signor, di lui!" (III. 3), is replaced with an aria in which he optimistically hopes that Tito will pardon Sesto: "Tu fosti tradito." This beautiful middle-style aria moves to high style at thoughts of betrayal and pain. Similarly, Servilia's "S'altro che lagrime," which also begs for pity for Sesto, is set in a beautiful middle style with a modicum of high style at the thought of cruelty.

Even the principals' arias in Act II use a mixture of styles, with the predominant *mezzo carattere* interwoven with high style. The arias stand out in contrast to those of the secondary characters primarily through their extremes of *chiaroscuro* and their passages in brilliant style, which attests to high rank. Light, military, and serious middle styles mediate between recurring sections in a whole gamut of high style *affetti*. In Sesto's and Vitellia's arias *chiaroscuro* becomes more important even than textual signs;

Mozart here composes music that seems counterindicative to the text.

Tito's "Se all'impero, amici Dei!" exhibits the high style with imperial trappings (prominent horn accompaniments, triadic melodies, syncopated, repeated-note accompaniments, strong accents, and long, challenging coloraturas). But as in his other arias, these signs are tempered with sprightly accompaniments and lovely melodies in middle style, as he expounds his philosophy of a stubborn generosity of spirit that will not be corrupted.

The arias for Sesto and Vitellia, "Deh, per questo istante solo" and "Non più di fiori," are both two-tempo *rondòs*. In addition to their dramatic functions, these numbers of great sentiment served to showcase the singer's prowess and to play on the spectators' emotions.[17] Both arias replaced Metastasian texts; Sesto's *aria patetica* "Vo disperato a morte" (III. 6), and Vitellia's simile aria "Getta il nocchier talora" (III. 11). In their new arias both characters pass from a serious middle style for thoughts of past happiness to an impassioned high style as they come to terms with the terrible reality of the present and the hopelessness of the future. In accordance with the formal type, the lively middle style returns at the end of the initial slow section, mediating between the horror of the present and the happiness of the past. The beginning of the ensuing fast section brings yet more tormented thoughts in high style. Now, however, comes an enigmatic third textual section in each final couplet: Sesto wonders how his heart can suffer such anguish without breaking; Vitellia comforts herself with the thought that her sufferings, if known, would surely inspire pity. In both cases Mozart departs entirely from previous styles, rejects a serious refrain, and sets the couplet in a light middle style, as if the protagonists had found solace, a certain detachment, in the process of coming to terms with their situations.[18]

The contrast seems particularly incongruous in Sesto's aria,

17 Rice, *Tito*, pp. 92–95.
18 One might compare this situation with that in the first movement of the "Jupiter" Symphony: in a context otherwise dominated by the *topos* of majesty, the closing theme is based on "Un bacio di mano," K. 541, composed as an insertion aria for Livigni's and Anfossi's *Le gelosie fortunate*.

Example 8.20 Mozart, *La clemenza di Tito*, Sesto, "Deh, per questo istante solo"

Sesto: A heart can suffer such torment, and yet not die of sorrow.

because the music appears out of keeping with the text: "Tanto affanno soffre un core, Né si more di dolor!" ("A heart can suffer such anguish and yet not die of sorrow"; Example 8.20). Yet this startling juxtaposition precisely in a climactic *rondò* dramatically hightlights the *chiaroscuro* of the plot. For the sake of his steadfast love, Sesto has lost both honor and friendship and, it appears, will soon lose his life. It is as if a point had been reached when sorrow is too great to bear, and a break in the prevailing seriousness is required before he can conclude his aria. This juxtaposition parallels the analogous one between low and high style in the overture.

These three *opere serie* of the last quarter of the eighteenth century demonstrate the many levels at which stylistic contrast operates within an opera. Haydn's *Armida*, in keeping with earlier practices, contrasts marches and the light middle style of the secondary characters with the otherwise serious high and middle styles. *Chiaroscuro* functions as an overall dramatic device, in that Act I lightens to celebrate the love of Armida and Rinaldo, and Acts II and III darken in response to their conflicts. Cimarosa's *Gli Orazi e i Curiazi* also moves, in the middle of Act I, from a predominantly light middle style to predominantly high style, which, in keeping with the darkening plot, remains dominant in Act II. But serious high style is lightened with middle style to such a degree that it tempers the plot's relentless progress toward its horrifying ending. Mozart's *La clemenza di Tito* uses *chiaroscuro* as a powerful dramatic device, moving from a predominantly light middle style to a serious, high style as the treasonous plot takes effect at the end of Act I. Act II returns to a predominantly middle style, reflecting the abiding goodness of Tito and the inevitability of a happy ending.

At the level of individual numbers, many topics and number types, including overture, march, minuet, and love song, elicit similar stylistic gestures regardless of genre. The choice of style in a given number may be determined by role, text, situation, characterization, or need for balance in the *chiaroscuro*. Some characters have a characteristic style: Rinaldo's mixed style reflects his indecision and inner conflicts; Armida's arias are all in high style; Orazia's middle style stands out, in her beautiful duo with Curiazio, aria of peace-making, and ironic duo with Marco Orazio. Contrasts in style within numbers may once again be a matter of number type (overture), a response to the text, a device used to delineate form (*rondò*, overture), or a means of balancing the *chiaroscuro*. Parlando, repetitive short phrases, staccato, short comments in dialogue, and other features normally associated with opera buffa are treated in an opera seria as compatible with serious sentiments and situations.

Despite the wide gulf that separates opera seria's Classical-heroic world from opera buffa's contemporary or exotic one, they share a wide range of musical styles, from the most pretentious high style to the commonest low style. Rather than looking to genre as a stylistic sign, we must consider topic, number type, rank, characterization, situation, textual interpretation, musical rhetoric, and the need for contrast – all as interactive determinants of style. To give only one example, the dominance of the middle style may have been a means towards, and a sign of, both genres' tendency to represent the triumph of goodness and social virtue, symbolized by their shared dependence on the *lieto fine*. Through such comprehensive approaches, a clearer picture of the interdependence of buffa and seria may begin to emerge.

9 | Figaro as misogynist: on aria types and aria rhetoric
Ronald J. Rabin

That opera buffa is a highly conventional genre is by now well established. Like other forms of comedy, opera buffa relies on stock characters and character configurations, familiar plot devices, and recurrent themes and motifs.[1] Recent scholarship has compared the genre to popular fiction (the modern romance novel or murder mystery) and popular entertainment (Hollywood movies).[2] It would appear, then, that a critical assessment of the role of convention in contemporary operas as well as in the Mozart-Da Ponte works is long overdue. Unfortunately, the task is complicated by the pejorative connotations of "convention" and "conventional," a legacy of nineteenth-century aesthetics that conflates "convention" with "formula" or "cliché"; as Harry Levin has argued with respect to the nineteenth century, "The recognition of convention . . . historically coincided with its repudiation."[3] Romantic aesthetics also shape our ideas about genre, especially the belief that a masterwork of necessity violates, transfigures, or dissolves genre conventions, as in Benedetto Croce's famous dictum that "Every true work of art has violated some established kind and upset the ideas of the critics."[4]

---

1 For an overview of plot structures, themes, and character-types in New Comedy and its descendants see Northrop Frye, "The Mythos of Spring," in *Anatomy of Criticism* (Princeton: Princeton University Press, 1957), pp. 163–86.

2 John Platoff, "The Buffa Aria in Mozart's Vienna," *COJ* 2 (1990), 99; Mary Hunter, *The Poetics of Entertainment: Opera Buffa in Vienna 1770–1790* (Princeton University Press, forthcoming).

3 Harry Levin, "Notes on Convention," in *Perspectives of Criticism*, ed. Harry Levin (Harvard: Harvard University Press, 1950), pp. 66–67.

4 Benedetto Croce, *Aesthetic as Science of Expression and General Linguistic*, rev. edn. trans. Douglas Ainslie (New York: Noonday Press, 1992), p. 37. On the opposition between convention and the individual in the Romantic period see Lawrence Manley, *Convention: 1500–1750* (Cambridge, MA: Harvard University Press, 1980),

The commonplace in the secondary literature is that Mozart does not adhere to or even transgress conventions, he "transforms" or "transcends" them. This view of Mozart as a genius among contemporaries who wrote "merely" conventional music invariably closes off the possibility of engaged comparative analysis. Even context-oriented studies that explore questions of genre and genre conventions maintain the duality of Mozart and the "others": Hermann Abert ends an excellent overview of Paisiello's style by claiming that Mozart is a more "realistic" artist than Paisiello; John Platoff concludes a recent inquiry into the *opere buffe* of Mozart's contemporaries with the question, "When was Mozart conventional and when original, and why?"[5] In order to understand how Mozart constructed drama of great power and immediacy from the conventional materials of opera buffa, we would do better to abandon such dichotomies as artificial/realistic, conventional/original, and concentrate instead on compositional techniques and artistic decisions. Rather than assume that Mozart's genius invariably led him to transform or transcend genre conventions, we might inquire instead how Mozart *exploits* them to suit his dramatic aims.

Consider, for example, the solo arias in opera buffa. Unlike ensemble numbers and finales, which tend to be closely tied to the dramatic context, distinctive and conventional aria "types" appear in opera after opera: the noble or heroic aria for the tenor, the comic aria for the *primo* or *secondo buffo*, and the *aria d'affetto* or

p. 3. The difficulties of discussing nineteenth-century opera within this aesthetic framework are addressed in James A. Hepokoski, "Genre and Content in Midcentury Verdi: 'Addio, del passato' (*La traviata*, Act III)," *COJ* 1 (1989), 249–76.

5 Hermann Abert, "Paisiellos Buffokunst und ihre Beziehungen zu Mozart," reprinted in *Gesammelte Schriften und Vorträge* (Halle: Niemeyer, 1929), pp. 395–96; John Platoff, "How Original was Mozart? Evidence from *Opera Buffa*," *EM* 20 (1992), 117. Platoff's question implies that we need not even inquire as to the originality of other composers of opera buffa. James Webster points out that in some German scholarship (including Abert) such assertions are bound up with nationalistic interpretations of Mozart's superiority to his Italian models. Webster, "Analysis," p. 102.

two-tempo *rondò* for the female protagonist are just some examples.[6] These aria types appear in the Mozart-Da Ponte operas as well. In fact, Mozart and Da Ponte often call attention to their use of conventional types – and they do so less by manipulating or transforming the characteristic features of their models than by deploying these arias in novel, and often striking, ways. In *Così fan tutte*, for example, there is little explicit parody of formal or gestural features in either Dorabella's "Smanie implacabili" or Fiordiligi's "Come scoglio"; rather, it is the disparity between the style of discourse and the dramatic context that raises the possibility of irony.[7] In *Don Giovanni*, Ottavio's tender love aria "Il mio tesoro" seems as incongruous in the shadowy moral climate of the opera as the character's belief in the noble virtues.[8] Even Don Giovanni's lyrical canzonetta "Deh vieni alla finestra" might be viewed as a sinister twist to a tradition of serenades in opera buffa.[9] This is not to suggest that all of these arias must be inter-

6 Some late eighteenth-century aria types are enumerated in Webster, "Analysis," pp. 105–14; cf. the discussion in Constantin Floros, *Mozart-Studien*, vol. 1, *Zu Mozarts Sinfonik, Opern- und Kirschenmusik* (Wiesbaden: Breitkopf und Härtel, 1979), pp. 84–129.

7 Mary Hunter, "*Così fan tutte* et les conventions musicales de son temps," *L'avant-scène opéra* no. 131–32, p. 164; Hunter, *Poetics of Entertainment*, ch. 5. Representative interpretations of "Smanie implacabili" as parodistic include Rodney Farnsworth, "*Così fan tutte* as parody and burlesque," *OQ* 6 (1988/89), 50–68; Bruce Alan Brown, *W. A. Mozart: "Così fan tutte"* (Cambridge: Cambridge University Press, 1995), pp. 127–30, 132–33. Although sometimes considered hyperbolic (see for example Sergio Durante's essay in this volume, p. 316), Dorabella's language in this aria is in keeping with the style of expression of opera seria; see, for example, Licida's aria "Gemo in un punto e fremo," which concludes Act II of Metastasio's *L'Olimpiade*.

8 My view of Ottavio as a displaced figure in the opera derives from Allanbrook, *Rhythmic Gesture* pp. 231–32; the idea was also captured in Peter Sellars's production set in Spanish Harlem, with Ottavio as a policeman – an ineffective, even outmoded symbol of moral authority surrounded by crime and drugs.

9 In addition to Count Almaviva's "Saper bramate" in ?Petrosellini's and Paisiello's *Il barbiere di Siviglia* (St. Petersburg, 1782; Vienna, 1783), serenades appear in, for example, Da Ponte's and Martín y Soler's *Una cosa rara* (Vienna, 1786), Mazzolà's and Rust's *Il marito indolente* (Vienna, 1784), and Chiari's and Paisiello's *La contadina di spirito* (St. Petersburg, 1779; Vienna, 1785). Da Ponte's first libretto for Salieri, *Il ricco d'un giorno* (Vienna, 1784), contains a double serenade, as two

preted ironically – only that the way the composer and librettist frame convention requires us to re-examine these aria types as signifiers.

Le nozze di Figaro is sometimes viewed as a more "realistic" drama than either the picaresque episodes of *Don Giovanni* or the carefully cultivated artifice of *Così fan tutte*. Yet here as well conventional aria types are prominent: revenge arias for Bartolo and the Count, a "pastoral" canzonetta for Susanna, an *aria d'affetto* for the Countess. Especially noteworthy in this respect are the arias for Marcellina and Basilio in Act IV, often singled out for criticism as much for their explicitly conventional subject matter as for the putatively inferior quality of their music. Many commentators echo Abert, who viewed these arias as obligatory numbers composed for the singers rather than for the drama.[10] But what of Figaro's Act IV aria, "Aprite un po' quegl'occhi"? In many ways it is just as conventional as the arias of Marcellina and Basilio that precede it: in its expression of misogyny (a frequent *topos* in opera-buffa arias), its address *ad spectatores*, and its artfully constructed images, which continue the animal metaphors of the two previous set pieces, and which appear in that most characteristic device of comic arias, the catalog.[11] No obligatory number for a secondary character, Figaro's aria is a defining moment in the drama: it crystallizes his lack of trust in Susanna, and thus prepares both her "Deh vieni" and the reconciliation of the couple in the finale. How does one analyze an aria that is at once highly conventional and pivotal?

brothers compete for the same woman. On Venetian serenades in opera buffa see Wolfgang Osthoff, "Gli endecasillabi villotistici in *Don Giovanni* e *Nozze di Figaro*," in Maria Teresa Muraro, ed., *Venezia e il melodramma nel settecento*, vol. 2 (Florence: Olschki, 1981), pp. 293–311.

10 Abert, *W. A. Mozart*, vol. 2 (Leipzig: Breitkopf und Härtel, 1921), pp. 288–9. Allanbrook (*Rhythmic Gesture*, pp. 160–67) offers an effective counterargument.

11 Allanbrook (*Rhythmic Gesture*, p. 358 n. 42) interprets the interplay of animal imagery as evidence that Da Ponte conceived the three arias as "a unified and significant sequence of texts."

I

Unlike studies of opera seria, in which the dramatic function of arias has always been a central concern, opera-buffa scholarship has only recently given much attention to arias, having long been pre-occupied with ensemble numbers and finales.[12] And while much of the literature on opera seria embraces the traditional notion that arias communicate primarily affective expression (albeit some-times clothed in rationalist garb), opera-buffa arias appear to be much more diverse in content and purpose. Affective expression may indeed be central to the Countess's "Porgi amor" or Fiordiligi's "Per pietà." But Leporello's catalog aria, Figaro's "Non più andrai," and Despina's "In uomini, in soldati" are spontaneous and exuberant performances, staged largely for the benefit of other characters; Susanna's "Venite, inginocchiatevi" and Don Giovanni's "Metà di voi" enact on-stage activities; and Anna's "Or sai chi l'onore" and Zerlina's "Batti batti" are both exhortations. This diversity of function suggests that equal attention needs to be devoted to the content of an aria and to the context and manner of its delivery. The combination of the two I will call aria rhetoric.

All arias contain an explicit argument, often one of persuasion. An aria may be addressed to other characters onstage, directly to the audience, or to an apostrophized figure (fate, Amor, an absent lover); or it may consist entirely of internal dialogue, akin to the soliloquy of spoken drama.[13] Some arias are explicitly rhetorical, even manipulative, while others are contemplative and pensive. Donna Anna's "Or sai chi l'onore" is an emotional appeal to Ottavio

---

12 On the function of arias in opera seria see, recently, Reinhard Strohm, "Händel-Oper und Regeldrama," in Hans Joachim Marx, ed., *Zur Dramaturgie der Barockoper: Bericht über die Symposien der Internationalen Händel-Akademie Karlsruhe 1992 und 1993* (Laaber: Laaber, 1994), pp. 35–37; Strohm, "Auf der Suche nach dem Drama im dramma per musica: Die Bedeutung der französichen Tragödie," in Peter Cahn and Ann-Katrin Heimer, eds., *De Musica et cantu: Studien zur Geschichte der Kirchenmusik und der Oper* (Hildesheim: Olms, 1993), pp. 481–93; Carl Dahlhaus, "What is a Musical Drama?," *COJ* 1 (1989), 95ff.

13 This aspect of rhetoric – aria as speech – is addressed in James Parakilas, "Mozart's *Tito* and the Music of Rhetorical Strategy," PhD diss., Cornell University, 1979.

for justice, which invokes her father's fatal wound and the blood-covered ground; Ferrando's "Un'aura amorosa" is a lyrical meditation based on a single metaphor, love as nourishment. Many arias depict self-persuasion: the Count's decision to seek revenge in "Vedrò mentr'io sospiro," or the Countess's rekindling of her hopes following the initial introspection of "Dove sono," are just two examples.

As with speeches or soliloquies in the theatre, the manner in which an argument is presented may be as important as the explicit subject-matter.[14] Invention is, after all, only one component of classical rhetoric; arrangement, style, and delivery all play a part in making an utterance persuasive. Eighteenth-century treatises that draw parallels between music and rhetoric often devote greater attention to the generative process of ordering, elaborating, and shaping musical ideas than to the ideas themselves.[15] The metaphor of rhetoric is a useful tool to probe issues like presentation and form: are the topics well chosen and effectively ordered? Do the parts form a coherent whole? Such questions can be asked of an aria as easily – perhaps even more easily – as of a symphony or string quartet. In opera-buffa arias, characters often reveal as much about themselves by their manner of expression as by their topic of discourse. What in instrumental music is normally an aesthetic question, namely the persuasiveness of the composer's musical language, in opera buffa becomes a dramatic question, the persuasiveness of a character's rhetoric.[16]

14 This point is related to Mary Hunter's argument that the musical form of an aria can play a crucial role in characterization; see her "Text, Music, and Drama in Haydn's Italian Opera Arias: Four Case Studies," *JM* 7 (1989), 30.
15 The relationship between music and rhetoric is of course complex; the goal of music is less that of persuading than of moving the listener. On rhetoric as an analytical tool for understanding eighteenth-century instrumental music see, recently, Mark Evan Bonds, *Wordless Rhetoric: Musical Form and the Rhetoric of the Oration* (Cambridge: Harvard University Press, 1991); Elaine R. Sisman, *Haydn and the Classical Variation* (Cambridge: Harvard University Press, 1993); Sisman, *Mozart: The Jupiter Symphony* (Cambridge: Cambridge University Press, 1993).
16 I assume that characters are responsible for the music as well as the text of their arias. The related but more complex question of whether characters are actually

Take arias written for the *primo buffo*. In the operas performed at the Burgtheater during Mozart's decade in Vienna, the *primo buffo* is typically one of three character types: a slow-witted rustic or lower-class character, a foolish guardian with designs on his ward or a paterfamilias with an obsessive desire to increase his social standing, or a foppish or ridiculous nobleman.[17] Sometimes the *primo buffo* functions as a "blocking character," impeding a young man's attempt to court a young woman (e.g. Bartolo in ?Petrosellini's and Paisiello's *Il barbiere di Siviglia*); sometimes he is merely a clown (Titta in Sarti's *Fra i due litiganti il terzo gode*).[18] Whatever his role in the plot, the *primo buffo* is nearly always absurd, a fool out of touch with other members of society. This is manifest in the low-style or comic rhetoric of his arias, which are often failed attempts at persuasion, argumentation, or explanation.[19] The character may try to relate plot events, or offer expert advice or opinions on topics like the collapse of values since the days of his youth or the best way to impress the ladies. Whatever the content, the attempt often falls victim to the character's fractured style of discourse.

One *primo buffo* who attempts a narration, with unfortunate results, is Don Demofonte in Palomba's and Cimarosa's *Li due baroni di Rocca Azzurra* (Rome, 1783; Vienna, 1789).[20] Demofonte's

conscious that they are singing, first addressed by Edward T. Cone, does not concern me here; see David Rosen, "Cone's and Kivy's 'World of Opera,'" *COJ* 4 (1992), 61–74.

17 Arias written specifically for the *primo buffo* at Vienna's Burgtheater, Francesco Benucci, are the subject of Platoff's "The buffa aria."

18 Both operas were first performed in Vienna in 1783, one year after their premieres in St. Petersburg (*Il barbiere di Siviglia*) and Milan (*Litiganti*) The term "blocking character" is used by Northrop Frye in *Anatomy of Criticism*, pp. 164ff.

19 Here and throughout I use "buffa aria" synonymously with "aria for the *primo buffo*." My repertory is broader than Platoff's ("The buffa aria"), as I include arias in operas imported into Vienna (and thus not written specifically for Francesco Benucci) as well as *primo buffo* roles performed by other singers (see below).

20 Demofonte was played in Vienna by Francesco Bussani, Mozart's first Bartolo and Alfonso as well as the Viennese Masetto. Normally cast as the *secondo buffo* (as in the Mozart-Da Ponte operas), Bussani occasionally took on *primo buffo* roles in operas in which Benucci did not appear.

plans to ennoble the house by having his nephew marry Madama Laura are thwarted when *two* women arrive at his doorstep, each claiming to be the intended. Near the end of the opera Demofonte is called upon to explain this bizarre situation, and he promises to narrate everything ("Vi narro tutto . . . il fatto com'è andato") even if it takes all day. While these prefatory remarks hint at the long-windedness of the aria that follows, they scarcely prepare one for the hopeless jumble that Demofonte makes from the already tangled events of the opera (see p. 240).

Demofonte begins to relate plot events (stanzas 1 and 2), but quickly becomes confused (stanza 3) and gropes for ideas (stanza 4, lines 15–24) before seizing on a ridiculous "conclusion" (lines 25–28). This degeneration in the argument is reflected in the rhyme scheme. The short initial stanzas contain a regular rhyme scheme; the extended final stanza, with the exception of the two *tronco* lines (lines 17 and 28), contains no proper rhymes but only similar-sounding words ("fisico," "topico," "Diavolo"; "concludere," "femmine," "topiche," "diavole," etc.). The shift from rhymed to unrhymed verse at line 15 coincides with a change of meter from *ottonari* to *settenari*, and from *piano* and *tronco* lines to almost exclusively *sdrucciolo* ones.[21] Thus the text accelerates, as happens in many male buffa arias:[22] it progresses from alternating rhymes to rhymed couplets to unrhymed single lines, from longer to shorter verse, and from *versi piani* to *versi sdruccioli*. Demofonte conceals the breakdown of his argument with bluster.

Just as Demofonte goes about his task in muddled fashion – he abandons his narration early on in favor of random thoughts about the female sex – his aria is muddled about its long-term goals (see the analysis in Figure 9.1). Cimarosa's setting is in two tempi, an Andante maestoso for the *ottonari* and initial *settenari* lines, and an

21 For an introduction to Italian prosody and its implications for musical settings, see for example Tim Carter, *W. A. Mozart: "Le nozze di Figaro"* (Cambridge: Cambridge University Press, 1987), pp. 76–87; Webster, "Analysis," pp. 133–40. In my renderings of aria texts, *tronco* lines are indicated by bold-face letters in the rhyme-schemes, *sdrucciolo* lines by underlinings.

22 Platoff, "The buffa aria," p. 105.

Palomba and Cimarosa, *Li due baroni* (Vienna, 1789), ii. 6

a	La Sposina s'attendeva		The little bride awaited
b	Del Barone, che sta lì;		The baron who is there;
a	E ricever la doveva		And she had to be accepted
b	Il Barone, che sta quì.		By the the baron who is here.
c	Ma la Sposa del ritratto,	5	But the bride of the portrait,
c	E la Sposa del contratto		And the bride of the contract
d	Spose, e mogli tutti due		Spouses and brides both
e	Quà si vennero a sposar.		Came here to marry.
f	Or se il Padre del Barone		Now if the father of the baron
g	Con il Padre della bella	10	With the father of the beauty
g	Contrattò prima con quella . . .		First made a contract with that one . . .
h	Cosa ci entra adesso questa . . .		How does that fit in with this here . . .
h	Ma sediamo, che la testa		But let us sit down, as my head
e	S'incomincia riscaldar.		Is beginning to get warm . . .
	(*si pone a sedere, ed il Bar. fa le stesse azioni*)		(*he takes a seat, as does the Baron*)
i	Mulier est mulier femina	15	Mulier est mulier: femina
i	Et homo est homo masculus,		Et homo est homo: masculus.
e	Ciò mi si può negar?		Who can deny me this?
k	Per questo il punto è fisico,		For this case the point is physical,
l	Fisico, cioè topico,		Physical, namely topical,
m	Critico, cioè Diavolo . . .	20	Critical, namely the devil . . .
n	Con ciò vengo a concludere,		With which I conclude
o	Che in general le femmine		That in general women
p	Son fisiche, son topiche,		Are physical, are topical,
q	Son critiche, son diavole . . .		Are critical, are devils . . .
r	Ergo sostengo, e pubblico,	25	Ergo I maintain, and divulge,
s	Ch'è un asino quel maschio,		That it is an ass of a man,
o	Che dalle donne femmine		Who lets himself, by female women,
e	Si faccia infinnochiar.	28	Be made a fool of.
	(*partono*)		(*exeunt*)

Example 9.1 Theme **B**, Palomba-Cimarosa, *Li due baroni*, "La sposina s'attendeva"
(source: A-Wn K.T.56)

[Andante maestoso]

Demofonte: Mulier est mulier femina et homo est homo masculus

Figure 9.1 "La sposina s'attendeva" (Source: A-Wn K.T. 56)

Andante maestoso

	Introduction			¶1 in I		¶2 = patter in V		"Conclusion" in I	
Measure	1	15	19	31	43	52	59	65	69
Material	A	Trans. B	⌣	A	Patter	Patter	Ext.	Trans. B	⌣
Text				1–4	5–8	9–12	13–14	15–17	
Local	I	on V		I	I–V^7–I in I	I–V^7–I in V	V	V^4_3/V–V	
D Major:	I			I	I^V	V	V^V	I	on V

Allegro

	Patter build-up		"Conclusion" + patter in V	
Measure	77		93	99
Material	Patter	⌣ "Ergo"	B'	Patter + Cadential
Text	18–24		25–28	
Local	I	V/V	V	$\flat\hat{6}$–$\hat{5}$–$\hat{1}$ in V
D Major:	I	on V/V	V	

	Back to I	Re-orientation		"Conclusion" + patter in I	
Measure	116	120		137	
Material	Patter	Patter	⌣ "Ergo"	B'	Patter
Text	9–10, 7–8	18–24		25–26	25–28
Local	V^7/I	I	V	I	I
D Major:	[–I]	I	on V	I	I

Local "Conclusion" + patter in I: $\flat\hat{6}$–$\hat{5}$–$\hat{1}$ in I

Note: x^V = half-cadence

Allegro for the remainder of the verse. The first vocal section begins with a distinctive opening theme (**A**; see Example 9.1) that disappears after m. 43 and never returns. Long stretches of patter follow, first in the tonic, then the dominant, leading to Demofonte's Latin phrases proclaimed triumphantly in the tonic over a *Trommelbass* (**B**). The first section concludes on the dominant, typical preparation for a second, faster section entirely in the tonic. But Demofonte traverses the same tonal goals in the Allegro that he explored in the Andante. After some initial patter in the tonic, he proclaims "Ergo" and restates the "conclusion" theme (**B**) in the wrong key, this time over thundering scales in the orchestra; additional patter leads to another "Ergo" and a final statement of **B** in the tonic. Indeed, **B** is not a logical culmination of Demofonte's arguments but only a way out of a mess. Nor is the theme, once attained, a self-sufficient unit, for it does not cadence without additional patter. Without large-scale goals, the aria relies for coherence on immediate connections: the repetition of blocks of music (mm. 43–51~52–59, 77–92~120–36, 93–115~137–59), and the periodic appearance of **B**, which functions as a tag. Overall, the aria depicts aimless wandering punctuated by occasional realignment. The setting mimics Demofonte's rhetoric, both his confusion and his attempt to cover it with sententiousness.

Demofonte concludes his arguments, but sometimes the *primo buffo* cannot and must admit defeat. Such breakdowns may be precipitated by plot events, by the character's excessive jealousy or suspicion, or simply by his own dull-wittedness. In Bertati's and Bianchi's *La villanella rapita* (Venice, 1783; Vienna, 1785), for example, when the peasant Pippo attempts in an aria to talk his way out of trouble, he eventually gives up, admitting that his brain cannot keep up with his tongue:

Ah m'imbroglio da ogni lato [Ah what an imbroglio from every
Mal s'io parlo, mal s'io taccio: side; it's bad if I talk, bad if I keep
Mi confondo povetaccio silent; Poor me I'm confounded,
E in cervello più no stò. And my head is spinning.] (I. 19)

In Mazzolà's and Salieri's *La scuola de' gelosi*, the jealous husband Blasio considers and rejects several schemes for dealing with his wife, concluding.

> Oimè che cosa è questa
> Che strana confusiona
> Non so dov'ho la testa
> Perduta ho la ragione
> Non veggo qual che faccio
> Comincio a delirar.   (II. 7)

> [Alas what a circumstance, what a strange confusion, I don't know where my head is at, I've lost my reason, I don't know what I'm doing, I'm beginning to lose control.]

Both numbers consist almost entirely of vocal patter, and both modulate frequently and lack clear tonal goals.

Of course, not all buffa arias feature meandering tonal schemes or extensive patter. Sometimes the comic effect is attained by a disjunction between the rhetoric of the aria and the dramatic situation. In Petrosellini's and Cimarosa's *L'italiana in Londra* (Rome, 1778; Vienna, 1783), Don Polidoro addresses a tender (and musically "straight") love aria to a beloved whom he believes has been rendered invisible and whom he unsuccessfully attempts to locate as he sings ("idol mio, sta qui oppur di la?").[23] Some arias parody high-style numbers. In Act II of Petrosellini's and Paisiello's *Le due contesse* (Rome, 1776; Vienna, 1787) the servant Prospero expresses inner turmoil with a high-style device, the simile aria.[24] But his comparisons are crude, even absurd, rather than elegant – he compares his turmoil to flying insects and bats – and instead of exploring a single telling image, he strings several together into a catalog.

---

23 "Dammi la mano, o bella," I. 10. Following the initial Larghetto, the aria becomes more explicitly comic; in the *secondo tempo*, an Allegro assai consisting mostly of patter, Polidoro confesses that he's worked up a sweat having to court an invisible (and elusive) quarry.   24 "Come girano i moschini," II. 2.

In Polidoro's and Prospero's arias, irony and parody, rather than musical style, suggest comic rhetoric.

As the embodiment of low-style or comic rhetoric, male buffa arias are the polar opposite of the high-style arias of serious characters. Table 9.1 is a comparison of the high and low styles, based on "ideal types" in Max Weber's sense rather than on particular arias in the repertory.[25] Arias for seria-like characters typically rely on formal clarity and the deployment of distinctive thematic material to project content: instead of short-term links between sections, tag themes, and frequent modulations, these arias contain well-defined spaces for tonic and dominant presentation as well as tonal return.[26] Like a well-constructed oration, high-style arias have a clear beginning, middle, and end – exactly what is lacking in male buffa arias. Indeed, the familiar buffo device of the repeated ineffectual cadence suggests the character's *ad hoc* struggle and failure to impose minimal structure (i.e. a point of articulation) on what is actually a free-form utterance.

Because of his jealousy, vanity, or some other vice, the *primo buffo* is frequently marginalized. Often he is the only character to speak in dialect, or to spout pseudo-Latin phrases; at the conclusion of many operas he must watch as the other characters celebrate what is frequently a double or even triple wedding.[27] His solo arias isolate him as well, marking his rhetoric as jumbled or incoherent or at least discursive and inelegant. Such a view is consistent with

25 On the "ideal type" see Carl Dahlhaus, *Analysis and Value Judgment*, trans. Siegmund Levarie (New York: Pendragon Press, 1983), pp. 45ff.; Philip Gossett, "Carl Dahlhaus and the 'Ideal Type,'" *19CM* 13 (1989), 49–56. On "middle" style as mediation between high and low, see Marita P. McClymonds's article in this volume.

26 Form in two high-style aria types, the *aria d'affetto* and the *aria di bravura*, is described in detail in my dissertation, "Mozart, Da Ponte, and the Dramaturgy of Opera Buffa: Italian Comic Opera in Vienna, 1783–1791" (PhD diss., Cornell University, 1996), pp. 161–208; on sonata-like procedures in opera buffa see Hunter, "Haydn's Aria Forms: A Study of the Arias in the Italian Operas Written At Esterháza, 1766–1783" (PhD diss., Cornell University, 1982), Chapter 9; Webster, "Mozart's Operas and the Myth of Musical Unity," *COJ* 2 (1990), 204; Webster, "Analysis," pp. 117–19.   27 Cf. Frye, *Anatomy of Criticism*, pp. 165–66.

Table 9.1. *High-style and low-style rhetoric in opera-buffa arias*

High-style rhetoric	Low-style (comic) rhetoric
Text	**Text**
Short (1 or 2 stanzas)	Longer than 2 stanzas
High language ("affano," "pene," "dolore," "pietà")	Low or comic language ("cervello," "confuso," "stordito," "pazzo")
Long statement, often a single or perhaps two sentences	Short statements, frequent self-interruption, asides, repetition or lists; sometimes confusion or breakdown
Ideas are concentrated	Ideas are diffuse
High sentiment (love, absence, hope, or – by extension – rage, vengeance)	Low sentiment or desire (misogyny, vanity, food, clichéd advice, boorish stories, fond reminiscence "in my youth")
Progression toward resolution or understanding of paradox, or steadfast (*aria di bravura*)	Degeneration into (further) confusion or anger, or misguided "conclusion"
Music	**Music**
Harmonically rich (chromaticism, augmented-sixth chords, secondary dominants)	Harmonically simple (alternation of tonic and dominant for long stretches)
Lyric, flowing lines, some melismas or coloratura; occasional interruption at a critical juncture (typically augmented-sixth to dominant with a fermata)	Syllabic text setting, "neutral" melodic lines, patter
Form clear, parts clearly articulated	Form frequently unclear, parts underplayed, disguised, or subverted
Inventiveness	Poverty of invention, or ideas superabundant and loosely organized
Restraint and control (*aria d'affetto*) or unbridled virtuosity (*aria di bravura*): compelling	Unrestrained, quasi-improvisatory, repetitious or tethered: incoherence

recent theories of comedy, including Michael Issacharoff's assertion that the comic sign in drama is somehow unbalanced or distorted, or Nina Ekstein's argument that narrative components in French seventeenth-century comedy feature distortion and disruption.[28]

I I

It is striking that when Mozart abandoned work on the two *opere buffe* that occupied him in late 1783 or early 1784, *L'oca del Cairo* and *Lo sposo deluso*, he also abandoned the standard practice of casting the *primo buffo* as an old guardian, country bumpkin, or foolish nobleman.[29] In the Mozart-Da Ponte operas, only the secondary characters Bartolo and Masetto resemble this character-type. This resemblance is seen in the low-style rhetoric of their arias as well as by their actions: Bartolo, incapable of even one effective modulation in "La vendetta," provides more comic relief than dramatic tension, despite his bluster; when Masetto faces a formidable enemy in "Ho capito," his thoughts scatter, as the circular deployment of thematic material makes clear.[30]

Figaro, however, is cast from a different mold. He possesses just those traits the *primo buffo* typically lacks: adaptability, quick wits, and above all, rhetorical brilliance. Allanbrook has called attention to Figaro's skills as a performer, including his ability to play Harlequin as well as to mime.[31] Role-playing is Figaro's métier. In the opening scene he continues the role he played in *Il barbiere di*

---

28 Michael Issacharoff, *Discourse as Performance* (Stanford: Stanford University Press, 1989), pp. 93–101; Nina Ekstein, *Dramatic Narrative: Racine's Récits* (New York: Peter Lang, 1986), pp. 123–49. Cf. Wolfgang Osthoff's comments on deviations from social norms as a source of humor and parody in opera buffa: "Die opera buffa," in *Gattungen der Musik in Einzeldarstellungen: Gedenkschrift Leo Schrade*, ed. Wulf Arlt, Ernst Lichtenhahn, and Hans Oesch (Berne: Francke, 1973), pp. 693–97.

29 Don Pippo in *L'oca del Cairo* and Sempronio in *Lo sposo deluso* are typical examples of the foolish paterfamilias.

30 On Bartolo see Rabin, "Dramaturgy of Opera Buffa," pp. 376–81; on Masetto see Allanbrook, *Rhythmic Gesture*, pp. 260–61.

31 Allanbrook, *Rhythmic Gesture*, pp. 77, 80–82, 167, and *passim*.

Siviglia, that of the nimble, good-natured servant: when he tells Susanna, in the duettino No. 2, ". . . in tre salti / Lo vado a servir" (". . . in three bounds / I'm at his service") he sings in the spirit of *Il barbiere di Siviglia*: "Pronto a servire / Vostra eccellenza" ("Ready to serve / Your excellency"). When Susanna reveals the Count's amorous intentions, everything changes. Figaro rejects the roles the Count has proposed:

> Voi ministro, io corriero, e la Susanna
> Segreta ambasciatrice . . .
> Non sarà, non sarà. Figaro il dice   (I. 2)

> [You as minister, I as courier, and Susanna your secret ambassadress . . .
> That shall never be; Figaro has said so.]

and casts himself as the Count's dancing master in "Se vuol ballare," the one who calls the shots. And in "Non più andrai" he serves as fraternal advisor to Cherubino, bidding farewell to the "amorous butterfly" by masterminding an impressive public send-off.[32] To the roles of dancing master and older brother, "Aprite un po'" adds the role of the cuckold. Like his other performances, it is a part he plays with self-awareness:

> Ed io comincio omai
> A fare il scimunito
> Mestiere di marito . . .[33]   (IV. 7)

> [And now I begin to take on the foolish role of the husband . . .]

The script is familiar. Unlike "Se vuol ballare" or "Non più andrai," in which Figaro's arguments have a fresh, improvisatory quality, "Aprite un po'" is constructed on a hoary theme – the faithlessness of women. Hardly surprising, then, that he should embrace convention here with a well-established aria type.

A number of misogyny arias in contemporary *opere buffe* resem-

---

32 Figaro's relationship to Cherubino is perceptively discussed in Allanbrook, *Rhythmic Gesture*, pp. 95–99.

33 Later in the finale (IV. 13) Figaro will style himself as Vulcan to Susanna's Venus and the Count's Mars.

ble "Aprite un po'." In Livigni's and Cimarosa's *Giannina e Bernardone* (Venice, 1781; Vienna, 1784), for example, the hot-tempered rustic Bernardone sympathizes with poor husbands whose wives make fools of them; in Petrosellini's and Paisiello's *Le due contesse* the nobleman Leandro brands all women lying seducers.[34] Like "Aprite un po'," these arias are positioned near the last finale in the opera, and are addressed explicitly to the men in the audience (Bernardone's to "Maritati poverelli," Leandro's to "noi . . . poverini," although later he also addresses the women). Like Figaro, Bernardone implores his listeners to open their eyes ("Gli occhi bene aprir potete"), and his aria, like Figaro's, contains references to "what you already know" ("già sapete") about women as well as the verbal-instrumental pun on the cuckold's horns.[35]

There is an essential difference between "Aprite un po'" and these arias, however. For Leandro and Bernardone, the misogyny aria is the culmination of a long sequence of jealous behavior, an expression of the true nature of the characters; both arias anticipate the difficulties the men will experience upon their reintegration into society in the *lieto fine*.[36] But for Figaro the misogyny aria is a misstep: Susanna is able to "pull him back."[37] A closer analogue to "Aprite un po'" is Sandrino's aria "Voi semplici amanti" from Casti's and Paisiello's *Il re Teodoro in Venezia* (Vienna, 1784).[38] Sandrino, like Figaro goaded by a misunderstanding involving his *sposa*, finds the role of misogynist late in the day; his lapse is doubly

34 Bernardone: "Maritati poverelli," II. 10; Leandro: "Son le donne quasi tutte," II. 13.
35 As given in the Venice 1781 libretto, the text of Bernardone's aria lacks the reference to "già sapete" as well as the cuckolding pun found in a number of contemporary scores (as well as the modern Ricordi score). I have not been able to determine whether the divergent text originates with Cimarosa's score or reflects a slightly later tradition.
36 In *Le due contesse*, Leandro decides to marry a servant rather than the betrothed who inspired his jealous rages; in *Giannina e Bernardone* Bernardone's jealousy ceases only when he is threatened with violence if he does not reconcile with his *sposa*.   37 Allanbrook, *Rhythmic Gesture*, p. 171.
38 Daniela Goldin suggests that "Voi semplici amanti," as well as a passage from Casti's *Poema tartaro*, were sources of inspiration for Da Ponte's verse. "Mozart, Da Ponte, e il linguaggio dell'opera buffa," in Muraro, ed., *Venezia e il melodramma*, vol. 2, pp. 246–48; reprinted in Goldin, *La vera fenice* (Turin: Einaudi, 1985), pp. 106–08.

striking, for Sandrino is a lyric tenor whose first number, a "heroic" metaphor aria, established him as a seria-like figure.[39] To work as effective dramatic vehicles, both "Voi semplici amanti" and "Aprite un po'" must convey debasement as well as anger.

The substance of Sandrino's argument, a warning to "simple lovers" about the inconstancy of women, is presented in the first of four stanzas of *senari*.

Casti and Paisiello, *Il re Teodoro in Venezia* (Vienna, 1784), II. 7

a	Voi semplici amanti	You simple lovers
b	Che a donne credete,	Who believe what women say,
a	Son tutte incostanti,	They are all inconstant,
b	L'esempio vedete,	Look to my example,
c	Specchiatevi in me.	5 See yourself in me.
d	Il moto dell'onda,	The motion of the waves
e	Il soffio dell'aria,	The blowing of the breeze,
d	La tremula fronda	The shaking of the leaves
e	Sì lieve, sì varia,	Such lightness, such variability
c	Sì instabil non è.*	10 Such instability pales in comparison.
f	Eppur francamente	And yet
f	Le udite sovente	You often hear them
g	Vantar fido core,	Boasting of a faithful heart,
g	Parlarvi d'amore	Talking to you of love
c	Promettervi fe.	15 Promising you faith.
a	Voi semplici amanti	You simple lovers
b	Che a donne credete,	Who believe what women say,
b	Da lor rivolgete	Turn away from them
c	Sollecito il piè.	Take to your heels right away.

* In Paisiello's setting the last two lines of the stanza are changed to "Più lieve, più varia / Più stabil non è."

The text is tightly organized: stanza 1 states the thesis, stanza 2 illustrates it with metaphors, stanza 3 refutes counter-arguments, and

---

39 Although Leandro in *Le due contesse* is also a tenor, the style of all three of his arias is declamatory rather than lyrical.

Figure 9.2 "Voi semplici amanti" (Source: A-Wn 17804)

Andantino espressiv o

Section	Introduction	Tonic par ag raph	Transition	Dominant par ag rapl
Measure	1	12	24	35
Text	—	1 – 5	6 –10	9 – 10
Material	A	A (lyrical)	A' (orch.: 32nds)	Color atur a
Key	I	I	I → V V/V	V

Section	Retr ansition
Measure	48
Text	6 – 10
Material	A''
Key	V → [I] on V

Allegro presto

Section	Tonal retur n			Primo tempo; Alleg ro prest· Coda
Measure	61	72	92	110 – 28
Text	11 – 15	16 – 19, 6 – 10	16 – 19	4 – 5
Material	Cells, scales	Cells, scales	Cells, scales	A; cadential
Key	I	I	I	I

stanza 4 reiterates lines 1 and 2 and concludes with advice. Although well argued, Sandrino's demonstration is essentially static; all we need to know appears in the first stanza. The use of a single meter throughout, especially one with a fixed stress pattern like *senari* (accents on syllables two and five), contributes to the static effect.

Despite the uniform text, Paisiello sets "Voi semplici amanti" in two tempi and two contrasting styles (see Figure 9.2). The opening Andantino espressivo contains tonic and dominant vocal paragraphs as well as a retransition. The lyrical character of this section is conveyed immediately by the expansive tonic paragraph, in which two identical statements of a cadential phrase frame a paired antecedent-consequent (see Example 9.2).

Text	Material	Harmony
1–2	a	$I-V^7-vi-ii^6-I^6_4-V-I$
3	b	$I-V$
4	b	V^7-I
4–5	a	$I-V^7-vi-ii^6-I^6_4-V-I$

Example 9.2 Casti-Paisiello, *Il re Teodoro*, "Voi semplici amanti" (source: A-Wn MS17804)

Example 9.2 (*cont.*)

- de - te   spec - - chia - te - vi in   me

Sandrino: You simple lovers who believe what women say, they are all inconstant, look to my example, see yourself in me.

The dominant paragraph maintains this lyrical quality with several extended passages of coloratura. The character of the set piece changes, however, with the Allegro presto and the tonal return: Sandrino abandons his melodic phrases for short rhythmic cells, scale patterns, and declamatory singing – in short, patter. In fact, one of the cells closely resembles the motive that launches Figaro's patter in "Aprite un po'" (see Example 9.3).[40] The Allegro presto remains in the tonic throughout, but it is no mere *stretta* or coda; it rivals or exceeds the opening section in intensity and dramatic weight.[41]

Thus it is Paisiello's setting rather than Casti's text that suggests a duality in "Voi semplici amanti." By having Sandrino establish (or confirm) his status as a seria-like tenor in the opening Andantino before descending to low-style patter singing in the Allegro presto, Paisiello conveys both the character-type and the dramatic situation – albeit in a successive rather than integrated fashion. In "Voi semplici amanti," the juxtaposition of high-style and low-style rhetoric suggests how far Sandrino has descended.

The text of Figaro's "Aprite un po'" is both longer and more

40 This resemblance is also noted in Abert, "Paisiellos Buffokunst," p. 392.
41 Cf. Platoff's description ("The Buffa Aria," 107–12) of the typical long concluding section in the tonic providing "structural balance" for an exposition.

caustic than that of "Voi semplici amanti"; it is also, unlike Sandrino's text, decidedly end-oriented.

Le nozze di Figaro, No. 26

a	Aprite un po' quegli occhi		Just open your eyes a bit
a	Uomini incauti, e schiocchi,		Rash and foolish men,
b	Guardate queste femmine,		Look at these women,
c	Guardate cosa son.		Look at what they are.
d	Queste chiamate Dee	5	These you call goddesses
e	Dagli ingannati sensi,		When your senses are overwhelmed,
e	A cui tributa incensi		To whom tribute is paid
c	La debole ragion.		By those of weak reasoning.
f	Son streghe che incantano		They are witches that cast spells
g	Per farci penar.	10	To cause us pain.
f	Sirene che cantano		Sirens that sing
g	Per farci affogar.		To make us drown.
h	Civette che allettano		Owls that entice us
i	Per trarci le piume,		To pluck out our feathers,
j	Comete che brillano	15	Comets that flash
i	Per toglierci il lume;		To take away our light;
k	Son rose spinose		They're thorned roses
k	Son volpi vezzose,		They're charming foxes,
l	Son orse benigne,		They're kind bears,
l	Colombe maligne,	20	Malicious doves,
m	Maestre d'inganni,		Masters of deceit,
m	Amiche d'affanni,		Friends of pain
n	Che fingono, mentono,		Who pretend, and lie,
n	Amore non sentono		Love is not felt by them
o	Non senton pietà,	25	They feel no pity,
p	Il resto nol dico		The rest I won't say
o	Già ognuno lo sa.		Everyone knows it already.

The introductory stanzas 1 and 2 set the tone for the entire number. While Sandrino simply offers advice based on his experience, Figaro's opening sentiments both attack the deceivers and indict the men – himself included – who allow themselves to be deceived.

Example 9.3 Patter cells, "Voi semplici amanti" (*Il re Teodoro*) and "Aprite un po'" (*Figaro*)

Sandrino: You simple lovers who believe what women say...
Figaro: They're thorned roses, they're charming foxes...

But his real fury is unleashed in stanza 3 and continues unabated until the closing envoi, "Il resto nol dico / Già ognuno lo sa." Stanza 5, at once longer and more compressed than the preceding stanzas, is the climax of the set piece: in this extended outburst Figaro's metaphors accelerate to one item per line, the rhyme scheme shifts to couplets, internal rhyme and alliteration appear ("rose spinose," "volpi vezzose"), and the passage culminates with three *sdrucciolo* words in two lines ("fingono," "mentono," "sentono"). The tag-line serves as both a concise dénouement ("there's more to be said") and a re-acknowledgment of the audience ("but everyone – including you, my listeners – know this already").

Together, the succession of images and the end-oriented structure create a more dynamic – or less "stylized" – effect than Sandrino's text; Da Ponte no doubt wanted to maintain some of the immediacy of both "Se vuol ballare" and "Non più andrai." The verse rhythms are crucial to this effect. The first two stanzas are set in *settenario*, a more flexible meter than the *senario* deployed by Casti, which allows Da Ponte to break the stress pattern in the second line, before reverting to the initial pattern to conclude:[42]

42 Also noted by Webster ("Analysis," p. 137).

> Aprite‿un po' quegli‿occhi (accents on 2 and 6)
> Uomini‿incauti,‿e schiocchi, (1 and 6)
> Guardate queste femmine, (2 and 6)
> Guardate cosa son. (2 and 6)

Only the key words are accented: "aprite," "uomini," "femmine" (the sole *sdrucciolo* word). "Guardate," the most important word in the stanza, appears twice at the beginning of lines, and is accented both times. Most poets would have matched the second stanza to the first, but Da Ponte again shifts the accents:

> Queste chiamate Dee (accents on 1 and 6)
> Dagli‿ingannati sensi, (2 and 6)
> A cui tributa‿incensi (2 and 6)
> La debole ragion. (2 and 6)

With Figaro's catalog in stanza 3 the verse locks into the more predictable rhythmic pattern of *senario*. But here as well Da Ponte maintains the pace: *versi sdruccioli* alternate first with *versi tronchi* (stanza 3) and then with *versi piani* (stanza 4), effective rhythmic preparation for the rhymed couplets (first *piani*, then *sdruccioli*) of the final stanza. The text of "Aprite un po'" builds inexorably to a climax: from a summons to attention and a bitter attack or self-recrimination (stanzas 1 and 2), to evocative descriptions (stanzas 3 and 4), an extended outburst (stanza 5), and the brief dénouement (stanza 6).

Mozart's setting suggests that he took pains to distinguish "Aprite un po'" from Figaro's other angry response to a perceived betrayal, "Se vuol ballare." Throughout "Se vuol ballare," Figaro keeps his fury tightly reined; his first vocal phrase, for example, is all the more menacing in its slow ascent to f^1, a goal carefully obtained by degrees. "Aprite un po'," however, begins with a barely controlled rush of invective, a driven antecedent-consequent that leads to an impatient chromatic ascent (mm. 34–35) in order to achieve closure:

Text	Material	Harmony (in I)
1	a	I
2	b	I–V^7
3	a'	V^7
4	C+ext.	V^7–I+V^2–I, chromatic ascent

Following this tonic paragraph Figaro moves immediately to the dominant ("Se vuol ballare" employs a more leisurely transition), and establishes the new key area with a vigorous dotted rhythm similar to the analogous spot in "Se vuol ballare" (mm. 31–32; compare Aprite un po'," mm. 37–38); yet the closing cadential phrase of the dominant paragraph is reminiscent not of Figaro as dancing master but of Bartolo's grandiose "La vendetta," especially in the orchestral accompaniment (mm. 5–13; compare "Aprite un po'," mm. 44–48).

In his earlier arias, Figaro demonstrates an awareness of form as a rhetorical tool – whether the calculated and dramatic return to the restrained introductory phrase of "Se vuol ballare," or the "evolving" rondo of "Non più andrai," which suggests Cherubino's approaching manhood.[43] Although Figaro doesn't entirely lose his grasp in "Aprite un po'" – the set piece never descends to tonal meandering – its loose formal structure comes closer to that of a buffa aria than do any of Figaro's other arias. Following short paragraphs in the tonic and dominant, the body of the aria consists of free tonal space for Figaro's patter, which unobtrusively returns to the tonic in midstream. Although the tonic has already been achieved, a "retransition" follows, modulating first to the dominant and then preparing for a more formal "tonal return," which essentially repeats the patter litany (see Figure 9.3).[44]

"Aprite un po'" preserves some of the rhetorical brilliance of "Se vuol ballare" and "Non più andrai." Yet the aria also conveys

---

43 On "Se vuol ballare" see Rabin, "Dramaturgy of Opera Buffa," pp. 381–85; on "Non più andrai" as a rondo, James Webster, "To Understand Verdi and Wagner We Must Understand Mozart," *19CM* 11 (1987), 181.

44 Platoff ("The Buffa Aria," 113–16) situates the tonal return in m. 49.

Figure 9.3 "Aprite un po'"

Section	Tonic paragraph	Dominant paragraph
Measure	24	37
Text	1–4	5–8
Material	A	A'
Key	I	V

Section	Body	Body
Measure	49	57
Text	9–16	17–27
Material	Neutral (a–c)	Patter
Key	V $\longrightarrow$ I	I

Section	"Retransition"
Measure	71
Text	1–4
Material	Neutral
Key	$\longrightarrow$ V I/V I$^\text{V}$

Section	"Tonal return"		Coda
Measure	77	85	102–11
Text	9, 11, 13, 15, +26	17–27	27
Material	Neutral (rep.)	Patter	Horn calls
Key	I	I	I

Figaro's readiness to embrace the low rhetoric of a *primo buffo*; it suggests the danger of his becoming the part rather than simply playing it. Spontaneity and exhibition are poised in uneasy equilibrium. The first time Figaro, spurred by anger and despair, produces his litany of images, we might be impressed at his verbal virtuosity; when he repeats it nearly verbatim (adding in asides, "Il resto nol dico") the utterance borders on caricature. Figaro's rhetoric here is both characteristic, and at the same time (and thus unlike Sandrino's aria) contorted to fit the shape of a conventional aria type. The drama of "Aprite un po'" arises from this tension.

III

Romantic aesthetics continue to influence the way we view the Mozart-Da Ponte operas. The valorization of organic unity, the orientation toward what is taken as naturalism and realism, and the assumption that great works of art always violate or transcend conventions are just some of the precepts that we have inherited from the previous century. As research continues into opera buffa in Mozart's Vienna, no doubt many of the old assumptions – that operas are "in" a key, that drama takes place primarily in realistic "action" arias and ensemble numbers, that sonata form is an ideal vehicle for conveying drama – will be abandoned.[45] Instead of developing a post-Romantic aesthetic framework, we might think about opera buffa in light of earlier views on art and convention. Before nineteenth-century writers constructed an opposition between convention and the individual, eighteenth-century theorists contrasted convention with universal nature. The arts were valued "as the product of human right reason in conformity with natural law and opposed to what man does merely willfully, arbitrarily, and habitually."[46] Thus the distinction between what eighteenth-century critics called "the rules" and what the Romantics called "conventions." The shift in terminology reflects the difference between a system understood to embody universal principles and one based only on general agreement; the new terminology "parallels the transition in political thought from natural law to the Rousseauistic doctrine of social contract."[47]

In the eighteenth century, the rules were still regarded as natural. But with the pragmatic orientation of neoclassical aesthetics – the belief that art was primarily a means to the end of pleasing and instructing an audience – the rules also functioned as a set of precepts for accomplishing a task; "emphasis on the rules and maxims of an art is native to all criticism that grounds itself in the demands of an audience."[48] The dual nature of the rules is expressed in the idea of the "individualized type." In depicting a

45 Many of these issues are addressed in Webster, "Myth of Musical Unity."
46 Manley, *Convention*, p. 10. On Aristotle's application of the same method to physical science, ethics, argument, and the arts, see Joseph Margolis, "Genres, Laws, Canons, Principles," in *Rules and Conventions*, ed. Mette Hjort (Baltimore: The Johns Hopkins University Press, 1992), pp. 130–66, especially pp. 130–37.
47 Levin, "Notes on Convention," p. 72.
48 M. H. Abrams, *The Mirror and the Lamp: Romantic Theory and the Critical Tradition* (1953, rpt. New York: Norton, 1958), p. 17.

character, the artist was obliged to express the essence of a type of human nature – in part because such a view of human character was in accordance with universal nature, in part because the artist would reflect the familiar and typical, both engaging the audience and ensuring the social relevance of the work. By creating the "individualized type," artists could simultaneously express what was common to the human experience while using their gifts to make the familiar and universal seem new and powerful.[49]

Aria types in opera buffa may be understood in the context of the "individualized type." On one hand, aria types offer a familiar framework for the listener: the recurrences of certain keys, scorings, meters, rhythmic *topoi*, and other parameters suggest common bases for comparing sentiments or arguments. On the other hand, the rhetoric of the character allows for individualized expression within this essentially fixed structure. In such a system an aria can be at once conventional and individual. In Sandrino's "Voi semplici amanti," this is accomplished by adjoining two distinct aria types – a lyric number and a low-comic number – to convey the character's debasement. In Figaro's "Aprite un po'," convention and rhetoric are more closely interwoven. The aria demonstrates just how easily Figaro's style of rhetoric can shade into the low style of a Bartolo. But Figaro's rhetoric is so distinctive – so individual – that even at his lowest, most conventional moment, he never ceases to be Figaro.

49 This paragraph is based on Abrams, *The Mirror and the Lamp*, pp. 38–42.

The alternative endings of Mozart's *Don Giovanni*

Michael F. Robinson

Of all Mozart's operatic finales none has drawn more criticism than the second-act finale of *Il dissoluto punito o sia il Don Giovanni*. The fault, if such it can be called, occurs in the last "scene" embracing the action following Don Giovanni's descent into hell. Having sorted out their marital and other affairs in a matter-of-fact way as though Don Giovanni's demise is good riddance to bad rubbish, the other characters conclude by taking the high moral ground in their tutti "Questo è il fin di chi fa mal." Julian Rushton says modern audiences may find this ending too neat, "a trivialization of the action."[1] Michael Beckerman calls the scene "somewhat hollow."[2] Successive critics, according to Wye Allanbrook, have found it "woefully inappropriate."[3]

If the scene is not up to the dramatic level of the rest of the finale, perhaps it should be removed. It was commonly cut in nineteenth-century productions. Nowadays it seldom is. Interestingly there is evidence that the composer and Da Ponte themselves intended to cut it at the time of the Vienna production in 1788. The 1788 Vienna libretto ends with Don Giovanni's death and with the other characters coming on just in time to witness it and to cry out in horror. The final scene is not there. Da Ponte was then official theatre poet and responsible for the printing of all librettos for the Burgtheater. It is hardly conceivable he would have authorized this version believing (at the time of printing at least) it was not to be performed that way.[4] Mozart abetted this ending by adding to his

---

1 Julian Rushton, *W. A. Mozart: "Don Giovanni"* (Cambridge: Cambridge University Press, 1981), p. 65.
2 Michael Beckerman, "Mozart's Duel with Don Giovanni," *MJb*, 1984–85, p. 14.
3 Wye J. Allanbrook, "Mozart's Happy Endings: A new Look at the 'Convention' of the 'Lieto Fine,'" *MJb*, 1984–85, p. 2.
4 I am grateful to Dorothea Link for confirming that Lorenzo Da Ponte was responsible for the publishing of librettos for the Burgtheater in 1788.

autograph, at some point in time, a full vocal chord in m. 596 on which the characters sing the syllable "Ah."[5] This is their cry of horror as they enter to see Don Giovanni disappearing. The fact that Mozart later crossed this chord out may be held to mean that he came to think this ending ineffective and that the last scene was not cut in 1788. However the intention of composer and librettist at some point in time to cut it seems clear.[6]

The fact that there are two alternative endings, both of which have been found more or less acceptable at different periods, has led modern commentators to consider the aesthetic qualities of each. In essence the arguments in support of one or other are as follows. If the opera ends with Don Giovanni's descent into hell, into which he plunges in spectacular fashion, his death and his behavior at the time are the audience's last and most vivid impression. In this circumstance "he becomes the hero, an object of awe and admiration."[7] This is also the ending likely to lead the imagination to dwell on man's irrationality and on his capacity to self-destruct – fascination with this aspect of the story may be one reason why nineteenth-century audiences preferred this ending to the other. The second alternative, the one that retains the final scene, ties the various dramatic loose ends more effectively together. It produces a calmer, more rational atmosphere. The spotlight moves from Don Giovanni to the other characters who react to his death by resolving their affairs in a reasonable way and by proclaiming in the tutti the lesson to be learned.[8] This close obeys the convention that a comic opera should terminate with a *lieto fine*, a happy finish.

---

5 See *NMA*, 11/5/17, xii–xiii.

6 Kunze, *Don Giovanni*, p. 56, also holds that Mozart thought of cutting the last scene.   7 Beckerman, "Mozart's Duel," p. 14.

8 Sabine Henze-Döhring, *Opera Seria, Opera Buffa und Mozarts "Don Giovanni,"* Laaber: Laaber, 1986 (*AnM*. 24), p. 251, argues that the final scene completes the span of action started by the act II sextet "Sola sola, in buio loco." The various characters wronged by Don Giovanni vow in the sextet to fight for justice. If the last scene of the finale were not there, she maintains, they would not have the opportunity to establish for themselves that their ambition is fulfilled.

Preoccupation with the aesthetic quality of the two endings has drawn attention away from the fact that both obey the structural procedures of a 1780s finale. It is the prime purpose of this article to review some of these procedures, and coincidentally to improve awareness of the options available to Mozart and Da Ponte when they came to create the last finale of a comic opera – and a comic opera on the subject of *Don Giovanni* in particular. This means examining the conventions affecting the final scenes both of comic opera in general in Vienna in Mozart's time and of particular settings of the *Don Giovanni* story prior to Mozart's (some seen in Vienna but others not), and seeing the extent to which the conventions are followed regardless of which ending is used.

What of the atmosphere generated by the two endings? That the final scene with its relatively "happy" denouement for the characters on stage is in the eighteenth-century tradition no one would deny. It is less easy to square the shortened ending with that tradition, for it is commonly associated with nineteenth-century interpretations of the opera which overlay the comedy with "Romantic" gloom and doom. Even to suggest that Mozart sanctioned the shortened version may be unacceptable to some, because of the possible implication that the composer had a "Romantic" view of the subject. In fact, as this article will make clear, there is a case for saying that eighteenth-century audiences would not have found the shortened, "tragic" close unconventional. The mistake is to imagine, against all the evidence, that any eighteenth-century opera that was officially "comic" had to end as comedy. This is nowhere more so than in the case of operas on the *Don Giovanni* story.

Both acts of an Italian comic opera of the 1780s–90s ended with a large, multi-sectional finale in which the large majority of the characters participated. This was indeed more than a convention; it was the rule. Da Ponte in an often-quoted passage refers to the necessity of bringing all characters on stage during a finale: "And if the plot of the play does not allow of it, then the poet must find a way to make it do so, in despite of good sense and reason and all the

Aristotles on earth."[9] Had he wished, Da Ponte could have invoked Aristotle's name again to make a crucial distinction between first-act and second-act finales. For while the finale in the first act left the plot unresolved, so that the drama could continue, that in the second contained the denouement. This involved use of what Aristotle called "peripeteia," that moment towards the end of a drama where there occurs a drastic change of fortune – usually the result of the discovery of new knowledge. Aristotle's own example of peripeteia is the arrival of the messenger in Sophocles' *Oedipus the King*.[10] One should remember that although Aristotle mentioned peripeteia specifically in relation to tragedy, Italian dramatists of the Renaissance onwards who were influenced by his writings employed peripeteia in all spheres of drama, comedy and comic opera included. Obviously the most suitable moment for a peripeteia was near the end of the final act, which in the case of comic opera before *c.* 1780 meant Act III. In third acts the moment of peripeteia and the subsequent denouement were commonly set as simple recitative. When however the number of acts of comic opera contracted from three to two, as happened in the 1780s,[11] the peripeteia and denouement necessarily shifted to the end of the second act, which already by custom had a large finale. For the first time therefore they were no longer set as recitative but as part of a large, lyrical ensemble.

The final tutti, also incorporated into the second-act finale in the 1780s, had an equally ancient ancestry. It can be traced back through Renaissance tragedies and pastoral plays ultimately to Sophoclean drama, which ended with a choral commentary. The appearance of choral commentaries at the end of late sixteenth-century pastorals (exemplified by Tasso's *Aminta* and Guarini's *Il pastor fido*) is particularly important, since early opera developed from the pastoral

9 *Memoirs of Lorenzo Da Ponte, Mozart's Librettist*, trans. L. A. Sheppard (London: Routledge, 1929), p. 114.   10 *Poetics*, 1452.[a-b]

11 Included in the general category of two-act operas are also operas in four acts, like *Le nozze di Figaro*, that end with a large finale. Single-act operas may also end with a large finale.

genre. For a variety of reasons it is worth while quoting the final
chorus of Guarini's play. The "pair" cited are the lovers Mirtillo and
Amarilli, who after many trials and tribulations receive permission
to marry in the closing pages.

> Oh fortunata coppia,
> Che pianto ha seminato e riso accoglie!
> Con quante amare doglie
> Hai raddolciti tu gli affetti tuoi!
> Quinci imparate voi,
> O ciechi e troppo teneri mortali,
> I sinceri diletti e i veri mali.
> Non è sana ogni gioia,
> Né mal ciò che v'annoia.
> Quello è vero gioire,
> Che nasce da virtù dopo il soffrire.

[O happy pair, who have shed tears and welcome laughter! How you
have softened your joys with sadness! So, blind and tender mortals, learn
[the difference between] true delights and falsehoods. Not every joy is
wholesome, nor is everything that annoys evil. True joy is what springs
from virtue after suffering.][12]

12 Battista Guarini, *Il pastor fido*, ed. J. H. Whitfield, Edinburgh Bilingual Library
   (Austin, 1979), p. 410; my translation. Comments by eighteenth-century writers on
   how a drama should finish are few and far between. However Francesco Saverio
   Quadrio, *Della Storia e della Ragione d'ogni Poesia*, Milan, vol. 3, part 2 (1744), pp.
   394–95, has this to say about the final chorus of Guarini's *Il pastor fido*:

   L'Epicharma [Ἐπίχαρμα], che vale quasi *Congratulazione*, non si dee
   considerare, come parte distinta dal Coro, ma è il Coro stesso, che come nelle
   Tragedie lugubri faceva il Commo, o Pianto, così nelle Favole di fine lieto si
   congratula, e allegrasi. Questo Epicharma fu anch'esso da alcuni Italiani nelle lor
   Pastorali usitato, come dal Guarini nel suo *Pastorfido* [*sic*]: poichè quel Coro, con
   cui termina la sua Favola, il quale incomincia, *O fortunata Coppia*, è propriamente
   un Epicarma [*sic*].

   (Epicharma . . . which almost means the same as *Celebration*, should not be
   considered as something different from the [end] chorus, but is itself the chorus.
   Just as [the end chorus] in sorrowful tragedies made the Commos, or song of
   lamentation, so in plays with a happy ending it celebrates and rejoices. This
   Epicharma was used by many Italians in their pastorals, including Guarini in his
   Pastor fido: for the chorus commencing *O fortunata Coppia*, which ends his play,
   is exactly an Epicharma.)

Guarini's play was standard reading in European literary circles until well into the nineteenth century. J. H. Whitfield has calculated that over forty editions of the text were printed in Europe between 1780 and 1820 alone.[13] The general message of the pastoral was thus very well known too: true joy is acquired only through a state of being virtuous, and becoming virtuous is acquired only through suffering. Nowhere is this message more clearly pronounced than in Guarini's final chorus. The same message was proclaimed time and again by eighteenth-century Italian dramatists of the Arcadian movement, and especially by Pietro Metastasio, the imperial *poeta cesareo*, whose "serious" opera librettos dramatize the heartaches of royal and imperial heroes as they are put under stress to behave virtuously, though their base inclinations prompt them to do otherwise.

Final choruses (or tuttis as I shall henceforth call them) of Italian eighteenth-century comic opera were as much derived from the pastoral as those of serious opera.[14] It cannot be said that the typical Metastasian tutti is strong in didactic content; most of his texts end with generalized statements about love and happiness. But there was even less incentive for librettists to finish comic operas with a strong moral message; comic opera, after all, was meant to be amusing. So the pastoral message was in comic opera very watered down. Vague echoes of the pastoral idea may be read in the third and fourth lines of Da Ponte's tutti to *Così fan tutte*:

Quadrio's definition of "Epicharma" [Ε'πίχαρμα] as celebration might make it a suitable term for the final "happy" choruses and tuttis of eighteenth-century comic opera. My slight reluctance to use the term in the comic-opera context stems from the definition of Epicharma in Henry George Liddell's and Robert Scott's *A Greek–English Lexicon*, new edn. (Oxford, 1940), p. 672, as "malignant joy" or "object of malignant joy." (Author's note)

13 *Il pastor fido*, p. 29.

14 There was no firm convention in the seventeenth century that an Italian opera should end with an ensemble or chorus. Many seventeenth-century operas finish with a duet or even with a solo aria. Why a concluding ensemble or chorus became *de rigueur* in all but a few *opere serie* after about 1700 requires investigation.

Fortunato l'uom che prende
Ogni caso pel buon verso
E tra i casi e le vicende
Da ragion guidar si fa. [italics added]

. . .

[Happy is the man who looks at everything on the right side *and through*
trials and tribulations makes reason his guide . . .][15]

But nine out of ten comic operas produced in Vienna in the 1780s
finish with tuttis of quite vacuous content that consists merely of
expressions of general rejoicing. The librettists' intention seems to
have been to express some joyful consensus of view that will send
an audience happily away from the theatre. Particularly revealing in
this respect is a comparison of the ending of Da Ponte's libretto of
Il pastor fido, based on Guarini's play and produced with Salieri's
music in Vienna in 1789, with Guarini's original. Da Ponte's plot is
simpler than Guarini's. The very trite tutti, which avoids all
mention of suffering, reads:

Selvaggio, Dorinda, Mirtillo, Amarilli	Vieni, o caro / cara a chi t'adora!
	Sia felice il nostro amor!
Tutti	O che coppie fortunate!
	Che felice genitor!
	A celebrar si vada,
	Sì fausto avvenimento;
	Suonin le vie d'Arcadia
	D'insolito contento;
	E tutte l'alme esultino
	In lor felicita! [*sic*].

[Come, dearest, to the one who adores you. May our love be happy! Oh
what happy couples! What a happy father! Let us go and celebrate such a
joyful event. Make the paths of Arcadia resound with perfect
contentment, and let every soul rejoice in their happiness.][16]

15 Translation [by Lionel Salter] from the libretto to Mozart, *Così fan tutte*
     (Deutsche Grammophon 2709–059. Polydor International GMb H, 1975).
16 The differences between Guarini's and Da Ponte's final lines occur in spite of Da
     Ponte's avowal printed at the end of his libretto (issued "Nella Imper. Stamperia
     dei Sordi, e Muti," Vienna, 1789):

Among the obvious exceptions to the observation that eighteenth-century comic opera ends in a mood of joyous celebration
are the works based on the subject of *Don Giovanni*.[17] These are
really black comedies, and they create a paradox. Although
officially "comic" their message is severer than the one customarily
found in contemporary serious and pastoral operas that dramatize
salvation through suffering. There is no salvation for the hero here.
Their last tuttis point out in unequivocal terms that the fate of Don
Giovanni is eternal damnation. Two quotations from tuttis will
suffice to reveal the substance of the *Don Giovanni* message, the first
from *Il convitato di pietra*, words by Pietro Pariati and music by
Giuseppe Calegari, produced in Venice in 1777:

Sorge ormai nel ciel l'aurora,
E rivolta a noi tremando
All'aspetto si scolora
Dell'Averno, e palpitando

Avendo io tratto questo Dramma dalla famosa Opera del C. [*sic*] GUARINI ho
cercato di lasciare, quant'ho potuto i versi stessi dell'Autore per non defraudare
il Pubblico di tutte quelle grazie e squisitezze ond'e [*sic*] ripiena quell'Opera.

[Having taken this drama from the famous work of C. [*sic*] GUARINI I have
tried, in so far as possible, to leave intact the author's own lines, so as not to
defraud the public of the many graces and subtleties found so plentifully in that
work.]

17 The most recent study of plays and operas on the subject of *Don Giovanni*
produced prior to October 1787, when Mozart's opera appeared, is by Charles C.
Russell, *The Don Juan Legend before Mozart* (Ann Arbor: UMI Research Press,
1993). It includes full texts of the following operas: *La pravità castigata* (music by
Eustachio Bambini, Brno, 1734), *Il convitato di pietra o sia Il dissoluto* (words by
Nunziato Porta, music by Vincenzo Righini, Prague, 1776), *Il convitato di pietra*
(words by Pietro Pariati, music by Giuseppe Calegari, Venice, 1777), *Il convitato di
pietra* (words by Giambattista Lorenzi, music by Giacomo Tritto, Naples, 1783), *Il
nuovo convitato di pietra* (words by Giuseppe Maria Foppa, music by Francesco
Gardi, Venice, 1787), and *Il capriccio drammatico* (words by Giovanni Bertati,
music by various composers, Venice, 1787) of which *Don Giovanni o sia Il convitato
di pietra* (music by Giuseppe Gazzaniga) forms Part II. From these it is possible to
study how different librettists treated Don Giovanni's fall. The book also
contains excerpts of the text of *Il Don Giovanni* (text based on Nunziato Porta's,
music by Gioacchino Albertini, ?1780).

A further opera on the same subject is *Il convitato di pietra* (text based on
Lorenzi's libretto, music by Vincenzo Fabrizi, Rome, 1787).

Mostra forse il nuovo dì.
Ma da notte sì terribile
Chiaro resta a noi visibile
Come un empio il Ciel punì.

[The dawn rises in the sky. Discoloured by [the fires of] hell, it turns to us, who are quaking at the sight, and timidly reveals the new day to us. But of the [preceding] night we still have the clear image how heaven punished an evil one.][18]

The second is from *Il convitato di pietra*, words by Giambattista Lorenzi and music by Giacomo Tritto first produced in Naples in 1783:

Ah! che il cor mi trema in petto!
Ahi! qual giel mi cadde sopra!
Ecco il fin di chi mal opra,
Ecco il Cielo che sà far.

[Ah how my heart trembles in my breast! Ah what ice descends upon me! This is the end of whoever exercises evil. This is how heaven acts.][19]

The similarity between Lorenzi's third line "Ecco il fin di chi mal opra" and Da Ponte's line "Questo è il fin di chi fa mal" is obvious, and raises the question whether Da Ponte knew the Lorenzi libretto. No question arises though as to which tradition the Da Ponte tutti follows. Hardly surprisingly its lineage may be traced to previous operas on the *Don Giovanni* theme.

The time has now come to look at Da Ponte's finale text itself. It is already clear that among the structural features of this piece he had to arrange for (1) a peripeteia, (2) a consequent unraveling of the plot, and (3) an end tutti expressing some consensus view among the characters. His choice of incident serving as peripeteia was the same as that of practically all dramatists who had previously used the theme: the appearance of the stone guest in response to Don Juan/Don Giovanni's invitation to dinner. Subsequent incidents, however, had to be carefully considered.

---

18 Russell, *The Don Juan Legend*, p. 275.   19 Ibid., p. 326.

Nearly every version of the *Don Giovanni* story involves the death of the hero and his descent into hell. Some spoken dramas on the subject place this event at the very end in the presence of a minimum number of onlookers. Molière's *Don Juan ou Le Festin de pierre* is a good example. An opera however could not end in precisely this way because of the need for a final tutti. Without several characters or a chorus present the tutti could not be sung.

Most librettists kept to the tradition of letting Don Giovanni die in front of the stone guest and one or two human witnesses, so they needed to bring the other characters back afterwards for the tutti.[20] Da Ponte followed this tradition too. How then was his action to close? One solution discovered by his predecessors was to create a spectacular vision of hell into which the hero has fallen and in which he is seen surrounded by devils. In the Pariati/Calegari and Lorenzi/Tritto works mentioned earlier the surviving mortals watch him suffering below and comment accordingly in their tutti. A similar vision appears at the end of *Il convitato di pietra, o sia il dissoluto*, produced in Prague in 1776 and Vienna in 1777 with words by Nunziato Porta and music by Vincenzo Righini. In this case though the chorus of devils takes over the function of the tutti, as none of Don Giovanni's earthly companions is present.[21]

The other solution was pioneered by Giovanni Bertati in his one-act *Don Giovanni o sia il convitato di pietra*, set to music by Giuseppe Gazzaniga and premiered in Venice in carnival time 1787. Put simply, he omitted the vision and let the surviving characters finish the action on their own. Da Ponte did the same. Hell manifests itself in both their texts, but only in the scene leading to the hero's fall. In the Bertati finale non-singing demons appear on stage at the moment of his death and accompany him below. In the Da Ponte finale an invisible chorus of demons chants "Tutto a tue colpe è

20 *Il nuovo convitato di pietra*, words by Francesco Gardi and music by Giuseppe Maria Foppa (Venice, carnival 1787), seems the one and only *Don Giovanni* opera to terminate with the death scene.

21 Gluck's ballet *Don Juan ou Le Festin de pierre*, produced in Vienna in 1761, also ends with the furies tormenting Don Juan in hell.

poco / Vieni c'è un mal peggior" ("All sins are small compared to yours. Come, there is yet worse for you") just before Don Giovanni disappears. Once Don Giovanni dies, however, all hellish apparitions cease. Left to their own devices Bertati's characters sing a "happy" tutti (unusual in an opera on this subject) in which, in such delight at the removal of Don Giovanni that they seem half-crazed, they imitate the sounds of musical instruments. Da Ponte's finish with a "moral" tutti, which, as we have seen, is more in the tradition of *Don Giovanni* tuttis over-all.

The important point to recognize is that, by choosing the less "tragic" solution, Da Ponte also chose the less spectacular. Had he concluded his libretto with the vision, he would have created opportunity for maximum stage spectacle at the end of the finale rather than in the middle of it (the scene of Don Giovanni's downfall). And he would have kept the spotlight on the hero at the close. These are actually the conditions that apply in the *shortened* version of his and Mozart's opera.

Before tackling musical aspects of the case, we should perhaps deal with the question whether, if the last scene is cut from performances of Mozart's *Don Giovanni*, the convention of the final tutti is ignored. In fact it can be said to have been obeyed, but only up to a point. Some may argue that the shorter alternative does not, and cannot, contain a tutti because Leporello is the only human left on stage at the final curtain. But there is a subterranean chorus singing "Tutto a tue colpe è poco" just before Don Giovanni disappears. And given that tuttis were sometimes sung by a chorus rather than by the soloists, it is possible to say that Mozart's chorus serves – just about – in this capacity. This is although it is in the background and is barely heard in many performances.

Cutting the last scene certainly blocks half the "unraveling of the plot." Don Giovanni's death is not affected, but how the others will resolve their affairs afterward remains uncertain if the curtain falls immediately after it occurs. The advantage of bringing on all the characters to witness his downfall – the device intended to be used by Da Ponte and Mozart at one time (see the Viennese 1788 libretto) is that we are assured they at least know it has happened. The fact that, in the original and longer version of the finale, they do not come on in time to see his demise is the one sure sign that librettist and composer had not already thought through the possibility that the work could end at this point. Had Da Ponte brought on the other characters a few seconds earlier, he might well have strengthened the shorter ending and almost made the longer one redundant. I say "almost," for the fate of the other characters would still be uncertain. Da Ponte could have introduced a scene earlier in the opera in which they discuss what they would do in the event of Don Giovanni's death. But if the intervention of hell was to retain its shock value, he could not forewarn them of it or indicate in advance what difference this might make to their behavior.

The music at the end of the shortened version is not *lieto*. But what about at the end of the longer? What interpretation are we to put on Mozart's setting of "Questo è il fin di chi fa mal"? His indication of Presto, his choice of D major and the predominantly diatonic style, the trills and sparkling eighth-note patterns of the accompaniment, induce many performers nowadays to interpret the music as one more expression of the normal joyousness of comic endings. Perhaps their view is correct. It means that Mozart played safe and put the happiest gloss on the *Don Giovanni* story. The one curious feature of this tutti is its semi-fugato opening; Donna Anna and Donna Elvira state the subject "Questo è il fin," etc., Zerlina repeats it in the dominant like a fugal answer, then Masetto and Leporello recommence it in the tonic – though it is this time modified. That is all the fugato there is. But why have a fugato at all? None of the tuttis to Mozart's other comic operas starts this way, and none written at the time by Salieri and Martín y Soler, his main composer contemporaries in Vienna, does either. There is no way of knowing whether Mozart attached any extra-musical significance to it. But it is worth noting that two other operas premiered in Vienna between 1784 and 1786 have tuttis with semi-contrapuntal beginnings, and both these tuttis have "other-than-happy" texts. Mozart's start, though apparently joyful, could be a commentary on his also "other-than-happy" message.

The two operas in question are Giovanni Paisiello's *Il re Teodoro in Venezia*, produced to Giambattista Casti's words in August 1784, and Stephen Storace's *Gli equivoci*, produced to Da Ponte's words in December 1786.[22] The tuttis of both works start with imitation, as Mozart's does. Both contain fast patter in the upper stringed accompaniment. The technical difference in the imitation is that whereas Mozart's voices enter alternately tonic-dominant, Paisiello's and Storace's enter all in the tonic (i.e. the voices' initial entries sound like the start of a canon). Casti's libretto is about a dethroned King Teodoro who lives in exile beyond his means and is thrown into prison for debt. At the end of the opera the other characters, instead of arranging for his happy release, leave him in prison with the following, rather cynical farewell:

Come una ruota è il mondo,
Chi in cima sta, chi in fondo,
E chi era in fondo prima,
Poscia ritorna in cima,
Chi salta, chi precipita,
E chi va in su, chi in giù.
Ma se la ruota gira
Lascisi pur girar,
Felice è chi fra i vortici
Tranquillo può restar.

[The world is like a wheel; whoever is at the top goes to the bottom, and whoever was at the bottom then goes to the top; whoever leaps falls, whoever rises descends. But if the wheel turns, let it turn. Happy is the one who can stay calm while it whirls.]

Paisiello's reaction to these words was to compose an opening motive with a long downward, then sharply upward swing – presumably inspired by the image of a wheel. The other voices then

---

22 Mozart saw *Il re Teodoro in Venezia* at least once; see Leopold's letter to Nannerl of 14 September 1784 (Mozart, *Letters*, p. 883; *Briefe*, vol. 3, p. 331).

Example 10.1 Paisiello, *Il re Teodoro*, Finale II (I-Nc Rari 3.3.2)

enter in groups creating a sort of musical "round" (see Example 10.1).

The tutti to Storace's opera, based on Shakespeare's *A Comedy of Errors*, is an elaborate one about how things are often the opposite of what they seem (see Example 10.2). It commences:

Si vede che nel mondo
S'equivoca assai spesso,
S'equivoca negli altri,
S'equivoca in se stesso.

Example 10.1 (*cont.*)

Lisetta, Belisa, Gafforio, Sandrino: The world is like a wheel; whoever is at the top goes to the bottom, and whoever was at the bottom then goes to the top; whoever leaps, falls.

[One sees that in the world one commonly makes mistakes. One is deluded about others, one is deluded about oneself.]

While musical style affects the atmosphere of a tutti, it does not create the conditions for a tutti to end an opera. The tonality chosen for the tutti is more important in this respect. One expects a last finale composed in the 1780s to have a multi-sectional structure, each section marked by a change of musical style, pace, and/or of key signature. John Platoff, in his own study of key patterns in Viennese finales, concludes that the commonest shift of key between sections is to a fifth away, less common but more dramatically striking are moves to a major or minor third away, and least common a move upward by a minor second.[23] There was no convention agreed upon by all composers about how often such shifts should occur or whether they should go more to the sharp or

23 John Platoff, "Music and Drama in the *Opera Buffa* Finale: Mozart and his Contemporaries in Vienna, 1781–1790" (PhD diss., University of Pennsylvania, 1984), pp. 22–23.

Example 10.2 Storace, *Gli equivoci*, Finale II (A-Wn K.T. 133)

Example 10.2 (*cont.*)

Tutti: One sees that in the world one commonly makes mistakes. One is deluded about others, one is deluded about oneself.

Table 10.1. *Sectional plan of Storace's* Gli equivoci *Act II finale*

Section	1	2	3	4	5	6	7	8	9
Time signature	3/4	4/4	3/4	4/4	3/4	4/4	4/4	3/4	2/2
Tempo indication	Allegro	Andante e staccato	Allegro	[recitative]	Allegro	Larghetto	Adagio quasi ad libitum	[no tempo]	Allegro assai

Key signature (A major, D major, G major, C major, F major, B♭ major, E♭ major): [graph — the graph does not indicate the relative length of each section; markings [P] = peripeteia above section 6–7, [T] = final tutti above section 9, ‖]

Notes:

The graph does not indicate the relative length of each section.

P = peripeteia

T = final tutti

flat side. All agreed however that a finale should begin and end in the same key.[24]

It is difficult to find a "typical" structure of a last finale composed in 1780s Vienna, for the form of each finale is different. Table 10.1 is a graph of the second finale of Storace's *Gli equivoci* showing the various changes of tempo and of time and key signatures within it. The complicated story of the opera concerns two sets of twin brothers, each twin being constantly confused with his double. None of them knows his brother is in the same town. This remains the situation till well into the second finale. Peripeteia occurs in

---

24 Though it is worth recording that Mozart was himself not entirely averse to giving a finale an irregular key structure. The finales to Acts I and II of his *La finta giardiniera* (1775) exceptionally begin in one key but end in another.

section 6 (Larghetto, note the effective change from D to E flat major!). Here for the first time all four come face to face, to their own and everyone else's astonishment. The other characters sort out their relationships with the twins in sections 7–8, and the tutti embraces section 9.

Storace's key changes are mostly on the flat side of the main tonality – Mozart's last-act finales also show a predilection for the flat side.[25] The detail that deserves more attention though is the return to the tonic in the middle (sections 3–5). Composers tended to avoid coming back to the tonic in the middle of a finale and then moving out of it again unless there was good reason.[26] Storace's choice of D major in sections 3–5 may have been affected by the need for trumpets (in those days generally in C or D) at the start of section 3 and by the calculation that a shift from D to E flat at the start of section 6 would be particularly effective. But what should one say about Mozart's return to the tonic minor in the middle of his *Don Giovanni* finale? He avoids the tonic (major or minor) in the middle of the last finales to *Le nozze di Figaro* and *Così fan tutte*, so what is the advantage of it here?

The plan of the last finale of *Don Giovanni* is shown in Table 10.2. The music veers to the flat side of the tonic (D major) during the three short wind serenades (sections 2–4) and remains so until the entry of the stone guest at the start of section 7, when the tonality returns to D (though this time to D minor, not D major). Throughout the dramatic episode between the stone guest, Don Giovanni, and Leporello (sections 7–9), the key remains officially D

25 Whether the music concentrates on the flat rather than the sharp side partly depends on the choice of tonic. The tonality of D major invites moves to the flatter keys more obviously than the tonality of E flat. Mozart's last finales of *Le nozze di Figaro* and *Don Giovanni* are both centered on D; that of *Così fan tutte* on C. The *Così fan tutte* finale is the only one of the three to exploit tonalities on the sharp side of the home key.

26 Few last finales in operas written for 1780s Vienna contain middle sections in the tonic. The last finales of Storace's *Gli sposi malcontenti* (produced June 1785), Martín y Soler's *Il burbero di buon cuore* (produced January 1786), and Salieri's *La cifra* (produced December 1789) have this feature. None offers the performers a suitable choice of alternative ending.

Table 10.2. *Sectional plan of Mozart's Don Giovanni Act II finale*

Section	1	2	3	4	5	6	7	8	9	10	11	12
Time signature	4/4	6/8	3/4	2/2	3/4	2/2	2/2	2/2	2/2	3/4	2/2	2/2
Tempo indication	Allegro vivace	[no tempo]	[no tempo]	[no tempo]	Allegro assai	Molto allegro	Andante	Più stretto	Allegro	Allegro assai	Larghetto	Presto

Key signature:
{ D major/minor
  G major
  C major
  F major
  B♭ major }

Graph labels: [major] [P] [minor] [T] [major]

Notes:

The graph does not indicate the relative length of each section.

P = peripeteia

T = final tutti

minor, though the music is so chromatic that it is more frequently out of the key than in it. The final scene, after Don Giovanni's disappearance (sections 10–12), starts in G but returns to D major for the tutti.

The crucial point is that Mozart ends section 9, the one in which Don Giovanni falls to his death, with a cadence on the tonic major chord. Admittedly the cadence is a plagal one, with a major third that sounds more like a "Tierce de Picardie" than a confirmation that D major has supplanted D minor. Nonetheless the reappearance of the tonic major chord coincides with the climax of the action, namely the disappearance of the hero. The action can end here, and the musical convention that a finale shall begin and end in the same key is not broken if it does so. A premature, yet satisfactory (or semi-satisfactory) close to the drama coinciding with a premature return to the tonic is rare in eighteenth-century last finales. No one seems yet to have pointed to a similar case.

However there is a similar case in at least one of the earlier operas on the subject of *Don Giovanni*. Tritto's finale to *Il convitato di pietra* (Naples, 1783) is in eight musical sections, as demonstrated in Table 10.3.[27] E flat major, the tonality at the start and finish of this piece, is also the key of the central episode (sections 5–6), during which Don Giovanni and his servant Pulchinella take supper in the presence of the stone guest. Don Giovanni dies at the end of this episode. The key shifts to G major at the start of section 7, when the other characters come on demanding to know where he is. It reverts to E flat in section 8, as they watch him suffering in hell.

This does not mean that there was a tradition of making Don Giovanni die in the home key. Exclusive of Tritto's and Mozart's works, we have music of two other *Don Giovanni* operas of the 1780s with finales that advance the action beyond the death scene. These are Gazzaniga's *Don Giovanni o sia Il convitato di pietra* and Vincenzo Fabrizi's *Il convitato di pietra* (Rome, autumn 1787). In neither of

27 MS I-Nc Rari 2.5.6. I am obliged to Eugenio Ottieri for pointing out to me the interesting structure of this finale.

Table 10.3. *Sectional plan of Tritto's* Il convitato di pietra *finale*

Section	1	2	3	4	5	6	7	8
Time signature	$\frac{3}{8}$	$\frac{4}{4}$	$\frac{4}{4}$	$\frac{4}{4}$	$\frac{4}{4}$	$\frac{4}{4}$	$\frac{4}{4}$	$\frac{4}{4}$
Tempo indication	Allegro	Recitativo	Allegro	[Allegro]	Andante	Allegro	[Allegro]	[Allegro]

Notes:
P = peripeteia
T = tutti

these cases is the death scene set in the tonic.[28] It is thus not easy to say whether Mozart did or did not have a model for the key scheme that he adopted at the end of his own opera.

I have here argued that the second-act finale of Mozart's *Don Giovanni* is constructed according to normal late eighteenth-century conventions. It has a peripeteia, subsequent unraveling of the plot, and a tutti. Some of its features, for instance the downfall of the hero and the moral tone of the tutti text, seem "serious" for a supposed comedy, but these are consistent with what is found in other operas on the same subject. Mozart's unusual setting of the tutti perhaps mirrors its moral message.

Finales of the 1780s began and ended in the same key. In this respect Mozart's finale ends conventionally enough. It is more

28 Gazzaniga's opera is published as *Don Giovanni, o sia, Il convivato di pietra*, ed. Stefan Kunze (Kassel: Bärenreiter, 1974). Fabrizi's finale is in MS GB-Lbl RM 22.c.6 (3).

remarkable to find that the shortened version of this piece also ends with the tonic chord. The fact that this version has its own tutti (or token tutti) in the form of an underworld chorus adds further to the argument that it violates none of the conventions as regards the structure of a last finale.

I have also maintained that at some point Mozart and Da Ponte proposed the use of the shortened version. (Whether the finale was performed thus in Mozart's lifetime is another matter.) By cutting the last scene they were in effect raising the heroic and tragic status of Don Giovanni, and removing all trace of a so-called *lieto fine*. Beyond the fact that previous operas on the *Don Giovanni* theme had also ended with a scene highlighting the discomfort of the hero, how might Mozart and Da Ponte have argued in favor of their shortened, "tragic" alternative?

A feature of the tragic close is that it creates both a very dramatic and a very scenic finish. Don Giovanni plunges to his death while flames flicker and the earth quakes about him. Stefan Kunze has built up a theory that the scenes of hell common to most eighteenth-century *Don Giovanni* operas were popular with audiences because they were stage spectacles, not because they were tragic. For Kunze these scenes are not tragic; they are merely variants, peculiar to *Don Giovanni* settings, of the pleasurable endings common to all comic operas. Thus the alternative endings of Mozart's finale are not tragic and comic either. For Mozart,

> the alternative was not comedy or tragedy, but simply the [differing] performing conventions relating to normal comic endings and to endings suitable for operas on the subject of the stone guest, which favored theatrically effective spectacle.[29]

Mozart's shortened ending, in other words, may be black comedy, but it is still comedy.

Eighteenth-century operas on the subject of *Don Giovanni* are technically "comic" because they depict characters of several different classes; "serious" operas by comparison depict only sove-

29 Kunze, *Don Giovanni*, p. 57.

reigns and members of the nobility. But if an eighteenth-century person of good education had been asked what subcategory of comedy the various *Don Giovanni* operas came under, it is unlikely he would have replied with an expression such as "black comedy." Such a categorization appears in no eighteenth-century theory book. It is more likely he would have considered these operas to contain elements of tragedy within comedy, in other words that they were close to dramas of mixed genre. Pastoral plays were other examples of mixed genre, though the formulas were different. The death of the hero/heroine at the end of a tragic drama was supposed – here we are back to Aristotelian theory – to induce catharsis and a feeling of compassion. If the death of Don Giovanni induces a similar feeling of compassion, then there is a case for saying that Mozart's shortened ending is in eighteenth-century terms tragic and not comic.

There are other eighteenth-century operas which end with a death combined with spectacle, and these are definitely not comedies. Metastasio's *dramma per musica Didone abbandonata*, set to music by Domenico Sarro in 1724 and then by a large number of other composers, is the most obvious case. Metastasio's storyline, based on the *Aeneid*, concerns the arrival of Aeneas at Carthage, his love affair with Queen Dido, and his abandonment of her in order to fulfill his destiny, which is the founding of Rome. As the future founder of Rome he is the one whom eighteenth-century audiences would have regarded as "heroic" and "virtuous." However the manner in which he abandons her tends to shift the audience's sympathy in her direction. In the final scene, in which she finds herself alone and commits suicide in the ruins of her burning city, she becomes a genuinely tragic figure, an object of compassion and pity.

The "Dido factor," the term I use to describe the ambiguity of feeling that may result when the wrong person acquires tragic status, and thus our sympathy, by suffering a scenically horrific death on stage, is also an element in dramatizations of the *Don Giovanni* story. Don Giovanni becomes the hero, although he in no way deserves this description save by the manner of his dying. The more the treatment concentrates on his death, and on his loneliness at the time of it, the more tragic and sympathetic he becomes. It is not suggested Mozart and Da Ponte were influenced by any particular tragic opera, say a setting of *Didone abbandonata*, when they considered cutting the final scene. But they were aware of the techniques of tragic endings, and the effects to be obtained by them. It is therefore a reasonable hypothesis that they proposed the shortened alternative believing (1) its scenic and dramatic impact was greater, and (2) it produced extra sympathy for Don Giovanni as a human being. The action, after all, revolves entirely around the hero, and it might not have done for the opera to be all about an unsympathetic person!

11 | *Don Giovanni*: recognition denied
Jessica Waldoff

Of all Mozart's operas, *Don Giovanni* is the most controversial. Neither *Le nozze di Figaro*, widely acclaimed in recent times as Mozart's greatest operatic achievement, nor *Die Zauberflöte*, often regarded as his most high-minded theatre piece, has a history of literary and critical response equal to that surrounding *Don Giovanni*. In addition, the opera has become the most influential version of the myth, forever changing the character of the legendary Don Juan. With the exception of Wagner's music-dramas, no opera rivals *Don Giovanni* for its influence on the history of ideas, or for a literature as vast as it is varied. Not only music critics and composers, but playwrights, novelists, and philosophers have responded to it, including E. T. A. Hoffmann, Pushkin, Kierkegaard, George Bernard Shaw, Henry James, and John Berger. More recently, in preparation for the Mozart year 1991, the director Jonathan Miller put together a collection entitled *The Don Giovanni Book: Myths of Seduction and Betrayal*, which features essays by prominent historians and critical theorists such as Roy Porter, Robert Darnton, and Peter Gay.[1]

Why does *Don Giovanni* have such a remarkable reception history? Why does this opera hold such a special, even peculiar, fascination for musicians and audiences, for historians and critics, and for writers and thinkers of all kinds? The nature of the character himself goes a long way toward explaining this fascination, for, as Peter Conrad suggests, Don Juan holds the appeal of the archetypal character who "wants to go everywhere, and to become everyone. He is less a person than a potential."[2] Posterity's attraction to such figures alone cannot explain the tremendous influence

1 London: Faber and Faber, 1990.
2 "The Libertine's Progress," in Miller, *The Don Giovanni Book*, p. 81.

of this particular version of the popular lothario. Why Don Giovanni and not Don Juan? Why Da Ponte's and Mozart's opera and not Tirso de Molina's *El burlador de Sevilla y Convidado de piedra* (1630), Molière's *Don Juan ou Le Festin de pierre* (1655), or Goldoni's *Don Giovanni Tenorio ossia il dissoluto* (1736), or for that matter the 1787 opera of Bertati and Gazzaniga on which Da Ponte based his libretto? Why was it Mozart's *Don Giovanni* and not some other version of the legend that moved Goethe to say that Mozart, had he lived, could have composed music in the same vein for *Faust*, and inspired Shaw's vision of Don Giovanni as a "philosopher . . . in the grip of the Life Force"?[3]

I

More than any other single issue, the problem of the ending – or, to be precise, the endings – has driven the controversy about the opera and inspired much of the commentary on it.[4] As it was originally conceived and produced, following Don Giovanni's descent into

3 Goethe's oft-cited remark appears in Johann Peter Eckermann, *Gespräche mit Goethe in den letzten Jahren seines Lebens*, ed. Fritz Bergemann (Wiesbaden: Insel-Verlag, 1955), p. 293. This statement is corroborated by a letter Goethe wrote to Schiller after attending a performance of *Don Giovanni* in 1797; see *Der Briefwechsel zwischen Schiller und Goethe*, ed. Emil Staiger (Frankfurt: Insel-Verlag, 1966), p. 530. The line from Shaw appears in *Man and Superman: A Comedy and a Philosophy*, ed. Dan H. Laurence (Harmondsworth: Penguin, 1946), p. 169.

4 See Hermann Abert, *Mozart's "Don Giovanni,"* trans. Peter Gellhorn (London: Eulenburg Books, 1976), p. 128–32, who was one of the first to inveigh against the notion that the music for the *scena ultima* was unworthy of Mozart; in this he differs from his predecessor, Otto Jahn, *W. A. Mozart*, 3rd edn., ed. Hermann Dieters (Leipzig: Breitkopf and Härtel, 1889–91), vol. 2, pp. 452–54. See also Irving Singer, *Mozart & Beethoven: The Concept of Love in their Operas* (Baltimore and London: The Johns Hopkins University Press, 1977), pp. 69–73; Julian Rushton, *W. A. Mozart: "Don Giovanni,"* Cambridge Opera Handbooks (Cambridge: Cambridge University Press, 1981), pp. 64–65; Michael Beckerman, "Mozart's Duel with Don Giovanni," *MJb* 1984–85, pp. 13–15; and Stefan Kunze, *Mozarts Opern* (Stuttgart: Philipp Reclam, 1984), pp. 340–44. Wye J. Allanbrook, "Mozart's Happy Endings: A New Look at the 'Convention' of the 'lieto fine,'" *MJb* 1984–85, pp. 1–5, is of special interest. See also Michael F. Robinson, elsewhere in this volume.

Hell there is a final scene that takes the form of the traditional *lieto fine* (or happy ending), in which the other characters appear on stage to discover his fate, to comment on their own futures, and finally to join in singing a conventional *lieto fine* tutti ("Questo è il fin di chi fa mal") that proclaims the moral of the piece – that this is the just end of all sinners. But early in the performance tradition – we cannot be certain how early – this final scene was cut: the opera now ended abruptly in a spectacle of hell-fire and brimstone – that is, with a scene in D minor as opposed to D major,[5] without explanation given to the other characters, without a moral, and without the customary bow to enlightenment wisdom. More important, it ended as eighteenth-century operas – almost by definition – would never have ended: without a *lieto fine*. It was this ending, which became standard by the nineteenth century, that gave rise to the Romantic interpretations of Don Giovanni's death as transcendence, influencing writers from Hoffmann to Hildesheimer.[6] (Hoffmann's story is particularly interesting in this connection, for, despite its romantic leanings, it includes the appearance of the other characters at the end of the opera.)

These two radically different endings are reflected in the Prague and Vienna librettos of 1787 and 1788, respectively,[7] and suggest the possibility that the opera may have been performed without the final scene as early as the first Vienna production. But these librettos alone cannot solve the mystery of how the opera was actually

5 The abruptness of this ending is accentuated by the fact that the scene culminates on a "Picardy" third.

6 See Christof Bitter, *Wandlungen in den Inszenierungsformen des "Don Giovanni" von 1787 bis 1928: Zur Problematik des Musikalischen Theaters in Deutschland* (Regensburg: G. Bosse, 1961); Karin Werner-Jensen, *Studien zur "Don Giovanni"-Rezeption im 19. Jahrhundert (1800–1850)* (Tutzing: Schneider, 1980); James Parakilas, "The Afterlife of *Don Giovanni*: Turning Production History into Criticism," *JM* 8 (1990), 251–65.

7 See facsimile editions of the original librettos in Warburton, vol. 2, pp. 189–91, which includes the entire *scena ultima*, and vol. 3, p. 474, which ends with the word "Fine" immediately after the chorus of devils takes Don Giovanni below with them. See also Daniel Heartz's discussion of an earlier *Don Giovanni* libretto, which, "poorly printed and proofread, looks very much like a hasty job concocted for submission to the censors" (*Mozart's Operas*, p. 163). In this earlier libretto, the *scena ultima* takes a slightly different form (pp. 172–74).

performed at any given place or time. For one thing, the autograph shows a cut of over sixty measures within the final scene, which Alan Tyson associates with the year 1788,[8] this implies that Mozart at least considered a shortened version of the final sextet – as opposed to its removal – for the Vienna production.[9] For another, the protean variability of eighteenth-century theatre doubtless produced still other versions of the ending, not preserved by the surviving paper trail. (In the nineteenth century, for example, variations on the ending included having Don Giovanni's house fall in and having Donna Anna brought on stage in a coffin to the accompaniment of mourners singing the "Dies Irae" from Mozart's *Requiem*.)[10] Further, the question of the opera's multiple endings is not merely a matter of a near-inscrutable historical record. Even if we could know for certain that during Mozart's lifetime *Don Giovanni* was always performed – shall we say – with the final sextet and *lieto fine*, we would still have to contend with the vast literary and critical response based on the other ending.

This problem of the ending, then, needs to be put in the larger context of uncertainties around which the critical literature on *Don Giovanni* has developed. Is Don Giovanni a hero or a villain? Is the opera a comedy or a tragedy?[11] And, does the conclusion dramatize

8 Alan Tyson, "Some Features of the Autograph Score of *Don Giovanni*," *Israel Studies in Musicology* 5 (1990), 12–13. The cuts mostly concern the Larghetto for Don Ottavio and Donna Anna and seem to involve the insertion of a ten-measure bridge (folio 263) that would connect m. 689 to m. 750: see the facsimile of the autograph, *Edition princeps: W. A. Mozart, Don Giovanni, Opéra en deux actes, Facsimile in extenso du manuscrit autographe conservé à la Bibliothèque Nationale* (Paris: La Revue Musical, n.d.).
9 It is possible that the cuts in the Anna and Ottavio Larghetto (see note 8 above) in the autograph were made to accommodate Francesco Morella, who took the role of Ottavio for the Vienna production and for whom "Dalla sua pace" was written. Indeed Ottavio's tessitura in this passage is similar to "Il mio tesoro," which was cut in Vienna, presumably because Morella's voice had different tessitura and capabilities from that of Antonio Baglioni, for whom the role was originally composed. I am indebted to Paolo Gallarati for this suggestion.
10 Abert, *Mozart's "Don Giovanni,"* pp. 128–29; from Jahn, vol. 2, pp. 453–54.
11 This question was long confused with that of whether the opera is best called "dramma giocoso," as appears on the title page of the libretto, or "opera buffa,"

a moral triumph over a justly-punished sinner, or does it celebrate the heroic defiance of an independent thinker reaching out toward Nietzsche's superman? The first two issues culminate in the third, for the questions of whether Don Giovanni is villain or hero and of whether the opera is comic or serious come to a climax in the complex and powerful scene in which the Don meets his end. To deal with the ending and the other questions the opera raises, we must acknowledge not only that meaning is ambiguous, and that complexity and contradiction are inherent in works of art, but that we have a particular fascination with the indeterminacy that often haunts great works. We are drawn to great works of art that appear to be divided against themselves, works that seem to undermine the very truths they attempt to assert. This is the appeal of *Don Giovanni*.

Much of that history centers on the character of the appealing, damnable, and elusive Don Giovanni himself. Interpreters have held that he is anything from a violent and aggressive rapist to the very embodiment of human desire, anything from a sinning blasphemer to a Promethean hero. The Romantics in particular, following Hoffmann, chose to view Don Giovanni as a Faustian figure, a tragic hero whose striving against the gods is a triumphant human achievement. In this century, many critics have chosen instead to see the Don as a confusing and enigmatic figure of dual nature, a combination of what is most and least admirable in human nature.[12] The difficulties of understanding the main character only make questions of the ending and its meaning more complex and urgent – a fact that is reflected in the critical literature.

as Mozart entered the work in his thematic catalog. While the question of how to reconcile the opera's comic and serious elements remains an important one, scholars have recently shown that the terms "dramma giocoso" and "opera buffa" were virtually synonymous. See Heartz, *Mozart's Operas*, pp. 195–205; Kunze, *Don Giovanni*; Sabine Henze-Döhring, *Opera seria, opera buffa und Mozarts "Don Giovanni": Zur Gattungskonvergenz in der italienischen Oper des 18. Jahrhunderts*, AnM 26 ([Laaber]: Laaber-Verlag, 1986).

12 For example, Rushton's *W. A. Mozart: "Don Giovanni,"* pp. 65, 103–9; Kunze's *Mozarts Opern*, pp. 319–25; and Allanbrook's view of the Don as "No-Man," *Rhythmic Gesture*, pp. 207–208.

But neither the problem of the ending nor the difficulties of understanding the main character can account for the remarkable reception history of *Don Giovanni*. Nor can the claim that it is *sui generis*.[13] In keeping with current literary and historical criticism that considers art to be both product and producer of culture, we can hardly attribute the matter to the sheer quality and effect of the opera. *Don Giovanni* is great art, to be sure, but its extraordinary appeal is something more, or at least something else. For the opera, divided in its sympathies, attempts to dramatize a moral affirmation that the titanic, heroic proportions of the Don's character bring into question and challenge. The crux of the drama comes in the spectacular scene near the end of the second act in which Don Giovanni is confronted by the ghost of the Commendatore, and in which the moral truth attempts to work its miraculous recognition: Don Giovanni must repent or perish. But at this moment, recognition is denied.

I I

Although it has never been acknowledged as such, this climactic scene is a recognition scene of the kind Aristotle describes in the *Poetics*, but one in which recognition ultimately fails to bring about its expected reversal. Recognition – as Aristotle defines it – is the shift from ignorance to knowledge, and involves the protagonist (and the audience) in a powerful reversal of former understanding. The finest recognition must come in conjunction with a peripeteia (recognition, peripeteia, and pathos are Aristotle's three constituent elements of plot). The paradigmatic example is *Oedipus Rex*: Oedipus sought to avoid fulfilling the prophecy of the oracle, but at the crux of the drama a powerful recognition scene reveals his actions to have brought about the very thing he feared; recognition brings knowledge, denouement, and conclusion.

Such moments of recognition are known to be an essential feature of plots in drama, fiction, and poetry, and they are funda-

13 Alfred Einstein, *Mozart: His Character, His Work*, trans. Arthur Mendel and Nathan Broder (New York: Oxford University Press, 1945), p. 442.

mental in opera as well. Mozart's operas dramatize recognition in a variety of ways, and at the levels of both plot and theme. Several culminate in a moment of climactic recognition, after which things are forever and significantly changed; many involve the use of disguise, which must later be discovered; and all involve several scenes in which one or more characters come to some significant realization on stage. More often than not, Mozart's operas turn explicitly on themes of knowledge, a fact that is particularly important to the ways in which these operas end. As with spoken drama and fiction, the plotting of an opera toward the illumination that comes at the end is built on climactic moments of recognition and reversal, which bring about the final denouement. The dramatization of the ascendance of light in the Act II finale of *Die Zauberflöte* is perhaps the most explicit representation of this effect, but nearly every contemporary opera ends with a bow to enlightenment teachings – whether it is dramatized primarily in domestic and private terms (as in *La finta giardiniera* and *Così fan tutte*) or with public rhetoric and spectacle (as in *Idomeneo* and *Die Zauberflöte*). The conclusions of these operas, whether buffa or seria, whether Italian or German, culminate in a truth that recognition brings, not for the individual alone, but for the whole stage and the world it represents.[14]

At the ends of operas, the rulers who have abused their power (or been tempted to) learn the virtues of benevolent rule; the characters who were motivated by rage or revenge confess their feelings, and become reconciled to the world they have wronged; the young nobles who have pursued innocent young women they never intended to marry are stopped before any actual harm is done; the lovers who were unfaithful (or very nearly so) return to their partners with new commitment. For the most part, these operas seek to reform the selfish, capricious, or foolish as well as the schemers, libertines, and traitors. There are a few exceptions, of course, characters who will not be reformed or reconciled to the general good –

---

14 Jessica Waldoff, "The Music of Recognition: Operatic Enlightenment in 'The Magic Flute'," *M&L* 75 (1994), 214–35; "The Music of Recognition in Mozart's Operas," PhD diss., Cornell University, 1995.

Electra in *Idomeneo* and the Queen of the Night are especially interesting examples. But in those cases, the threat the character poses to the social and moral order is eventually removed in some other way. Indeed, in *Die Zauberflöte*, the defeat of the Queen and the darkness she represents is central to the opera's enlightenment allegory.

In contrast, when the dark and compelling Don descends through a similar trap door in an even more spectacular manner, as the opera's main protagonist he takes our sympathy and interest with him. And herein lies a crucial structural and generic problem. Don Giovanni is a most unusual protagonist in the context of late eighteenth-century opera, one who does not finally capitulate to the greater good, which must triumph in the end without him. He is a protagonist who is neither reformed nor forgiven by the end of the opera – one who refuses to embrace the enlightenment and join in the *lieto fine*.

This refusal flouts the conventions of how operas end. In late eighteenth-century opera studies the conventions governing the relation of denouement to *lieto fine* have not been codified,[15] but generally the denouement unfolds into the *lieto fine*, which culminates in – but must not be seen as restricted to – a final tutti. In the largest sense the *lieto fine* may be understood as the happy ending itself and all that goes with it: an entirely separate scene, as in *Don Giovanni*; or the aftermath of a *deus ex machina*, as in *Idomeneo*; or even the denouement itself, as in *Le nozze di Figaro*. As it is used in criticism, the term thus refers both to the fact of the happy ending and to the final celebratory tutti; the slippage lies in the term itself, and often, as in *Don Giovanni*, both senses are relevant. In what follows I distinguish between these two meanings with the words *"lieto fine"* (the happy ending) and final tutti (its culmination). The

15 See Frederick W. Sternfeld, "The Birth of Opera: Ovid, Poliziano, and the *lieto fine*," in *Studien zur Italienisch-Deutschen Musikgeschichte*, vol. 12, AnM 19 (Köln: Arno Volk Verlag, 1979), pp. 30–47; Allanbrook, *Rhythmic Gesture*, pp. 322–25; Allanbrook, "Mozart's Happy Endings"; Kunze, *Mozarts Opern*, pp. 325–30; Bernard Williams, "Mozart's Comedies and the Sense of an Ending," MT 122 (1981), 451–54.

most important concerns raised by the *lieto fine* and its tutti, however, are not those of the internal workings of the final scene alone. The *lieto fine* needs to be understood in relation to the denouement it follows and to the opera as a whole. That in *Don Giovanni* is no exception.

Don Giovanni concludes the *action* with a powerful denouement and concludes the *opera* shortly afterwards with a *lieto fine*, which culminates in a joyful tutti, the "antichissima canzon." As Wye Jamison Allanbrook has pointed out, it is quite common for *opere buffe* of this period to end with a moment of tutti affirmation that takes the form of joyous song, a moment "when music is named – when attention is drawn to the celebratory human habit of music-making."[16] *Le nozze di Figaro*, Cimarosa's *Il matrimonio segreto*, Martín y Soler's *Una cosa rara*, among many others, end in a similar manner. But in one important way the ending of *Don Giovanni* (and that of its immediate predecessor, Bertati's and Gazzaniga's *Don Giovanni Tenorio*) is fundamentally different. While ordinarily the happy ending confirms the discoveries of the opera's central climax, in this instance the *lieto fine* seems to be at odds with the opera's catastrophic denouement.

In his writings on the origins of the *lieto fine*, Frederick W. Sternfeld draws an important distinction between "the main plot, [or] the myth (favola) of the protagonists," and "the dramatic frame-work which encloses the story."[17] The *lieto fine* is of course best understood as a function of the latter; when the denouement and the *lieto fine* confirm the same human truth, as they usually do, there is no perceived conflict between convention and art. The *lieto fine* follows the denouement, reaffirming whatever knowledge the opera has dramatized, and serves as the conventional ending to a work that is all but complete without it. And thus, to modify Sternfeld slightly, the *lieto fine* is part of both the drama and the framework. As the characters sing the moral of the drama, often rejoicing among themselves in the self-conscious way Allanbrook

16 Allanbrook, "Mozart's Happy Endings," p. 3.
17 Sternfeld, "The Birth of Opera," p. 44.

describes, they also turn to face the audience, opening the opera and its conventional moral wisdom to all those present in the theatre.

But what of *Don Giovanni*, in which the denouement and subsequent *lieto fine* appear to be in conflict? As Allanbrook suggests, in the face of such problematic works, "we romantic moderns all too often make the tacit judgment that the conventions of eighteenth-century opera buffa are hollow devices – 'mere conventions.'"[18] It was in part this perception that the final sextet of *Don Giovanni* with its *lieto fine* was "mere convention" that led to its omission in the nineteenth century and, more recently, to the ongoing disputes about the dramatic integrity and function of the *scena ultima*.[19] The problem lies in the expectations one brings to bear on the conventions of ending, and especially on the relation of *lieto fine* to denouement. The *lieto fine* with its affirmation of a righteous social and human order cannot overcome the compelling sense of disorder created by the opera's denouement. But perhaps the true source of discomfort is the belief that if order is to be restored, it should be accomplished without contradiction or complication. "Comedy ends with the assertion of the proper orders," Allanbrook tells us, "but this assertion may not necessarily be the crown of a serene and sane society; it may indeed be a lid clapped on disorder and despair."[20]

Given that the legend dictates that Don Giovanni must be defeated, and bearing in mind the conventions of the *lieto fine*, any opera on the Don Juan legend is bound to be unconventional in this way. (For a discussion of the endings of other Don Juan operas, see Michael F. Robinson's essay elsewhere in this volume.) As Byron quips about the hero of his own *Don Juan*, "We have all seen him, in the pantomime, / Sent to the Devil somewhat ere his time."[21] The

---

18 Allanbrook, "Mozart's Happy Endings," p. 1.
19 See Allanbrook, *Rhythmic Gesture*, pp. 322–25, "Mozart's Happy Endings";
    Williams, "Mozart's Comedies."
20 Allanbrook, "Mozart's Happy Endings," p. 5.
21 *Don Juan*, ed. Leslie A. Marchand, Riverside Editions (Boston: Houghton Mifflin,
    1958), Canto I, verse i, p. 10.

legend itself precludes the reform of the protagonist. Indeed, such a reform seems as undesirable as it is impossible. Don Juan stories of every stripe, however different in matters of form and style, are all built on the same legend, in which an elusive and appealing libertine – after serving as the primary agent of a remarkable entertainment – is forced to pay for his sins in a spectacular scene of "pantomime devilry."[22]

Don Giovanni, as Bernard Williams puts it, "is as unambiguously and magnificently removed from despair and boredom as it is possible to be."[23] Indeed, we must assume that the exploits and excesses of the protagonist were largely responsible for the popularity of the tale. There were countless versions, from what Goldoni liked to call "the bad Spanish play" of Tirso de Molina (1630) to the plays of Goldoni, Shadwell, and Molière, to the puppet shows and burlesques of the eighteenth century, to the 1787 opera of Bertati and Gazzaniga.[24] Protagonist and audience alike could for a time enjoy the abandonment of self to pleasure – could enjoy the pleasures of a life lived outside the ordinary social and moral constraints, as long as they took place within the confines of a carefully constructed stage which, as Thomas Bauman has recently argued, was committed to the goals of "moral edification and aesthetic order" so common in eighteenth-century theatre.[25] The moral is clear in the very title of so many of the versions, *Il dissoluto punito*, "the profligate punished." The recognition that comes in the last scene is not intended for Don Giovanni; it is rather the moral of his tale, intended for the other characters and the audience.

22 Julian Rushton, *W. A. Mozart: "Don Giovanni,"* p. 6.
23 Bernard Williams, "Don Giovanni as an idea," in Rushton, *W. A. Mozart: "Don Giovanni,"* p. 81.
24 For the comment from Goldoni's *Mémoires*, see Heartz, *Mozart's Operas*, p. 161. For a study of earlier Don Juan operas see Kunze, *Don Giovanni*. For an extraordinary catalog of literary, theatrical, and other accounts of Don Juan, see Leo Weinstein, *The Metamorphoses of Don Juan* (Stanford: Stanford University Press, 1959), pp. 187–214, where he lists 490 different versions of the tale.
25 Thomas Bauman, "The Three Trials of Don Giovanni," in Peter Ostwald and Leonard Zegans, eds., *The Pleasures and Perils of Genius: Mostly Mozart*, (Madison, CT: International Universities Press, 1993), p. 143.

Yet, as I have already suggested, in damning Don Giovanni the opera's resolution attempts to dramatize a moral affirmation that his compelling if villainous character brings into question and complicates. Our identification with the protagonist is thus at odds with the central theme of the work. Don Giovanni's death is the literal dramatization of the moral given at the very end – all sinners get what they deserve – but the tremendous force of his character throughout undermines the effect of his spectacular damnation and offers a serious challenge to the recognition that comes at the end. The enlightenment morality that governs this work has met in Don Giovanni a most formidable adversary – one whose will cannot be bent, one who refuses even in the face of death to reconcile himself to the social and moral order, one who refuses to recognize any truth but his own. Just as surely as Don Giovanni is undone by the truth he denies, the truth the opera's conventional ending attempts to establish is undone by the fact that Don Giovanni refuses to acknowledge it.

III

Before turning to *Don Giovanni*'s catastrophic recognition scene, let me consider the way in which it is prepared by the events of the opera. Recognition is always built upon earlier moments of individual or partial recognition, upon the shifts, discoveries, and reversals of which all plots are made. *Don Giovanni* is no different. The opera moves steadily toward moments of confrontation and discovery. In the first scene, Don Giovanni is pursued by Donna Anna and challenged by her father, the Commendatore, whom he is reluctant to fight. As the opera develops, Don Giovanni meets with a new challenge in practically every scene. Leporello accuses him of "forcing the daughter and murdering the father"; Elvira accuses him of leaving her; Anna recognizes him as her attacker and reveals his identity to Ottavio; he is caught red-handed in the Act I finale trying to force himself on Zerlina. And yet he will not acknowledge his crimes.

In this succession of scenes, the dramatic action repeatedly points toward recognition. At first, Don Giovanni is challenged by individuals (Anna and the Commendatore) when his identity is concealed by disguise and the cover of darkness. But soon, unmasked, he is confronted by Leporello and Elvira. Then steadily Anna, Ottavio, Masetto, and Zerlina realize what Don Giovanni is, until in the Act I finale he is publicly confronted by all. There is a clear intensification from the cover of disguise and night to the reality of identity and daylight, from private recrimination to public accusation. But still Don Giovanni will not repent.

The second act depicts a different progression, from the attempted retribution of the social order he threatens (and evades) through the promise of vengeance in the cemetery scene to the confrontation with the supernatural in the finale. Overall, the progression is from private to public, from concealment to exposure, from the powers of human morality and law to the power of a divine order that will triumph over the flesh even where it cannot over the spirit. Don Giovanni's confrontation with the ghost is carefully prepared and seems near the end of Act II to have become inevitable.

Given the plot's steady progression towards a moment of catastrophic recognition, the earlier scenes in which Don Giovanni is confronted with his actions and given the opportunity to move in the direction of awareness become vital to our understanding of the ending. Four moments are especially important: (1) the duel with the Commendatore in the Introduzione, (2) the conclusion of the Act I finale, in which Don Giovanni is accused of his crimes, (3) the confrontation and capture of the false "Don" Leporello in the Act II sextet, and (4) the episode in the cemetery. In each of these scenes, the events of the plot conspire to confront Don Giovanni with what he has done, to force him to acknowledge the error of his ways and capitulate to moral and social law, yet in each scene the recognition is denied.[26] In addition, each scene involves textual and musical indicators that point to its role in the succession of events

26 Bauman, "The Three Trials."

that move towards the opera's inevitable conclusion. In three of these moments Don Giovanni is confronted directly and challenged; the sextet differs in this regard, since it advances the tide against Don Giovanni without his knowledge.

The duel presents the first challenge. Several of its musical features have long been considered harbingers of the Don's fate: the key of D minor, the sword motifs (which return in the Act II finale), the diminished seventh chord on which the Commendatore falls wounded in m. 175 (which returns with the appearance of the ghost of the Commendatore at m. 433 of the Act II finale),[27] and what Rushton calls the "chromatic moan" at the Commendatore's death (mm. 190–94), which "hovers over unresolved harmony, leaving the end of No. 1 open."[28]

During the F minor trio, Don Giovanni, while he does not seem to recognize how wrong his actions have been, at least seems to reflect his regret over the duel with his eerie minor rendering at m. 178 of Anna's melodic line at m. 102.[29] But this tragic scene, though it certainly offers him cause to do so, does not force him to rethink his actions, let alone his way of life. The proof lies in the close of the Introduzione, as many commentators have suggested, none more eloquently than Bauman:

> The "Moonlight Trio's" final, thwarted cadence tells us that the opera's initiatory dream has *not* concluded: Giovanni does *not* respond to this brief window of opportunity; he does *not* reflect on the meaning of his actions, and the day of reckoning is once more put off. This act of delay and of self-deception that we witness on stage is underscored in our ears by Mozart's deceptive cadence. In consequence, we along with Giovanni

27 This diminished seventh on B is spelled with a G$\sharp$ for the A$\flat$ when it returns in the Act II finale. See Rushton, *W. A. Mozart: "Don Giovanni,"* pp. 115–21.

28 Ibid., p. 117. Rushton goes on to connect this unresolved sixth on B to the opening of No. 2 on the same chord; in musical terms, Anna and Ottavio pick up at exactly the moment of the Commendatore's death. He also points to the appearance of the "chromatic moan" in No. 2 and in the Act II finale (pp. 117–18). Allanbrook calls this chromatic descent "the flight of the soul from the body" (*Rhythmic Gesture*, p. 214).

29 Among others, see Frits Noske, *The Signifier and the Signified: Studies in the Operas of Mozart and Verdi* (The Hague: Nijhoff, 1977), p. 51.

are forced to carry this moment and its unresolved psychic meaning through the activities of the following day to the second nocturnal visitation of the Commendatore that concludes the drama.[30]

At the moment of denouement in the Act I finale, Don Giovanni is caught attempting to force himself on Zerlina, who, hidden from view, first calls out for help and then cries "Scellerato" on a diminished seventh chord, *crescendo* (at m. 477), making clear that she now realizes what he is. When the three maskers and Masetto finally break the door down, Don Giovanni is caught in the act: he is revealed before all for who and what he is. Now confronted by his peers and by the moral law and social order they represent, he will not acknowledge the nature of his actions. First Ottavio and then Elvira and Anna unmask, but the discovery does not bring its accustomed result; Don Giovanni recognizes their identities, but nothing else. He attempts to blame his assault on Leporello, but the company responds: "Tutto[,] tutto già si sa" ("Everything, everything we already know").

In terms of moral and social law, this confrontation is fully adequate to bring about his downfall. He is discovered not by one nobleman but by the entire society (as represented by this strange ball where peasants, bourgeoisie, and nobles alike share a dance floor). Knowledge of his crimes is then followed by the promise of retribution: "Trema[,] trema scellerato" ("Tremble, tremble, villain"). Don Giovanni realizes the threat that faces him, but it does not move him to self-reflection. He meets the accusation and the promise of punishment with declarations of courage, and at the end of the finale he escapes with Leporello. The parallels between this moment and the confrontation with the ghost of the Commendatore in the Act II finale, as well as the large-scale structural parallels between the two finales, have received much attention.[31] Here in the realm of the moral and social order, Don

---

30 Bauman, "The Three Trials," p. 140.
31 See Christoph Bitter, *Wandlungen in den Inszenierungsformen des "Don Giovanni,"* pp. 17–24; Rushton, *W. A. Mozart: "Don Giovanni,"* pp. 46–47, Table 1; Kunze, *Mozarts Opern*, pp. 346–70; and Allanbrook's excellent discussion, *Rhythmic Gesture*, pp. 275–325.

Giovanni is able to escape human law; but later, in the presence of supernatural forces, he will not be able to escape divine law.

With the conclusion of Act I, the attempts of the moral and social order to overcome Don Giovanni have already reached a point of climax. If the human powers of that order were capable of restraining him, they would have done so. He is next confronted in the cemetery, this time by supernatural powers, the instrument of a higher order. This scene is parallel to the duel in Act I.[32] It repeats the delivery of an insult, for here Don Giovanni offers the disrespect to the dead that he earlier offered to the living; and it repeats the issue of a challenge, for the statue of the Commendatore picks up in death where he left off in life: "Di rider finirai pria dell'aurora" ("You will cease laughing by morning"). This recitative in the graveyard marks the first appearance of the Commendatore's trombones, which feature prominently in the Act II finale. As Abert suggests, this scene owes much of its effectiveness to the different reactions it provokes in servant and master:

> The words of the statue at once arouse superstitious fears in Leporello. Don Giovanni, however, takes it all as a jest made by someone quite outside his own world and tries to humour him with his invitation. Thus even the final catastrophe is introduced in the buffo manner, and the irony is further emphasized by the fact that it is Leporello, trembling with fear, who delivers the invitation to the Statue.[33]

Of course at the moment the statue accepts the invitation in "O statua gentilissima," the unexpectedness of the answer is reflected in the music, which immediately turns from the tonic E major of the statue's "Si" to C, flat VI; even Don Giovanni is at first taken aback by this turn of events and reacts *mezza voce*. But the effect is short-lived and, once again, he observes events that directly concern him without recognizing their significance.

The sextet, finally, is a thwarted climax, a moment of false

---

32 Luigi Dallapiccola makes the point that this scene, like that of the duel, involves three basses in a private, dark setting, and draws other parallels as well; see "Notes on the Statue Scene in *Don Giovanni*," *Music Survey* 3 (1950), 91ff.

33 Hermann Abert, *Mozart's "Don Giovanni*," p. 116.

recognition (paralogismos). Ottavio, Anna, Zerlina, and Masetto, having lost Don Giovanni after the Act I finale, believe that they have found him again; this time he is cornered and cannot get away. In many textual, structural, and musical details this ensemble reflects the developments of the overall action thus far and antici- pates the real dénouement in the Act II finale. Before the "Don" is discovered, Anna turns to D minor with her entrance at "Lascia almen alla mia pena" (which recalls with both words and pitch outline her angry exclamation of grief to Ottavio in their recitative [No. 2], "Fuggi, crudele, fuggi: lascia che mora anch'io" ["Leave me, cruel one, leave me: let me die too"]).[34] On the word "pianto" ("weeping") she seems to recall the "chromatic moan" of the Commendatore's death. The chromatic descent of the repeating eighth-note motive with sixteenth-note anacrusis that now enters in the strings also reflects the chromaticism of the Commendatore's death. The violins descend angrily on the "Don" with thirty-second-note runs reminiscent of those in the duel and Anna, Ottavio, Masetto, and Zerlina resolve on immediate justice: "Morà!" ("Let him die!"). The key, significantly, is not D minor, but G minor. This scene may look and feel like the moment of retribu- tion, but, despite the several points of similarity, it does not sound like real dénouement (which will occur in D minor). The passage is repeated, arriving once again on "Morà!", and the chromaticism of the duel appears now in the winds in preparation for the death blow.

The four now seize him and have the satisfaction of hearing their culprit beg for mercy, but their "Don" reveals himself to be Leporello. Their surprise is reflected in the music with a striking deceptive cadence. The moment of discovery is followed by a *sotto voce* reaction that, to borrow John Platoff's terminology, we might think of as a "shock tutti."[35] Recognition and dénouement are unsuccessful here because the social order has only the power to

34 See Noske, *The Signifier and the Signified*, p. 54.

35 See John Platoff, "Musical and Dramatic Structure in the Opera Buffa Finale," *JM* 7 (1989), 219–22; on the sextet, see also Platoff in this volume.

catch the wrong man. This ensemble, an extraordinary little drama
in its own right, is in part a comic enactment of the recognition
scene yet to come (as we will see below) and in part a repetition of
the thwarted denouement at the end of Act I. This concluding
Molto allegro is parallel dramatically to the final Allegro of the Act
I finale; in both instances the villain is discovered and confronted,
but manages to escape. Leporello even models his reaction on that
of his master a few hours earlier.

LEPORELLO (Sextet)

Mille torbidi pensieri	A thousand confused thoughts
Mi si aggiran per la testa;	Are churning in my head;
Se mi salvo in tal tempesta	If I save myself in this storm
È un prodigio in verità!	In truth, it will be a miracle.

DON GIOVANNI (Act I finale)

È confusa la mia testa[,]	My head is confused
Non so più quel ch'io mi faccia,	I no longer know what I do,
E un horribile tempesta	And a horrible storm is
Minacciando oddio mi va.	Threatening me, Oh God!

The progression from confusion to the conceit of the storm is
common to both servant and master, emphasized by the repetition
of the "testa"/"tempesta" rhyme. But, unlike his master, when the
stretto ends, Leporello acknowledges his wrongs and begs their
forgiveness in his aria, "Ah, pietà, Signori miei!" He then makes his
way to the door in the wall, and, following his master's example
once again, manages to escape.

IV

Don Giovanni's confrontation with the ghost of the Commendatore in the Act II finale has all the hallmarks of a climactic
recognition scene. It comes just before the end of the opera, as
recognition scenes so often do, and it possesses all four characteristics that, as I have argued elsewhere, one often finds in conjunction with recognition scenes in Mozart.[36] First, it is set apart, by the

36 As in note 14.

entrance of the statue ghost, by the shift to *alle breve*, to full orchestration (with trombones), and to D minor. Second, the central shifts in action within the scene are accompanied by musical shifts of key, texture, melodic line, dynamics, and orchestration, with the effect that the intensity of the scene is vividly depicted in the music. Third, the moment of discovery depends for its meaning on the unfolding of the plot, which itself serves as an explanatory narrative. The significance of the recognition depends for its meaning on the very story being enacted on the stage, and most particularly the episodes involving the duel and Don Giovanni's blasphemous denial of supernatural retribution in the cemetery scene.

Finally and most important, as is well known, there is a great deal of musical repetition. The key of D minor returns from the overture, the duel scene, Anna's and Ottavio's vengeance duet, and elsewhere. The Commendatore enters on the very diminished chord on which he was mortally wounded in the duel.[37] The Andante of the overture returns, with its dotted rhythms, syncopations, and chromatic scales.[38] Re-enacted as it is recomposed, the music of the overture now clearly signals the crux of the drama, but Don Giovanni stands firm. Soon the orchestra jabs at Don Giovanni with sword motives from the earlier duel, but he remains unflinching, unmoved. It is not so much that he lacks understanding, for the terror of the scene does eventually produce some effect upon his lines, but that he refuses to acknowledge the significance of the Commendatore's return. In no other scene in Mozart is recognition so overdetermined. And yet, here, just where text, music, and tremendous stage spectacle unite powerfully in an attempt to bring it about, recognition is denied. For the Romantics

---

37 In addition, the knocks on the door at mm. 407–08 and following repeat the orchestral gesture at the beginning of the closing Allegro (m. 533) of the Act I finale. This of course was the moment at which Don Giovanni was accused of crimes but escaped punishment. Supernatural retribution enters where human efforts leave off.

38 Among others see Rushton, *W. A. Mozart: "Don Giovanni,"* p. 116, and Allanbrook, *Rhythmic Gesture*, pp. 293–319.

this strength of will makes Don Giovanni a hero of tragic proportions. But the true tragic hero – Oedipus, Hamlet, Othello, Faust – always has his moment of recognition. Don Giovanni is no tragic hero. Heroic though his defiance may seem, he stands in the place where a hero should be. Somehow reconciling what is heroic with its opposite, he combines villainy and heroism. Don Giovanni is an enigma, an anti-hero.

V

Writing about the last scene of *Don Giovanni*, Joseph Kerman chafes at what he calls the opera's "accidental and unformed ambiguity,"[39] and he blames Da Ponte for the questions the opera raises: "Certainly the epilogue answers none of [these questions]; it only goes to show how drab life is without the Don."[40] But perhaps this is the point. Bernard Williams suggests, "The [final] sextet is . . . absolutely essential, as defining – in a sense – a 'return to normal', something which itself helps to define the meaning of previous events and of Giovanni himself."[41] The fascination of this work lies in the way in which its two endings (one for the protagonist and one for everyone else) face in opposite directions.

What exactly happens at the end of the opera, at least in its original 1787 configuration? Don Giovanni is engulfed in flames as demons drag him down to Hades, after which spectacle the opera must conclude. The lights come up as the other characters rush in to discover Don Giovanni's fate. They each explain the end of their own stories, after which all join in singing the *lieto fine* tutti:

Questo è il fin di chi fa mal:	This is the end of those who do wrong:
E de[´] perfidi la morte	And the wicked shall die
Alla vita è sempre ugual.	As befits the way they lived.

39 Joseph Kerman, *Opera as Drama*, rev. edn. (Berkeley and Los Angeles: University of California Press, 1988), p. 103. 40 Ibid.
41 Williams, "Mozart's Comedies," p. 453.

Of course, this is a stock ending. More important, in the eighteenth century it was the expected ending. And yet, in the case of *Don Giovanni* it has long been regarded as inappropriate and contrived, a cardboard convention. When the *lieto fine* is omitted, ironically, an unexpected, new "happy" ending is created, one in which Don Giovanni is saved from his fate. Damnation is transformed into transcendence. Of course, this sort of happy ending is more commensurate with nineteenth- than eighteenth-century aesthetics. And that is how Shaw's play *Man and Superman* finds Don Giovanni on his way to Heaven, to join Mozart in the "home of the masters of reality."[42]

My suggestion is that the *lieto fine* with its final recognition for the other characters and the audience is as necessary as it is conflicted. We should not wish to dispense with it any more than we should wish Don Giovanni would reform. But I would argue that one cause of the residual feeling among critics that this opera's *lieto fine* is unsuccessful, despite the opera's persistent appeal, is its highly unusual recognition scene. Although Don Giovanni's confrontation with the ghost has never before been acknowledged as a recognition scene, it is recognition that has engendered the long history of controversy. The opera culminates – as most dramas do – in a moment of climactic recognition, and this scene, as one would expect, is both the heart of the opera and the place where the issues are most forcefully dramatized. But while recognition usually brings resolution, here it brings the opposite: in *Don Giovanni*, recognition – and its denial – deepen the conflict already inherent in the work.

The issues I mentioned earlier all turn on this conflict. Is Don Giovanni hero or villain? Is the opera comedy or tragedy? And, most important, does the conclusion dramatize moral triumph or heroic defiance? These questions do not lend themselves to easy answers. Indeed, the questions themselves are far more interesting than any answers one could provide for them. The opera, like its

42 Shaw, *Man and Superman*, p. 139.

defiant protagonist, refuses to capitulate to the conventional order set by the example of others. The conflicted ending preserves something contradictory and uncertain in human nature. In attempting to be true to the complexity of human nature, the opera resists a neat, moral conclusion. It is this tension born of the conflict between Don Giovanni's damnation and the *lieto fine* that is most compelling in the opera. To disrupt the balance between recognition denied and exalted would be to set the opera out of joint. For it is this very indeterminacy that has fascinated musicians, writers, and audiences for two hundred years.

PART III

Analytical and methodological issues

**Analysis and dramaturgy: reflections
towards a theory of opera**
Sergio Durante

A methodological reflection focusing on a particular genre (opera
buffa) and a particular cultural milieu (Vienna, in Mozart's time) is
ideally placed at a crossroads between two fields of research:
theory of opera and research on Mozartean theatre. This is true
especially because of the excellence of recent studies in both fields.
The most significant recent contribution to operatic theory is probably Carl Dahlhaus's "Drammaturgia dell'opera italiana," which
will provide a strong theoretical foundation for a long time to
come.[1] Recent analytical research on Mozartean opera also reveals
a breadth of approach and intellectual subtlety that leave little to be
desired. However, these two fields do not represent a coordinated
whole, nor are they homogeneously oriented. Their differences are
perhaps best captured by a juxtaposition of the terms "dramaturgy" and "analysis." This study is in part a reflection on the
distinctions and overlaps between them, as well as on the problems
involved in a synthetic approach to the study of opera.

ANALYSIS AND DRAMATURGY

While it would be incorrect to characterize the recent analytical
research on eighteenth-century opera and Mozart as a homogene-

1 Carl Dahlhaus, "Drammaturgia dell'opera italiana," in Lorenzo Bianconi and
Giorgio Pestelli, eds., *Storia dell'opera italiana*, vol. 6, *Teorie e tecniche, immagini e
fantasmi* (Turin: EDT/Musica, 1988). Also of importance are more recent studies
departing from or commenting on Dahlhaus, such as Fabrizio Della Seta,
"Affetto e azione: Sulla teoria del melodramma italiano dell'Ottocento," in
Angelo Pompilio et al., eds., *Atti del XIV congresso della Società internazionale di
musicologia: Trasmissione e recezione delle forme di cultura musicale* (Turin:
EDT/Musica, 1990), vol. 3, *Free papers*, pp. 395–400; Luca Zoppelli, *L'opera come
racconto: Modi narrativi nel teatro musicale dell'Ottocento* (Venice: Marsilio, 1994).

ous "trend," a few general traits can be identified: the overcoming of traditional analytical and aesthetic categories (in particular, the sonata-form paradigm, the various myths of "unity," and perhaps even the hypostatization of musical form);[2] a balanced approach to all the elements in opera (according to an oft-quoted expression: text, music, and drama); a deeply felt need for analytical thoroughness; a hermeneutic intention (in the sense that the goal is to connect and interpret the individual aspects); and finally, the analysis of set pieces as the central methodological principle.[3] The centrality of music is a basic concept for Dahlhaus as well, although his focus on dramaturgy implies that the analytical experience is not an end in itself, but instrumental to a broad discourse on opera (far broader than the word "Italian" in his title would imply).

The understanding of Mozart's operas (or opera in Mozart's time) can thus rely on both broad and focused tools which, interestingly, were developed approximately in the same years (middle and late 1980s) in Europe and America. As recently as 1987, James Webster could still invoke the maturation of a discourse on opera that would not merely simulate existing discourses on spoken theatre or on instrumental music as a project for the future (albeit the immediate future):

> Operatic analysis will have to develop its own (partly new) explanatory models, idiomatic to the genre. But (and this is only a superficial paradox) these will be fully effective only when they have become sufficiently powerful and, at least implicitly, sufficiently general to induce people to apply them to *other* repertories [than late eighteenth-century opera].[4]

2 "In many Mozart arias, 'the' form does not exist": Webster, "Analysis," p. 122. Cf. Webster, "Mozart's Operas and the Myth of Musical Unity," *COJ* 2 (1990), 197–218.

3 That analysis, especially of set pieces, should be the central moment of a discourse on opera has not always seemed obvious. In the past, critical reflection on opera depended on selective (i.e. non-multivalent) literary and dramatic (and even moral) concepts, and was pursued primarily by literati and dramatists; indeed this remains true to a considerable extent.

4 James Webster, "To Understand Verdi and Wagner We Must Understand Mozart," *19CM* 11 (1987–88), 193; compare his article in this volume.

The quest for "idiomatic" methods is indeed fundamental, and corresponds to the classical dictum that every thing must be judged according to its own principles. Although the call for idiomatic explanatory models does not imply a devaluation of the immense corpus of writing on opera, from many different perspectives, it does imply that, beyond opera's role as a stimulating subject for cultural investigation, an understanding of its aesthetic nature will increasingly be associated with analytical scrutiny.

Webster's remarks also imply the standing need for a more or less explicit theory of opera, one that could be applied not only to Mozart but to the entire genre (and its various subgenres). Dahlhaus's "Drammaturgia dell'opera italiana" (published in 1988) addressed this need; as he explained in another context, "Musical analysis . . . is either a means or an end. It aims at theory and is thus its first step; or it tries to do justice to a musical work as a particular individual formation."[5] Dahlhaus's own work clearly follows the former path. On the other hand, although many of the recent detailed North American studies imply a theoretical basis or bases, their principal aim is not the production of a general theory, but the inductive investigation of classes of pieces or selected cases.[6] Not that they have been pursued in a theoretical vacuum. John Platoff, for example, takes the "action-expression cycle" as a general explanatory principle for both ensembles and finales in opera buffa;[7] and Webster elaborates on the concepts of "type" (of set piece and of form) and "network" (a way of organizing our understanding of different numbers), proceeding to an explanation of the "analytical domains," and demonstrating the explanatory potential of detailed investigation of their relationships.

---

5 Carl Dahlhaus, *Analysis and Value Judgment*, trans. Siegmund Levarie (New York: Pendragon, 1983), p. 9.

6 For example, Webster, "Mozart's Arias"; Mary Hunter, "Text, Music, and Drama in Haydn's Italian Opera Arias: Four Case Studies," *JM* 7 (1989), 29–57; "Some Representations of *Opera Seria* in *Opera Buffa*," *COJ* 3 (1991), 89–108; John Platoff, "The Buffa Aria in Mozart's Vienna," *COJ* 2 (1990), 99–120.

7 Mary Hunter later applied the more convincing pairing of "action-reflection" ("Text, Music, and Drama," 31).

Nevertheless, the theoretical principles adumbrated are presented in such a way as to satisfy the needs of the particular objects of investigation (finales and arias in particular), without necessarily aiming towards a general theory.

This does not diminish the importance of these studies. For example, the reappraisals of the "sonata-form" approach to the finale and of the dramatic relevance of arias[8] – as opposed to the traditional "Wagnerian" elevation of ensembles and finales to privileged locations within the drama – marks the removal of a no longer tenable critical bias.[9] In this stimulating landscape, it may seem tempting patiently to pursue one's analytical work, on the reasonable hypothesis that the analysis of opera – or more precisely of the "musicodramatic text" that begins with the overture and ends with the last finale – is the cumulative result of the analysis of its individual set pieces, considered within their respective dramatic contexts.

Nevertheless, a more convincing perspective might emerge if one considered the other end of the methodological spectrum and established links – or located possible frictions with – Dahlhaus's theoretical approach. The following passage seems the most relevant for a reflection on analysis:

> The thesis that locates into the music the fundamental and constituent element of the peculiar drama called opera – a thesis that goes well beyond the acknowledgment of the preponderance of music – entrusts to the dramaturgy of music the duty to define which relationships are established, case by case, between the music and the other partial factors converging in the composite artistic *opus*.
>
> To define these relationships means to determine a hierarchy with different degrees of prominence and subordination. One can in fact take for granted, even before detailed analysis, that the relationship (the proximity or distance) between music and *fabula* or plot, music and

---

8 Webster concludes that in Mozart, "aria is drama" ("Analysis," p. 199). On the dramaturgical and rhetorical significance of arias see also the essay by Ronald J. Rabin in this volume.

9 See Carolyn Abbate and Roger Parker, "Dismembering Mozart," *COJ* 2 (1990), 187–95.

conceptual structure of the drama, music and the constellation of the
characters, music and scenic action, music and active or expressive-
contemplative discourse, music and "inner action," music and staging,
will be extremely different, when we examine both each individual case
(an individual opera or type), and the global phenomenon (i.e. "opera
theatre" as a whole or by genre).[10]

Dahlhaus here provides a list of binary relationships between
music, which is made the pivot of a signification system, and a
number of abstractly defined but directly relevant operatic elements. At the same time he suggests that different hierarchical relationships (of prevalence or subordination) can be established
between the elements in play. But how would this theoretical
model apply to the "detailed analysis" that Dahlhaus takes for
granted?

To be sure, recent Mozartean analysis shares a clear perception
of the multiplicity of the elements in play. Yet in a study focused on
individual set pieces the different threads of the web – which we
may as well name "analytical domains" – receive a somewhat
unequal treatment. I quote again from Webster's study on Mozart's
arias:

> Since stage-action, characterization, and plot-development cannot be
> "analyzed" in any conventional sense, for our purposes here [the analysis
> of Mozart's arias] the multivalent nature of arias can be understood in
> terms of three primary domains: text, voice, and orchestra.[11]

The idea of a hierarchy enters the theoretical frame in a pre-defined
manner: a division between elements that are subject to analysis
(i.e., have undergone a process of formalization) and those that are
not. Although the set piece is not considered in isolation, the notion
of dramatic context, which provides the connection between the
individual piece and the opera as a whole, is seen as a synthesis of
elements from different domains.

10 Dahlhaus, "Drammaturgia," p. 83 (internal paragraph-break added).
11 Webster, "Analysis," p. 122.

AN EXAMPLE: DORABELLA AND FIORDILIGI

Let us examine a *locus classicus* of the buffo repertoire, the two arias of Dorabella and Fiordiligi in the first act of *Così fan tutte*. While Dorabella's "Smanie implacabili" is patently parodistic, Fiordiligi's "Come scoglio" leaves space for different interpretations. Both internal evidence and various contextual elements direct our interpretation. In "Smanie implacabili" the parody is emphasized by the hyperbolic language of the text; however, regarding "Come scoglio," some argue that the wide leaps of the Andante maestoso are meant as parodistic, while others disagree.[12] A musical detail of importance (see Example 12.1) is the "death figure" at mm. 32–37, at the lines "e potrà la morte sola / far che cangi affetto il cor" ["And perhaps only death can make the heart change its affections"], reiterated five times; it is patently related to the identical figure at m. 76 of the Act I finale (where it appears at a sudden modulation to B flat, the key of "Come scoglio"), when the Albanians pretend to drink poison.

This also implies that when Fiordiligi invokes death in "Come scoglio," she is not exaggerating, but foretelling the truth: Ferrando's attempted suicide, shortly thereafter, will produce the possibility of a change of mind. The two musical forms also differ conspicuously in their observance of aria types: "Smanie implacabili" reflects a long-standing model (and if conventionality were equated with superficiality or untruthfulness this might mean something), while "Come scoglio" is unique.[13] (Note, however, that

12 The first and more generally accepted view is stated by, among others, Stefan Kunze, *Mozarts Opern* (Stuttgart: Reclam, 1984), pp. 521–22, and Rodney Farnsworth, *"Così fan tutte* as Parody and Burlesque," *OQ* 6 (1988–89), 60–61; the second by Constantin Floros, "Stilebenen und Stilsynthese in den Opern Mozarts," in Floros, *Mozart-Studien*, vol. 1, *Zu Mozarts Sinfonik, Opern- und Kirchenmusik* (Wiesbaden: Breitkopf und Härtel, 1973), p. 98. A balanced approach to the question is found in Hunter, "Some Representations," pp. 106–08; see also Rabin's essay in this volume, p. 234.

13 Within the Mozartean corpus, the nearest one could come to an analogy would be Elettra's "Tutte nel cor vi sento" in *Idomeneo*, No. 4. While "Come scoglio" could be considered an elaborated variant of a two-tempo type, it can also be perceived simply as an "exceptional" form (compare Webster's suggestion in "Analysis," p. 116, Table I, note g).

Example 12.1a Mozart, *Così fan tutte*, Fiordiligi, "Come scoglio"

Fiordiligi: And perhaps only death...

a "conventional" number-type can nonetheless be written and composed as a dramatic and psychological climax. This is particularly true of the *rondò*; for example, Fiordiligi's "Per pietà.")

We might also expand the context visually: "Smanie implacabili" is characterized by the incongruity (or oxymoron) between

Example 12.1b Mozart, *Così fan tutte*, Act I Finale

Ferrando, Guglielmo: Leave me alone!
Don Alfonso: Wait!
Ferrando, Guglielmo: Arsenic will free me from such cruelty.

the "low" register of the chocolate thrown on the floor and the "high" one of the ensuing recitative and aria. Moreover, the parody is reinforced by Dorabella's being prevented from exiting following her aria (a feature of the type); instead, the stage-direction implies farce ("si metton a sedere in disparte da forsennate" ["They sit down on one side, in desperation"]).[14] At the end of "Come scoglio" the exit convention is reintroduced, but again revoked: the ladies "van per partire" ["set out to leave"], but are made to stay by Ferrando and Guglielmo.

Within the plot, Dorabella's aria follows an "interruption and inversion" of the dramatic mood (we could see it as an allusion to a new narratological "motif"; that is, a series of acts or events having a common expository purpose):[15]

(a) departure of the lovers (scenes 5–6)

(b) Don Alfonso's "anticipation" (scene 7) and presentation of Despina (scene 8) = mood inversion

(c) entrance of the ladies (scene 9) and follow-up to the mood in (a).

On the other hand, "Come scoglio" is relatively consequential to the immediately preceding situation.[16] Not that the comic side is

---

14 The presence of two listeners on stage, during a type of aria that was usually sung as a soliloquy, is generically incongruent as well.

15 By "motif" (not to be confused with a musical motive in the sense of a small unit of material) I mean something close to Gerald Prince's *motif* or "minimal thematic unit" (*A Dictionary of Narratology* [Lincoln: University of Nebraska Press, 1987], p. 55) or Elisabeth Frenzel's "small thematic unit which is not capable of embracing the whole of a plot or of a fabula but which already represents an element of content and of situation," in *Stoff-, Motiv- und Symbolforschung* (Stuttgart: Metzler, 1963), p. 29; quoted from Cesare Segre, *Introduction to the Analysis of the Literary Text*, trans. John Meddemmen (Bloomington: University of Indiana Press, 1988), p. 284. On the relationship between motif and *fabula* (the "represented" time as opposed to its representation in the work) see also Segre, *Teatro e romanzo* (Turin: Einaudi, 1984), pp. 22–26; for an extensive discussion of the terms motif and theme, with musicological implications, see Segre, *The Literary Text*, pp. 277–99.

16 Note, however, that from the point of view of the *fabula*, Dorabella's aria follows the Terzettino *immediately*, skipping over the farcical element exposed by Despina to the audience. In fact, in part owing to the change of scene, the latter is "contemporaneous" with the Terzettino within the "represented time."

lacking: the oxymoronic juxtaposition of Guglielmo's "farfallette amorose agonizzanti" ["agonizing amorous butterflies"] and Fiordiligi's "l'alito infausto degli infami detti" ["the ill-starred breath of the infamous deeds"] is no less comical than Dorabella's invocation of the Eumenides. Nevertheless, the former marks only the beginning of an *accompagnato*, which rapidly evolves to a more serious tone.

Perhaps only consideration of the conceptual structure of the drama, with the progressive individualization of the two sisters during the second act, confirms that "Come scoglio" is a "double" of "Smanie." This interpretation might also make sense of Fiordiligi's slightly unexpected use of the plural in her second stanza ("con noi nacque quella face / che ci piace e ci consola" ["That fire was born with us that pleases and consoles us"]), reinforcing the notion that the two ladies are still one and the same "actant." It would follow that the musicodramatic text implies parody throughout both arias, which differ perhaps only in degree. If this example demonstrates the relevance of the different components (textual discourse, plot, conceptual structure, visual action, characterological development; as well as music, in its composite agency of signs, motives, *topoi*, keys, and forms), it also indicates how problematic it can be to determine their hierarchical status. Our rhetorical interpretation of the parodistic element may influence, or even direct, our understanding of individual musical features: once we accept that parody is present, there will be little room for a "psychological" interpretation of Fiordiligi's music (and conversely).[17]

Of course, most arias do not present such strong ambiguities. Still, the close relationship between the different domains in this case raises several issues. First, how shall we determine the relative hierarchical status of the different domains? While it might seem legitimate to erect a pre-defined hierarchy in the case of an individual study of arias, various elements of the larger dramatic context

17 "An essential aspect of musical parody is that our recognition of it often depends not so much on 'purely musical' excess or inappropriateness as on an incongruity between the music and dramatic or textual factors" (Webster, "Analysis," p. 112).

may be paramount for a definition of the very conceptual frame within which the "primary domains" will be understood in the first place. (The hierarchy might even be reversed, such that any domain could be granted "primary" status.) Second, the resistance of certain domains (for example, stage-action or plot-development) to formalization and analysis seems a consequence more of the segmentation based on the set pieces (notably arias), than of any inherent qualities in those domains.

TENTATIVE FORMALIZATIONS: STAGE-ACTION

Using narratological and semiotic procedures (suitably altered to the operatic context),[18] it is in fact possible to abstract and graph the stage-action corresponding to a given set piece. (By "stage-action" I designate the combined operations prescribed by the text and para-text.)[19]

To begin, we must determine the appropriate level of abstraction.[20] Our guiding principle will be the goal-orientation of a certain action at the highest level of abstraction, which allows us to locate within our repertory two general classes (to be further articulated at lower levels):[21] (1) acts of *persuasion*, request, inducement,

18 Whereas the principles of formalization for spoken theatre are numerous and well suited to dramatic texts, I have not found significant investigations of opera using such techniques. Nevertheless, the latter genre exhibits a degree of convention that makes it a relatively easy case for narratological analysis. On the other hand, the temporal expansion of speech acts through music presents specific problems that seem not to be discussed in the narratological literature.

19 By para-text I mean all the scenic directions prescribed or implied by the text. (It would be possible to analyze individual performances or performing traditions rather than the musicodramatic text, but this is not my primary concern here.)

20 The "stage-action," as defined here, partially overlaps with one of Webster's primary domains, the text ("Analysis," pp. 122ff.). However, it seems to me that to include the latter as a primary domain distinct from the stage-action produces an artificial separation between the "poetic" text and the text as a component of a performative act (see Segre, *Teatro e romanzo*, pp. 7–11).

21 This subdivision does not precisely reflect any current narratological formalization, although it resembles Austin's two classes of actions (Keir Elam, *The Semiotics of Theatre and Drama* [London: Methuen, 1980], pp. 157 ff.). The possibility of elaborating categories appropriate for a particular corpus is stressed in Segre, *The Literary Text*, ch. 3.

and so forth, and their opposites; and (2) acts of *representation* or ostension involving objects, states of mind, visual images, narrations, etc.

Both persuasion and representation establish a relationship between a character (or group) and another character (present or absent), or with him- or herself, or with the audience.[22] Any of these acts may (or may not) involve speech acts, of either realistic or metaphorical nature, and any act is placed within the narrative time in such a way as occasionally to produce prospective and/or retrospective connections with other acts.[23]

The Terzetto No. 3 in *Così fan tutte* (see Figure 12.1) embeds a representation of facts that are supposed to happen in the future ("Una bella serenata / far io voglio alla mia dea" ["I want to sing a beautiful serenade to my goddess"]). "Porgi amor" (No. 10 in *Figaro*) embeds a prayer (and therefore an act of persuasion) to a symbolic character (Cupid). Fiordiligi's *rondò* No. 25, "Per pietà," embeds an act of persuasion directed at an absent character. Donna Anna's *rondò* No. 23, "Non mi dir," also embeds an act of persuasion, but one directed at a character who is present on stage. Contrasting or opposed acts of persuasion/dissuasion are portrayed in the Duet No. 14 in *Don Giovanni*, "Eh, via buffone," and the Duettino No. 5 in *Le nozze di Figaro*, "Via resti servita" (in a different stylistic register). "La mia Dorabella," No. 1 in *Così fan tutte*, portrays a contrast

22 Segre (*Teatro e romanzo*, p. 11) names this case "fuga di notizie" (information leakage), and locates it in asides as well as in monologues. It is very common and structurally relevant in opera, where it obviously assumes different profiles (or styles) in monologues and asides.

23 In the figures the letters represent characters; an absent character is indicated by parentheses, a temporarily silent one by circled letters; "X" designates a metaphorical character (e.g. Cupid); an arrow indicates an act as well as the relationship consequently established. A pair of opposed arrows indicates reciprocal actions of similar quality (an arrow with a double diagonal slash indicates a difference in the quality of the symbolized action). A curved arrow indicates that the action involved is respectively an anticipation (if directed towards the right-hand side) or a retrospection (left-hand side). Letters designating characters are grouped together when the latter cumulatively develop the same action.

I thank M. Barollo for assistance with the figures in this article.

Figure 12.1 Formalization of acts

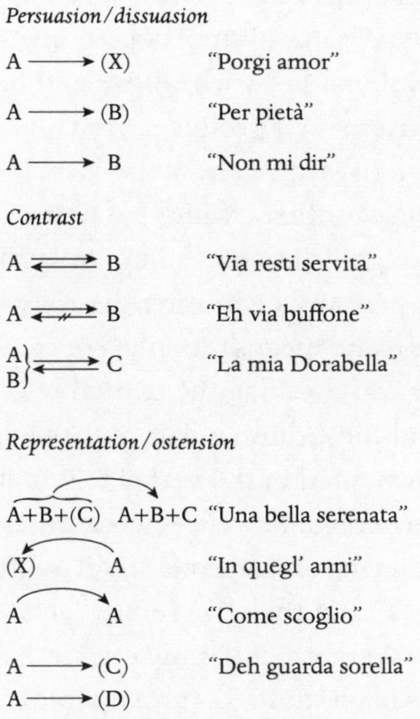

Persuasion/dissuasion

A ⟶ (X)   "Porgi amor"

A ⟶ (B)   "Per pietà"

A ⟶ B   "Non mi dir"

Contrast

A ⇌ B   "Via resti servita"

A ⇌ B   "Eh via buffone"

A⎫
 ⎬ ⇌ C   "La mia Dorabella"
B⎭

Representation/ostension

A+B+(C) A+B+C "Una bella serenata"

(X)   A   "In quegl' anni"

A   A   "Come scoglio"

A ⟶ (C)   "Deh guarda sorella"
A ⟶ (D)

between a pair of undifferentiated characters[24] and an antagonist. Basilio's "In quegl'anni," No. 26 in *Le nozze di Figaro*, is a representation of past experience reported in metaphorical terms.[25]

Although other categorizations could be essayed, this one at least satisfies the requisites of pertinency (with respect to the corpus) and flexibility (the level of abstraction is sufficiently high to fit the codes in play).[26] Application of these concepts does not entail

24 The narratological term "actant" suits this case, as well as the numerous operatic situations where two or more characters are grouped together and assigned similar or identical musical materials. This usage should be distinguished from Webster's suggestion of "agency" for purely instrumental ideas ("Cone's 'Personae' and the Analysis of Opera," *CMS* 29 [1989], 51).

25 A similar case, presented however as a realistic narrative, is Da Ponte's "In quegl'anni in cui solea" (Martín y Soler, *Una cosa rara*, No. 11). The gnomic texts so frequent in opera can be interpreted as belonging to the first category, in that the character is attempting an act of self-persuasion.

26 On this point see Segre, *The Literary Text*, § 3.4, "The Scale of Generalization."

a new understanding of set pieces, but it does have heuristic value for refining our analytical tools. For if an act is a syntactic component of the "action,"[27] it is important to investigate both its elements and its relational network, above and beyond its analytical interest or the excitement it produces on stage.

This formalization stresses how the visual and textual components relate to each other, while retaining a degree of independence. Although the prevailing relationship is one of parallelism (thus perhaps suggesting the fully synthetic nature of each "act"), this is by no means the rule. For example, the visual and musical elements can override the textual one. The duel between Don Giovanni and the Commendatore is seen and heard, but it is not narratively presented in the verbal text (a first degree of independence). Moreover, while we are accustomed to think about the visual element in terms of consequentiality with respect to the text – a character "says" and then/therefore "acts" – the contrary can occur as well. The Terzetto No. 7 in *Le nozze di Figaro*, "Cosa sento! tosto andate," has been studied as an example of musical manipulation, in that the Count's orders are "disobeyed," by subtle tonal and motivic means.[28] But this divergence of the textual and musical codes is parallel to that between the textual and visual codes: the Count's order to Basilio is not followed by his exit. Another different case is "Venite inginocchiatevi" (*Le nozze di Figaro*, No. 12), where the text can be understood as an accessory of the action rather than its originator. (This is at least in part the case also with "realistic" music.)[29]

27 See entry "Action" in Prince, *Dictionary*, p. 3.
28 See David Lewin, "Musical Analysis as Stage Direction," in Steven Paul Scher, ed., *Music and Text: Critical Inquiries* (Cambridge: Cambridge University Press, 1992), pp. 163–176.
29 By "realistic" music I mean "music that ideally would be sung even in a spoken drama" (Webster, "Analysis," p. 108), such as No. 11, "Voi che sapete," in *Le nozze di Figaro*, or most serenades, marches, and choruses. However, the class thus defined encompasses very different situations: for example, Cherubino's song projects the character's subjective point of view and therefore "acts" differently from an on-stage orchestra. In any case, opera as a genre does not ordinarily allow for visual action protracted over a long period of time. In the first finale of

While one could select a larger number of categories, the point is that each act is mediated by the causal (or merely temporal) chain in which it occurs.[30] Beyond this basic level of segmentation and classification, we must investigate the relationship between the formal nature of these acts, their individual connotations, and their consequences within the drama. For instance, insofar as the elements in play have a metaphorical or symbolic nature (if text), or represent an evocation (if visual), their expository function within the drama will be other than the "logical-causal" one. While in "Non mi dir" Donna Anna addresses Don Ottavio in order to obtain something from him (his assent to a delay in their marriage), Fiordiligi in "Per pietà" does not really mean to inform Guglielmo of anything (her newly acquired consciousness expresses a line of conduct for the immediate future). The Countess describes through her invocation a relatively stable condition (her husband's loss of interest in her): this "action" has the longest-lasting effect within the expository development, because its consequence occurs only at the denouement. In these examples, the combined textual and visual elements delineate a scale of dramatic "reality" that ranges from objective stage-presence (Ottavio), to recall (Guglielmo), to pure imagination (Cupid). The actions embedded in the set pieces have consequences, which can be either immediate or remote, and differ in degree rather than in quality. This suggests a slightly more complicated notion of "act" than the usual one (the actions of the characters on stage), both because it differentiates among the media (visual and/or verbal, and/or musical), and because it relates actions to their consequences, and thus offers the opportunity to qualify them. (Conversely, other acts, though qualifying a set piece as an "action number," may have minor consequences within the drama.)

Così fan tutte, for instance, the "doctor's" visual operations are verbally described as they occur; this is superfluous from a purely dramatic standpoint, but was evidently considered necessary for the sake of textural and stylistic continuity.

30 I use the term "chain" without necessarily implying that all the acts are connected through cause-effect relationships.

Let us further explore the explanatory value of such artificially isolated acts.[31] They represent a very high level of abstraction even by narratological standards, so that the immediate advantages for the analyst are not clear, beyond the clarification of general relationships between textual, musical, and visual codes. In fact, the most evident connections between analytical domains are established at other levels. Musical *topoi*, affects, tonality, even form: all relate to the domain of stage-action at levels of formalization that concern less general qualities of the acts. An act of persuasion usually bears no special musical character until it is particularized, for example as an incitement to commit a crime (or a love-persuasion), and this in turn produces a state of agitation (or tenderness), along with the corresponding musical *topos*:[32]

Persuasion → crime   agitation → musical topos
Persuasion → love   tenderness → musical topos

Accessory qualifications often involve the local (seaside vs. garden), the ritual (serenade vs. private talk), the status of the characters (higher vs. lower class), and so forth. A complete set of qualifications will thus involve numerous elements from different domains and at various levels of abstraction.[33]

The choice (or elaboration) of a certain musical form, for example, generally results from a combination of factors. Thus a *rondò* usually is assigned to a noble character (or the *prima donna*)

31 The genuinely "idiomatic" object of operatic analysis would be the combination of primary and secondary domains (or, if one prefers, the scenical act as regulated by the music). This sort of act is much more complex than the stage-action (the operations prescribed by the text and para-text). It follows, however, that the visual aspect must be included in any adequate consideration of set pieces.

32 This does not eliminate the possibility of establishing connections at other levels. For example, in the first section of Vitellia's "Deh se piacer mi vuoi" (No. 2 in *Tito*) the main relationship between the quality of the action and the music is established at the highest level, in that the temporary goal of the action is the blind persuasion or fascination of Sesto per se; see Julian Rushton, "Mozart's Art of Rhetoric: Understanding an opera seria ('Deh se piacer mi vuoi' from *La clemenza di Tito*)," forthcoming in *The Contemporary Music Review*.

33 See Webster, "Analysis," p. 131.

and marks a highpoint within the plot.[34] However, an element in a given domain can potentially connect with any other domain, as long as the elements in question signify in the appropriate manner. The formal, tonal, and registral features of a given set piece (and especially its variance with respect to a "type") have been persuasively interpreted as representing a character's psychological condition, as in Hunter's study of Flaminia's "Ragion nell'alma siede" in Haydn's *Il mondo della luna* and Webster's of "Porgi amor" in *Le nozze di Figaro* and "Vo pensando" in Salieri's *La locandiera*.[35] This is a rewarding field of exploration, especially with respect to arias that may seem "dramatic." However, this does not imply a link between formal types and characterological implications. The musical parameters can interact with any of the domains, at any level. In *Così fan tutte*, the trio "È la fede delle femmine" (No. 2) is based on the relationship between the near-quotation from Metastasio in the text and the varied da capo form associated with the classic Metastasian aria; the psychology of the characters plays only a secondary role.[36] An analogous example from Paisiello's *Il re Teodoro in Venezia* (1785) is Teodoro's heroic-comic aria "Io re sono e sono amante," in which allusions to opera seria (a paraphrase of a Metastasian first line and a suggestion of da capo form) are combined with features characteristic of male buffa arias (a long text and a climactic ending); see Figure 12.2.[37]

34 For our purposes, the term "highpoint" is generic. In the late eighteenth century the *rondò* was generally reserved for a phase of the plot-development enclosed within the "descendant action" of Freytag's pyramid (see "Freytag's Pyramid," in Prince, *Dictionary*, pp. 36–38).

35 Hunter, "Text, Music, and Drama," pp. 31–38; Webster, "Analysis," pp. 151–69; see also his essay in this volume.

36 The textual allusion is from Metastasio's *Demetrio* (1731), III.3: "È fede degli amanti / Come l'araba fenice" ["The faith of lovers is like the Arabian phoenix"]; it was a familiar *topos* (employed as well by Goldoni); see Heartz, *Mozart's Operas*, p. 229, and Bruce Alan Brown and John A. Rice, "Salieri's *Così fan tutte*," *COJ* 8 (1996), 17–43.

37 The paraphrase is of "Son regina e sono amante," sung by the heroine in *Didone abbandonata*, likewise known throughout the eighteenth-century operatic world. The form of Paisiello's aria, in two movements separated by a short Largo, combines the da capo and rondo principles in a rather original structure:

Figure 12.2 Casti/Paisiello, *Il re Teodoro in Venezia*, aria of Teodoro, "Io re sono e sono amante": formal design

	Allegro moderato							Largo 3/4	Allegro C	
			II	III		IV	V	VI	VII	VIII
Measures	1 3 5 7 9 11	13 15 17 19 21 23 25 27 29 31 33 35	37 39 41 43 45	47 49 51 53 55	57 59 61 63 65 67 69 71 73 75	77 78 80	82 84 86 88 90 92 94 96 98 100 10:
Vocal par.	1 '						
Text-lines	1	2	3a–3b 4a–4b 5	5 6 7	6	8 9 10 11 12	13 14 15	16 17 18 19 20 17–20'	1 2	3a–3b 4a–4b 4	5 6 6 10	11 12 10 11 12
Ideas (voice)	1*	1' 2 4 5	6 6 7a 7b	9	11	12* 12	1' 2 4	1' 2 4	5	13	7a 7a	8 8
Ideas (orch.)	1	1' 3	1 1 7a 7b	8		12	10	1' 3	1' 3	7a 7a	8 8
Phrasing	2+2]1+2]2+2 2+1	2+2 2+2 2+2 1×4+4	3+4	4×2	1×4	2+2 2+2 2+2+1 3	2+4	5×1	2+(2×3) 3+4
Structure						anticipation	
Harmony	ii–V		bVI	VII9		I7 IV7 IV II	
Tonality	I [V—I V—I] V	V	V	V	I	V—I—I] V—I	V I	I
Sections	A	B	C	D	E	A'	C'	VI	I

From a theoretical perspective, this means that two different hierarchies have been established, in both of which the domain of musical form is subordinate. In "Ragion nell'alma siede" it is dominated by the domain of character (at the level of the individual).[38] In "È la fede delle femmine," by contrast, the domain of musical form (specifically da capo form) is dominated by that of text (at the level of intertextuality). In the latter case we might as well say that the textual quotation and the musical form are related by a historical association that marginalizes the customary organization of a Terzetto.[39]

Formal abstraction can thus regularly be applied to the so-called secondary domains, albeit with a utilitarian approach that tends to underplay certain theoretical aspects. Concepts associated with stage-action, such as motivation, dramaturgical function, feeling, and so forth, might as well be construed as combinations of distinct if interacting domains (the stage-action in its verbal and visual components, the characters, the plot-development, the epistemic system, the time system, etc.). Whether or not such extensions of the theoretical framework will foster our understanding of the principal domains (and of opera *tout court*) is a different question. In any case, I see no cogent reason for applying different formalization standards to different domains.

TENTATIVE FORMALIZATIONS: PLOT-DEVELOPMENT

Notwithstanding the utility of abstracting "acts," most set pieces – to be precise: many arias, most ensembles, and all finales – embed

A(I)–B(V)–C(I–V)–A'(I)–D(I)–C'(I). On male comic arias see Platoff, "The buffa aria"; on mixtures of seria and buffa, see Hunter, "Some Representations," as well as Marita P. McClymonds's article elsewhere in this volume.

38 As opposed for instance to character at the level of "type," such as the masks of the commedia dell'arte.

39 The piece could be described as an arietta *con pertichini* ("with understudies"; i.e., with interpolated comments by other characters). Analogous cases are Donna Elvira's "Ah chi mi dice mai" and the Terzetto No. 10 in *La clemenza di Tito*.

situations that cannot be thus reduced, but are constituted as a chain of acts, evolving (or merely succeeding one another) in time. A formalization must therefore account for a number of connected acts (see Figure 12.3). These can be grouped into discrete units or motifs.[40] At this point, the conflicts between purely narrative (or dramatic) and operatic segmentation become evident: although a chain of acts within a single set piece may constitute an expository unit on musical grounds, it may or may not correspond to a *narrative* motif or "movement."[41] In other words, a segmentation of the plot-development on the basis of individual set pieces may correspond to the autonomous narrative or expository structures less closely than to the conventions of the genre; that is, the division into set pieces and recitatives, as well as the criteria for such divisions in different historical periods or genres. (Otherwise we would be applying narratological criteria to opera as if it were nothing more than a story or a play.)

Nevertheless, a purely narrative segmentation may interact in some relevant way with peculiarly operatic segmentation.[42] At the beginning of *Così fan tutte*, for example, we can distinguish different narrative motifs (see Figure 12.4): the "bet," which concludes in No. 3 with an initial "anticipation" of victory (i.e., an ostension projected in the future); and the ladies' "virtual courting" of their lovers' portraits, also concluded by an (unwitting) "anticipation" of change (the Allegro of the duet No. 4: "Se questo mio core / mai cangia desio / Amore mi faccia / vivendo penar" ["If my heart ever changes its desire, may Love make me suffer while I live"]). Notwithstanding their differences, these two motifs cohere across the strong visual articulation of the change of scene, thanks to a double parallelism: between the men's verbal representation of the ladies at the very beginning and the ladies' representation of the

40 On motifs, see n. 15 above.

41 The narratological notion of "movement" is used in Segre's magisterial analysis of the *Maistre Pathelin*, in *Teatro e Romanzo*, pp. 27–50.

42 In particular, the temporal span of a narrative movement is much longer than most segments corresponding to a set piece (with the possible exception of finales).

Figure 12.3 Formalization of "chains of acts"

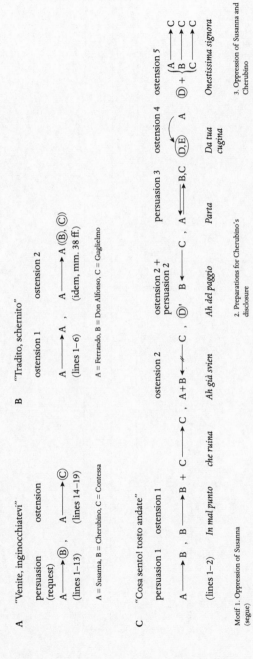

Figure 12.4 *Così fan tutte*: dramatic motifs (Act I, scenes 1–3)

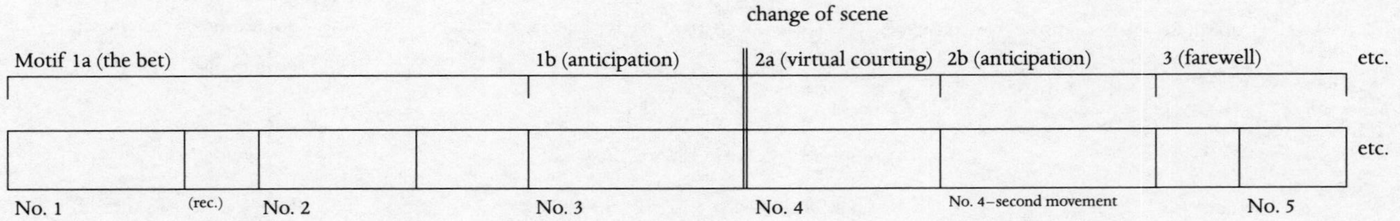

men (visually "reinforced" by the portraits); and between the two anticipations. The ensuing, much longer "farewell" or "departure" motif, on the other hand, produces a sudden and drastic modification of these expectations.

Indeed, these narrative structures may influence the musical form of the sisters' duet. The two-movement accelerating sequence and the ample virtuosic expansion of the Allegro (73 measures for the last four lines, as opposed to 71 for the fourteen lines of the Andante) relate not so much to the poetic structure – the stanzas comprise 4+4+4+6 lines, with the Allegro entering at the third line of the concluding sestet – as to the disposition of the speeches (the last two couplets are *à due*). The fast movement is certainly a valuable joint characterization of the two coquettes, who sing brilliant, light, schematically undifferentiated parts to a text that might have suggested a more serious approach. However, its climactic, "ending" character might appear inappropriate, since it immediately follows a change of scene and another ensemble (the Terzetto No. 3, also a strong point of articulation both instrumentally and tonally).[43] The segmentation of the plot, however, suggests that the Allegro of No. 4, independently of the first part of the duet, serves the articulatory function of an "anticipation," and is thus analogous to No. 3. What happens immediately following is thus marked as a new beginning, the first stage of the "complication" of the plot.[44]

Plot-development can also provide clues to a deeper understanding of set pieces; for example, those that resist categorization according to types or forms and hence are not easily subjected to comparative analysis. This is often the case with ensembles, whose formal outline reflects the layout of the verbal text (albeit to different degrees).[45] The sextets in Act II of *Don Giovanni* and Act I of *Così*

43 It is the first number after the overture to use trumpets and timpani; also, it resumes the key of the overture (C), following the first two Terzetti in G and E.
44 Complication is one of Labov's and Waletzky's five formal generalizations of plot-elements (Orientation, Complication, Evaluation, Resolution, Coda); cited from Segre, *The Literary Text*, p. 95 and n. 46.
45 For Mozart's compositional habits in this respect, see John Platoff's contribution

fan tutte have in common not only the number of singers but the progressive accumulation of characters on stage, a central position within their respective acts, and a size and construction reminiscent of finales. Although their position with respect to the expository process, the dramatic mechanism, and the constellation of the characters is entirely different, both are based on an accelerating structure in two or three movements. Although both dramatic expositions turn on a problem of identity, during the *Don Giovanni* sextet Leporello's identity is revealed, whereas in *Così fan tutte* the false identity of the "Albanians" is reinforced by repeated "proofs." The difference is obviously connected with the position of the two sextets within the plot (the first is close to the "resolution," the second occurs during the "complication").

Indeed the sextets function differently with respect to the segmentation of their respective plots (see Figure 12.5). Whereas the one in *Don Giovanni* participates in two different motifs, which I name "identity exchange" and "vindication," that in *Così fan tutte* belongs to only one, "introduction of the Albanians," which continues on after the sextet. Despite this difference, both ensembles present a turning point, best considered in the context of the characters' belief systems. In *Don Giovanni*, the revelation of Leporello's identity under threat of imminent death causes a complete alteration of the system (with the exception of Leporello himself): not only does it modify the attitude of those present toward him but, more notably, it has a prolonged dramatic consequence with respect to the Don, whose guilt is now beyond dispute for all. At the same time, however, the object of indignation is removed, and this creates the prospect of a delayed punishment in the future.[46] Although the situation may be termed "dramatic" in a general sense (the 5+1 final grouping of the voices appears to reflect an

to this volume; also Ronald J. Rabin, "Mozart, Da Ponte, and the Dramaturgy of Opera Buffa: Italian Comic Opera in Vienna, 1783–1791," PhD diss., Cornell University, ch. 4, and Hunter, *The Poetics of Entertainment: Opera Buffa in Vienna, 1770–1790* (Princeton University Press, forthcoming), ch. 4.

46 The visual element plays a relevant but static role, in that darkness (reinforced by the textual incipit) is the condition that permits this sort of action.

Figure 12.5 A comparison of two sextets

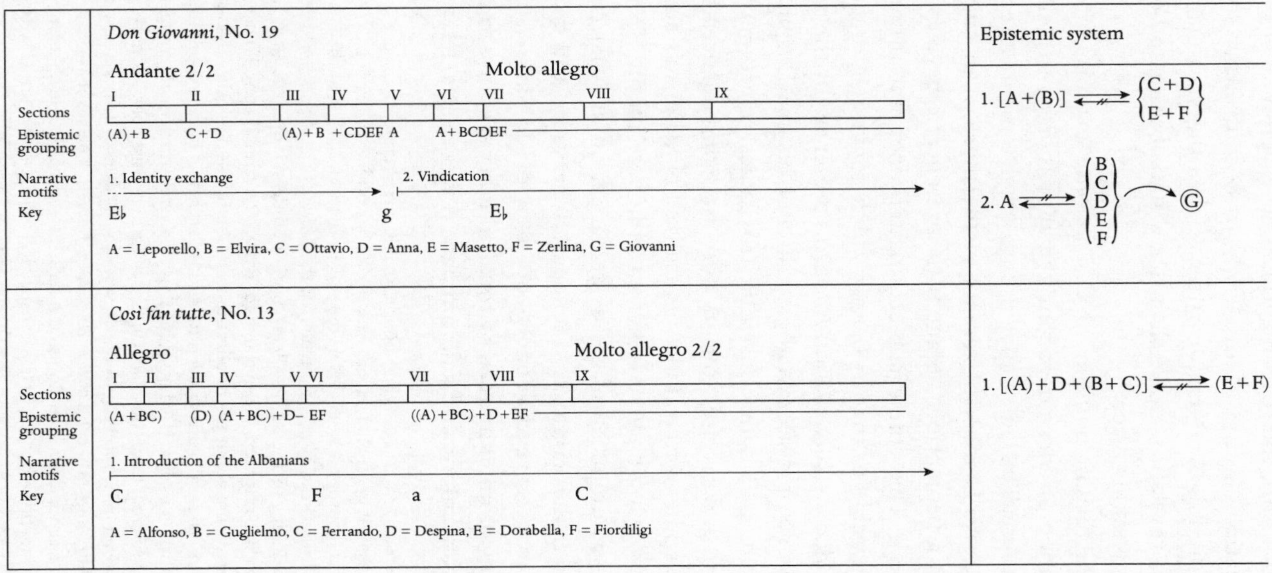

	Epistemic system
Don Giovanni, No. 19	
Andante 2/2 Molto allegro	1. $[A+(B)] \not\rightarrow \begin{cases} C+D \\ E+F \end{cases}$
Sections: I II III IV V VI VII VIII IX	
Epistemic grouping: (A)+B C+D (A)+B +CDEF A A+BCDEF	2. $A \rightleftharpoons \left.\begin{matrix} B \\ C \\ D \\ E \\ F \end{matrix}\right\} \rightarrow \text{Ⓖ}$
Narrative motifs: 1. Identity exchange 2. Vindication	
Key: E♭ g E♭	
A = Leporello, B = Elvira, C = Ottavio, D = Anna, E = Masetto, F = Zerlina, G = Giovanni	
Così fan tutte, No. 13	
Allegro Molto allegro 2/2	1. $[(A)+D+(B+C)] \not\rightarrow (E+F)$
Sections: I II III IV V VI VII VIII IX	
Epistemic grouping: (A+BC) (D) (A+BC)+D- EF ((A)+BC)+D+EF	
Narrative motifs: 1. Introduction of the Albanians	
Key: C F a C	
A = Alfonso, B = Guglielmo, C = Ferrando, D = Despina, E = Dorabella, F = Fiordiligi	

antagonism), the real antagonist has evaporated with Leporello's revelation. A sign of this is the two contrasting stylistic levels (Leporello's "low" comic patter vs. the others), which, by the time of the revelation, make clear that a juxtaposition rather than a real clash is taking place.[47]

The turning point in the *Così fan tutte* sextet is represented by a violation of social decorum: the admission of the Albanians into the house. The ladies' fury rises to a high temperature through two successive changes of tempo; furthermore, their coloratura provides a perceptibly antagonistic presence, especially in the final section. The comic subject matter does not provide a frame comparable to that in *Don Giovanni*; comic reinforcement is also provided visually by Don Alfonso's presence "by the door," as well as by the precise textual ostension of his and Despina's asides. It remains an "action" ensemble (the ladies' rejection of the men is strong and precise), but its potential consequences for the plot-development are rapidly neutralized by Alfonso's ensuing recitative, which still pursues the "introduction" motif.

As a complication and systematization of what can be understood as the "context" of an operatic set piece, this discussion may help to interpret the concept of "principal domains." In both sextets the highpoint is marked by tonal mobility around a foreign key (the mediant minor and subdominant respectively), but while in *Don*

---

47 Platoff's criticism (in this volume) of Mozart's return to the tonic in this sextet must not go unchallenged. The strong harmonic articulation, V/vi–I, can be seen as an appropriate parallel to the stage situation, so long as the latter is examined in its entirety. While it is true that the "shock" has already occurred, the beginning of the Molto allegro is not eventless: it dramatizes the *effects* of the shock. Until then, the five antagonists of Giovanni/Leporello have been wondering about the implications of Leporello's disclosure ("Stupida/o resto . . . Che mai sarà!"); the sudden turn to E flat from a distant chord thus reflects a return to reality. Furthermore, a visual as well as dramatic component must be considered: until the cadence, five characters have been addressing Giovanni/Leporello; now, however, each of them turns to a new focal point, addressing either the audience or him/herself. The suspension of the characters' interaction calls attention to the suddenly "absent" Don Giovanni, determining an indefinite but important prospection: one does not know what will happen next. (Compare Platoff's comment at his p. 402, n 37.)

Giovanni the high situational tension is sustained only by tonal and motivic means, in *Così fan tutte* the fundamental rhythmic shift to 3/4 marks the intensifying entrance of two new characters. The new tempo also sets the stage for the later reinterpretation of its opening motif in free augmentation as a ritual imploration in minor by the Albanians and Despina (mm. 82ff.). The rhythmic and textural differences of these highpoints are evident, but their respective quality of "tonal mobility" should also be considered: in *Don Giovanni*, an underlying three-part structure based on C minor (endpoints around mm. 61 ff. and 121 ff.);[48] in *Così fan tutte*, a linear rather than a closed structure (from m. 54 on: F major, C major, A minor, and the home dominant, preparing the Molto allegro in C major). Such different tonal outlines can be seen as reflecting each sextet's "epistemic" system, which changes during that in *Don Giovanni* but remains constant in *Così fan tutte*. Although both ensembles can be defined as dramatic "in the sense of being theatrically exciting or in the sense of embodying or representing action,"[49] one must still distinguish between different components of the dramatic domain.

Beyond the investigation of "acts," with their qualitative determinations (and relative hierarchies), and of chains of acts (narratological motifs), we must also acknowledge that the hierarchical network of analytical relationships is itself subject to occasional changes, even within one and the same set piece.[50] One evident example is found in the Quintet No. 8a in *Così fan tutte*, where the visual component of the action is so dominant as to permit the annihilation of the text through the broken, "pointillistic" presentation of the words ("Di . . . scri- . . . ver- . . . mi" etc.). Immediately afterwards, however (mm. 7–11), subjective expres-

48 Platoff gives a formal diagram of the sextet.

49 Hunter, "Text, Music, and Drama," p. 38 (contrasting it with the different type of "dramaticity" embodied in arias such as "Ragion nell'alma siede"). These features, combined with a "Wagnerian" orientation, are the traditional grounds for the high critical reputation of ensembles.

50 Solos and ensembles alike can encompass one or more "acts," although it is rare for an ensemble to embed only one simple act (an example of the latter is the Terzettino No. 10, "Soave sia il vento," in *Così fan tutte*).

sion comes to the fore.[51] We could describe what happens in the latter section as the momentary dominance of the characters' domain (assigning one half-phrase to each sister, consistent with their incomplete subjectivization at this stage of the plot-development.)[52]

THE ROLE OF THEORY

If we accept this kaleidoscopic variability of hierarchies as a feature of composite aesthetic artifacts (such as opera), our analytical efforts will be at once complicated and clarified. A musicodramatic text embraces domains that, although apparently peripheral and often secondary for the music, can occasionally be located at the top of the ideal pyramid of signifying elements. This need not imply an overevaluation of certain domains, or endanger the centrality of music in a discourse on opera; on the contrary, it provides a suitable theoretical framework even for those "purely musical" aspects of the musicodramatic text that are not easily interpreted in terms of dramatic functions. (One example is the final sections of climactic ensembles, where the syntactic expansion of the music corresponds to the indefinite reiteration of the same words, and therefore to a neutralization or suspension of verbal signification, and in some cases of the action as well.)

This step adds a hierarchical element to the analytical paradigm of "multivalence," which holds that the various domains of an opera (text, action, music, etc.) are "not necessarily congruent and may even be incompatible; and that the resulting complexity or lack of integration is often a primary source of their aesthetic effect."[53] While this widely accepted point of view greatly expands the

51 As Kunze has stressed: *Mozarts Opern*, pp. 497 ff.
52 A piece in which the "belief system" of the characters determines the structure of the whole middle section is the Quintet No. 6 in *Così fan tutte*. The men and the ladies are juxtaposed twice in an A-B-(A') structure (mm. 36–46 and 65–75): the "pathetic" section for the two ladies is isolated from the men's asides, so that the music reflects and emphasizes mechanically the epistemic condition of the two groups.   53 Webster, "Mozart and the Myth of Unity," p. 198.

analytical vision, it runs the risk of turning the interpretive process into a mere census of unordered observations (which we are consequently compelled to describe as "exceptional"). From this perspective, a complication of the theoretical framework may alleviate the risk of analytical or interpretive impasses.

My purpose in this tentative application of formalization principles to various domains has not been to encourage a blind trust in the supposed power of an ever more systematic methodology. The explanation of a work of art, "finished model of an infinite world" (Jurij M. Lotman),[54] is an endless aspiration, half rational exercise, half a form of devotion. Setting up a theory represents more the selection of a useful narrative strategy than the solution to a problem. It is from this perspective that I find relevant a closer scrutiny of fundamental concepts such as "drama" and "action": they remain an important basis of our appreciation system, even if their formulation within opera studies has often been inadequate. On the other hand, many of my observations imply a reformulation of notions that already belong to the heritage of Mozartean research. Perhaps they can reinforce detailed multivalent analyses by clarifying the nature of the musicodramatic text and by offering a means of negotiating between the analysis of individual set pieces and of whole operas. The distinction between these attitudes reflects different subjective interests, mirrored in the decision to posit a relatively stable hierarchical model of the relationships between distinct operatic domains, as opposed to an infinitely variable one. While the two approaches do not imply any opposition, it is doubtful whether they will soon converge. But this is a problem of creativity rather than criticism.

54 Quoted from Segre, *Teatro e romanzo*, p. 21.

James Webster

In the mid-1980s, the analysis of operatic music was catapulted into musicological discourse as a central issue, notably with the publication of *Analyzing Opera: Verdi and Wagner*.[1] Not surprisingly, the approaches were decidedly mixed: some contributors adopted or adapted methods that for generations had been applied to "absolute" instrumental music; others, notably Carolyn Abbate and Roger Parker, sharply criticized such methods and called for new ones.[2]

Today, such revisionist stances have become the norm in operatic studies. However else they may differ, most if not all scholars of eighteenth-century opera would agree on the following theses: (1) The eighteenth-century operatic "work" was multifarious and contingent. An opera had multiple authors, including not only the composer, but also the impresario, librettist and stage-director,[3] set-designer, and especially the principal singers, whose "performative" activity centrally defined the experience of the work.[4] By the same token, an opera had no fixed text; it was always subject to change, whether through substitution of arias more to singers'

1 Ed. Carolyn Abbate and Roger Parker (Berkeley: University of California Press, 1989); see especially the editors' introduction. These essays, like those in the present volume, originated as contributions to an international conference at Cornell University (held in 1984; hence the phrase "mid-1980s").
2 My contribution to the same conference was likewise of mixed character, although my main concern was not so much the putative differences between operatic and instrumental analysis as the lack of analytical attention to Mozart's operas. It was published as "To Understand Verdi and Wagner We Must Understand Mozart," *19CM* 11 (1987–88), 175–93.
3 On the librettist's function as stage-director, see Heartz, *Mozart's Operas*, ch. 5.
4 On the importance of singers and especially their performative function, see, for example, Heartz, "When Mozart Revises: Guglielmo in *Così*," in Sadie, *Wolfgang Amadè Mozart*, pp. 155–61, as well as his essay in this volume; Mary Hunter, *The Poetics of Entertainment: Opera Buffa in Vienna, 1770–1790* (Princeton University Press, forthcoming), ch. 3.

liking, or wholesale revision in new productions.[5] (2) Opera's mutability is not merely a matter of what happened two hundred years
ago. An opera is a dramatic action; it lives not only through music,
but also plot, characterization, staging, ideational content, and so
forth. Hence, although any operatic number can indeed be analyzed, its form – that is, the resolution of one's analytical results
into a coherent image that can be described in prose or represented
in a diagram, or that seems to exemplify a well-defined type –
remains fluid and contingent.[6] (3) In addition, operatic numbers
must be interpreted. Our sense of the meaning of a given number
depends not only on analytical results but also, again, on many
other things that cannot be analyzed in any ordinary sense:[7] which
character sings it and with what motivation, the dramatic context,
how it is performed; and beyond, to the role it plays in our view of
the work as a whole.[8] (4) All eighteenth-century operas (including
Mozart's) were composed and understood in the context of powerful conventions of genre; today as well, an adequate knowledge of
the generic context is essential for understanding.[9] (5) As public,

5 This applied to Mozart no less than to other composers. The 1789 revival of *Le
   nozze di Figaro* included substitutions for both of Susanna's arias, in order to
   accommodate Adriana Ferrarese (who also created the role of Fiordiligi), while
   the differences between the 1787 Prague and 1788 Vienna productions of *Don
   Giovanni* (neither of which corresponds to the current standard version) continue
   to exercise scholars and critics; see the debate between Wolfgang Rehm and
   Stefan Kunze as to whether the original (Prague) version should count as the
   (only) "authentic" one, in "'Don Giovanni': Prag 1787 – Wien 1788–1987," *MJb*,
   1987–88, pp. 195–221; see also the articles by Michael F. Robinson and Jessica
   Waldoff in this volume.
6 For a comprehensive methodological discussion see Webster, "Analysis."
7 Admittedly, the import of "ordinary" can be contested; for an expansive view
   of operatic analysis, notably as regards semiotic and dramaturgical aspects, see
   Sergio Durante's important methodological essay in this volume.
8 This is not to endorse the older view that an eighteenth-century number-opera
   can be profitably *analyzed* as a whole, as in Siegmund Levarie's notorious
   representation of an entire work as a single four-chord progression; see his
   Mozart's "Le nozze di Figaro": A Critical Analysis (Chicago: University of Chicago
   Press, 1952), pp. 233–45.
9 John Platoff, *Mozart and Opera Buffa in Vienna, 1783–1791* (Oxford University Press,
   forthcoming); see also the introduction to this volume.

342 | James Webster

theatrical events, operas both reflected and created social meanings, more directly than instrumental music ever could.[10]

For all these reasons (the consensus runs), the study of operatic music must be *contextualized*. Operas are fundamentally different from works of absolute music, a category dependent on the concepts of the perfect, timeless artwork and the single, visionary author of genius.[11] Not only the methods associated with the analysis of absolute music, but the very traditions and ideologies that animate and sustain such analysis – notably their grounding in the search for unity – are seen as suspect in the multifarious and contingent (and therefore contested) worlds of opera.[12] Hence operatic analysts must develop new, "idiomatic" methods; in particular, they must avoid the uncritical use of terms and concepts drawn from traditional instrumental analysis.[13]

However, despite its virtues this new consensus seems to me in some important respects problematical.[14] In this essay I will inter-

10 Martha Feldman, "Magic Mirrors and the *Seria* Stage: Thoughts towards a Ritual View," *JAMS* 48 (1995), 423–84; Hunter, *The Poetics of Entertainment*, chs. 1–2.
11 Carl Dahlhaus, *The Idea of Absolute Music*, trans. Roger Lustig (Chicago: University of Chicago Press, 1989). The classic postmodern problematizations of author and artwork are Roland Barthes, "The Death of the Author," in *Image – Music – Text*, trans. Stephen Heath (New York: Hill and Wang, 1977), pp. 142–48; "From Work to Text," ibid., pp. 155–64, and in Josué V. Harari, ed., *Textual Strategies: Perspectives in Post-Structuralist Criticism* (Ithaca: Cornell University Press, 1979), pp. 73–81; Michel Foucault, "What is an Author?" ibid., pp. 141–60; see also Jacques Derrida, "Parergon," in *The Truth in Painting*, trans. Geoff Bennington and Ian McLeod (Chicago: University of Chicago Press, 1987), pp. 15–147; "Restitutions of the Truth in Pointing [*pointure*]," ibid., pp. 255–382. For an incisive summary see Donald Preziosi, *Rethinking Art History: Meditations on a Coy Science* (New Haven: Yale University Press, 1989), ch. 2.
12 See Abbate and Parker, *Analyzing Opera* (n. 1).
13 Among eighteenth-century scholars Platoff in particular has repeatedly insisted on the latter difference; see his article in this volume.
14 I say this notwithstanding the unity-bashing in my polemical "Mozart's Operas and the Myth of Musical Unity," *COJ* 2 (1990), 197–218, and the fluidity of formal interpretation in my "Analysis" ("Any notion of 'the' analysis of a Mozart aria is a chimera"; "In many Mozart arias, 'the' form does not exist"; pp. 105, 122). The key word is "uncritical" (at the end of the preceding paragraph); about the continuing centrality of analysis to operatic understanding there can be no doubt.

rogate it in two ways: by attempting to deconstruct the binary opposition between "instrumental" and "operatic" analysis, and by raising the issue of value.[15]

To begin with the latter: recent writings on opera buffa have tended to avoid explicit value-judgments. The reason (I would speculate) is not so much mere cultural correctness, as the inherent tension between their focus on contextualization and the inescapable presence of Mozart. This binary opposition, "Mozart vs. the 'others,'" is one of the most powerful in musicological culture.[16] Even the most knowledgeable and sympathetic students of this repertory treat Mozart as a special, privileged case.[17] Similarly, the great majority of detailed analyses of later eighteenth-century Italian opera have been devoted, not to Piccinni, Salieri, Paisiello, or Cimarosa, but to Mozart and Haydn. (As an operatic "other" to Mozart, Haydn is the exception who proves the rule: although analyses of his operas continue to proliferate,[18] his status as a musical dramatist remains uncertain. Presumably, the analyses have come into being because of both his privileged position in the canon and the sheer availability of his music; however,

---

15 The most penetrating musicological discussion of value remains Dahlhaus, *Analysis and Value Judgment*, trans. Siegmund Levarie (New York: Pendragon, 1983).

16 It has been especially characteristic of German-language scholarship (and Anglo-American scholarship dependent on it), which has favored nationalistic and idealistic interpretation of Mozart's operas as having "transcended" the Italianate "models" that "prepared" them. A variant of this attitude, transferred to the realm of drama in general, can be seen in Paolo Gallarati's essay elsewhere in this volume, while most of the remaining contributions either problematize, or contextualize, the issue of Mozart vs. the "others."

17 For example, Platoff, "How Original Was Mozart? Evidence from *opera buffa*," *EM* 20 (1992), 105–17.

18 Reinhard Strohm, "Zur Metrik in Haydns und Anfossis 'La vera costanza,'" in Eva Badura-Skoda, ed., *Joseph Haydn: Bericht über den internationalen Joseph Haydn Kongress Wien . . . 1982* (Munich: Henle, 1986), pp. 279–94; Hunter, "Haydn's Sonata-Form Arias," *CM* 37/38 (1984), pp. 19–32; Hunter, "Text, Music and Drama in Haydn's Italian Opera Arias: Four Case Studies," *JM* 7 (1989), 29–57; Caryl Leslie Clark, "The Opera Buffa Finales of Joseph Haydn," PhD diss., Cornell University, 1991; Regina Wochnik, *Die Musiksprache in den opere semiserie Joseph Haydns unter besonderer Berücksichtigung von L'incontro improvviso* (Eisenach-Hamburg: Wagner, 1993); Rebecca Green, "Power and Patriarchy in Haydn's Goldoni Operas," PhD diss., University of Toronto, 1995.

these advantages derive not from the prestige of his operas, but from that of his instrumental music, supplemented by the *Creation* and the late masses.) In short, notwithstanding their common opposition to the bad old traditions of opera criticism, the calls for close analysis and those for contextualization have so far been motivated by different concerns and have had little effect on each other.[19]

In what follows, I will attempt to bring these two new traditions into a more nearly explicit relation, by undertaking a close analysis of a number by a buffa composer other than Mozart or Haydn: an aria from Salieri's opera buffa *La locandiera* ("The Innkeeper"; Vienna, 1773).[20] I selected it from no other motive than that it appealed to me greatly during a recent survey of *opere buffe*, based on available recordings, undertaken pursuant to the conference from which the present volume emerged.[21] The choice seemed propitious in other ways as well. From an institutional point of view, Salieri was the key figure in Viennese opera during Mozart's time: he was active there more or less continuously from the late 1760s into the nineteenth century, and as *Hofkapellmeister* exercised immense influence throughout the period.[22] *La locandiera* dates from the first flowering of Viennese opera buffa, a period associated primarily with Florian Leopold

19 The same point is made in Durante's study in this volume, except that the opposite to analysis has become "dramaturgy."

20 As far as I am aware, this is the first such analysis in English. Nor are such analyses common in German; a notable exception (albeit more impressive for length than insight) comprises the Anfossi analyses in Volker Mattern, *Das Dramma Giocoso: La finta giardiniera: Ein Vergleich der Vertonungen von Pasquale Anfossi und Wolfgang Amadeus Mozart* (Laaber: Laaber, 1989). Platoff discusses Salieri's aria "L'anno mille settecento" from *La cifra* (1789; libretto by Da Ponte) in "The Buffa Aria in Mozart's Vienna," *COJ* 2 (1990), 105–12, albeit without pretensions to detailed analysis.

21 *La locandiera*: Nuova Era compact discs, cat. 6888–89.

22 On Salieri see Rudolph Angermüller, *Antonio Salieri: Sein Leben und seine weltlichen Werke unter besonderer Berücksichtigung seiner "großen" Opern*, 3 vols. (Munich: Katzbichler, 1971), as well as John A. Rice's forthcoming monograph (University of Chicago Press).

Gassmann and the young Salieri himself; it was contemporaneous with Haydn's *L'infedeltà delusa* and preceded Mozart's *La finta giardiniera* by only two years. It thus exemplifies an important and relatively little studied stage of buffa history in the Habsburg realm.[23]

Finally, my aria has numerous points of contact with others, including some by Mozart, so that a comparative discussion will be possible. However, in contrast to the usual practice when comparing Mozart to his contemporaries, I will not assume that the differences necessarily signify Salieri's inferiority. This will entail (among other things) an attempt to separate out those aspects of Mozart's musical virtuosity *that can be analyzed* – the qualification is essential – from his other, "operatic" virtues. This distinction will clarify some of the (often unconscious) presuppositions that govern the belief in Mozart's operatic superiority, and will thus pose the issue of value in a novel manner. But since most analytical practice relates specifically to traditions of instrumental music, this questioning of the primacy of analysis in an operatic context will also cast doubt on the supposed general distinction between operatic and instrumental analysis.[24] What these two issues – the problem of value and operatic vs. instrumental analysis – have in common is that neither can be understood unless one has sorted out the relations between analysis and interpretation. Indeed, I will argue that an understanding of those relations is essential not only in the study of opera, but in musicological discourse generally.

23 This period is briefly discussed in the articles by Daniel Heartz and Bruce Alan Brown elsewhere in this volume.
24 Although I agree with Platoff that the analytical methods in general use were developed primarily with respect to instrumental music and therefore ought not to be applied to opera uncritically, I cannot accept his premise that instrumental and operatic "thinking" constituted opposed categories of composition in Mozart's time. See his article elsewhere in this volume.

II

The libretto of *La locandiera* was adapted from Goldoni's play of the same name by Domenico Poggi, a bass-turned-impresario. The storyline is simple: Mirandolina, an innkeeper, is courted by two minor noblemen, the rich but foolish Count Albafiorita ("flowery dawn"), and the grandiloquent but poor and cowardly Marquis Forlimpopoli. However, she sets her sights on yet a third personage, Cavaliere Ripafratta ("bramble-bank") – not because she is in love with him, but because he is a misogynist, and she wants to demonstrate, to him and to the world, that he is no more immune to feminine charms than any other male. In the end, she spurns all three worthies and marries her faithful employee Fabrizio. (In anticipation of Giuseppe Sarti's popular *Fra i due litiganti il terzo gode* ["Between the two contestants the third wins out"], the opera could just as well have been titled *Fra i tre litiganti il quarto gode*.)[25]

The opera is remarkable for its positive portrayal of the heroine: intelligent and resourceful, yet sufficiently proud and manipulative to be a credible character rather than a mere stick-figure;[26] her virtues shine all the more brightly in comparison to the four fallible male characters. During Act I, Mirandolina begins to apply her blandishments to the Cavaliere; predictably, after an initial period of resistance he becomes intrigued, and is soon hooked. As the curtain rises on Act II we see him alone, pacing back and forth, attempting to make sense of his feelings. The attempt naturally takes the form of an aria, "Vo pensando." This event confirms the

25 Sarti's opera, premiered in Milan in 1782, was produced in Vienna in 1783, during the first season of the new opera buffa troupe founded by Joseph II. It not only supplied one of the dinner-music tunes in the Act II finale of *Don Giovanni* (as is well known) but, as Silke Leopold argues in a study forthcoming in *AnM*, may have been an important source for *Le nozze di Figaro* as well.

26 This notwithstanding Goldoni's (presumably disingenuous) comment in his preface that this play was his most moral and instructive because it denounces female hypocrisy! On gender issues see the papers by Marvin Carlson and Tia DeNora in this volume.

Cavaliere's central status; a soliloquy-aria with no preceding recitative at the beginning of Act II was a privileged moment (think of "Porgi amor"; as we shall see, this comparison is pertinent in other ways as well).

"Vo pensando" belongs to a loosely definable group (it is not quite a genuine aria type), which Stacy Moore has dubbed the *indecision aria*.[27] In these arias "a character, often in distress," manifests "two simultaneous and contradictory states of mind," but cannot resolve this conflict by an act of will. The arias tend either to be *di mezzo carattere* (like "Vo pensando"), or to mix "high" seria style with agonized or incoherent outbreaks (Haydn/Porta, *Orlando Paladino*: Medoro's "Parto. Ma, oh Dio, non posso" and "Dille che un infelice"). Often the love-conflict involves an inappropriate class-relation (Martín y Soler/Da Ponte, *Una cosa rara*: the Prince's "Seguir degg'io chi fugge?"). A related situation is that of the "seductee" in the opening section of a seduction duet; for example, Zerlina's first line in "La ci darem la mano" is "Vorrei, e non vorrei."[28] Indecision arias often seem to be simultaneously "straight" and ironic, comic and serious, in ways that are not easy to pin down. They are often constructed in several contrasting sections, and exhibit an unusual degree of independent orchestral material. Because of this dramatic and musical complexity, indecision arias often seem central to the overall meaning of the operas in which they occur; they permit, indeed encourage, multiple interpretations.

---

27 Moore, "'E risolvermi non so': Representations of Indecision in Opera Buffa Arias," unpublished paper, Cornell University, 1994, p. 5. I am very grateful to Ms. Moore for permission to refer to it here.

  On aria types see Webster, "Analysis," §1. For detailed treatment of particular types see Platoff, "The buffa aria"; Helga Lühning, "Die Rondo-Arie im späten 18. Jahrhundert: Dramatischer Gehalt und musikalischer Bau," *Hamburger Jahrbuch für Musikwissenschaft*, 5 (1981), 219–46; Rice, "Rondò vocali di Salieri e Mozart per Adriana Ferrarese," in Muraro, *I vicini*, vol. 1, pp. 185–210.

28 See Richard Stiefel, "Mozart's Seductions," *CM* 36 (1983), 151–66.

Poggi and Salieri, *La locandiera* (Vienna, 1773), II. 1

Il Cavaliere passeggiando pensieroso.[*]   *The Cavaliere pacing pensively.*

[Ottonario]

Vo pensando, e ripensando;	I'm thinking and reflecting;
Son così fra il si, e il no.	I'm trapped between Yes and No.
Che far debbo a me domando,	I wonder what I should do,
E risolvermi non so.	But I can't make up my mind.

[Versi sciolti]

Io non so se m'inganno;	I don't know if I'm mistaken,
Ma giurerei, che sono innamorato.	But I would swear that I'm in love.
Tal caldo inusitato	Such an unaccustomed fire
Mi sento insinuar entro le vene,	I feel stealing into my veins
Che riposo non ho.	That I find no rest.
La pace antica	The former tranquility
Del mio cor dove andò?	In my heart, where has it gone?
La bella Locandiera	The fair innkeeper
M'incantò, mi sedusse . . .	Has charmed me, has seduced me . . .
Ma quest'affanno	But this turmoil,
Non potria derivar d'altra	Could there be no other reason
cagione?	for it?
Un effetto di bile esser potria;	It could be an effect of bile;
Esser potrebbe ancor ipocondria.	Or it might be hypochondria.

[Settenario]

Ma se tu fossi, Amore,	But if you, Love, are
Cagion del mio penar,	The cause of my distress,
Nasconditi nel core,	Hide yourself in my heart,
E non ti palesar.	And don't reveal yourself.

[*] Text according to the libretto printed in the recording, Nuova Era 6888–89 (altered in a few details to reflect the spelling and punctuation of the autograph); translation adapted from that by Timothy Alan Shaw.

The text of "Vo pensando" comprises two quatrains at the beginning and end, enclosing a longer middle section in *versi sciolti* (free, seven- and eleven-syllable lines intended to be set as recitative). In the first stanza, the Cavaliere is consumed by self-centered ambivalence; the subject "I" appears in every line, and yet he cannot even name his problem.[29] This he does at the beginning of the middle section: "I would swear that I'm in love"; after which he expounds on this at length. In the last stanza, he finally invokes "Love" by name, but by means of a remarkable image: still resisting, he asks Love to "hide" – but where? – "in his heart"! Indeed Love is now the subject of the Cavaliere's discourse; he has abandoned his own agency, indeed has already succumbed. This process is foreshadowed in the middle section, in which the last occurrence of "I" as subject (in the middle) comes only in a dependent clause ("I find no rest"). The subject of the next sentence is already the more abstract "tranquility"; and immediately thereafter comes the decisive shift: "The fair innkeeper" (subject) "has seduced me" (object).

Salieri dramatizes this scene imaginatively and resourcefully (see the score provided in Example 13.1).[30] The aria, in the key of E flat, is through-composed, with three sections corresponding to the three textual divisions. Perhaps its most striking event is the concluding line of the first stanza, "E risolvermi non so" (prefigured in the introduction, mm. 7–8). The dominant demonstratively fails to resolve; the leading-tone D (m. 7) slides down chromatically to D♭, producing a B flat minor chord, and on to a deceptive cadence – not,

29 In another sense, as Arthur Groos kindly informs me, the Cavaliere's impasse in the second line, "Son così fra il Sì e il No," can be understood as invoking (or parodying) the scholastic method of argumentation, still common in the eighteenth century, in which one's interlocutor was forced to respond to each in a sequence of propositions by "Yes" or "No," until the desired logical conclusion was achieved.

30 The opera is unpublished; this reduction was made by ear and later checked against Salieri's autograph (A-Wn, Mus. Hs. 16179). I thank John A. Rice for making a microfilm available, as well as for information supplied from his forthcoming biography of Salieri. (Rice had independently concluded that "Vo pensando" is of unusual beauty and interest.)

Example 13.1 Salieri, "Vo pensando": vocal score (for source see n. 30)

Il Cavaliere passeggiando pensieroso.

Example 13.1 (*cont.*)

Example 13.1 (cont.)

Example 13.1 (*cont.*)

Example 13.1 (*cont.*)

Example 13.1 (*cont.*)

Example 13.1 (*cont.*)

Recitativo

Io non so se m'in-gan-no, Ma giu-re-re - i che so-no in-na-mo-ra-to.

Tal cal-do in-u - si-ta-to mi sen-to in-si-nu-ar; en-tro le

più adagio

ve-ne, che ri - po-so non ho.

Example 13.1 (*cont.*)

La pa-ce an - ti - ca del mio cor do-ve an-dò?

La bel-la lo-can-die-ra m'in-can-

rinf. [*p*] *rinf.*

- tò, mi se-dus-se... Ma quest'af-fan-no de-ri-var non po-

p *f* *p*

Example 13.1 (*cont.*)

-tri-a d'al-tra ca-gio-ne? Un ef-fet-to di bi-le es-ser po-

- tri- a; Es-ser po-treb-be an-cor i-po-con-dri-a.

Tempo primo

sotto voce

Ma se tu fos - si, A-mo - re, Ca - gion del mio pe -

Example 13.1 *(cont.)*

Example 13.1 (*cont.*)

Example 13.1 (*cont.*)

however, on the relative minor, or even V of V, but on the sub-dominant, a grammatically "incorrect" chord in this context. We see and hear the Cavaliere swoon, in the sickening realization that he is in danger of succumbing.

Although the vocal form of the first section closes normally (m. 48), the section as a whole does not; the postlude breaks off in the middle and leads chromatically to the middle section, set as accompanied recitative. In the course of this section the strings introduce a new, dotted figure, *y* (m. 60), which alternates between drooping *piano* and resolute *forte*, while its persistent descent symbolizes the Cavaliere's "fall" – into love, and out of his cherished independence. The final section shows him in a state of pronounced agitation. It begins as an arioso: not in the tonic, but on the dominant of C minor, with syncopated strings, at first in unison but then dissonant, and at first without bass. Moreover, the Cavaliere resumes singing at once, without orchestral preparation, on a downbeat (the only downbeat line-beginning in the aria), again on a word that crystallizes his state of mind: "But." Not until the last text-line does the music broaden (mm. 83 ff.) and head for a firm cadence in E flat; however, this is undercut by a deceptive cadence, again on C (m. 87). The entire subsection is thus governed as much by C minor and its dominant as by E flat; "E risolvermi non so" still holds, on the largest scale. Owing to this renewed lurch into indecisiveness the Cavaliere must now begin over (m. 88), again in *accompagnato*, on a variant of the recitative motive *y*. This leads to a free repetition of the entire subsection, beginning however on the home dominant (m. 91); the music is scored more brilliantly and with richer harmonies (mm. 94–97), and the number closes with the first and only perfect authentic cadence in the entire final section.

So far, this overview has been couched in a more or less traditional, "mixed" musicological discourse: garden-variety analytical remarks, comparative statements (aria types, etc.), and straightforward interpretation ("of two minds"; "swooning"; "falling"; etc.). How would "Vo pensando" fare if subjected to the full range of "close" analytical techniques?

With respect to the first part: the vocal section exhibits clear binary form (mm. 11–23+30–48, plus the linking 26–29). The introduction presents the primary thematic material, which comprises three visual–rhetorical figures: "walking" (mm. 1–4, as the Cavaliere paces back and forth, halting at each arrival at tonic or dominant); "recollection" (mm. 5–6, the tender motive *x* in strings alone); and "swoon." Moreover, the same sequence of topics defines the course of both the exposition and the reprise as a whole; in particular, the swoon-plus-cadence configuration from mm. 7–10 ends both large subsections (mm. 20–23, 45–48), and the initial orchestral phrase begins the postlude.[31] Thus the introduction

---

31 The recapitulation is expanded from one paragraph into two, by the extension of mm. 34 ff. to the cadence in m. 38 and an expanded treatment of the recollection motive *x*.

functions as a ritornello with respect to the section as a whole.[32] In addition, it establishes the aria's "rhythmic profile":[33] two-measure phrases beginning with a two-note upbeat, to accommodate the *ottonario* text-lines:

"Vo pen- | *san*-do e ri-pen- | *san*-do"; etc.

Indeed almost every vocal phrase in the first section is two or four measures long; the only exceptions are three-measure phrases in mm. 19–21 and 36–38, again on "E risolvermi non so."

In some passages the aria exhibits an independent instrumental "persona."[34] The tender sixteenth-motive x (mm. 5–6) returns several times, but usually in the orchestra: in mm. 18–19, the violins must induce the Cavaliere to sing it, and in mm. 23–25 and 38–41 he ignores it entirely, in favor of long-note ruminations. Even when he finally sings both measures of x (mm. 43–44), thus achieving his only four-measure phrase, a new bass version of the motive is required to spur him on (m. 42). (In the postlude, the same urgent bass motive instigates the recitative, and hence the next phase of the scene.) In the final section, his agitation is conveyed primarily by the orchestra, which creates both the instability at the beginning of each subsection and the increased breadth and richness just before the cadences. By contrast, the Cavaliere still sings mainly in two-measure phrases; the only exceptions are three-measure phrases at each increase in breadth (mm. 83–85, 96–98; they are followed without pause by two-measure confirmations, producing five-measure compound phrases). I interpret this as "protesting too

---

32 A ritornello-like function for buffa aria introductions is not uncommon, especially before 1780; see Hunter, "Haydn's Aria Forms: A Study of the Arias in the Italian Operas Written at Eszterháza, 1766–1783," PhD diss., Cornell University, 1982, ch. 4; Webster, "Analysis," pp. 124–25, 144, 160–61, 179, 182; Webster, "Are Mozart's Concertos 'Dramatic'? Concerto Ritornellos and Aria Introductions in the 1780s," in Neal Zaslaw, ed., *Mozart's Concertos: Text, Context, Interpretation* (Ann Arbor: University of Michigan Press, 1996), pp. 107–37.

33 On the concept of the rhythmic profile, see Webster, "Analysis," pp. 133–37.

34 Edward T. Cone, *The Composer's Voice* (Berkeley: University of California Press, 1974), especially chs. 1–2; Webster, "Cone's 'Personae' and the Analysis of Opera," *CMS* 29 (1989), 44–65.

much" – as his conscious effort to maintain control while threatened with seduction. But this hope is belied by the syncopations throughout the final section: the violins know perfectly well that he has already succumbed. (This passage thus resembles the famous one in Gluck's *Iphigénie en Tauride*, where Orestes's vain hope, "Le calme rentre dans mon coeur," is belied by the syncopated monotone in the violas.)

Finally, let us examine the vocal line, specifically its structural–tonal voice-leading and "high-note" organization.[35] The background headnote is clearly 3̂, or G. But the Cavaliere has difficulty singing high G (g^1, notated g^2) in a convincing manner.[36] Like so much else in this aria, this difficulty is prefigured in the introduction (see Example 13.2). The first four measures ascend confidently from 1̂ through 2̂, to 3̂, but only in the lower octave; high f^2 (upbeat to m. 3) goes nowhere, and high g^2 appears only in passing (m. 5, where it is structurally subordinate to eb^2).[37] In the Cavaliere's first vocal phrase (structurally identical to mm. 1–4), this problem is posed in a much more obvious manner. In the first measure, he mounts into the upper octave, where he rises from high Eb (m. 11) to F (m. 13), as if heading for a structural high G. Instead, he leaps down to the lower octave and cadences on low G in m. 14. When he does manage high G (mm. 19, 22, 26), it is too late; the music is already in the dominant and thus cannot establish g^2 as a background headnote.[38] Indeed, although he finally sings

35 On this methodology, see Webster, "Analysis," pp. 166–69.
36 To be sure, the creator of the role, the tenor Domenico Guardasoni (who later, as impresario in Prague, commissioned *Don Giovanni*) had an especially effective lower range. However, this point is of little consequence, because all three of the Cavaliere's other arias not only attain, but surpass, high G (see nn. 4, 49). On the use of tessitura for purposes of characterization, see Julian Rushton's article elsewhere in this volume.
37 The problematical status of G also marks the swooning "E risolvermi non so": although it resolves down to F, the latter cannot descend, for the subverted cadence kicks the line *above* G, to Ab, from where it eventually descends to Eb.
38 Admittedly, such a phenomenon is theoretically possible (the 3̂ over V being understood as a middleground suspension of a notional 3̂ over I in the background), but there is no reason to credit this possibility here.

Example 13.2a Salieri, "Vo pensando": analysis

(a)

Example 13.2b Salieri, "Vo pensando": analysis

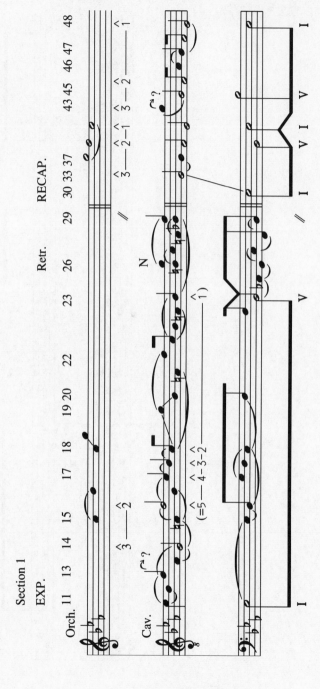

Example 13.2c Salieri, "Vo pensando": analysis

one high G in the key of E flat (m. 43), it comes only in the structurally underarticulated context of motive x. And even if we were to grant this g^2 background status, it could not be the source of any background descent in that register, because he again moves into the lower register for his swoon onto A♭ and the cadence.

In the recitative, the pitch-class G plays no structural melodic role. The final section reasserts its primacy; yet initially it is merely the dominant of C minor, as the Cavaliere blankly intones, "Ma se tu fossi, Amore" on low G; the entire orchestra is low as well. Only in the broadening passage (mm. 83 ff.) does he open up registrally; indeed he actually attains high G – but only on the last sixteenth of m. 83, from where he immediately skips down a major seventh to a♭^{1} (part of a larger-scale descending line from high F; see Example 13.2), and on to another low cadence. By contrast, when this passage is repeated (m. 96), it leads to the Cavaliere's only strong high G in the entire aria: in m. 100, he cadences on g^1, and immediately leaps up an octave to g^2, on the beat, in vigorous "Scotch snap" rhythm. And yet even here, the final descent takes place in the lower register.

There is no question as to the tonal cogency of "Vo pensando." The pitch-class G is strongly and interestingly established as the headnote; it serves as the basis for a firm *Ursatz* structure, enriched by the various deceptive cadences and especially the massive off-tonic prolongation in the first half of the final section. On the other hand, high G never initiates a prominent descent in that register. This does not imply an analytical problem (still less a compositional deficiency); as shown in Example 13.2b, we simply take the lower register as the "obligatory" one, such that g^2 appears as a "reflection" of the background g^1.[39] The question is rather: what does this mean?

---

39 In Schenkerian practice, the background descent of the *Urlinie* to î must take place in a single, specifiable octave, called the "obligatory register."

III

Close study of Salieri's aria thus ineluctably leads back to the general issue of the relation between analysis and interpretation of operatic numbers. Moreover, since interpretation is always at least implicitly comparative, we may also focus on a much-analyzed aria by Mozart that has many points of contact with "Vo pensando": the Countess's "Porgi amor" in *Le nozze di Figaro*.[40]

The first section of "Vo pensando" in particular has a good deal in common with "Porgi amor." As noted above, both are soliloquies that open Act II; both are in E flat (the most common key for *arie d'affetto*);[41] both set a single quatrain of *ottonario* (eight-syllable) verse; both are relatively short and self-contained, with deliberate movement and relatively little coloratura; both combine the "slow march" and *affetuoso* topics;[42] their "rhythmic gestures" are closely related (Larghetto; *alla breve* in Salieri, 2/4 in Mozart);[43] the instrumentation is similar (two oboes in Salieri, two clarinets in Mozart, otherwise horns, bassoons, and strings); and so forth.

40 Obviously, "Vo pensando" could appropriately be compared with many arias, the majority of them by composers other than Mozart. However, because of the familiarity of Mozart's music, as well as his dominance of our reception of opera buffa, any such comparisons will inevitably involve him (again, even if only implicitly), at least until a reasonably large repertory of *opere buffe*, and of analyses of numbers by other composers, have become available.
   "Porgi amor" itself has been the focus of comparative treatments; see Heartz's discussion (*Mozart's Operas*, pp. 141–42) of Rosina's "Una voce poco fa" from Paisiello's *Il barbiere di Siviglia*, and the "network" of Mozart arias described in Webster, "Analysis," pp. 113–14, 169–70.

41 On the *aria d'affetto* see Wolfgang Osthoff, "Mozarts Cavatinen und ihre Tradition," in Wilhelm Stauder et al., ed., *Festschrift Helmuth Osthoff zum siebzigsten Geburtstag* (Tutzing: Schneider, 1969), pp. 139–77; Heartz, *Mozart's Operas*, pp. 38–40, 141–43, 240–41. Obviously, "Vo pensando" deviates from the type for dramatic reasons (on such deviations generally see Webster, "Analysis," pp. 109–13). "Vo pensando" is *La locandiera*'s first number in E flat (this does not apply to "Porgi amor").

42 For "Porgi amor," see Allanbrook, *Rhythmic Gesture*, pp. 101–04; in "Vo pensando" a similar mixture is represented by the "pacing" music of mm. 1–4 and the tender, reflective motive *x*.

43 Although the Countess's initial downbeat rhythmic profile differs strongly from the Cavaliere's upbeat one, she later changes to a profile very like his; compare, for example, her mm. 39–40 to his mm. 13–14.

Furthermore, both arias are "about" their characters' struggle to attain high G (see Example 13.3). Unlike the Cavaliere, however, the Countess will discover that high G is something she must (eventually) sing, that this note is her tonal/vocal destiny.[44] Although she too at first can rise only as far as f^2 and must cadence in the lower octave (note the similarity between Example 13.3, mm. 18–25, and Example 13.2, mm. 11–14), by the end she has worked through her problem (the psychologizing metaphor is precisely appropriate) in such a way as to be able to articulate high G as climax and to achieve a background descent in that register (compare Example 13.3, mm. 46–47, with Example 13.2, mm. 45–48).

Now the usual comparative move at this point would be to emphasize that "Vo pensando" is musically less complex than "Porgi amor": that although its topical variety (particularly in the introduction) is scarcely less than Mozart's, overall it is motivically less dense and developmental; that its harmonic language is less rich and varied (the final section, which seems so rich in this context, would seem ordinary in a Mozart number); that although the orchestra has much independent material, overall the instrumental writing is less independent, both texturally and in its tendency to fall silent during the vocal pauses at phrase-endings (except, again, in the final section, where the only interstitial silence, at the deceptive cadence in m. 81, is precisely appropriate [compare "Porgi amor," mm. 13, 43]); that the rhythmic profile exhibits less variety, both overall and in the degree of directed change between one paragraph and another; and that notwithstanding the resourceful treatment of G, the voice-leading is less complex. And the reprise (m. 30) seems inadequately prepared: the

---

44 I do not mean to endorse Edward T. Cone's controversial view that operatic characters know that they are singing – that they are "composers"; see "The World of Opera and its Inhabitants," in Cone, *Music: A View from Delft* (Chicago: University of Chicago Press, 1989), pp. 125–38. But insofar as we take musical features of operatic numbers as dramatizing or symbolizing the characters' feelings and motivations, we may certainly conflate analytical description and psychological interpretation.

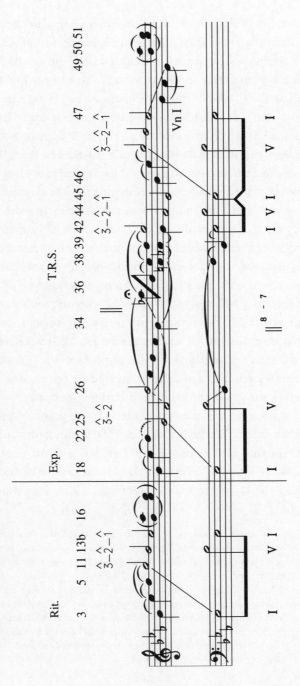

Example 13.3 Mozart, *Le nozze di Figaro*, "Porgi amor": analysis. From James Webster, "The Analysis of Mozart's Arias," in Cliff Eisen, ed., *Mozart Studies* (London: Oxford University Press, 1991). p. [167]. Reproduced by permission.

putative retransition (mm. 26–29) remains in the key of B flat, rather than transforming it into the home dominant.

Suppose (to repeat) I concluded that, musically, "Vo pensando" is less complex than "Porgi amor," less interesting, less rewarding to analyze. Would this demonstrate that "Porgi amor" is a better aria? No – and this holds whatever we may mean by "better." (Of course, this question is not at all the same as posing a straight value-judgment, such as: Is "Porgi amor" a finer aria than "Vo pensando"? Is *La locandiera* a greater opera than *Le nozze di Figaro*?) My point is not that we should avoid value-judgments (we cannot, even when we try), but that analysis is not the means by which we arrive at them, and the results of analysis cannot legitimately be used to support them.[45] Mozart's superiority as an operatic composer (if it is that) does not depend primarily on purely musical virtues (more precisely, on virtues that are amenable to analysis),[46] but on what I previously referred to as "operatic" factors: his librettos (for which he was partly responsible, of course), his theatricality, his sense of plotting, his gift of characterization, his quicksilver psychology, and many other things. More important, in a genre as inherently multivalent and critically contested as opera, one cannot determine any single cause for his putative superiority.[47]

In opera, the analysis *is* the interpretation. Sometimes this is obvious. In "Vo pensando," the deceptive cadence onto the subdominant on "E risolvermi non so" cannot be understood in "purely musical" terms; it makes sense only in connection with the text, the Cavaliere's ambivalent feelings, and the dramatic context.

45 For a detailed exposition of this position, see Webster, "Ambivalenzen um Mendelssohn: Zwischen Werk und Rezeption," in Christian Martin Schmidt, ed., *Felix Mendelssohn Bartholdy: Kongreß-Bericht Berlin 1994* (Wiesbaden: Breitkopf und Härtel, 1997), §4.

46 Whereby "musical" virtues include those that may emerge over spans larger than a single number: tonal and topical organization, connections in material and instrumentation, and so forth; these cannot be considered here.

47 For a formal presentation of this principle of operatic mutability, see Jessica Waldoff and James Webster, "Operatic Plotting in *Le nozze di Figaro*," in Sadie, *Wolfgang Amadè Mozart*, pp. 248–93.

(In fact, we almost never encounter passages of such weirdness in instrumental works of the 1770s – not even in Haydn – and when we do, as for example in the "Farewell" and "Distratto" Symphonies, we seek, and usually find, "extramusical" explanations.)[48] But although "E risolvermi non so" may be an exceptionally clear example of the impossibility of analyzing without interpreting, the principle applies generally. It was not merely my garden-variety summary of "Vo pensando" that conflated analytical and inter-pretative modes of discourse; my detailed analytical discussion did so as well: the new, bass form of motive *x* "spurs the Cavaliere on" and "instigates" the recitative, in the final section he "protests too much," and so forth.

In particular, my treatment of that problematic high G was explicitly interpretative, and necessarily so. The orchestra's initial ascent to G is "confident," but the Cavaliere only "manages" to sing high G "too late," in the dominant; his only high G in the tonic is "underarticulated"; in the final section, he "blankly intones" low G and "opens up" only later; and so forth. In fact, high G becomes a problem for interpretation by its very existence. Why, given that the Cavaliere sets it up as a potential background goal and fleetingly sings it several times, does he never use it for a complete tonal structure? It's not that Guardasoni's voice wasn't up to it (see n. 36), or that Salieri wasn't capable of composing out a registrally complex background. Rather, it must be a question of the Cavaliere's character and motivation, and the dramatic situa-tion. As he says, he is "trapped between Yes and No"; the reason he can't belt out 3̂–2̂–1̂ in the high register is that to do so would be to admit, indeed to welcome, the fact that he was falling in love. (By comparison, Tamino, in "Dies Bildnis," does belt out 3̂–2̂–1̂ in

---

48 See Elaine R. Sisman, "Haydn's Theater Symphonies," *JAMS* 43 (1990), 311–20; Webster, *Haydn's "Farewell" Symphony and the Idea of Classical Style: Through-Composition and Cyclic Integration in his Instrumental Music* (Cambridge: Cambridge University Press, 1991), chs. 4, 7; Gretchen A. Wheelock, *Haydn's Ingenious Jesting with Art: Contexts of Musical Wit and Humor* (New York: Schirmer, 1992), pp. 154–71; Richard James Will, "Programmatic Symphonies of the Classical Period," PhD diss., Cornell University, 1994.

the high register, in the very first bars and repeatedly thereafter, because he welcomes the fact of having fallen in love with every fiber of his being.)[49]

The fact that an operatic analysis automatically entails interpretation does not imply a marginalization of analysis. On the contrary, a good analysis often suggests points of interpretation that would never be dreamed of by conventionally postmodern critics or genre-oriented historians. "Vo pensando" is such a case: the Cavaliere's failure to sing a complete background progression in the high register – something we know he would ordinarily be capable of doing (he has already done so in Act I) – dramatizes his ambivalence about falling in love. On the other hand, we can determine the *value* of "Vo pensando" only on the basis of our assessment of its degree of success in articulating that dramatic action, in the context of a staged performance of the entire opera. What could any conclusion that it was analytically less interesting than "Porgi amor" contribute to such a value-judgment? The hope would be as vain as the attempt to argue that the greater analytical interest of the music in *Fidelio*, compared to that in *Der Freischütz*, could tell us which was the better opera.

I V

No less than musicology in general, the analytical and theoretical community has learned in recent years to see itself as moving within an unstable field, created by the tension between a modernist, work-immanent, absolute-musical aesthetics and various newer, contextualized, postmodernist ones. And yet this must be a false dichotomy; so crude a binary opposition ought to self-decon-

49 To judge from the tessitura, Benedikt Schack, the first Tamino, must have had a wonderful high G (and the ability to maintain it throughout the evening), and this presumed fact helps to explain how Tamino's tessitura came to be what it is. But such facts neither prescribe, nor proscribe, any specific interpretations; in particular, we would not be satisfied with an explanation of Tamino's character that was restricted to a description of Schack's vocal characteristics. See also nn. 4, 36.

struct before even being thought through.[50] But then are not all the other binary oppositions so characteristic of recent operatic discourse – analysis vs. interpretation; Mozart vs. the "others"; operatic vs. instrumental composition (or analysis) – equally suspect?

Whereas five years ago I too emphasized operatic analysis's differences from the unity-valorizing analysis of instrumental music, now I would say simply that the possibility of meaning is open with respect to all music – whether we locate that meaning in the individual work (hermeneutics), in performance, in musical tradition (intertextuality), in genre, in reception, or in "music as cultural practice."[51] Moreover, as even many theorists now acknowledge, no analysis, not even one devoted exclusively to the musical structure of an "absolute" instrumental work, is innocent or objective. Every analysis tells a story, in its mode of presentation, narrative style, and so on;[52] every analysis implicitly (when not explicitly) conveys its author's motives and "covert values";[53] authors of analyses are no less subject to "anxieties of influence" and the vicissitudes of status and reputation than famous poets. (It follows that there can be no opposite to an analysis "in context." What could that be – an analysis "out of context"? As Derrida would say if this issue came to his attention, the analysis and interpretation of music are "always already," always have been, one and the same.)[54]

---

50 Not that most "new" musicologists evince much awareness of the dialectical complexities of the relations between "modernism" and "postmodernism"; for a brief but cogent survey of this issue, see Fredric Jameson, *Postmodernism: Or, The Cultural Logic of Late Capitalism* (Durham, NC: Duke University Press, 1991), ch. 2.

51 The title of Lawrence Kramer's frequently cited volume (Berkeley: University of California Press, 1990).

52 V. Kofi Agawu, "Schenkerian Notation in Theory and Practice," *MA* 8 (1989), 275–301.

53 Janet M. Levy, "Covert and Casual Values in Recent Writings about Music," *JM* 6 (1987), 3–27.

54 This point is not entirely new, even in the context of instrumental analysis; see Dahlhaus, *Absolute Music*, pp. 27–41.

Even from this perspective, however, operatic analysis might seem to have a special role to play. From a previously marginal position, it may be moving, not merely to its "rightful" place in musicological discourse, but to a privileged one. The prestige and influence of operatic studies are at present arguably higher than those of any other musicological subdiscipline. And of all musical genres, opera is best situated to teach us how to deal with music in context (in the traditional sense of that concept). Whereas instrumental analyses "in context" currently do no more than contest absolute-musical ones, in operatic analysis no such contestation can even arise: the absolute-musical view is irrelevant.

On the other hand, the majority of the recent studies responsible for opera's prestige are not primarily analytical in nature.[55] Indeed, the "new" musicology has in general focused largely on the nineteenth century, secondarily on the twentieth and on popular music, very little on the art-music of the eighteenth century, and least of all on eighteenth-century opera, about which (always excepting Mozart) most musicologists remain blissfully ignorant. It is in part for this reason that I argue for a more ecumenical approach to both analysis and interpretation, in both operatic and instrumental studies: the new musicologists need analysis at least as much as Mozartians need "context."

Ten years ago, I predicted that in order "to attain maturity and autonomy, operatic analysis will have to develop its own (partly new) explanatory models, idiomatic to the genre." So far, so good. But I continued by speculating that these new models "will [become] fully effective only when they have become sufficiently powerful and . . . general to induce people to apply them to *other*

---

55 To cite one prominent case: the musical examples in Abbate's *Unsung Voices: Opera and Musical Narrative in the Nineteenth Century* (Princeton: Princeton University Press, 1991), as indeed in most of her writings, comprise solely quotations from scores, without analytical intervention save for occasional and elementary motivic bracketings or chord-labels. For a prominent (and not hidebound) theorist's reservations about such analytical reticence, see Arnold Whittall, " 'Forceful Muting' or 'Phatic Dithering'? Some Recent Writing on Opera," *M&L*, 71 (1990), 67–69.

repertories . . . when I [can] learn about Haydn's string quartets by reading [an] analysis of *Otello* – and . . . about *Rigoletto* by analyzing Haydn's string quartets."[56] Such a prospect has not yet been realized; I myself then called it "farfetched," and concluded with a more conventional plea that Mozarteans and nineteenth-century operatic scholars should talk to each other. Today, however, any supposed dichotomy of principle between operatic and instrumental analysis seems increasingly irrelevant. For if all music, including instrumental music, is seen as potentially productive of meaning, the notion that interpretations of opera might prove fruitful for our understanding of instrumental music no longer seems farfetched at all. But if this is so, it follows that studies of instrumental music will doubtless continue to provide useful stimuli for the understanding of opera as well.

56 "To Understand . . . Mozart," pp. 192–93. In the quoted passage I was referring to Harold S. Powers's adumbration, in a 1984 study of *Otello* (still unpublished), of "multivalent" operatic analysis – a concept to which I am obviously much indebted.

14 | Operatic ensembles and the problem of the *Don Giovanni* sextet

John Platoff

The "problem" of my title is actually my problem: the great sextet from the second act of *Don Giovanni* has always seemed a little strange to me. This ensemble occurs at the climax of the initially comic subplot involving Leporello's disguise as Don Giovanni. Having led Donna Elvira off into the darkness, Leporello here attempts to get away from her. But his escape is blocked by the arrivals, first of Donna Anna and Don Ottavio, then of Zerlina and Masetto. When they discover Leporello he reveals himself – after nearly being killed by Don Ottavio – and pleads cringingly for his life. These events occur in a single musical movement, a long Andante that creates an atmosphere of increasing darkness, mystery, and tragic intensity. This is, of course, an atmosphere far removed from the unshadowed comedy of the typical opera buffa ensemble.[1] But after the five characters react in shock to Leporello's unmasking, the Andante gives way to the energetic Molto allegro of a typical stretta movement; the dark mystery of this extraordinary ensemble snaps suddenly back to routine comic frenzy, in a shift that seems disruptive and unconvincing. It is almost as though the first movement has raised questions that the second movement is utterly unable to answer, or even to address. The problem is made only more acute by the tonal shift that connects these two movements – from the end of the Andante, with its strongly marked cadence on the dominant of C minor, to the Molto allegro in the tonic key of E flat.

The dissatisfaction I feel with this ensemble, or more precisely with this particular spot, has led me to think about the nature of

---

1 Even in *opere buffe* with serious elements, the ensembles – above all, the larger ones, from quartets to septets – are almost universally comic. The only exception known to me is the quintet "Deh lasciate ch'io respiri" from Cimarosa's and Casti's *Il matrimonio segreto* (1792).

Mozart's decision-making process. Asking why Mozart made a particular decision is not very common, not only because answering the question is so difficult but because his decisions so frequently seem to be perfect: they do not invite questioning. In what follows, I hope to suggest at least some of the reasons why the sextet is structured as it is, and above all why Mozart employed the shift from V/vi to I. In brief, my answer will be that his choices were shaped in part by his experience as a composer of instrumental music. Second and more broadly, my investigation will demonstrate how a contextual study, grounded in an awareness of what contemporary composers were doing, can give us additional insights into Mozart's own music. In particular, it permits us to form conclusions about whether certain musical choices are typical or unusual. Whether or not my views on the sextet are persuasive, it will be clear that much of the information I draw upon in developing those views arises from just such a contextual approach.

Let me begin with a general characterization of opera buffa ensembles. It is a truism that, unlike arias, which are generally devoted to the expression of feelings, ensembles combine dramatic action with continuous music. But while many ensembles work in just this way, they do not consist entirely of action. Most are constructed using two distinct poetic and musical styles, which I label *active* and *expressive*. In the first, dialogue among the characters on stage moves the story forward; in the second, the characters sing together in a tutti that ceases to move the action forward and instead expresses their feelings. The first phase is itself frequently subdivided: it may begin with a solo stanza for each character, in which his or her initial activity or emotional position is made clear. After these stanzas, which set the stage for dramatic action, true dialogue takes place in shorter interchanges among the characters.[2]

---

2 Ronald J. Rabin, writing about the same phenomenon, describes it somewhat differently: he sees three distinct phases (called respectively Statements, Dialogue, and Tutti), the first of which may be omitted. See "Mozart, Da Ponte, and the Dramaturgy of Opera Buffa: Italian Comic Opera in Vienna, 1783–1791," PhD diss. Cornell University, 1996, pp. 287ff.

Collectively, the ensembles of Viennese opera buffa range from pieces (such as "Soave sia il vento" from *Così fan tutte*) consisting entirely of a single expressive tutti, to those that comprise a single action/expression cycle (such as "Cinque – dieci", the opening duet from *Le nozze di Figaro*), to larger and more complex pieces made up of a series of cycles. The most elaborate and lengthy ensembles are finales, which may comprise eight or more cycles of active dialogue and expressive tutti.[3] Other ensembles do not reach this size, but pieces comprising two or three cycles are not uncommon.

The creation of these structures began, of course, with librettists. By writing active scenes in dialogue and punctuating them with expressive tutti passages, they enabled composers to vary both the dramatic pace and the musical texture of ensembles. And the punctuating tuttis could also make a musical number that actually contained rather little stage-action seem more substantial and interesting. For example, in the Act II trio of *Le nozze di Figaro*, "Susanna, or via sortite," the Count commands Susanna first to come out of the closet, and later to speak so that he can hear her voice. Each command is countermanded by the Countess, followed immediately by an expressive tutti. In this way Da Ponte and Mozart created an ensemble of two parallel cycles of action and expression, when what actually takes place could quite easily have occurred in one rather concise cycle.

It must be noted that the "active" and "expressive" qualities of dialogue and tutti passages respectively are not always as pure as I have suggested. Not every bit of dialogue is as clearly active as "Stop, you rogue! Where are you going?" nor every tutti as obviously expressive as "What! [It's] Leporello! What trickery is this? I am amazed. What now?" (both from the *Don Giovanni* sextet). Taken line by line, active passages frequently contain emotional expression, while expressive ones may include a plan, or the hope of some future event. Yet structurally, because of the consistent organization by which dialogue is followed by tutti, the distinction

3 See John Platoff, "Musical and Dramatic Structure in the Opera Buffa Finale," *JM* 7 (1989), 191–97.

between action and expression is clearly maintained – and when it is underlined by the music, the shift from one to the other may be easily recognized.[4]

Librettists used other means as well as the shifts from dialogue to tutti to create articulations. Longer ensembles frequently contain changes of poetic meter, sometimes between a dialogue and the following tutti but most typically between the end of one action/expression cycle and the start of the next. When the plot permits, the number of characters may change, as in the *Don Giovanni* sextet, which actually begins as a duet and continues as a quartet until m. 70. A more subtle but occasionally important articulating device is a change in the end-rhyme used to close each stanza of text in an ensemble.[5]

But with respect to all these devices we may say that "the librettist proposes, the composer disposes"; or to quote Joseph Kerman, "the dramatist is the composer."[6] For every point of articulation made available by the libretto – a shift from dialogue to tutti, a new poetic meter, a character's entrance or exit – the composer has complete control to highlight, obscure, or simply overrule it. For instance, a change of poetic meter typically leads a composer to switch to a new movement (see below), thus creating an important articulation; but the composer may ignore this poetic cue and set the new text to more of the old music.[7] Conversely, a change of tempo and meter within a passage in a single poetic meter has the effect of producing more sections than the librettist provided. For that matter, a tutti may be created where the librettist did not write one, simply by repeating earlier lines and having characters sing

4 For a discussion of the musical styles used in active and expressive passages, see ibid., 197–227.

5 Tim Carter, *W. A. Mozart: "Le nozze di Figaro"* (Cambridge: Cambridge University Press, 1987), pp. 80–87.

6 Joseph Kerman, *Opera as Drama* (New York, 1956; rev. edn., Berkeley: University of California Press, 1988), p. 91.

7 See, for example, the opening duet from *Le nozze di Figaro*: the final tutti quatrain changes from *ottonario* lines to *decasillabo*, a change carefully hidden by Mozart's musical setting. James Webster, "To Understand Verdi and Wagner We Must Understand Mozart," *19CM* 11 (1987–88), 184.

them together. Sometimes an ensemble whose text provides a single action/expression cycle can be lengthened into two cycles, by the simple expedient of using some or all of the active dialogue and then the expressive tutti a second time. In all these ways the composer has the final say over the number of active and expressive passages, their relative length and importance, and the resulting form and sense of pace in the ensemble.

A brief digression is called for here, to explain my concentration on "movements," by which I mean relatively lengthy passages of music in a single tempo and meter.[8] Points of articulation within an operatic number exist along a continuum of strength, from the smallest gesture to the most shocking and dramatic break in the musical flow. Composers create articulations at different levels of the musical structure in all sorts of ways: with cadences, dynamic changes, alterations in texture, new melodies or accompanimental motives, and so on. And features of the stage-action and the poetry – plot events, entrances or exits of characters, changes in poetic meter, and the like – create articulations as well, which may or may not coincide with points of musical articulation.[9] In my view the single most powerful articulating device is a change from one movement to another, by which I mean the shift from music in one tempo and meter to new music in a perceptibly different tempo and/or meter. Such articulations obviously vary in impact, depending, for example, on whether they occur congruently with articulations in the poetry and/or stage-action, whether they occur *attacca* or after a pause, whether they involve a full or half-cadence or no cadence at all, whether a small or large tonal shift also occurs, and so on. Yet while tempo and meter changes vary in articulating strength, they consistently affect the musical flow

8 This would exclude, for example, calling a six-measure passage in a new tempo a movement. I differ here from Webster, who argues for a distinction between "movements" and "sections" in which the former, unlike the latter, "articulate a complete formal design." See *Haydn's "Farewell" Symphony and the Idea of Classical Style* (Cambridge: Cambridge University Press, 1991), pp. 186–87.
9 This "multivalence" in Mozart's operas is discussed in Webster, "Analysis," pp. 103–4 and *passim*.

more strongly than any other single element. One can therefore view the number of movements in an ensemble as a key aspect of its structure – though certainly not the only important one – and examine a large operatic repertory in terms of this variable, as I will do in this study.

In the sextet from Act I of *Così fan tutte*, we can see how Mozart alters Da Ponte's implied structure in two principal ways. The text consists of 46 lines,[10] all in *ottonario* and relying on a single end-rhyme. In the first 25 lines only four characters sing, Fiordiligi and Dorabella not yet having entered. The text contains no tutti passage in this part of the scene, just one for all six characters at the end (lines 38–46). Mozart, however, sets the sextet not as one continuous movement but in three movements. The initial Allegro in common time changes to a 3/4 Allegro when the sisters enter, thus highlighting the separation between two distinct phases of the action. And a 2/2 Molto allegro begins at the final tutti, making that expression of feelings into an exciting and relatively lengthy stretta. Mozart's other change articulates the sextet, whose text can be read as a single action/expression cycle, into two cycles. In lines 17–19 in the first section, after Despina has responded laughingly to the appearance of Ferrando and Guglielmo in disguise, the two men join Don Alfonso in singing "Now matters are settled; if she doesn't recognize us/them, there's nothing to fear." These lines may seem to suggest an expressive tutti; but such remarks, when made by some but not all of the characters on stage, are often set within an ongoing active dialogue. Instead Mozart makes a decisive tutti (in mm. 38–48): to the texture of the three male voices he adds Despina, who repeats her lines 10–12 (see lines 20–22). As a result the quartet portion of the ensemble contains not merely action but a full action/expression cycle. Mozart's decisions – to divide the sextet into three movements, and to create a tutti at the end of the first of these – make more distinct the two phases of the action, the

10 This includes three repeated lines, which I discuss below. The text is laid out as in the original printed libretto, which is reprinted in facsimile in Warburton, vol. 3, pp. 218–20.

first being the encounter of the disguised lovers with Despina and the second their meeting with the outraged sisters.[11]

Così fan tutte, Sextet No. 13

	DON ALFONSO	Alla bella Despinetta	
		Vi presento, amici miei;	
		Non dipende che da lei	
		Consolar il vostro cor.	
5	FERRANDO	) Per la man che lieto io bacio,	*(con tenerezza*
	GUGLIELMO	) Per quei rai di grazie pieni,	*affetata)*
		Fa che volga a me sereni	
		I begli occhi il mio tesor.	
	DESPINA	Che sembianze! che vestiti!	*(da se,*
10		Che figure! che mustacchi!	*ridendo)*
		Io non so se son Vallacchi,	
		O se Turchi son costor.	
	DON ALFONSO	Che ti par di quell'aspetto?	*(piano a*
			Despina)
	DESPINA	Per parlarvi schietto, schietto,	
15		Hanno un muso fuor dell'uso,	
		Vero antidoto d'amor.	
	FERRANDO	) Or la cosa è appien decisa;	
	GUGLIELMO	) Se costei non li/ci ravvisa,	
	DON ALFONSO	) Non c'è più nessun timor.	
		)	
20	DESPINA	) Che figure! che mustacchi!	
		) Io non so se son Vallacchi,	
		) O se Turchi son costor.	
	FIORDILIGI	) Ehi Despina! olà Despina!	*(dentro le*
	DORABELLA	)	*quinte)*
	DESPINA	Le padrone!	
	DON ALFONSO	Ecco l'istante!	*(a Despina)*
25		Fa con arte; io qui m'ascondo.	
			(Si ritira.)
	FIORDILIGI	) Ragazzaccia tracotante,	

11 Tim Carter has also noted Mozart's overriding of the structure proposed by Da Ponte's poetry; he sees this sextet as an example of "Mozart's eagerness to explore . . . looser, more progressive structures . . . [as] alternatives to sonata-form organization." "Mozart, Da Ponte and the Ensemble: Methods in Progress?" in Sadie, *Wolfgang Amadè Mozart*, p. 247.

	DORABELLA	)	Che fai lì con simil gente?
			Falli uscire immantinente,
			O ti fo pentir con lor.
30	FERRANDO	)	Ah madame perdonate!
	GUGLIELMO	)	Al bel piè languir mirate
	DESPINA	)	Due meschin, di vostro merito (*s'inginocchiano*)
			Spasimanti adorator.
	FIORDILIGI	)	Giusti numi! cosa sento?
35	DORABELLA	)	Dell' enorme tradimento,
			Chi fu mai l'indegno autor?
	DESPINA	)	Deh calmate quello sdegno!
	GUGLIELMO	)	
	FERRANDO	)	
	à 6		
	DORABELLA	)	Ah, che più non ho ritegno!
	FIORDILIGI	)	Tutta piena ho l'alma in petto
40			Di dispetto, e di furor.
			Ah perdon, mio bel diletto;
			Innocente è questo cor.
	GUGLIELMO	)	Qual diletto è a questo petto
	FERRANDO	)	Quella rabbia e quel furor.
45	DESPINA	)	Mi dà un poco di sospetto
	DON ALFONSO	)	Quella rabbia e quel furor.

These aspects of compositional decision-making pertain to the *Don Giovanni* sextet, of course, since we are concerned with the particular decisions Mozart made in that piece. These decisions must be seen not only in light of what else he might have done, and, in fact, did do in other ensembles, but also in view of what contemporary composers typically did. And from these perspectives, the structure of the sextet reveals connections to procedures found rarely in opera, but quite often in instrumental music.

Finding a link to instrumental music in a Mozart opera should not be a great shock. Unlike nearly all his operatic competitors in Vienna, Mozart was much more experienced in the composition of instrumental music than opera buffa.[12] Between his move to Vienna in 1781 and the composition of *Don Giovanni*, he had written

12 The only clear exception is Karl Ditters von Dittersdorf, who succeeded in Vienna with German Singspiel but had little success in opera buffa.

only two full-scale operas, one of them in the quite different genre of Singspiel.[13] During the same period he had composed three symphonies, fifteen piano concertos, seven string quartets, ten sonatas for violin and piano, six larger pieces of chamber music with piano, and numerous other instrumental works. In this light it would be more surprising if his operas did *not* reflect the perspective of instrumental music.

I will not offer here a full-scale analysis of the sextet; but a brief discussion of the text and Mozart's setting of it can provide the necessary background for the points I address below. Da Ponte's text is organized in three distinct sections, each with its own poetic meter (*ottonario, quinario* at line 21, and *ottonario* again at line 43). The first section is initially a duet and then a quartet, with quatrains for Donna Elvira, Leporello, Don Ottavio, and Donna Anna, in turn, followed by shorter utterances for the first two as they try to leave the courtyard.[14] This section has no closing tutti: the action is meant to continue directly into the next section. And the entrance of Zerlina and Masetto, marked by the shift to *quinario*, does continue the action, as all confront the supposed Don Giovanni and demand his death, despite Elvira's pleas for mercy. After Leporello reveals himself there follows a quatrain of shocked response to be sung tutti by the others (lines 39–42). The final section, back in *ottonario*, is another expressive tutti with complementary words for Leporello and the other five characters. This second tutti is clearly provided to permit an extended, energetic musical conclusion to the sextet, like the stretta of a typical act finale, since its words – except for allowing Leporello to express his terror – add nothing new to the dramatic situation.

13 The two are *Le nozze di Figaro* (1786) and *Die Entführung aus dem Serail* (1782). Mozart also wrote a one-act Singspiel, *Der Schauspieldirektor* (1786), and made false starts on two *opere buffe*: *L'oca del Cairo* and *Lo sposo deluso*. In these last two Mozart fully or partially drafted a total of ten numbers.

14 These opening quatrains exemplify what Rabin calls the "Statements" phase of an ensemble (see n. 2 above), and what I have described as the first of two phases in the active dialogue.

Don Giovanni, Sextet No. 19

[OTTONARIO]

DONNA ELVIRA	Sola, sola in bujo loco,	
	Palpitar il cor mi sento,	
	E m'assale un tal spavento	
	Che mi sembra di morir.	
5 LEPORELLO	Più che cerco, men ritrovo	
	Questa porta sciagurata:	
	Piano, piano, l'ho trovata,	
	Ecco il tempo di fuggir.	(*sbaglia la porta*)
DON OTTAVIO	Tergi il ciglio, o vita mia,	(*entrano*
10	E dà calma al tuo dolore,	*vestiti a lutto*)
	L'ombra omai del genitore	
	Pena avrà de' tuoi martir.	
DONNA ANNA	Lascia almen alla mia pena	
	Questo picciolo ristoro,	
15	Sola morte, o mio tesoro,	
	Il mio pianto può finir.	
DONNA ELVIRA	Ah dov' è lo sposo mio?	(*senza esser vista*)
LEPORELLO	Se mi trova son perduto:	(*dalla porta senza esser vista*)
à 2	) Una porta là veggio	
20	) Cheto cheto io vo partir.	(*Nel sortire s'incontrano in Zerl. e Mas.*)

[QUINARIO]

ZERLINA	) Ferma, briccone,	
à 2	) Dove ten vai!	(*Lep. s'asconde la faccia*)
MASETTO	)	
DONNA ANNA	) Ecco il fellone.	
à 2	) Come era quà!	
DON OTTAVIO	)	
25 à 4	) Ah mora il perfido	
	) Che m'a tradito!	

	DONNA ELVIRA	È mio marito,	
		Pietà! pietà!	
	DON OTTAVIO	) È Donna Elvira	
30	ZERLINA	) Quella ch'io vedo?	
	à 4	) Appena il credo;	
	MASETTO	) No no, morrà!	(*in atto di*
	DONNA ANNA	)	*ucciderlo*)
	LEPORELLO	Perdon perdono,	(*Lep. si scopre,*
		Signori miei,	*e si mette*
35		Quello io non sono.	*in ginocchio*
		Sbaglia costei;	*davanti gli*
		Viver lasciatemi	*altri*)
		Per carità!	
	TUTTI [*à* 5]	Dei! Leporello!	
40		Che inganno è questo;	
		Stupido/a resto,	
		Che mai sarà!	

[*OTTONARIO*]

		Mille torbidi pensieri
		Mi s'aggiran per la testa;
45		Che giornata, o stelle, è questa!
		Che impensata novità!
	LEPORELLO	Mille torbidi pensieri
		Mi s'aggiran per la testa;
		Se mi salvo in tal tempesta
50		È un prodigio in verità!

Mozart's setting comprises only two movements rather than the three suggested by the text. That is, the entrance of Zerlina and Masetto, which accompanies a change of poetic meter from *ottonario* to *quinario*, is not marked by a new tempo or meter. Instead the initial Andante persists all the way to the start of the final tutti in *ottonario*, which is set as a Molto allegro. But Mozart did not ignore Da Ponte's point of articulation; instead he treated it more subtly, not as a change of direction but as an interruption within the ongoing flow of the Andante. The brilliant result is a long, continuous, and foreboding movement whose atmosphere darkens as it progresses.

Figure 14.1 charts the course of the Andante movement.[15] Not surprisingly its motivic and tonal relationships are quite complex – I have recorded here only those features relevant to my argument. Arrows mark the principal points of foreground articulation. In a manner typical of ensembles, Mozart set the first quatrain (for Elvira) in the tonic and the second (for Leporello) moving to and cadencing in the dominant. The quatrains for Don Ottavio and Donna Anna follow, after a stunning modulation to D by means of an augmented-sixth chord, supported by *piano* trumpets and timpani – one of the most celebrated moments in the opera. Ottavio sings in D, Anna in D minor modulating through B flat to C minor. Her music makes a remarkable transition, darkening the tone of the ensemble from the rather conventional initial paragraphs for Elvira and Leporello into something quite gripping.

At m. 61, where Anna concludes, begins a passage that skillfully knits together various signs of beginning and ending, initiating a second phase of the Andante without a big articulation and without a clear division of the movement into separate sections. This process involves ambiguous relations between the events at m. 61 and those at m. 70. The organization of the text (see p. 387) suggests one sort of change at m. 61: the series of opening quatrains concludes, followed by the shorter exchanges characteristic of dialogue. On the other hand, the initial *ottonario* has not changed, nor has the end-rhyme; true dialogue cannot be said to be occurring, since Elvira and Leporello are speaking to themselves; and their joint couplet suggests a tutti *a due*, and thus a subsequent point of closure in the text. Moreover, that textual articulation – at m. 70 – is far more dramatic than Anna's conclusion at m. 61. The poetry changes to *quinario*, with a new end-rhyme; Zerlina and Masetto enter; all the characters become aware of one another for the first time; and the central action of the ensemble begins – the discovery

---

15 My analysis borrows in part from one provided as Table 2 by Lawrence Schenbeck in a talk entitled *"Ecco il fellone*: Leporello as Picaresque Hero," presented at the Hofstra University Mozart Conference, Hempstead, NY, February 9, 1991.

Figure 14.1 *Don Giovanni*: sextet, mm. 1–130

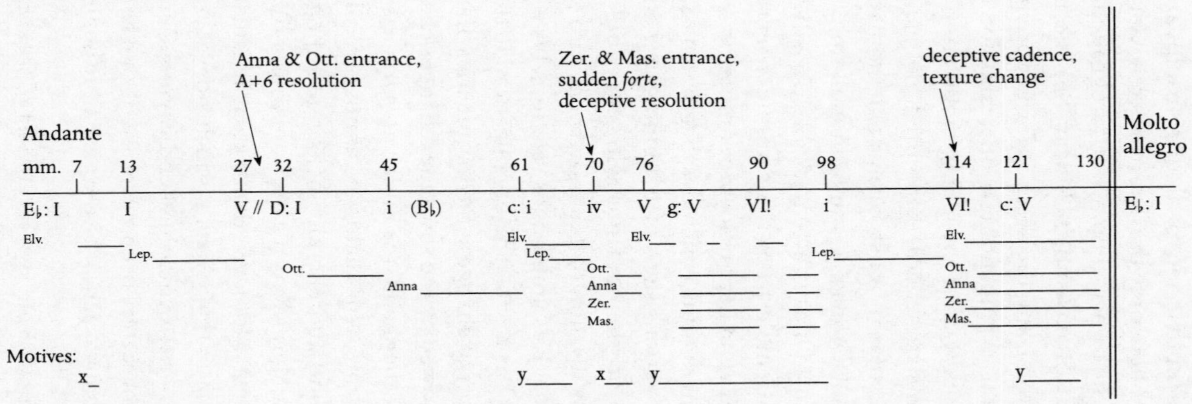

Andante

mm. 7   13   27   32   45   61   70   76   90   98   114   121   130

Molto allegro

E♭: I   I   V // D: I   i (B♭)   c: i   iv   V   g: V   VII!   i   VII!   c: V   E♭: I

Anna & Ott. entrance, A+6 resolution (→ 27)

Zer. & Mas. entrance, sudden *forte*, deceptive resolution (→ 70)

deceptive cadence, texture change (→ 114)

Elv.   Lep.   Ott.   Anna   Elv.   Lep.   Ott.   Anna   Zer.   Mas.   Elv.   Lep.   Elv.   Ott.   Anna   Zer.   Mas.

Motives:

x   y   x   y   y

of "Don Giovanni," followed by the revelation that he is actually Leporello.

Mozart's musical setting creates articulations that interact multivalently with those in the text to create an overall musical continuity, rather than decisively suggesting a break at either point. Measure 61 is marked tonally and motivically as the beginning of a new phase in the movement. Tonally, mm. 61–130 stay close to C minor and G minor, with the central segment (mm. 80–120) in the latter key. This relative tonal stability, despite several deceptive cadences, contrasts with the range of modulation earlier, not only at mm. 27–28 but within Donna Anna's quatrain. (Of course such tonal stability can only be perceived retrospectively.) More immediately apparent is the chromatically descending figure in a dotted rhythm, played by strings alone (labeled y in Figure 14.1), which recurs throughout mm. 61–130. This figure stands out from its first appearance, contrasting strongly with the accompanimental patterns played by the strings (with woodwind support) during Ottavio and Anna's quatrains.

The moment of Zerlina's and Masetto's entrance (m. 70) is highlighted musically in several ways. First, it is preceded by the obviously cadential tutti *a due* for Leporello and Elvira (which rhymes musically with Leporello's earlier cadence at mm. 25–27). Measure 70 itself is marked by a deceptive resolution, a momentary inflection towards F minor, a sudden *forte* outburst, and the reappearance of an orchestral motive from early in the movement (*x*). Yet despite these features Zerlina's and Masetto's entrance – clearly the start of something new from the point of view of the stage action – is treated musically more as an interruption than as a new section. This is confirmed at m. 76 by the return both of the *piano* dynamic and of the dotted figure (*y*), which controls the music for the next 22 measures. The perceived meter also suggests an interruption: mm. 70–76 seem to insist on 4 / 4, while measure 76 returns to the 2 / 2 feeling of the rest of the Andante. The newly arrived characters, after their angry initial statement, are palpably pulled back into the suspenseful, slower-moving musical atmosphere that prevailed before their entrance.

The last important articulation in the Andante, the tutti expression of shock at Leporello's unmasking (mm. 114ff.), is likewise a momentary interruption contained within the ongoing motivic pattern.[16] The strong deceptive cadence and new orchestral texture at m. 114, marked also by dynamic changes and chromatic harmonies in the following seven measures, are subsequently re-integrated by the return of the controlling dotted figure at m. 121. So although mm. 114–30 serve as a brief shock tutti,[17] their separation from the preceding music is carefully minimized. Given the structure of the text to this point, a composer would normally have created two distinct movements, with the change coming at m. 70; instead, Mozart has used various means to maintain musical and what might be called "atmospheric" continuity throughout this long Andante.

Separation is maximized, though, by the sudden tonal shift that begins the Molto allegro, from a half cadence in C minor to the vigorous opening in E flat, the tonic key of the sextet. This stretta movement has much in common with the final stretta of the Act 1 finale, above all the consistent textural device of having Leporello chatter frantically in eighth-note patter, while the other five characters sing together and generally in much longer notes (in the finale both Leporello and Don Giovanni sing the patter).

How does this brief analysis of the form of the sextet suggest Mozart's experience as a composer of instrumental music? I see two of Mozart's compositional decisions – one of these very effective, the other clumsy and unconvincing – as related to the procedures of instrumental music. The first involves the division of the piece into only two movements, rather than the three clearly suggested by the libretto. The second, discussed below, involves the tonal shift from V/vi to I.

16 The lapse of dramatic realism at this moment – since Leporello sings for a full 16 measures before the others react in shock – is discussed in John Platoff, "How Original was Mozart? Evidence from *Opera Buffa*," *EM* 20 (1992), 113–15.

17 For a discussion of the shock tutti see Platoff, "Musical and Dramatic Structure," pp. 219–23.

What factors might lead a composer to create more or fewer movements in an ensemble? In general, a smaller number of movements enhances continuity; it also makes an ensemble more like an instrumental movement, which only rarely has multiple sections in different tempos or meters.[18] Moreover, ensembles in a single movement allow for the possibility of a sonata-like formal plan, or at least one in which a highly articulated double return of the tonic and the initial thematic material can occur. If the latter portion of an ensemble is in a different tempo or meter, such a double return is far less likely. On the other hand, new movements in an ensemble can suggest or highlight changed circumstances or even psychological progression, both of which are of prime importance in an opera. For example, in "Là ci darem la mano" the change to 6/8 coincides with and confirms Zerlina's capitulation to Don Giovanni's seduction. Generally speaking, then, more movements in an ensemble might offer advantages in terms of operatic drama, while fewer movements make possible the use of formal plans like those found in instrumental music.

Examining a substantial number of operas by Mozart's Viennese contemporaries enables one to make meaningful comparisons between his works and those by other composers. Here I draw upon information about the ensembles in Mozart's three Da Ponte operas and in nineteen works by other composers.[19] Mozart's ensembles in the Da Ponte operas contain strikingly fewer move-

18 The sonata-form first movement with slow introduction is an obvious exception.
19 In pursuing this line of research, I have developed a data-base containing information on each musical number in over two dozen *opere buffe* – by both Mozart and his contemporaries – performed in Vienna during the 1780s. In all, the data-base comprises more than 700 musical numbers. The non-Mozart operas included in this study are: Bárta/?Bussani (after Goldoni), *Il mercato di Malmantile*; Cimarosa/Bertati, *Il matrimonio segreto*; Dittersdorf/Brunati, *Democrito corretto*; Gazzaniga/Da Ponte, *Il finto cieco*; Martín y Soler/Da Ponte: *Il burbero di buon cuore*, *Una cosa rara*, and *L'arbore di Diana*; Paisiello/Petrosellini, *Il barbiere di Siviglia*; Paisiello/Casti, *Il re Teodoro in Venezia*; Righini/Da Ponte, *Il demogorgone*; Rust/Mazzolà, *Il marito indolente*; Salieri/Da Ponte: *Il ricco d'un giorno*, *Il talismano*, and *La cifra*; Salieri/Casti, *La grotta di Trofonio*; Sarti/an unknown librettist (after Goldoni), *Fra i due litiganti*; Storace/Brunati, *Gli sposi malcontenti*; Storace/Da Ponte, *Gli equivoci*; Weigl/Mazzolà, *Il pazzo per forza*.

Figure 14.2 Number of movements in ensembles: Mozart and his Viennese contemporaries

ments than those in the operas of his Viennese contemporaries, as may be seen in Figure 14.2. 76 percent of Mozart's ensembles comprise a single movement, compared to only 45 percent for other composers. Conversely only 6 percent of Mozart's ensembles (2 of 34) have more than two movements, compared to 24 percent for other composers. These differences, analyzed by means of a Chi-square test, are significant at the 1 percent level, meaning that the likelihood of Mozart's ensembles having this pattern of fewer movements purely by happenstance is less than 1 in 100.[20]

Since composers typically were guided in subdividing ensembles by cues in the libretto – above all by changes of poetic meter – we can also compare Mozart's response to the texts of his ensembles with the practices of his contemporaries (Figure 14.3). Mozart used fewer movements in an ensemble than there were poetic meters 15 percent of the time (in 5 numbers), while other composers did this even more rarely (9 percent). But only 12 percent of the time did

20 The Chi-square test is a common measure of the degree of independence between two variables in a population. Very simply, the test gives a measure of the likelihood that the given distribution – here, the frequency of ensembles with one, two, or three or more sections – might occur simply by chance. A result is usually considered to be statistically significant if the probability of the given result occurring by chance is less than .05 (or .01); that is, if it would occur fewer than five times (or once) in a hundred.

Figure 14.3 Number of movements in ensembles vs. number of poetic meters:
Mozart and his Viennese contemporaries

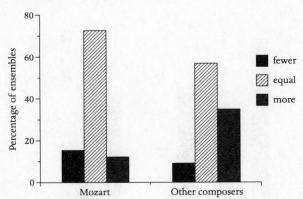

Mozart create *more* movements than there were poetic meters,
while other composers did this in over one-third of their ensembles. The differences in Figure 14.3 are significant at the 5 percent
level.[21]

This analysis can be carried a bit further by examining Mozart's
approach in each of the three Da Ponte operas (Figures 14.4 and
14.5). The nine ensembles of *Le nozze di Figaro* are all in a single
movement,[22] even though two of them feature texts with two
poetic meters. One of these is the Act III sextet; in the other, the
opening duet, Mozart's suppression of a potential change of tempo
or meter clearly creates a more instrumentally organized piece,
with the final tutti making a last reprise of one of the principal

21 This means of course that the differences are less strongly suggestive than those
in Table 1. On the other hand, Mozart did not frequently overrule his librettist in
either direction – note that Mozart and Da Ponte "agreed" 73 percent of the
time, compared to just 57 percent for other composers and their librettists.
Mozart worked extensively with his librettists in the creation of their texts, and
he surely collaborated with Da Ponte to produce ensemble texts that would
conform to his musical plan for setting them.
22 See above for a definition of "movement" as I use it here. This is not to say that
there are no important articulations in these ensembles; see for example the
passage of accompanied recitative in the Act I trio of *Le nozze di Figaro*, "Cosa
sento!"

Figure 14.4 Number of movements in ensembles: Mozart's three Da Ponte operas

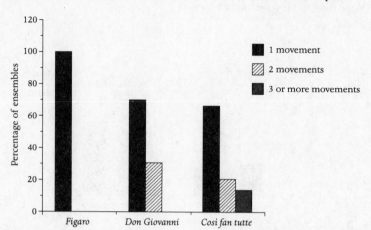

themes of the ensemble.[23] In *Don Giovanni* seven of the ten ensembles are in a single movement and three in two movements, but two of the two-movement pieces have texts with *three* poetic meters (the *introduzione* and our sextet) – there too Mozart suppresses textual points of articulation.[24] The first-act quartet, "Non ti fidar, o misera," despite also having a text with three poetic meters, is written in a single movement. Only one piece in the opera, "Là ci darem," has more movements than poetic meters (see Figure 14.5). But the picture is quite different in *Così fan tutte*, written more than two years later. While ten of its ensembles use a single movement, the other five include pieces with three and even four movements.[25] It is also striking that *Così fan tutte* contains three ensembles with more movements than poetic meters.[26] These somewhat over-

23 See n. 7 above. Of course, this does not mean that the decision is not dramatically effective, or that it was not made at least in part for reasons of operatic characterization. Any such choice can be made for various reasons, and have various effects.

24 The other ensemble in two movements is "Là ci darem."

25 These are, respectively, the Act I sextet and the Fiordiligi/Ferrando duet in Act II. The three two-movement ensembles are the Fiordiligi/Dorabella duet in Act I, the quintet and chorus in Act I, "Di scrivermi ogni giorno!" and the Act II quartet "La mano a me date."

26 These are the sisters' duet in Act I, the Act I sextet, and the Fiordiligi/Ferrando duet.

Figure 14.5 Number of movements in ensembles vs. number of poetic meters: Mozart's three Da Ponte operas

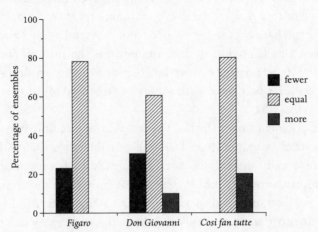

simplified criteria suggest that the ensembles in *Così fan tutte* may reflect a more purely operatic approach by Mozart, one less concerned with the kinds of formal issues that are central in instrumental music.

This suggestion is bolstered by the history of the search for sonata form in Mozart's ensembles. Those critics eager to find sonata-form or sonata-form-like structures in Mozart's operas (most notably Kerman and Charles Rosen) have cited only a limited number of ensembles, and significantly they are all in *Le nozze di Figaro* or *Don Giovanni*.[27] The absence from their lists of any ensem-

---

27 The examples in *Le nozze di Figaro* include the Act I trio, "Cosa sento," and the sextet in Act III, along with the Act II finale, well-known for its allegedly sonata-like tonal shape (but see Webster, "Mozart's Operas and the Myth of Musical Unity", *COJ* 2 [1990–91], 205–7, and John Platoff, "Tonal Organization in 'Buffo' Finales and the Act II Finale of 'Le nozze di Figaro'", *M&L*, 72 [1991], 387–403). In *Don Giovanni* writers have cited, besides the present sextet, the trio in Act II, "Ah taci, ingiusto core." To this list should be added the Act II trio from *Le nozze di Figaro* cited above, which is in a two-part, exposition-recapitulation form. On sonata form in Mozart's operas, see, e.g., Kerman, *Opera as Drama*, pp. 63–68; Rosen, *The Classical Style: Haydn, Mozart, Beethoven* (1971; New York: Viking, 1972), pp. 290–302; Carter, "Figaro", pp. 88–104. See also Carter, "Mozart, Da Ponte and the Ensemble," p. 249.

bles from *Così fan tutte* corroborates the view that Mozart has moved in that work away from instrumentally influenced thinking. This is *not* to say, incidentally, that sonata-form is a particularly useful explanatory concept even for musical numbers in *Le nozze di Figaro* or *Don Giovanni*. Rather, the point is that in *Così fan tutte*, Mozart's structures have moved further away from any design that could be described, even with somewhat tortured logic, in sonata-form terms.

The organization of the *Don Giovanni* sextet into only two movements, then, can be viewed as one possible sign that Mozart's compositional thinking has been influenced by his experience in writing instrumental music. This is not in itself a bad thing: the linking of so many disparate dramatic elements in the long Andante movement is a brilliant achievement, creating one of the most gripping passages in the opera. More generally, finding a connection to instrumental music in this sextet, or in some aspect of it, is not linked to any value judgment about the piece or the specific aspect. But it *is* relevant, in seeking to understand why Mozart did what he did, to explore all possible influences and evaluate their effects in each individual case.

The second manifestation of a connection to instrumental music in the sextet is the dramatic and highly articulated shift from a half-cadence in the relative minor to the tonic at the start of the Molto allegro. The issue is not, of course, that the ensemble returns to and closes in its original tonic key, a practice nearly universal in late eighteenth-century opera. It is rather that Mozart accomplishes this return by means of a tonal shift extremely rare in the operatic repertory of his time, though it is familiar enough in instrumental writing. Rosen, incorrectly in my view, sees in this return the principles of sonata form, and views the lengthy second movement as a kind of recapitulation or resolution (in sonata terms) of the tonal issues earlier in the sextet.[28] However we interpret the return in the sextet, though, the ensembles of Mozart's

28 Rosen, *The Classical Style*, p. 301.

contemporaries show far less concern for such resolutions: they frequently return to the tonic in a more routine and less highly articulated manner, making clear that while an ending in the tonic is necessary, the *moment* of return need not be of any particular significance.[29]

In about 90 percent of the multi-movement ensembles I have examined, the last movement begins in the tonic; in over half of these, however, this follows a penultimate movement that closes in the tonic, with either a full or a half-cadence. In other words, the return to the tonic key has already occurred; the start of the last movement marks a point of rhythmic articulation, but not a tonal return like that in most instrumental forms. In most of the remaining ensembles the penultimate movement cadences in the dominant, and is followed by the final movement in the tonic, either immediately or after a brief transition.

In short, the V/vi–I shift by which Mozart's sextet returns to the tonic is extremely rare in this repertory. (In fact, conspicuous or highly articulated returns to I from any key besides V are quite rare, as are returns following a half-cadence in any key besides the tonic.) Apart from *Don Giovanni*, where it occurs no fewer than three times,[30] I have found only five examples in ensembles or finales, and all five are by just two composers: two are from operas by Vincenzo Righini, and the other three from *Democrito corretto* by Dittersdorf, who was, like Mozart, an experienced and talented composer of instrumental music.[31]

If we search outside the operatic repertory, tonal shifts from V/vi to I – whether within a movement or between movements – are, of course, not hard to find. In many Baroque concertos, the slow movement is in the relative minor, and may close on its domi-

29 This is also true in many arias, as I have argued elsewhere: see John Platoff, "The Buffa Aria in Mozart's Vienna," *COJ* 2 (1990), 105–16.

30 The other two cases besides the sextet are discussed below.

31 In all, these five examples – four are in ensembles and one in a finale – come from over 550 transitions between sections of an ensemble or finale; and in only three of them does the shift to the tonic occur at the start of the last movement, as in the *Don Giovanni* sextet.

nant. The start of the succeeding movement back in the tonic key produces exactly the juxtaposition found in Mozart's sextet.[32] And the case for Mozart's familiarity with Baroque instrumental music, above all that of J. S. Bach, is not hard to make. But a source closer to home for this tonal shift is the Classic sonata form: there are numerous examples of development sections concluding on V/vi, followed by recapitulations that begin back in the tonic.[33]

It is crucial to recognize, however, how differently this tonal move functions in an operatic as opposed to an instrumental context. In a sonata-form movement the return from V/vi to I, accompanied by the restatement of the opening theme, represents a return to the stability and familiarity of the beginning. In such a double return the thematic return clarifies the meaning of the tonal shift, confirming that it really does go back to the tonic. In addition, V/vi has been heard as a "point of furthest remove,"[34] arrived at through a series of rapid modulations; it does not normally function as a half-cadence in a fully established local tonic. But in an operatic context the shift is a surprise. There is no thematic return,

32 Examples include such familiar works as the Bach Brandenburg concertos Nos. 1, 3 (with just two chords standing between the outer movements, clearly implying some sort of improvisation on a Phrygian cadence to V/vi), and 4. In the sixth Brandenburg the slow movement also concludes on V/vi, even though most of the movement is in IV. Looking at Corelli's trio sonatas, one finds eight examples in Opp. 3 and 4 alone (Op. 3 Nos. 2, 6, and 8; Op. 4 Nos. 1, 4, 7, 9, and 10).

33 Among others, see the first movement of the Dittersdorf Symphony in C Major (publ. 1785), the first of his set based on Ovid's *Metamorphoses*. The development leads to a prominent half-cadence on V/vi, followed after a rest by the start of the recapitulation in the tonic. The first movement of Haydn's Symphony No. 85 in B flat, "La Reine," does virtually the same thing, with two notes by unaccompanied first violins providing the slightest possible connecting thread. Mozart adopts this approach in the Presto finale of the Symphony in G, K. 199. Webster, *Haydn's "Farewell" Symphony*, pp. 134–45, discusses the V/vi–I juxtaposition at the point of recapitulation and cites a number of examples from Haydn's symphonies. See also the first movement of Haydn's Quartet Op. 64, No. 6 (cited by Webster in "Sonata Form," *The New Grove Dictionary of Music and Musicians*, ed. Stanley Sadie, vol. 17, p. 502) and Michael Haydn's Symphony in E flat of 1783 (cited by Rosen in *Sonata Forms* [New York: Norton, 1980], p. 255).

34 See Leonard Ratner, *Classical Music: Expression, Form, and Style* (New York: Schirmer, 1980), p. 226.

since the new movement following the shift does not restate material heard before. And there may be no reason to understand the shift as a tonal return, either. In fact just the reverse is true in Mozart's sextet. C minor has controlled a good part of the lengthy Andante movement; it is a well-established key in mm. 121–30. Moreover the *topos* of these measures (above all in mm. 127–30) is that of a slow introduction to an instrumental Allegro: what is clearly expected is a fast continuation in C minor (or perhaps C major). The leap from the dominant of C minor to the key of E flat is a contradiction of the listener's (or at least this listener's) tonal expectations; it has an effect not of resolution, as asserted by Rosen, but of misdirection. Consider by contrast the approach to the similar stretta movement that ends the finale to Act I (as Jessica Waldoff notes, the two movements are "parallel dramatically . . . in both instances the villain is discovered and confronted, but manages to escape").[35] There Mozart wrote a massive half-cadence in C (mm. 526–32), with something of the same introductory *topos*, to prepare the stretta in the same key. The stretta begins with a feeling of tonal stability and solidity, not because it is the key in which the finale opened – most listeners cannot hear that – but because of the solid dominant preparation. In short, Mozart's sextet seems to employ a procedure from sonata form, but it has a much different and perhaps even unintended effect in this context.

Might we argue that this tonal misdirection in the sextet is called for by the dramatic situation? This is plausible in principle; in finales, as I have shown elsewhere, Mozart and other composers distinguished routine tonal moves between movements (usually up or down a fifth) from more distant, usually chromatic ones, with the latter serving to mark new phases of the action or to highlight surprising events.[36] But in the sextet nothing happens between the end of the Andante and the start of the Molto allegro. As we have seen, Leporello's unmasking has already elicited a shocked response from

35 See her essay elsewhere in this volume. She also points out the similarity of Leporello's lines in the sextet stretta to those of Giovanni in the stretta of the Act I finale.   36 See Platoff, "Tonal Organization in 'Buffo' Finales," pp. 390–93.

the other characters, with an appropriate musical reaction, in mm. 114–30. Their shock is signaled not only in the seventeen-measure passage as a whole, but in the deceptive resolution and change of texture in m. 114. The text of the Molto allegro changes nothing, instead expressing the sort of conventionalized consternation typical of stretta movements. So the claim that a surprising change of key is dramatically appropriate here is unconvincing.[37]

This is especially true by contrast to the two other places in *Don Giovanni* where Mozart uses the same tonal shift: once in each of the two finales. (As I have indicated, Mozart never used this shift between movements anywhere in the other Da Ponte operas.) Near the end of the finale to Act I, a half-cadence in D minor leads to a movement in F when, with everyone rushing to Zerlina's aid, Don Giovanni emerges, unexpectedly claiming that Leporello was her assailant. This *is* a surprise – a bit of misdirection by Don Giovanni, one might say – that justifies the surprising tonal move. In the Act II finale the same shift, from V/d to F, occurs when Leporello, sent to see why Donna Elvira screamed, returns in terror to say that the statue of the Commendatore is coming. Here too the tonal surprise coincides with an event that, if not surprising to the audience, is at least out of the ordinary! But in the sextet, as we have seen, the tonal shift does not coincide with a new phase of the action or with a surprise. Instead it stands – ineffectively in my view – at the point where a more typical dominant preparation would have better served to make the beginning of the E-flat stretta sound like the home key.[38] If my claim about the borrowing of this tonal shift

---

37 Elsewhere in this volume (p. 336, n. 47), Sergio Durante argues that the tonal shift is "an appropriate parallel to the stage situation." But he is wrong in claiming that "until the cadence [at m. 130], five characters have been addressing Giovanni/Leporello": their words clearly express shock addressed to no one in particular, just like the words they sing in the stretta.

38 In rejecting Rosen's sonata-form view of the sextet, Julian Rushton makes the extraordinary statement that "the dramatic effect [of the sextet] would be the same if it ended in C rather than E flat major, a licence the harmonic situation before the Allegro (a dominant of C minor) would certainly permit, exceptional though such a procedure would have been." "Mozart," *The New Grove Dictionary of Opera*, ed. Stanley Sadie (London: MacMillan, 1992), vol. 3, p. 494.

from an instrumental context is correct, there is an irony in the fact that the gesture, which indicates tonal resolution in that context, here undermines it instead.

I am not arguing that the stretta itself is unnecessary. While no new action takes place in it – and while its words do not add particularly to our understanding of the characters' feelings – it is nonetheless true that their shock requires time for adequate expression, and that m. 114–30 have not been nearly sufficient. In the musical world of eighteenth-century opera buffa, far less significant recognition scenes than this one often receive lengthy musical treatment in a movement like the Molto allegro. But to me, both the key and the tone of this stretta are misjudged. The key-change makes the reaction in the stretta sound non-consequential, less related to the shocking revelation that precedes it. (Compare again the logical and persuasive relationship between the penultimate and final movements of the Act I finale.) As for its tone, the conventional stretta gestures of the movement undermine the importance of the dark experiences we have just witnessed; in Sergio Durante's words "the introduction of two stylistic levels (with the 'low' characterizaton of Leporello's comic patter) reinforces the hypothesis that a comic juxtaposition, rather than a real clash, is taking place between the servant and the others on stage."[39] Yet as we have seen, the Andante surely insists that far more than a comic juxtaposition is at stake. In other words, and as I suggested at the outset, Mozart's stretta simply does not seem up to the task of adequately dealing with the challenges presented by the Andante. An opera buffa ensemble, the stretta seems to admit, is after all no place for anything deeper than light comedy.[40]

---

39 See his essay elsewhere in this volume, text corresponding to his n. 47.
40 Waldoff makes the insightful point that the sextet "is in part a comic enactment of the recognition scene yet to come and in part a repetition of the thwarted denouement at the end of Act I." (See p. 303.) This may be part of the explanation for its mixture of the serious and the conventionally comic, a mixture I find unsuccessful. For a more admiring view see Hermann Abert, *Mozart's "Don Giovanni"* (trans. Peter Gellhorn) (London: Eulenburg, 1976), pp. 105–12.

My goal in this paper, beyond presenting a view of the *Don Giovanni* sextet that I hope will be persuasive or at least provocative, has been to indicate what can be learned about Mozart's operatic music by putting it in a larger context. There is ample evidence that, of all the great composers, Mozart was one of the most interested in the music of his contemporaries. Letters and other documents attest to his attendance at concerts and operatic performances and rehearsals. We know a great deal about his opinions of other composers and their works; and there is every reason to view his Da Ponte operas as having been written with a keen understanding of what other opera composers in Vienna were doing, and what the Viennese public liked to see and hear on the stage of the Burgtheater. All the more crucial, then, that we study these operas with the same broad musical perspective, the same knowledge of other operatic works, that Mozart brought to the composing of them.

Considering the sextet in this way has led to the hypothesis that some of Mozart's musical choices in his Da Ponte operas reveal the influence of his experience as an instrumental composer. A corollary to this hypothesis is the claim that the connection to instrumental music is strongest in *Le nozze di Figaro* and *Don Giovanni*, while this influence has diminished in importance by the time of *Così fan tutte*.[41] Although I certainly do not regard this paper as having proved the proposition, there seems to be sufficient evidence to warrant considering the matter further. And, for those inclined to reject it out of hand, I close with a question: since it is accepted scholarly practice to cite "operatic" elements in Mozart's instrumental music,[42] why should we be

---

41 Cf. Carter, "Mozart, Da Ponte and the Ensemble," p. 249: "If *Figaro* is an eminently 'instrumental' opera, *Così* is eminently operatic."

42 See for example Reinhard Strohm, "Merkmale italienischer Versvertonung in Mozarts Klavierkonzerten," in Friedrich Lippmann, ed., *Colloquium "Mozart und Italien" (Rom 1974) (AnM*, vol. 18 [1978]) pp. 219–36. References to opera buffa style abound particularly in discussions of Mozart's piano concertos: see among others Albert Einstein, *Mozart: His Character, his Work*, trans. Arthur Mendel and

surprised to discover evidence of musical connections running in the opposite direction?[43]

Nathan Broder (New York: Oxford University Press, 1945), pp. 305, 309; Cuthbert Girdlestone, *Mozart and his Piano Concertos*, 2nd edn. (London: Cassell, 1958), pp. 254, 345; Rosen, *The Classical Style*, pp. 226–67; Robert Levin, "Concertos," in H. C. Robbins Landon, ed., *The Mozart Compendium* (New York: Schirmer, 1990), pp. 263–64.

43 My thanks to Janet M. Levy, Leonard B. Meyer, Ruth R. Montgomery and Ronald J. Rabin for intellectual and technical advice.

From an early stage in his operatic career Mozart was concerned to fit arias to his singers as a tailor fits a suit: "Wolfgang refuses to do the work twice over and prefers to wait for [the primo uomo's] arrival so as to fit the costume to his figure."[1] No doubt he also wanted his ensemble writing to fit the singers; and no doubt Salieri, Paisiello, and Cimarosa felt the same. Over the course of a work composed for virtuosi, if not in its every section, an eighteenth-century composer would normally aim to display the performer's strengths to the full. But composers also welcomed their operas being transferred to other theatres, as when Paisiello's *Il barbiere di Siviglia* and Mozart's *Don Giovanni* were performed in Vienna. For this to work, the music must be aimed at *voice types*, which, in the new production, could be appropriately matched to the music already written. It appears, therefore, that voice types, if not indi-vidual singers, and the way in which they are exploited, are a significant variable which should affect opera analysis and particu-larly the analysis of character.

The singers known to Mozart whose music uses the bass clef are variously described in modern reference books as bass, baritone, or bass-baritone.[2] A contemporary might prefer to distinguish singers as buffo and serio – Mozart referred to Francesco Benucci not as the bass but as "the buffo."[3] Distinctions could be blurred: among

1 Leopold Mozart, letter of 24 November 1770 (*Letters*, p. 171; *Briefe*, vol. 1, p. 405). The occasion was an opera seria, *Mitridate re di Ponto*, but the principle holds for opera buffa.

2 See Owen Jander, Lionel Sawkins, J. B. Steane, and Elizabeth Forbes, "Baritone" and "Bass" in Stanley Sadie, ed., *The New Grove Dictionary of Opera* (London: Macmillan, 1992), vol. 1, pp. 323 and 339.

3 Letter of 7 May 1783; quoted in the final paragraph of Daniel Heartz's essay in this volume. It is notable that the letter precedes by three months the Viennese premiere of Paisiello's *Il barbiere di Siviglia*.

tenors, Michael Kelly was not only buffo; Antonio Baglioni created Mozart's Ottavio and Tito; Vincenzo Calvesi as Ferrando could act the sentimental lover in a buffo context.[4] The Vienna company could normally field three or four male buffo singers, with at least three distinct possibilities of range which today would be called tenor, baritone, and bass. I have taken data mainly relating to three singers, Stefano Mandini, a singer whose great Mozart role (Conte Almaviva) we would now classify as baritone, and two classifiable as basses, Francesco Bussani and the nonpareil Benucci. Baritone roles suggest a lighter vocal coloring, in contrast to the bass: less than in tenor-bass duets (Ferrando and Guglielmo), but still noticeable with, for instance, the composer and the poet in Salieri's *Prima la musica* or the duets of Don Giovanni and Leporello (much of the slapstick humor of their exchange of clothes depends on their voices *not* being naturally alike).[5] The list of roles (see Table 15.1) is selective, but it includes some not created by these singers. Paisiello's *Il barbiere di Siviglia* is included for its well-attested influence on Mozart.[6] *Don Giovanni* is included because Mozart wrote it for the singers he had heard in the Prague *Figaro*, who took over roles created by the Vienna singers; the duet "Per queste tue manine" (K. 540b) was written for Benucci, who sang Leporello in Vienna. When Mozart composed *Don Giovanni* he must have had a future Vienna production in mind, and he was surely unaware that

4 On singers see individual entries in *The New Grove Dictionary of Opera*; Peter Clive, *Mozart and his Circle: A Biographical Dictionary* (London: Dent, 1993); and articles by Bauman, Gidwitz, Campana, and Heartz in *EM* 19 (1991), 557–90.

5 In a surprising internal contradiction in *The New Grove Dictionary of Opera* (see note 2 above), "Baritone" (p. 323) has Figaro, Leporello, and Guglielmo "often considered baritone roles," adding that "heavy baritone would not seem tautologous" (presumably meaning not an oxymoron). "Bass" (p. 339) has Almaviva, Giovanni, and Guglielmo as "nominally for bass" but "now regarded as equally baritone" roles; characters of lower station (Leporello, Figaro) "are essentially *basso buffo* roles."

6 On Mozart's debt to Paisiello, see "Constructing *Le nozze di Figaro*," in Heartz, *Mozart's Operas*, pp. 133–55. Figaro's music in Mozart owes something to Benucci's role, Bartolo, in *Il barbiere*, as noted by Heartz, pp. 145–46 (see also John Platoff, "The Buffa Aria in Mozart's Vienna", *COJ* 2 [1990], 103 and 112), but also something to Figaro's, sung in Paisiello by Bussani.

Table 15.1. *Roles examined*

	Benucci	Bussani	Mandini
Paisiello: *Il barbiere di Siviglia* 1783 (Vienna)	Dr Bartolo	Figaro	Conte Almaviva
Mozart: *Lo sposo deluso* 1783–84	Bocconio	Pulcherio	Asdrubale
Mozart: additions to Bianchi: *La villanella rapita* (1785)	Biaggio		[Pippo played by Paolo Mandini]
Salieri: *Prima la musica* (1786)	Maestro di musica	[director]	Poeta
Mozart: *Le nozze di Figaro* 1786	Figaro	Dr Bartolo and Antonio	Conte Almaviva
Mozart: *Don Giovanni* 1788 (Vienna)	Leporello	Masetto and Commendatore	[Don Giovanni: Albertarelli]
Mozart: *Così fan tutte* 1790	Guglielmo (officer)	Alfonso ("philosopher")	
Cimarosa: *Il matrimonio segreto* 1792	Count Robinson	[did *not* sing Geronimo]	

Mandini would leave Vienna early in 1788: though created in Prague by Luigi Bassi, the role of Giovanni is perfectly tailored for Mandini.

To focus my argument, which is based on incomplete, but still profuse and potentially conflicting data, I shall first pose three problems relating to these singers' roles within Mozart's output, and return to them by way of conclusion.

The first problem concerns *Lo sposo deluso*. As is well known, Mozart attached the names of singers to the roles of this unfinished opera buffa. Benucci as Bocconio presents no problem; the pretentious bourgeois wanting to marry late in life is a stock buffo type like others in Benucci's repertoire, notably Paisiello's Bartolo. But the other male singers are notated in the tenor C-clef. Don Asdrubale is assigned to Benucci's sparring partner, Stefano Mandini, and Pulcherio to Francesco Bussani. Their most celebrated Mozart roles are respectively Almaviva and Bartolo, both notated in the bass clef. Mandini played Almaviva in *Il barbiere di Siviglia*, nominally a tenor role later taken over by Michael Kelly. But this role lies low for a tenor, and is of remarkably narrow range. Mandini did not have to extend down far to remain Almaviva in Mozart's *Le nozze di Figaro*. In the progress from *Il barbiere di Siviglia* to *Le nozze di Figaro*, Bussani and Benucci exchanged personalities. The title-role in Paisiello's opera is clearly inferior to that of Bartolo, whereas Mozart's Bartolo is a comparatively minor figure; so Benucci as *primo buffo* became Figaro. Analysis of the most celebrated music composed for them by Mozart suggests that as voice-types Benucci and Bussani were virtually indistinguishable: Bartolo's aria in *Le nozze di Figaro* would have suited Benucci to perfection. So why does Bussani appear in *Lo sposo deluso* apparently as a tenor?

The second problem concerns the key of Masetto's aria "Ho capito, Signor, si." In the context of Mozart's normal habits, the previous recitative, by cadencing in D major, prepares for an aria in G or, marginally less likely, D; but the aria is in F. Such a contradictory harmonic situation does not occur elsewhere in *Don*

Giovanni.[7] Because the paper suggests a later date of composition than the rest of Act I, Alan Tyson suggested that an aria in G major may have been intended, and the piece "transposed down to suit the singer." Daniel Heartz makes it clear that there is no evidence for this.[8] In any case "Ho capito," with a range of one octave, is within the scope of almost any male singer, whether in F or G. Elsewhere Masetto ranges a third higher and a third lower (i.e. from A to e[1]), and the singer was expected to double the Commendatore. Masetto, in fact, though created in Prague by Giuseppe Lolli, appears a typical Bussani role. But the case remains odd; why should Masetto, of all people, occasion a harmonic non-sequitur?

The third problem concerns Guglielmo, a role created by Benucci. Mozart wrote a grand aria for him in Act I, "Rivolgete a lui lo sguardo" (K. 584), but removed it from *Così fan tutte*, entering it separately in his catalogue with the legend "für Benucci". The obvious explanation for this change of mind is probably the best; "Rivolgete" is far too long for its dramatic context.[9] The replacement is clearly superior as a vehicle for getting the outraged sisters off the stage before the brilliant laughing trio. The omission leaves Guglielmo with two arias, but the Act I substitute, "Non siate ritrosi," is tiny, and, unusually, is in the same key as the other, "Donne mie la fate a tanti." Why should Mozart thus short-change his leading buffo?

These problems bear closely on my particular preoccupation, which is the association between tessitura and characterization. Mozart's choices of range and tessitura within a vocal line function

7 Normally in *Don Giovanni*, recitative cadences occur in the same key as that of the ensuing set pieces or its dominant; more rarely, as before the inserted aria "Dalla sua pace," its subdominant. The same is generally true of the Mozart-Da Ponte operas, and indeed the whole repertory.

8 "Ho capito" was written down on Prague paper: see Alan Tyson, "*Le nozze di Figaro*: Lessons from the Autograph Score," *MT* 122 (1981), 456–61, and (without, however, any suggestion of transposition to suit a singer) "Some Features of the Autograph Score of *Don Giovanni*," *Israel Studies in Musicology* 5 (1990), 11–12; Heartz, *Mozart's Operas*, pp. 176–77.

9 Heartz reaches this conclusion in "When Mozart Revises: Guglielmo in *Così*," in Sadie, *Wolfgang Amadè Mozart*, pp. 355–61; see also Heartz, *Mozart's Operas*, p. 243.

rhetorically like other more familiar variables such as topics and instrumentation. In his major study of Mozart's arias, James Webster has already drawn attention to the significance of vocal high points.[10] Exactly how these signs function may depend upon the individual performance, but should not vary widely if the appropriate voice type is selected for the role (the question of including performance variables in an analytical discussion cannot be considered here). In addition, range and tessitura certainly have a bearing on the vexed question of Mozart's choice of keys, especially for arias. It may not always be possible to decode these signs with precision, but I suggest they play a significant role in enhancing our sense of Mozart's characters; or in Peter Kivy's terminology, in *animating* characters.[11] Kivy has claimed that at best, musical beauty creates the illusion of animation. He rests his case on a persuasive critique of comments which claim powers of animation for music, but which are, in fact, essentially founded on the libretto. Kivy calls "characterization" what music can undoubtedly evoke through topical allusion, for instance, or by tempo and modal distinctions; music can produce a two-dimensional characterization – his term – but not, he claims, that three-dimensionality which he calls animation.[12] In short, Kivy suggests, music can create types, but not characters; which is why I think his terminology should be revised. Henceforward when I say characterization I mean what Kivy means by animation: the creation of personality rather than mere typicality in the humans within the fictional world of an opera.

There is no reason to exclude any variable in a demonstration of music's powers of characterization, but particular value may be

10 Webster, "Analysis," pp. 166–69 and passim.
11 Peter Kivy, "How did Mozart do it," in *The Fine Art of Repetition: Essays in the Philosophy of Music* (Cambridge: Cambridge University Press, 1993), pp. 160–77. On characterization see also Kivy, *Osmin's Rage: Philosophical Reflections on Opera, Drama, and Text* (Princeton: Princeton University Press, 1988), particularly pp. 263–75; Allanbrook, *Rhythmic Gesture*.
12 This formulation owes something to a classic discussion of characterization by E. M. Forster in *Aspects of the Novel*.

attached to elements which can be shown (statistically or otherwise) to be *not necessarily or intrinsically conventional*: shown, in fact, to be elements of compositional *choice*. These certainly include the style and tonality of arias. Salieri's comments are revealing: in settling down to convert a libretto into an opera, "I decided first on the key appropriate for the character of each vocal piece."[13] I agree with John Platoff that his laying out of tonalities implies not a formal intention, but rather a characterizing intention.[14] Keys are chosen partly by conventional associations, and by the requirements of the appropriate instrumentation; but these elements themselves contribute to the dramatic goal which, in part, is characterization.

But the choice of key must also depend on the desired voice type, and in Mozart's case on the range and tessitura of particular singers. Bussani or Lolli could probably have sung Masetto's aria as much as a third higher or lower, but a wider-ranging aria is less susceptible of transposition, and may only be singable in one key or those semitonally adjacent to it. The relation of key to tessitura is associated with stress points in the voice, usually high and low pitches whose function will vary according to key. For example, the sisters' arias in *Così fan tutte* alternate high and low tonic and dominant: "Come scoglio" gives Fiordiligi a high tonic, $b\flat^2$, "Per pietà" a high dominant, b^2; whereas for Dorabella the key of B flat has a high dominant, f^2, with climactic uses of its upper neighbor g^2 and its

---

13 Quoted Heartz, *Mozart's Operas*, p. 139 (German translation of Salieri's original, p. 154).

14 I am grateful to John Platoff for sending me in advance of publication the draft of a chapter in his study of Viennese opera buffa concerned with tonal organization. Part of this material has appeared as "Myths and Realities about Tonal Planning in Mozart's Operas," *COJ* 8 (March, 1996), 3–15. Webster discusses the characterizing significance of keys in "Analysis." For divergent views on tonal organization in Mozart's *opere buffe* see Siegmund Levarie, *Mozart's "Le nozze di Figaro": A Critical Analysis* (Chicago: University of Chicago Press, 1952); Tim Carter, *W. A. Mozart: "Le nozze di Figaro"* (Cambridge: Cambridge University Press, 1987); Andrew Steptoe, *The Mozart-Da Ponte Operas* (London: Oxford University Press, 1988); Heartz, *Mozart's Operas*, pp. 148–50; Webster, "Mozart's Operas and the Myth of Musical Unity," *COJ* 2 (1990), 205–16; Julian Rushton, "Mozart," *The New Grove Dictionary of Opera*, vol. 3, p. 95.

neighbor $a_\flat^2$; g^2 is the high point of her E flat aria, where it is the mediant. The great Benucci role, Figaro, includes three arias, in F, C, and E flat, differentiated in range as well as key. In "Se vuol ballare," Figaro only occasionally hits the high tonic f^1: the aria is more concerned with the high, but not strained, dominant pitch, c^1, and its upper neighbor d^1. The arpeggio melody of "Non più andrai" sails up to the major mediant, e^1. This accords with the positive subtext of the aria: Figaro's plans are maturing, he is even enjoying himself. But in "Aprite un po' quegl' occhi," Figaro's spirits are cast down. The highest note is the regularly available tonic, $e_\flat^1$, but rather than use it as a glorious climax, as in "Come scoglio," Mozart treats it as a frequent point of stress, with, in the coda, heart-stopping falls to $d_\flat^1$. This music would lie high for Benucci in F, and perhaps in E; it would be less effective in D, although Benucci possessed the requisite bottom G. Other reasons militate against D major for Figaro here, including the presence of two angry D major arias earlier in the opera (for Bartolo and the Count). In all these arias, if tonality is chosen for its contribution to affect, that contribution is intimately associated with matters of range and tessitura.

It is necessary to distinguish these terms, particularly as Webster, in his otherwise comprehensive discussion, does not.[15] Range is the distance between bottom and top notes; tessitura is where the voice lies within that range, and should be defined as the part of the voice most persistently exploited.[16] Range and tessitura are readily distinguished by looking at the "Benucci" and "Mandini" roles, if they may be so termed, in *Don Giovanni*. In the C major sections of the first finale their *range* is the same: c to e^1. Leporello reaches the top in the "Viva la libertà" fanfare (m. 387), following Giovanni's lead, and then in unison with Giovanni but in opposition to the other characters (m. 550). Elsewhere Leporello is

---

15 Webster, "Analysis," p. 170, where the "tessitura" of the Countess's arias is described in terms of range, i.e. the distance between top and bottom notes. Tessitura and range are not included in the list of variables on p. 131.

16 See Owen Jander and J. B. Steane, "Tessitura," in *The New Grove Dictionary of Opera*, vol. 4, p. 703.

persistently heard *below* Giovanni, even though Mozart assigned the lowest bass-clef line to Masetto (the "Bussani" role). Leporello's tessitura is therefore lower. The same difference in tessitura is apparent in the buffo duets "Eh via buffone," in which they share material, and "O statua gentilissima," where the material is markedly individualized. Nevertheless their frequent coupling and sharing of pitches has led to misunderstanding of the distinction between Giovanni and Leporello as voice types.[17]

The difference between range and tessitura derives from a conflict between the physical possibilities of a voice type and the general widening of ranges characteristic of eighteenth-century virtuoso singing. In *Don Giovanni*, all three bass-clef singers move freely through the major ninth c to d[1]; in D major and G major they occupy mainly the d–d[1] octave. Their upper range is not much different: all three go to e[1]. What mainly distinguishes them is extension downwards: Masetto to G, Leporello twice to F.[18] But Giovanni lacks low notes; exceptionally, in the quartet, he descends to B♭, but usually he goes no lower than c.[19] In ensembles his higher range derives from his aristocratic right to sing above his servant, but a higher tessitura is equally evident in his arias. The question is mildly confused in *Le nozze di Figaro* by the extension downwards of the Mandini role to A, and the extension upwards of the Benucci role to f[1], although Figaro's f[1] occurs only as a bell tone (No. 2) or an

17 James Parakilas points out that Giovanni was taken over early in the nineteenth century by tenors such as Garcia and Nourrit. After a baritone period typified by Verdi's first Iago, Victor Maurel, the role has been adopted by basses such as Pinza and Raimondi. "The Afterlife of *Don Giovanni*: Turning Production History into Criticism," *JM* 8 (1990), 251–65. *The Viking Opera Guide*, ed. Amanda Holden, (London: Viking, 1993) lists Giovanni as bass or baritone, but Almaviva (who goes lower) as baritone; "baritone" in *The New Grove* (see note 2 above) has Giovanni "perhaps" but is unequivocal about Almaviva. Both dictionaries appear to be concerned with modern rather than historic practice.
18 Optionally, just before the Commendatore enters; and in the piece written specifically for Benucci, "Per queste tue manine."
19 Parakilas (see note 17) gives Giovanni's range as G to e[1]; but G is confined to a spurious passage in certain vocal scores (first finale, mm. 408–13, the opening strain of the Minuet).

indignant shout ("Se vuol ballare"). Nevertheless, in tessitura these roles are not the same at all.[20]

Tessitura should not be crudely represented by the median, the half-way point between the highest and lowest notes. Like range, on which it partly depends, it may vary in the course of a movement. Extension may run parallel with harmonic intensification, but harmonic intensification may occur without extension: the tessitura is not necessarily raised, for instance, by a modulation to the dominant. Extension of range sometimes accompanies a change in singing style. For example, it often occurs in what one might call the fanfare sections in the closing phase of an aria, where the voice tends to emphasize the notes of the tonic triad; this tendency is most marked in bass-clef roles in ensembles where the singer doubles the harmonic bass, but it also occurs in arias, even "Non più andrai" where the principal idea is already an arpeggio.[21]

Paisiello's Bartolo aria "Veramente ho torto, è vero" is a useful paradigm. In Webster's classification, it is a binary form with tonal return.[22] In the "exposition" the fully-closed tonic section, apart from two cadential uses of B♭, is confined to the range d–b♭.[23] In the dominant section, mm. 21 to 52, the same range is used but the tessitura actually sinks a little; the finely varied second part grows increasingly excited, but it is the fanfare, presented in patter singing, which takes off from the bottom of the register and rises to e♭[1]; near the cadence the low A♭ completes the range of a twelfth

20 Mozart avoided the low A in writing for the original Giovanni; did Bassi find the bottom of Almaviva's role difficult? Mozart made no adjustments to the role for Vienna, but composed an aria for the Vienna Giovanni, Francesco Albertarelli ("Un bacio di mano," K.541), with the range B–e[1].

21 The fanfare coda is a phenomenon of bass-clef vocal music; it is not an aspect of the characterization of Giovanni, as Steptoe implies (*The Mozart-Da Ponte Operas*, p. 194). In ensembles, the bass naturally concentrates on dominant and tonic, but even in arias where the voice is the main melodic part final sections tend to privilege notes of the tonic triad.

22 Webster, "Analysis," p. 115, the example being "Aprite un po' quegl' occhi."

23 The Ricordi vocal score (edited by Mario Parenti, 1960) replaces both instances of B♭ by d, but earlier sources consulted confirm B♭, doubling the orchestral bass.

Table 15.2. *Arias in E♭ sung by Benucci*

	Key	Range	Tessitura as Pitch Center of Gravity (PCG)	
A Bartolo (*Il barbiere di Siviglia*)				
Aria: "Veramente ho torto"	E♭	A♭–e♭^{1}	below f♯	(11·87)
Section in tonic 1–20		B♭–b♭	f♯/g	(12·3)
Section going to V 20–34		d–b♭	f/f♯	(11·4)
Section in V 34–52		B♭–b♭	f/f♯	(11·5)
Reprise in tonic 52–72		B♭–b♭	f	(11·3)
Coda 72–end		A♭–e♭^{1}	f♯	(12·4)
B Figaro (*Le nozze di Figaro*)				
Aria: "Aprite un po"	E♭	B♭–e♭^{1}	above a♭	(14·3)
Section in tonic 1–14		d–e♭^{1}	below a♭	(13·8)
Section in V (a) 14–25		B♭–e♭^{1}	below a♭	(13·8)
Section in V (b) 26–47		e♭–e♭^{1}	a♭/a	(14·6)
Reprise in tonic 48–62		B♭–e♭^{1}	f♯/g	(12·5)
Coda 62–end		e♭–e♭^{1}	a/b♭	(15·8)

(see Table 15.2A). Yet a calculation of tessitura shows it to be more or less constant throughout the aria.

This calculation of tessitura is presented in the tables as an average represented by a number and the name of the nearest pitch: in Bartolo's aria this is f♯, a pitch not actually used. The tessitura fluctuates less than the median, and is unmoved by Bartolo's growing excitement. Is this an indication of the impotence of his fury? Certainly other examples show tessitura changing in the course of an aria or ensemble much more than this. Figaro's "Aprite un po' quegl' occhi" may be partly modeled on "Veramente ho torto," but it handles range and tessitura very differently. B♭ is reached in the second section and e♭^{1} is present from the start (see Table 15.2B). The incidence of both extremes increases as the aria proceeds; nevertheless the last section, from m. 62, shows a marked rise in tessitura, while the previous measures, 48–62, plumb the depths. The opening of the aria has a tessitura centered just below a♭; mm. 48–62 it is below g; and from 62–85 it rises nearly to b♭ (see Table 15.2B).

Table 15.3. *Don Giovanni*

Arias in F sung by lower-caste characters	Range (median)	PCG
A Masetto (Lolli: Bussani) "Ho capito, Signor, si"	c–c¹ (f♯)	f♯/g (12·6)
B Leporello (Ponziani: Benucci) "Notte e giorno faticar"	A–c¹ (e/f)	f (10·9)

The calculation of tessitura as a pitch-sign marking the center of the comfortable range I owe to Richard Rastall's conception of a Pitch Center of Gravity (PCG).[24] The PCG is an average obtained by computing the amount of time the singer actually dwells on each note. The PCG is theoretically distinct from the median, even if often similar in practice. The median may be distorted by a single high or low note. The PCG covers statistically erratic extensions of range by including them in a complete calculation averaging pitch and duration. This gives an imprecise, but still truer, picture of the lie of a voice, its tessitura, than does the observation of extremes of range, and the calculation permits the demonstration of fine distinctions. Leporello, in "Notte e giorno faticar," goes no higher than Masetto in his aria in the same key; but Leporello's range extends a third lower (see Table 15.3). Both the median and the PCG are lower by a good three-quarters of a tone. But the lowering of the median would occur if Leporello had touched bottom A only once: the calculation of tessitura shows that the entire section lies lower. The difference need not be great to be significant. We all know how precise singers often are about the keys in which they are willing to perform certain music. It is not the outer extremities which cause a singer to transpose, for instance, a Schubert song, but

24 Rastall has devised what he describes as "a purely numerical manipulation [which] permits objective calculation of a point-tessitura," achieved by calculations in the pitch–time dimension. Richard Rastall, "Vocal Range and Tessitura in Music from York Play 45," *MA* 3 (1984), 181–99, quoted from p. 192. In order to reach the figures in the tables, each pitch is assigned a numeral, with low G 1, f♯ 12, g 13, and so on.

Table 15.4. *Early Benucci roles by Mozart*

	Key	Range (median)	PCG	
A Bocconio (*Lo sposo deluso*)				
No. 1 (Quartet: lowest voice)	D	A–e^1 (f$_\sharp$–g)	above a	(15·3)
No. 4 Trio	E$\flat$	A$\flat$–e$\flat^1$ (f–f$_\sharp$)	e/f	(10·5)
B Figaro (*Le nozze di Figaro*)				
Duet No. 1	G	d–d^1 (g$_\sharp$)	g$_\sharp$/a	(14·5)
Duet No. 2	B$\flat$	A–f^1	below f$_\sharp$	(11·9)
Part I 1–96		B$\flat$–f^1	above a	(15·3)
Part II 97–end		A–b$\flat$	below d	(8·7)
Aria No. 3 "Se vuol ballare"	F	c–f^1 (g$_\sharp$–a)	below g$_\sharp$	(13·86)
Minuet sections		c–f^1		(13·73)
Contredanse		c–d^1	above g$_\sharp$	(14·19)
Aria: "Non più andrai"	C	c–e^1	f$_\sharp$/g	(12·6)
Refrain	C	c–e^1	above f$_\sharp$	(12·3)
Dominant material	G	d–d^1	above g$_\sharp$	(14·4)
Other tonic material	C	c–e^1	a	(15·1)

the *comfort* of the voice throughout the whole piece; and comfort is part of the definition of tessitura.[25]

Change of range or tessitura is an obvious way to make a dramatic point. Mozart particularly relished the versatility of Benucci in this respect and exploited it in the first music he wrote for him (Table 15.4). The PCG drops with the spirits of Bocconio in the Trio of *Lo sposo deluso*, when compared to his confidence in the *introduzione*. The second duet in *Le nozze di Figaro* divides in two. Figaro is confident at first, then as he understands what Susanna is saying he is horrified: his tessitura falls by a fifth. That the first section includes a little top f^1 (the bell-imitation, possibly taken falsetto), and that the last section is mainly a duet (with Figaro much the lower voice), does not sufficiently account for this unusually drastic change.

25 Jander and Steane define tessitura in terms including "lie" and "comfortable": see note 16. See also Julian Rushton, "Villains and Voice-Types: Towards a Methodology of Operatic Characterization," paper delivered at the conference "Signs in Opera," Imatra, July 1993, forthcoming in *Acta Semiotica Fennica*.

I now return to my three problems. Benucci and Bussani may have been far apart in artistic quality but in the Mozart-Da Ponte operas they appear practically interchangeable as vocal types. Yet in *Lo sposo deluso* the role of Pulcherio lies almost as high as that of Asdrubale, itself the highest music Mozart ever wrote for Mandini or those who covered similar roles, such as Bassi and Albertarelli. It appears, however, that Bussani did in fact sing tenor roles, including those of lovers.[26] Mozart did not (as one might be tempted to conclude) make a mistake, but selected from possible voice types which inhabited the same body, that of Francesco Bussani; such versatility was doubtless more practicable in the small theatres of the time. For we cannot confuse Figaro in *Il barbiere di Siviglia*, which is assumed to have influenced Mozart so much, with a tenor: the voice type is totally different from that of Pulcherio. This emphasizes that the subject under discussion is not after all the individual singer, tantalizingly lost to posterity, but the voice type. Mozart evidently came to prefer the baritone or bass Bussani and composed a lower tessitura both for him and Mandini in the second number of *Lo sposo deluso* – but not strikingly so, and they remain in the tenor C-clef (see Table 15.5). The two ensembles Mozart wrote for Bianchi's *La villanella rapita* (1785) already display Bussani (Biaggio) as a basso buffo.[27]

Turning to "Ho capito," to choose F rather than G would hardly change the voice type suited to the aria from baritone to bass, and the key was not altered to suit any singer's limitations. But with the aria in G, there would be great emphasis on the high dominant, d^1; in F, this emphasis moves down to c^1. Giovanni himself and the Commendatore make great play with d^1, so the choice of F major might have been intended to prevent Masetto sounding like his

---

26 I owe this information to Dorothea Link (personal communication): on 22 April 1783 Zinzendorf heard Bussani sing in *La scuola de'gelosi*, referring to him as "le primo amoroso" and comparing him unfavorably with the tenor Calvesi. Bussani sang the tenor role of Nardone in *La frascatana* in Turin in 1775.

27 There may have been a role in this revival for Stefano Mandini but it appears that the tenor/baritone role of Pippo, for which Mozart composed, was played by his brother Paolo (I am indebted to Dorothea Link for this information).

Table 15.5. *Lo sposo deluso* (Benucci's role, see Table 15.4)

	Key	Range (median)	PCG	
Asdrubale (Mandini)				
No. 1 Quartet	D	$e–g^1$ (b/c^1)	above $c_\sharp^1$	(19·2)
No. 4 Trio	E♭	$d–e♭^1$ ($g_\sharp/a$)	below a	(14.8)
Pulcherio (Bussani)				
No. 1 Quartet	D	$e–g^1$	$c^1–c_\sharp$	(18.5)
No. 3 Aria	G	$c_\sharp–f_\sharp^1$	$a_\natural–b$	(16·4)

social superiors.[28] But this does not explain why, if Mozart planned an aria in F, he prepared in the recitative for one in a sharp key. The local conflict between D major and F major chords (not tonalities) may itself be an aspect of characterization, intended momentarily to animate the confrontation between Don Giovanni's flashing sword and the unfortunate peasant.[29]

This view derives some support from considering the other bass-clef voices when they use the same key, F major (see Table 15.6A). Leporello, in "Notte e giorno faticar," extends the range downwards, with an appreciably lower PCG: this represents the natural voice of the character, in soliloquy. "Per queste tue manine" is in C major, the key of Benucci's exultant "Non più andrai," but Leporello is tied up and awaiting punishment; the upward extension is more than compensated for by low notes, and overall the tessitura is gloomy. Leporello's two arias in sharp keys lie markedly higher.[30] Like the duet which replaced it, "Ah, pietà Signori miei" is

28 On the use of d^1 in the role of Giovanni see Steptoe, *The Mozart-Da Ponte Operas*, pp. 193–94. Tyson's hypothetical transposition might have been intended to support this characterization.

29 Heartz (*Mozart's Operas*, pp. 176–77) observes that Mozart seldom has consecutive numbers in the same key (the preceding chorus is in G). He also argues that the move D–F "is not a strange relationship in this opera" (e.g. the overture and *introduzione*); nevertheless it remains eccentric as a shift from recitative to aria.

30 A performance including "Per queste tue manine" should not also include Leporello's G major aria. On the two versions of the opera see Julian Rushton, *W. A. Mozart: "Don Giovanni"* (Cambridge: Cambridge University Press, 1981), pp. 20–22, 53–57.

Table 15.6. *Don Giovanni*

	Range (median)	PCG
A *Don Giovanni*: arias in F		
Leporello (Ponziani: Benucci)	A–c^1 (e/f)	f (10·9)
"Notte e giorno faticar"		
Masetto (Lolli: Bussani)	c–c^1 (f$\sharp$)	f$\sharp$/g (12.6)
"Ho capito, Signor, si"		
Giovanni (Bassi: Albertarelli)		
"Metà di voi quà vadano"	c–e^1 (g$\sharp$)	below g$\sharp$(13·8)
B Other sections of Giovanni's music		
Duet: "Là ci darem la mano" (in A)	e–e^1 (b$\flat$)	above b$\flat$ (16·3)
Quartet: "Non ti fidar" (in B$\flat$)	B$\flat$–e$\flat^1$	below g (12·8)
Aria: "Fin ch'an dal vino" (in B$\flat$)	d–e$\flat^1$ (g$\sharp$/a)	above a (15·3)
Trio: "Ah taci, ingiusto core" (in A)	c$\sharp$–d^1 (e^1 x ♪)	a (15·1)
Serenade (in D)	d–d^1 (e^1 x ♪)	above b$\flat$ (16·3)

a plea for mercy, but Leporello is free-moving and escapes at the end. As for "Madamina, il catalogo è questo," he is, if not imitating Giovanni in D major, at least empathizing with him; the PCG is noticeably higher than is normal for Leporello.

The other F major aria is Giovanni's "Metà di voi quà vadano," in which the range extends a third higher than the other bass-clef pieces in F. The median is correspondingly higher; but the tessitura is only a semitone higher than Masetto's, and is generally lower than the rest of his role (see Table 15.6: Giovanni lies unusually low in the Quartet, where he is the lowest voice and must talk under his breath). Even in the dominant area of "Metà di voi," when the tessitura rises sharply, it remains lower than Giovanni's most exultant utterance, "Fin ch'an dal vino." Doubtless this is because, in the F major aria, he is imitating Leporello. Within the aria, the PCG for different sections of the aria varies significantly: when Giovanni is fully in (Leporello's) character, it remains at a fairly normal "Mandini" level which is also the level of Leporello in his sharp-key arias. But when, in the dominant key, Giovanni narcissistically describes himself, his hat, and his sword (currently worn by Leporello), he rises frequently to his favorite high d^1 and even e^1. In a concinnity of parameters, this section places exceptional emphasis on G major (V of V); presumably it is this point that Edward J. Dent interpreted as Giovanni almost forgetting his disguise.[31] The effect in "Metà di voi" results from Mozart's manipulation of range and tessitura; it is not an inevitable result of the conditions of his musical language. One might expect the tessitura to rise when the music modulates to the dominant, if only because one constituent pitch is sharpened, often two; higher intensity may be recognized in the tonicization of the dominant pitch. But in Masetto's aria, although the dominant C is clearly tonicized, with even a passing F$\sharp$ in the orchestral melody, the section in the dominant is barely higher in tessitura than the opening; there is a greater rise at the dominant preparation for the reprise.[32] And in Bartolo's aria, as already noted, the tessitura is actually a little higher in the tonic sections.

Tessitura, therefore, remains one of the composer's areas of choice. Another effective example is Bartolo's fruitless search for the paper dropped by Rosina; this section of their F major duet is largely in the subdominant, and Paisiello uses the same range as the tonic sections, but with the tessitura nearly a semitone down. Mozart's drastic manipulation in Figaro's second duet with Susanna, described above, remains exceptional in degree rather than in kind. Extension of range of voice in the closing section of an aria is an obvious rhetorical device; equally rhetorical is the way Masetto sticks obdurately to his octave in "Ho capito," even for the fanfare coda. The question of key, therefore, may be resolved without hypotheses about transposition, or reference to long-range structural considerations. The character of the music would

31 Dent, *Mozart's Operas: A Critical Study*, 2nd edn. (London: Oxford University Press, 1947), p. 166. Abert suggests the mask falls at measure 15, at "ferite pur, ferite" (*Mozart's "Don Giovanni"*, trans. Peter Gellhorn [London: Eulenburg, 1976], pp. 102–03). Such emphasis on V/V is unusual in arias and almost without parallel in *Don Giovanni*.

32 The opening section, 12.3; the dominant section 12.6; the retransition 13.1; the reprise 12.8; the coda 12.6.

come over equally strongly in G, but having the aria in F, and the obtuse tonal juxtaposition with D, characterize Masetto, and in this particular situation: the voice part, in particular, resists the flamboyant possibilities available from the original singer. Mozart's procedures here – key, range, and tessitura, harmonic non-sequitur, instrumentation – go beyond conventional animation and characterize Masetto as surely as "Fin ch'an dal vino" and, I would suggest, "Metà di voi" characterize Giovanni.

The problem of Guglielmo may also be referred to the needs of characterization. In ensembles Guglielmo is the lowest voice, with Bussani as Alfonso lying above, so that the positions of Benucci and Bussani in *Le nozze di Figaro* and the Vienna *Don Giovanni* were reversed (even in Alfonso's little aria "Vorrei dir" Bussani was asked for a consistently higher tessitura, though not as high as the aborted role of Pulcherio; Mozart presents Alfonso as a baritone and surely if the chance had been offered he would have written it for Mandini). Guglielmo's G major arias both exploit the high dominant d^1 without stress; and, descending only to B, neither employs Benucci's lowest notes. Thus both predominantly use the d–d^1 octave and have a PCG in the region of a (Table 15.7), which is almost identical to that of the rejected D major aria, "Rivolgete a lui lo sguardo." But "Rivolgete" exploits the high *tonic* d^1 from the outset, and to enliven the closing fanfare Mozart has recourse to several extended high mediants: $f\sharp^1$ rather than the e^1 of "Non più andrai." Mozart's previous piece for Benucci, "Per queste tue manine," uses the range F–e^1; Mozart asked of Benucci as Guglielmo a range higher by a whole tone than what his other music implies was comfortable (the repeated high f^1, in "Se vuol ballare" is surely not meant to be comfortable). Was "Rivolgete" then cut because it was too high "für Benucci"?[33] Surely it is hardly conceivable that Mozart would make such a mistake about a singer

33 The PCG of "Rivolgete" is affected by an extension of range downwards in the closing stages, as well as upwards: nevertheless the closing section rises to the highest level (see Table 15.7).

Table 15.7. *Così fan tutte*: Guglielmo (Benucci)

	Key	Range	PCG	
No. 1 Trio	G	B–e^1	f♯/g	(12·5)
No. 2 Trio	E	d♯–e^1	g♯	(14·3)
No. 3 Trio	C	c–e^1	g/g♯	(13·4)
Aria: "Non siate ritrosi"	G	d–e^1	a	(15·02)
Duet: "Il core vi dono"	F	c–d^1	below g♯	(13·8)
Aria: "Donne mie a tanti"	G	B–e^1	below b♭	(15·8)
1st half (includes section in V)			a/b♭	(15·4)
2nd half (from measure 87)			b♭	(16)
Aria: (rejected) "Rivolgete a lui lo sguardo"	D	G–f♯^{1}	a	(15·1)
Tonic section 1–30		c♯–d^1	below f♯	(11·9)
Dominant section 31–70		c♯–e^1	a	(15·1)
X section 71–128		c♯–e♭^{1}	below b♭	(15·88)
Allegro molto (tonic return)		G–f♯^{1}	above b♭	(16·03)

he knew this well, and other evidence suggests that Benucci could employ higher notes still when required.[34] So why do his Mozart roles, including Guglielmo in the final version, not exploit this ability to the full?

Mozart was no doubt intending a particular characterization of Guglielmo, and the tessitura is one result. Guglielmo's arias are baritonal, but in ensembles he functions as a bass with a correspondingly lower range and PCG. The marvelous Benucci presumably took this in his stride. Mozart's rhetorical purposes in exploiting this singer, and Bussani, in particular ways were surely concerned with character and class. A bass sound and tessitura are

---

34 Kay Lipton informs me that when singing Picchanillo in Guglielmi's *Le vicende d'amore* (Rome, 1784, in the presence of the Austrian emperor) Benucci reached g^1 (see Lipton, "The *opere buffe* of Pietro Alessandro Guglielmi in Vienna and Eszterháza: Contributions to the Development of *opera buffa* between 1768 and 1793," PhD diss., UCLA, 1995). Was this falsetto? When this opera was sung in Vienna he sang a different, and lower, role, so his g^1 was not then on display to Mozart.

associated with the plebeian or peasant class: Leporello, Masetto. Alfonso is a middle-class intellectual; Guglielmo is an officer. Of course Bartolo, whom both singers had impersonated, was a middle-class professional, but he was also a buffoon, and Mozart does not intend us to understand Guglielmo or Alfonso that way. This interpretation is borne out by Cimarosa's role for Benucci, Count Robinson in *Il matrimonio segreto*, an opera without servant characters. Robinson lies generally above Geronimo in ensembles; nevertheless his tessitura is not high, with a PCG generally in the region of f#. It rises distinctly in more soloistic utterances, including the duet with the tenor, Paolino. Both upper-crust and a buffoon, Robinson is a summation of Benucci's abilities. Cimarosa requires a notated range of over two octaves, although the bottom E is obviously a joke and there is only a little, but full-voiced, f^1.

In conclusion, there appears to be a distinction in late eighteenth-century practice between high, middle, and low male voices; but in certain circumstances that distinction becomes blurred. Singers whose abilities we think we know from one role are deliberately exploited in a different way in another context, and thus appear to have been capable of functioning as two distinct voice types; but when a role has been composed, it implies, as it were for future use, only one voice type. The tessitura and range of sung passages is a variable like any other, under the rhetorical control of the composer (failure to understand this has led to such modern aberrations as bass Alfonsos and Giovannis). Mozart was lucky in that both Bussani and Benucci could cope with baritonal roles or at least baritonal sections within bass roles, and his exercise of choice in the matter is part of his manipulation of musical material to a dramatic end. We should modify our view of Mozart the bespoke tailor, and perhaps reflect on the unexpected level of creative control he exercised in his mature opera buffa, for it is clear that for purposes of characterization he sometimes deliberately avoided exploiting the full potentialities of his singers.

Abbate, Carolyn. *Unsung Voices: Opera and Musical Narrative in the Nineteenth Century*. Princeton: Princeton University Press, 1991.

Abbate, Carolyn, and Roger Parker, eds. *Analyzing Opera: Verdi and Wagner*. Berkeley and Los Angeles: University of California Press, 1989.

"Dismembering Mozart." *COJ* 2 (1990): 187–95.

Abert, Hermann. "Paisiellos Buffokunst und ihre Beziehungen zu Mozart." *AMw* 1 (1918–19): 402–21. Reprinted in Abert, *Gesammelte Schriften und Vorträge*. Halle, 1929. Reprint Tutzing: Schneider, 1968.

Mozart's "Don Giovanni". Trans. Peter Gellhorn. London: Eulenburg Books, 1976.

Abrams, M. H. *The Mirror and the Lamp: Romantic Theory and the Critical Tradition*. New York: Oxford University Press, 1953.

Accorsi, Maria Grazia. "Teoria e pratica della «variatio» nel dramma giocoso: a proposito della 'Villanella rapita' di Giovanni Bertati." In Muraro, *I vicini*.

Adams, Charles Francis. *Familiar Letters of John Adams and His Wife Abigail Adams, During the Revolution*. New York: Hurd and Houghton, 1876.

Agawu, Kofi. "Schenkerian Notation in Theory and Practice." *Music Analysis* 8 (1989): 275–301.

Allanbrook, Wye Jamison. *Rhythmic Gesture in Mozart: Le nozze di Figaro and Don Giovanni*. Chicago: University of Chicago Press, 1983.

"Mozart's Happy Endings: A New Look at the 'Convention' of the 'Lieto Fine.'" *MJb* 1984–85, 1–5.

"Human Nature in the Unnatural Garden: *Figaro* as Pastoral." *CM* 51 (1993): 82–93.

Alpers, Svetlana. *The Art of Describing: Dutch Art in the Seventeenth Century*. Chicago: University of Chicago Press, 1988.

Angermüller, Rudolph. *Antonio Salieri: Sein Leben und seine weltlichen Werke unter besonderer Berücksichtigung seiner "großen" Opern*. 3 vols. Munich: Katzbichler, 1971.

Anglani, Bartolo. *Goldoni: il mercato, la scena, l'utopia*. Naples: Liguori, 1983.

Arney, William Ray. *Power and the Profession of Obstetrics*. Chicago: University of Chicago Press, 1982.

Balet, Leo, and E. Gerhard. *Die Verbürgerlichung der deutschen Kunst, Literatur und Musik im 18. Jahrhundert*. Strasbourg: Heitz & Co., 1936.

Baratto, Mario. *Tre studi sul teatro (Ruzante – Aretino – Goldoni)*. Vicenza: Neri Pozza, 1964.

Barthes, Roland. "The Death of the Author." In *Image – Music – Text*. Trans. Stephen Heath. New York: Hill and Wang, 1977.

  "From Work to Text." In *Image – Music – Text*.

  "The Grain of the Voice." In *Image – Music – Text*.

Bauman, Thomas. "The Three Trials of Don Giovanni." In *The Pleasures and Perils of Genius: Mostly Mozart*, ed. Peter Ostwald and Leonard Zegans. Madison, CT: International Universities Press, 1993.

Beaumarchais, Pierre-Augustin, Caron de. *Le Mariage de Figaro ou la Folle Journée*. Ed. Jean Meyer. Paris: Editions du Seuil, 1953.

Becker, Howard. *Art Worlds*. Berkeley and Los Angeles: University of California Press, 1982.

Beckerman, Michael. "Mozart's Duel with Don Giovanni." *MJb* 1984/85, 9–15.

Bitter, Christof. *Wandlungen in den Inszenierungsformen des "Don Giovanni" von 1787 bis 1928: zur Problematik des musikalischen Theaters in Deutschland*. Regensburg: G. Bosse, 1961.

Blood, Elizabeth. "From *canevas* to *commedia*: Innovation in Goldoni's *Il servitore di due padroni*." *Annali d'italianistica* 11 (1993): 111–19.

Bloom, Harold, ed. *Poets of Sensibility and the Sublime*. New York: Chelsea House Publishers, 1986.

Bonds, Mark Evan. *Wordless Rhetoric: Musical Form and the Rhetoric of the Oration*. Cambridge, MA: Harvard University Press, 1991.

Bourdieu, Pierre. "Intellectual Field and Creative Project." *Social Science Information* 8.2 (1969): 89–119.

Boyle, Nicholas. *Goethe: the Poet and the Age*. Vol. I: *The Poetry of Desire (1749–1790)*. Oxford: Clarendon Press, 1992.

Braunbehrens, Volkmar. *Maligned Master: The Real Story of Antonio Salieri*. Trans. Eveline L. Kanes. New York: Fromm, 1992.

Brissenden, R. F. *Virtue in Distress: Studies in the Novel of Sentiment from Richardson to Sade*. New York: Barnes and Noble, 1974.

Brockway, Lucile H. *Science and Colonial Expansion: The Role of the British Royal Botanical Gardens*. New York: Academic Press, 1979.

Brown, Bruce Alan. "Beaumarchais, Mozart and the Vaudeville: Two Examples from *The Marriage of Figaro.*" MT 127 (1986): 261–65.

 Gluck and the French Theatre in Vienna. Oxford: Clarendon Press, 1991.

 W. A. Mozart: "Così fan tutte." Cambridge: Cambridge University Press, 1995.

 "Beaumarchais, Paisiello, and the Genesis of *Così fan tutte.*" In Sadie, *Wolfgang Amadè Mozart.*

Brown, Bruce Alan, and John A. Rice. "Salieri's *Così fan tutte.*" COJ 8 (1996): 17–43.

Brown, John. *Letters upon the Poetry and Music of the Italian Opera.* Edinburgh: Bell and Bradfute, 1789.

Bryant, David, ed. *La farsa musicale.* Vol. 2 of Muraro, *I vicini.*

Carter, Tim. *W. A. Mozart: "Le nozze di Figaro."* Cambridge: Cambridge University Press, 1987.

Chiarini, P. Introduction to *Drammaturgia d'Amburgo*, by G. E. Lessing. Rome: Bulzoni, 1975.

Cibotto, Gian Antonio, Filippo Pedrocco, and Danilo Reato, eds. *La maschera e il volto di Carlo Goldoni: Due secoli di iconografia goldoniano.* Vicenza: Neri Pozza, 1993.

Clark, Caryl Leslie. "The Opera Buffa Finales of Joseph Haydn." PhD diss., Cornell University, 1991.

Clive, Peter. *Mozart and his Circle: A Biographical Dictionary.* London: Dent, 1993.

Cone, Edward T. *The Composer's Voice.* Berkeley and Los Angeles: University of California Press, 1974.

 "The World of Opera and its Inhabitants." In *Music: A View from Delft: Selected Essays*, ed. Robert P. Morgan. Chicago: University of Chicago Press, 1989.

Croce, Benedetto. *Aesthetic as Science of Expression and General Linguistic.* Rev. and trans. Douglas Ainslie. New York: Noonday Press, 1922.

Da Ponte, Lorenzo. *Memoirs of Lorenzo Da Ponte, Mozart's Librettist.* Trans. L. A. Sheppard. London: Routledge, 1929.

 Memorie. Ed. Cesare Pagnini. Milan: Rizzoli, 1960.

 An Extract from the Life of Lorenzo Da Ponte. New York: The Author at No. 54 Chapel St. ..., 1819. Trans. Marina Maymone Sinischalchi; ed. Marina Maymone Sinischalchi and Franco Carlo Ricci. Naples and Rome: Edizioni Scientifiche Italiane, 1989.

Dahlhaus, Carl. "'Si vis me flere.'" *Die Musikforschung* 25 (1972): 51–52.

Analysis and Value Judgment. Trans. Siegmund Levarie. New York: Pendragon Press, 1983.

"Drammaturgia dell'opera italiana." In *Storia dell'opera italiana*, ed. Lorenzo Bianconi and Giorgio Pestelli. Vol. 6, *Teorie e tecniche, immagini e fantasmi*. Turin: EDT/Musica, 1988.

The Idea of Absolute Music. Trans. Roger Lustig. Chicago: University of Chicago Press, 1989.

"What is a Musical Drama?" *COJ* 1 (1989): 95–111.

Dahlhaus, Carl, ed. *Die Musik des 18. Jahrhunderts*. Laaber: Laaber Verlag, 1985.

Dallapiccola, Luigi. "Notes on the Statue Scene in Don Giovanni." *Music Survey* 3.2 (Dec. 1950): 89–97. Repr. in *Dallapiccola on Opera: Selected Writings*, trans. Rudy Shackelford. n.p.: Toccata Press, 1987.

Della Corte, Andrea. *Paisiello; con una tavola tematica*. Turin: Fratelli Bocca, 1922.

L'opera comica italiana nel Settecento: studi ed appunti. Bari: Laterza, 1923.

Piccinni (settecento italiano): con frammenti musicali inediti e due ritratti. Bari: Laterza, 1928.

Della Seta, Fabrizio. "Affetto e azione: Sulla teoria del melodramma italiano dell'Ottocento." In *Atti del XIV congresso della Società internazionale di musicologia: Trasmissione e recenzione delle forme di cultura musicale*, ed. Angelo Pomilio et al. Vol. 3. Turin: EDT/Musica, 1990.

DeNora, Tia. "The Musical Composition of Social Reality? Music, Action, and Reflexivity." *The Sociological Review* (1995): 296–315.

Dent, Edward J. *Mozart's Operas: A Critical Study*. Second edition. London: Oxford University Press, 1947.

Derrida, Jacques. *The Truth in Painting*. Trans. Geoff Bennington and Ian McLeod. Chicago: University of Chicago Press, 1987.

Deutsch, Otto Erich. *Mozart: A Documentary Biography*. London: Black, 1965.

Deutsche Bibliothek der schönen Wissenschaften Halle 2 (1768). Cited in Arnold E. Maurer, *Carlo Goldoni: seine Komödien und ihre Verbreitung im deutschen Sprachraum des 18. Jahrhunderts*. Bonn: Herbert Grundmann, 1982.

Diderot, Denis. *De la Poésie dramatique*. In *Oeuvres ésthetiques. Textes établis, avec introductions, bibliographies, notes et relevés de variantes*. Paris: Garnier, 1959.

Donnison, Jean. *Midwives and Medicine Men: A History of the Struggle for the*

Control of Childbirth. Second edition. London: Historical Publications, 1988.

Edge, Dexter. "The Original Performance Material and Score for Mozart's *Le nozze di Figaro.*" Paper presented at the annual meeting of the American Musicological Society, Minneapolis, MN, November 1995.

Ehrenreich, Barbara and Dierdre English. *Witches, Midwives, and Nurses: A History of Women Healers*. Old Westbury, NY: Feminist Press, 1973.

Einstein, Alfred. *Mozart: His Character, His Work*. Trans. Arthur Mendel and Nathan Broder. New York: Oxford University Press, 1945.

Ekstein, Nina. *Dramatic Narrative: Racine's Récits*. New York: Peter Lang, 1986.

Elam, Keir. *The Semiotics of Theatre and Drama*. London: Methuen, 1980.

Emery, Ted A. *Goldoni as Librettist: Theatrical Reform and the "drammi giocosi per musica.*" New York: Peter Lang, 1991.

"Goldoni's *Pamela* from Play to Libretto." *Italica* 64 (1987): 572–82.

Erämetsä, Erik, "A Study of the Word 'Sentimental' and of Other Linguistic Characteristics of Eighteenth-Century Sentimentalism in England." Thesis, University of Helsinki, 1951.

Farnsworth, Rodney. "*Così fan tutte* as Parody and Burlesque." *OQ* 6 (1988/89): 50–68.

Favart, Charles-Simon. *Mémoires et correspondances littéraires, dramatiques et anecdotiques*. 3 vols. Paris: Collin, 1808.

Feldman, Martha. "Magic Mirrors and the *Seria* Stage: Thoughts Toward a Ritual View." *JAMS* 48 (1995): 423–84.

Fido, Franco. *Guida a Goldoni: Teatro e società nel Settecento*. Turin: Einaudi, 1977.

Floros, Constantin. *Zu Mozarts Sinfonik, Opern- und Kirchenmusik*. Vol. 1 of *Mozart-Studien*. Wiesbaden: Breitkopf und Härtel, 1979.

Ford, Charles. *Così? Sexual Politics in Mozart's Operas*. Manchester: Manchester University Press, 1991.

Foucault, Michel. *The Order of Things*. New York: Pantheon, 1970.

"What is an Author?" In Harari, *Textual Strategies*.

Frängsmyr, Tore, ed. *Linnaeus: The Man and his Work*. Berkeley and Los Angeles: University of California Press, 1983.

Frenzel, Elisabeth. *Stoff-, Motiv- und Symbolforschung*. Stuttgart: Metzler, 1963.

Frevert, Ute. *Women in German History: From Bourgeois Emancipation to Sexual Liberation*. Trans. Stuart McKinnon-Evans. Oxford: Berg, 1989.

Fried, Michael. *Absorption and Theatricality: Painting and Beholder in the Age of Diderot*. Berkeley and Los Angeles: University of California Press, 1979.

Frye, Northrop. *Anatomy of Criticism*. Princeton: Princeton University Press, 1957.

"Towards Defining an Age of Sensibility." In Bloom, *Poets of Sensibility and the Sublime*.

Fyfe, Gordon and John Law, eds. *Picturing Power: Visual Depiction and Social Relations*. London: Routledge, 1988.

Gallarati, Paolo. *Musica e maschera. Il libretto italiano del Settecento*. Turin: EDT, 1984.

"Music and Masks in Lorenzo Da Ponte's Mozartian Librettos." *COJ* 1 (1989): 225–47.

La forza delle parole: Mozart drammaturgo. Turin: Einaudi, 1993.

Gerber, Ernst Ludwig. "Etwas über den sogenannten Musikalischen Styl." *AMZ* 2.19 (Feb. 6, 1799): 295–96.

Gidwitz, Patricia Lewy. "'Ich bin die erste Sängerin': Vocal Profiles of Two Mozart Sopranos." *EM* 19 (1991): 565–79.

"Vocal Profiles of Four Mozart Sopranos." PhD diss., University of California, Berkeley, 1991.

Girdham, Jane Catherine. "Stephen Storace and the English Opera Tradition of the Late Eighteenth Century." PhD diss., University of Pennsylvania, 1988.

Girdlestone, Cuthbert. *Mozart and His Piano Concertos*. Second edition. London: Cassell, 1958.

Goehring, Edmund J. "Despina, Cupid and the Pastoral Mode of *Cosi fan tutte*." *COJ* 7 (1995): 107–35.

Goethe, Johann Wolfgang von. *Gespräche mit Goethe in den letzten Jahren seines Lebens / Johann Peter Eckermann*, ed. Fritz Bergemann. 2 vols. Wiesbaden: Insel-Verlag, 1955.

Goldin, Daniela. "Mozart, Da Ponte e il linguaggio dell'opera buffa." In *La vera fenice: Librettisti e libretti tra sette e ottocento*. Turin: Einaudi, 1985.

"In margine al catalogo di Leporello." In *La vera fenice*.

Goldoni, Carlo. *Tutte le opere di Carlo Goldoni*. Ed. Giuseppe Ortolani. 14 vols. Milan: A. Mondadori, 1952.

The Comic Theater. Trans. John W. Miller. Lincoln: University of Nebraska Press, 1969.

Green, Rebecca Lee. "Power and Patriarchy in Haydn's Goldoni Operas," PhD diss., University of Toronto, 1995.

Greenblatt, Stephen. "Towards a Poetics of Culture." in *The New Historicism Reader*, ed. H. Aram Veeser. New York: Routledge, 1989.

Grundsätze zur Theaterkritik, über Einsicht Sprache und Spiel in Menschenhaß und Reue. Vienna: Joseph Georg Oehler, 1790.

Hadamowsky, Franz. "Das Spieljahr 1753/4 des Theaters nächst dem Kärntnerthor und des Theaters nächst der K. K. Burg." *Jahrbuch der Gesellschaft für Wiener Theaterforschung* 11 (1959): 3–21.

Die Wiener Hoftheater (Staatstheater) 1776–1966. Verzeichnis der aufgeführten Stücke mit Bestandnachweis und täglichem Spielplan. 2 vols. Vienna: Prachner, 1966.

Hagstrum, Jean. *Sex and Sensibility: Ideal and Erotic Love from Milton to Mozart*. Chicago: University of Chicago Press, 1980.

Harari, Josué, ed. *Textual Strategies: Perspectives in Post-Structuralist Criticism*. Ithaca: Cornell University Press, 1979.

Heartz, Daniel. "Opera and the Periodization of Eighteenth-Century Music." *Report of the Tenth Congress of the International Musicological Society, Ljubljana 1967*. Kassel: Bärenreiter, 1970.

"The Creation of the Buffo Finale in Italian Opera." *PRMA* 104 (1977–78): 67–78.

"Goldoni, *Don Giovanni* and the *dramma giocoso*." *MT* 120 (1979): 993–98. Rev. in Heartz, *Mozart's Operas*.

"Vis comica: Goldoni, Galuppi and *L'arcadia in Brenta* (Venice 1749)." In *Venezia e il melodramma nel settecento* ed. Maria Teresia Muraro, vol. 2. Florence: Olschki, 1981.

"Nicolas Jadot and the Building of the Burgtheater." *MQ* 68 (1982): 1–31.

"Haydn und Gluck im Burgtheater um 1760: Der neue krumme Teufel, Le Diable à quatre, und die Sinfonie 'Le Soir.'" In *Bericht über den Internationalen Musikwissenschaftlichen Kongress Bayreuth 1981*, ed. Christoph-Hellmut Mahling and Sigrid Wiesmann. Kassel: Bärenreiter, 1983.

"Constructing *Le nozze di Figaro*." *JRMA* 112 (1987): 77–98. Repr. in Heartz, *Mozart's Operas*.

"An Iconography of the Dances in the Ballroom Scene of *Don Giovanni*." In Heartz, *Mozart's Operas*.

Mozart's Operas. Edited, with contributing essays, by Thomas Bauman. Berkeley and Los Angeles: University of California Press, 1990.

Haydn, Mozart and the Viennese School 1740–1780. New York: Norton, 1995.

"When Mozart Revises: Guglielmo in *Così*." In Sadie, *Wolfgang Amadè Mozart*.

Henze-Döhring, Sabine. *Opera Seria, Opera Buffa und Mozarts "Don Giovanni."* Laaber: Laaber Verlag, 1986. *AnM* 24 (1986).

Hepokoski, James. "Genre and Content in Mid-Century Verdi: 'Addio del passato' (*La Traviata*, Act III)." *COJ* 1 (1989): 249–76.

Herbert, Christopher. *Trollope and Comic Pleasure.* Chicago: University of Chicago Press, 1987.

Hildesheimer, Wolfgang. *Mozart.* Frankfurt am Main, 1977. Trans. Marion Faber. New York: Farrar, Straus, and Giroux, 1981.

Hill, George Birkbeck, ed. *Boswell's Life of Johnson.* Oxford: Clarendon Press, 1887.

Honolka, Kurt. *Papageno: Emanuel Schikaneder, Man of the Theater in Mozart's Time.* Trans. Jane Mary Wilde. Portland, OR: Amadeus, 1990.

Hume, Robert D. *The Rakish Stage: Studies in English Drama, 1660–1800.* Carbondale, IL: Southern Illinois University Press, 1983.

Hunter, Mary. "Haydn's Aria Forms: A Study of the Arias in the Italian Operas Written at Eszterháza, 1766–1783." PhD diss., Cornell University, 1982.

"Haydn's Sonata-Form Arias." *CM* 37/38 (1984): 19–32.

"'Pamela': the Offspring of Richardson's Heroine in Eighteenth-Century Opera." *Mosaic: A Journal for the Interdisciplinary Study of Literature* 18 (1985): 61–76.

"The Fusion and Juxtaposition of Genres in Opera Buffa 1770–1800: Anelli and Piccinni's Griselda." *M&L* 67 (1986): 363–80.

"Text, Music, and Drama in Haydn's Italian Opera Arias: Four Case Studies." *JM* 7 (1989): 29–57.

"Così fan tutte et les conventions musicales de son temps." *L'avant-scène opéra*, no. 131–2, 158–64.

"Some Representations of *Opera Seria* in *Opera Buffa*." *COJ* 3 (1991): 89–108.

"Landscapes, Gardens and Gothic Settings in the Opere Buffe of Mozart and his Italian Contemporaries." *CM* 51 (1993): 94–104.

"Rousseau, the Countess and the Female Domain." In *Mozart Studies* 2, ed. Cliff Eisen. London: Oxford University Press, 1997.

The Poetics of Entertainment: Opera Buffa in Vienna 1770–1790 (Princeton University Press, forthcoming).

Issacharoff, Michael. *Discourse as Performance.* Stanford, CA: Stanford University Press, 1989.

Jacquin, Nikolaus. *Anleitung zur Pflanzenkenntniss nach Linnés Methode: Zum Gebrauche seiner theoretischen Vorlesungen.* Vienna: Christian Friedrich Wappler, 1785.

Jahn, Otto. *W. A. Mozart*. Third edition, ed. Hermann Dieters. Leipzig: Breitkopf und Härtel, 1889–91.

Jameson, Frederic. *Postmodernism: Or, The Cultural Logic of Late Capitalism*. Durham, NC: Duke University Press, 1991.

Jordanova, L. J. "Naturalizing the Family: Literature and the Bio-Medical Sciences in the Late Eighteenth Century." In *Languages of Nature: Critical Essays on Science and Literature*, ed. L. J. Jordanova. New Brunswick, NJ: Rutgers University Press, 1986.

   Sexual Visions: Images of Gender in Science and Medicine between the Eighteenth and Twentieth Centuries. Madison: University of Wisconsin Press, 1989.

Kaunitz, Wenzel. "Reflexions sur les spectacles de la Ville de Vienne 1765." Quoted in Oscar Teuber, *Das k.k. Hofburgtheater seit seiner Begründung*. 2 vols. Vienna: Gesellschaft fur vervielfältigende Kunst, 1903–06.

Kelly, Michael. *Reminiscences of Michael Kelly, of the King's Theatre, and Theatre Royal Drury Lane, Including a Period of Nearly Half a Century: With Original Anecdotes of Many Distinguished Persons, Political, Literary and Musical*. 2 vols. London: H. Colburn, 1826.

Kerman, Joseph. *Opera as Drama*. Revised edition. Berkeley and Los Angeles: University of California Press, 1988.

Khevenhüller-Metsch, Rudolf and Hanns Schlitter, eds. *Aus der Zeit Maria Theresias: Tagebuch des Fürsten Johann Josef Khevenhüller-Metsch, kaiserlichen Obersthofmeisters 1742–1776*. 8 vols. Vienna: Holzhausen, 1907–25.

Kimbell, David. *Italian Opera*. Cambridge: Cambridge University Press, 1991.

Kivy, Peter. *Osmin's Rage: Philosophical Reflections on Opera, Drama, and Text*. Princeton: Princeton University Press, 1988.

   "Opera Talk: A Philosophical 'Phantasie.'" *COJ* 3 (1991): 63–77.

   "Composers and 'Composers': A Response to David Rosen." *COJ* 4 (1992): 179–86.

   "How Did Mozart Do It?" In *The Fine Art of Repetition: Essays in the Philosophy of Music*. Cambridge: Cambridge University Press, 1993.

Kramer, Lawrence. *Music as Cultural Practice*. Berkeley and Los Angeles: University of California Press, 1990.

Krebs, Roland. *L'Idée de «Théâtre National» dans L'Allemagne des Lumières: théorie et réalisations*. Wiesbaden: Harrassowitz, 1985.

Kritsch, Cornelia, and Herbert Zeman. "Das Rätsel eines genialen Opernentwurfs – Da Pontes Libretto zu *Così fan tutte* und das literarische Umfeld des 18. Jahrhunderts. "In *Die österreichische Literatur:*

ihr Profil an der Wende vom 18. zum 19. Jahrhundert (1750–1830), ed.
Herbert Zeman. Graz: Akademische Druck- und Verlagsanstalt,
1979.

Kunze, Stefan. *Don Giovanni vor Mozart: Die Tradition der Don-Giovanni-
Opern im italienischen Buffa-Theater des 18. Jahrhunderts*. Munich: Fink,
1972.

Mozarts Opern. Stuttgart: Reclam, 1984.

Landon, H. C. Robbins. *Mozart: The Golden Years*. New York: Schirmer,
1989.

Laqueur, Thomas. *Making Sex*. Cambridge, MA: Harvard University Press,
1990.

Lea, K. M. *Italian Popular Comedy: A Study of the Commedia dell'arte,
1560–1620, with Special Reference to the English Stage*. New York: Russell
and Russell, 1962.

Lessing, Gotthold Ephraim. *Selected Prose Works of G. E. Lessing*. Trans.
Helen Zimmern. London: G. Bell, 1913.

Hamburgische Dramaturgie. Ed. Otto Mann. Stuttgart: Kröner, 1963.

"Gotthold Ephraim Lessings theatralische Bibliothek: Lustspiel-
Abhandlungen." In *Gotthold Ephraim Lessing Werke*, vol. 4,
Dramaturgische Schriften, ed. Karl Eibl. Munich: Carl Hanser, 1973.

Levarie, Siegmund. *Mozart's "Le nozze di Figaro": A Critical Analysis*.
Chicago: University of Chicago Press, 1952.

Levin, Harry. "Notes on Conventions." In *Perspectives of Criticism*, ed.
Harry Levin. Cambridge, MA: Harvard University Press, 1950.

Levin, Robert. "Concertos." In *The Mozart Compendium*, ed. H. C. Robbins
Landon. New York: Schirmer, 1990.

Levy, Janet M. "Covert and Casual Values in Recent Writings about
Music." *JM* 6 (1987): 3–27.

Lewin, David. "Musical Analysis as Stage Direction." In *Music and Text:
Critical Inquiries*, ed. Steven Paul Scher. Cambridge: Cambridge
University Press, 1992.

Link, Dorothea. "The Da Ponte Operas of Vicente Martín y Soler." PhD
diss., University of Toronto, 1991.

"L'arbore di Diana: A Model for *Così fan tutte*." In Sadie, *Wolfgang Amadè
Mozart*.

Lipton, Kay. "The *Opere Buffe* of Pietro Alessandro Guglielmi in Vienna
and Eszterháza: Contributions to the Development of *Opera Buffa*
between 1768 and 1793." PhD diss., UCLA, 1995.

Lühning, Helga. "Die Rondo-Arie im späten 18. Jahrhundert:

Dramatischer Gehalt und musikalischer Bau." *Hamburger Jahrbuch für Musikwissenschaft* 5 (1981): 219–41.

Mackenzie, Barbara Dobbs. "The Creation of a Genre: Comic Opera's Dissemination in Italy in the 1740s." PhD diss., University of Michigan, 1993.

Manley, Lawrence. *Convention: 1500–1750.* Cambridge, MA: Harvard University Press, 1980.

Mann, William. *The Operas of Mozart.* New York: Oxford University Press, 1977.

Margolis, Joseph. "Genres, Laws, Canons, Principles." In *Rules and Conventions*, ed. Metje Hort. Baltimore: The Johns Hopkins University Press, 1992.

Marshall, David. *The Surprising Effects of Sympathy: Marivaux, Diderot, Rousseau and Mary Shelley.* Chicago: University of Chicago Press, 1988.

Mattern, Volker. *Das Dramma Giocoso: La Finta giardiniera: Ein Vergleich der Vertonungen von Pasquale Anfossi und Wolfgang Amadeus Mozart.* Laaber: Laaber Verlag, 1989.

Michtner, Otto. *Das alte Burgtheater als Opernbühne.* Vienna: Böhlaus, 1970.

Miller, Jonathan, ed. *The Don Giovanni Book: Myths of Seduction and Betrayal.* London: Faber and Faber, 1990.

Mitchell, David. "The Truth about 'Così.'" In *A Tribute to Benjamin Britten on His Fiftieth Birthday*, ed. Anthony Gishford. London: Faber and Faber, 1963.

Moore, Stacy. "'E risolvermi non so': Representations of Indecision in Opera Buffa Arias." Unpublished paper, Cornell University, 1994.

Muraro, Maria Teresa and David Bryant, eds. *I vicini di Mozart: Il teatro musicale tra Sette e Ottocento.* 2 vols. Florence: Olschki, 1989.

Nagel, Ivan. *Autonomy and Mercy: Reflections on Mozart's Operas.* Trans. Marion Faber and Ivan Nagel. Cambridge, MA and London: Harvard University Press, 1991.

Nicoll, Allardyce. *The World of Harlequin: A Critical Study of the Commedia dell'arte.* Cambridge: Cambridge University Press, 1963.

Noske, Frits. *The Signifier and the Signified: Studies in the Operas of Mozart and Verdi.* The Hague: Nijhoff, 1977.

Oakley, Ann. *The Captured Womb: A History of the Medical Care of Pregnant Women.* New York: Blackwell, 1984.

Osthoff, Wolfgang. "Mozarts Cavatinen und ihre Tradition." In *Festschrift Helmuth Osthoff zum siebzigsten Geburtstag*, ed. Wilhelm Stauder et al. Tutzing: Schneider, 1969.

"Die Opera Buffa." In *Gattungen der Musik in Einzeldarstellungen: Gedenkschrift Leo Schrade*, ed. Wulf Arlt, Ernst Lichtenhahn and Hans Oesch, vol. 1. Berne and Munich: Francke, 1973.

"Gli endecasillabi villotistici in *Don Giovanni* e *Le nozze di Figaro*." In *Venezia e il melodramma nel settecento*, ed. Maria Teresia Muraro, vol. 2. Florence: Olschki, 1981.

Parakilas, James Paul. "Mozart's *Tito* and the Music of Rhetorical Strategy." PhD diss., Cornell University, 1979.

"The Afterlife of *Don Giovanni*: Turning Production History into Criticism." *JM* 8 (1990): 251–65.

Parnell, Paul. "The Sentimental Mask." *PMLA* 78 (1963): 529–35.

Payer von Thurn, Rudolph. *Josef II als Theaterdirektor: Ungedruckte Briefe und Aktenstücke aus den Kinderjahren des Burgtheaters*. Vienna: Heidrich, 1920.

Pezzl, Johann. *Skizze von Wien*. 6 issues. Vienna, 1786–1790. Translated in H. C. Robbins Landon, *Mozart and Vienna*. New York: Schirmer, 1991.

Pichler, Caroline. *Denkwürdigkeiten aus meinem Leben*. Ed. Emil Karl Blümml. 2 vols. Munich: Georg Müller, 1914.

Planelli, Antonio. *Dell'opera in musica*. Naples, 1772. Quoted in Enrico Fubini, *Music and Culture in Eighteenth Century Europe*, trans. Bonnie J. Blackburn. Oxford: Oxford University Press, 1994.

Platoff, John. "Music and Drama in the Opera Buffa Finale: Mozart and His Contemporaries in Vienna." PhD diss., University of Pennsylvania, 1984.

"Musical and Dramatic Structure in the Opera Buffa Finale." *JM* 7 (1989): 191–230.

"The Buffa Aria in Mozart's Vienna." *COJ* 2 (1990): 99–120.

"Tonal Organization in 'Buffo' Finales and the Act II Finale of 'Le nozze di Figaro.'" *M&L* 72 (1991): 387–403.

"How Original was Mozart? Evidence from *Opera Buffa*." *EM* 20 (1992): 105–18.

"A new history for Martín's 'Una cosa rara.'" *JM* 12 (1994): 85–115.

"Myths and Realities about Tonal Planning in Mozart's Operas." *COJ* 8 (1996): 1–16.

Mozart and Opera Buffa in Vienna, 1783–1791. Oxford University Press, forthcoming.

Powers, Harold S. Unpublished study of Verdi's *Otello*, 1984.

Preziosi, Donald. *Rethinking Art History: Meditations on a Coy Science*. New Haven: Yale University Press, 1989.

Prince, Gerald. *A Dictionary of Narratology*. Lincoln, NE: University of Nebraska Press, 1987.

Quadrio, Francesco Saverio. *Della storia e della ragione: D'ogni poesia*. 3 vols. Milan: Agnelli, 1744.

Rabin, Ronald J. "Mozart, Da Ponte, and the Dramaturgy of Opera Buffa: Italian Comic Opera in Vienna, 1783–1791." PhD diss., Cornell University, 1996.

Rand, Erica. "Depoliticizing Women: Female Agency, the French Revolution, and the Art of Boucher and David." *Genders* 7 (1990): 47–68.

Rastall, Richard. "Vocal Range and Tessitura in Music from York Play 45." *Music Analysis* 3 (1984): 181–99.

Ratner, Leonard. *Classic Music: Expression, Form, and Style*. New York: Schirmer, 1980.

Regn, Gerhard. "Jenseits der 'commedia borghese': Komödienspiel, Karnevalisierung und moralische Lizenz in Goldonis 'Locandiera.'" *Germanisch-Romanische Monatsschrift*, n.s., 44 (1994): 324–44.

Rendle, A. B. "Letters of J. F. von Jacquin (1788–90)." *The Journal of Botany* 61 (1923): 287–90.

Rice, John A. "Rondò vocali di Salieri e Mozart per Adriana Ferrarese." In Muraro, *I vicini*.

"Vienna under Joseph II and Leopold II." In *Man and His Music: The Classical Era: From the 1740s to the End of the 18th Century*, ed. Neal Zaslaw. Englewood Cliffs, NJ: Prentice Hall, 1989.

W. A. Mozart: "La clemenza di Tito." Cambridge: Cambridge University Press, 1991.

"Mozart and his Singers: the Case of Maria Marchetti Fantozzi, the first Vitellia." *OQ* 11 (1995): 31–52.

Antonio Salieri and Viennese Opera. University of Chicago Press, forthcoming.

Richardson, Samuel. *Pamela; Or, Virtue Rewarded*. Ed. Peter Sabor. New York: Penguin, 1980.

Richter, Joseph. "Ein Beytrag zum Patriotismus und Theatergeschmack der Wiener." In *Der Zuschauer in Wien, oder Gerade so sind die Wiener und Wienerinnen*. Third edition, in 6 vols. Vienna: Hochenleitter, 1790. Vol. 5, pp. 13–22.

Riedt, Heinz. *Carlo Goldoni*. Trans. Ursule Molinaro. New York: Ungar, 1974.

Robinson, Michael F. *Naples and Neapolitan Opera*. Oxford: Clarendon Press, 1972.

Robinson, Michael F., with the assistance of Ulrike Hofmann. *Giovanni Paisiello: A Thematic Catalogue of his Works*. 2 vols. Stuyvesant, NY: Pendragon Press, 1991–94.

Rosand, Ellen. "Operatic Ambiguities and the Power of Music." *COJ* 4 (1992): 75–80.

Rosen, Charles. *The Classical Style: Haydn, Mozart. Beethoven*. New York: Viking, 1971.

Rosen David. "Cone's and Kivy's 'World of Opera.'" *COJ* 4 (1992): 61–74.

Rushton, Julian. *W. A. Mozart: "Don Giovanni."* Cambridge: Cambridge University Press, 1987.

"Mozart's Art of Rhetoric: Understanding an Opera Seria ('Deh se piacer mi vuoi' from *La clemenza di Tito*)." *Contemporary Music Review*, forthcoming.

"Villains and Voice Types: Towards a Methodology of Operatic Characterization." In *Acta Semiotica Fennica*, forthcoming.

Russell, Charles C. *The Don Juan Legend before Mozart; With a Collection of Eighteenth-Century Opera Librettos*. Ann Arbor: University of Michigan Press, 1993.

Sadie, Stanley, ed., *The New Grove Dictionary of Opera*. 4 vols. London: Macmillan, 1992.

Wolfgang Amadè Mozart: Essays on his Life and his Music. Oxford: Clarendon Press, 1996.

Sartori, Claudio. *I libretti italiani a stampa dalle origini al 1800*. 7 vols. Milan: Bertola and Locatelli, 1990–95.

Scheibe, Johann Adolph. *Der critische Musikus*. Second edition. Leipzig, 1745. Facs. reprint Hildesheim: Olms, 1970.

Schenbeck, Lawrence. "*Ecco il fellon*: Leporello as picaresque hero." Paper presented at *Mozart: 200 Years of Research* at Hofstra University, February 1991.

Schiebinger, Londa. "The Private Life of Plants: Sexual Politics in Carol Linnaeus and Erasmus Darwin." In *Science and Sensibility: Gender and Scientific Inquiry, 1780–1945*, ed. Marina Benjamin. London: Blackwell, 1991.

"Why Mammals are called Mammals: Gender Politics in Eighteenth-Century Natural History." *American Historical Review* 98 (1993): 382–421.

Schindler, Otto G. "Das Publikum des Burgtheaters in der Josephinischen Ära: Versuch einer Strukturbestimmung." In *Das Burgtheater und sein Publikum*, ed. Margret Dietrich. Vienna: Verlag der Österreichischen Akademie der Wissenschaften, 1976.

Segre, Cesare. *Teatro e Romanzo*. Turin: Einaudi, 1984.

Introduction to the Analysis of the Literary Text. Trans. John Meddemmen. Bloomington: University of Indiana Press, 1988.

Singer, Irving. *Mozart & Beethoven: The Concept of Love in their Operas*. Baltimore and London: The Johns Hopkins University Press, 1977.

Sisman, Elaine R. "Haydn's Theater Symphonies." *JAMS*, 43 (1990): 292–352.

Haydn and the Classical Variation. Cambridge, MA: Harvard University Press, 1993.

Mozart: The "Jupiter" Symphony. Cambridge: Cambridge University Press, 1993.

Smith, Adam. *The Theory of Moral Sentiments*. London, 1759. Reprinted New York: Garland, 1971.

Sonnenfels, Joseph von. *Briefe über die wienerische Schaubühne von J.v.: Sonnnenfels*. Vienna: C. Konegen, 1884.

Briefe über die Wienerische Schaubühne. Ed. Hilde Haider-Pregler. Graz: Akademische Druck- und Verlagsanstalt, [1988].

Stafleu, Frans. *Linnaeus and the Linnaeans: The Spreading of their Ideas in Systematic Botany 1735–1789*. Utrecht: A. Oosthoek's Uitgeversmaatschappij N.V. for the International Association for Plant Taxonomy, 1971.

Staiger, Emil, ed. *Der Briefwechsel zwischen Schiller und Goethe*. Frankfurt: Insel-Verlag, 1966.

Steptoe, Andrew. *The Mozart-Da Ponte Operas: The Cultural and Musical Background*. Oxford: Clarendon Press, 1988.

Sternfeld, Frederick. "The Birth of Opera: Ovid, Poliziano and the *lieto fine*." *Studien zur italienisch-deutschen Musikgeschichte* 12: 30–47. Cologne: Arno Volk, 1979. *AnM* 19.

Stiefel, Richard. "Mozart's Seductions." *CM* 36 (1983): 151–66.

Strohm, Reinhard. "Merkmale italienischer Versvertonung in Mozarts Klavierkonzerten." *AnM* 18 (1978): 219–36.

Die italienische Oper im 18. Jahrhundert. Wilhelmshaven: Heinrichshofen, 1979.

"Zur Metrik in Haydns and Anfossis 'La vera costanza.'" In *Joseph Haydn: Bericht über den internationalen Joseph Haydn Kongress Wien . . . 1982*, ed. Eva Badura Skoda. Munich: Henle, 1986.

"Auf der Suche nach dem Drama im dramma per musica: Die Bedeutung der französischen Tragödie." In *De Musica et Cantu: Studien zur Geschichte und der Oper*, ed. Peter Cahn and Ann-Katrin Heimer. Hildesheim: Olms, 1993.

"Händel-Oper und Regeldrama." In *Zur Dramaturgie der Barockoper: Bericht über die Symposien der Internationalen Händel-Akademie Karlsruhe 1992 und 1993*, ed. Hans Joachim Marx. Laaber: Laaber Verlag, 1994.

Sulzer, Johann Georg. *Allgemeine Theorie der schönen Künste*. 2 vols. Leipzig: Weidmann, 1771–74.

Till, Nicholas. *Mozart and the Enlightenment: Truth, Virtue, and Beauty in Mozart's Operas*. London and Boston: Faber and Faber, 1991.

Todd, Janet M. *Sensibility: an Introduction*. London: Methuen, 1986.

Troy, Charles R. *The Comic Intermezzo: A Study in the History of Eighteenth-Century Italian Opera*. Ann Arbor: UMI Press, 1980.

Tyson, Alan. "'Le nozze di Figaro': Lessons from the Autograph Score." *MT* 122 (1981): 456–61.

Mozart: Studies of the Autograph Scores. Cambridge, MA: Harvard University Press, 1987.

"Some Features of the Autograph Score of *Don Giovanni*." *Israel Studies in Musicology* 5 (1990): 7–26.

Van Sant, Ann Jessie. *Eighteenth-Century Sensibility and the Novel: The Senses in Social Context*. Cambridge: Cambridge University Press, 1993.

Waldoff, Jessica. "The Music of Recognition: Operatic Enlightenment in *The Magic Flute*." *M&L* 75 (1994): 214–35.

"The Music of Recognition in Mozart's Operas." PhD diss., Cornell University, 1995.

Waldoff, Jessica and James Webster. "Operatic Plotting in *Le nozze di Figaro*." In Sadie, *Wolfgang Amadè Mozart*.

Warburton, Ernest, ed. *The Librettos of Mozart's Operas*. 5 vols. New York and London: Garland, 1991.

Wasserman, Earl. "The Sympathetic Imagination in Eighteenth-Century Theories of Acting." *Journal of English and Germanic Philology* 46 (1947): 264–72.

Webster, James, "To Understand Verdi and Wagner We Must Understand Mozart," *19CM* 11 (1987–88): 175–93.

"Cone's 'Personae' and the Analysis of Opera." *CMS* 29 (1989): 44–65.

"Mozart's Operas and the Myth of Musical Unity." *COJ* 2 (1990): 197–218.

"The Analysis of Mozart's Arias." In *Mozart Studies*, ed. Cliff Eisen. Oxford: Clarendon Press, 1991.

Haydn's "Farewell" Symphony and the Idea of Classical Style: Through-Composition and Cyclic Integration in his Instrumental Music. Cambridge: Cambridge University Press, 1991.

"Are Mozart's Concertos 'Dramatic'? Concerto Ritornellos and Aria

Introductions in the 1780s." In *Mozart's Concertos: Text, Context, Interpretation*, ed. Neal Zaslaw. Ann Arbor: University of Michigan Press, 1996.

"Ambivalenzen um Mendelssohn: Zwischen Werk und Rezeption." In *Felix Mendelssohn Bartholdy: Kongreß-Bericht Berlin 1994*, ed. Christian Martin Schmidt. Wiesbaden: Breitkopf and Härtel, 1997.

Weinbrot, Howard. "Northrop Frye and the Literature of Process Reconsidered." *Eighteenth Century Studies* 24 (1990–91): 173–95.

Weinstein, Leo. *The Metamorphoses of Don Juan*. Stanford: Stanford University Press, 1959.

Weiss, Piero. "Carlo Goldoni, Librettist: The Early Years." PhD diss., Columbia University, 1970.

Werner-Jensen, Karin. *Studien zur "Don Giovanni"–Rezeption im 19. Jahrhundert (1800–1850)*. Tutzing: Schneider, 1980.

Wheelock, Gretchen A. *Haydn's Ingenious Jesting with Art: Contexts of Musical Wit and Humor*. New York: Schirmer, 1992.

"*Schwarze Gredel* and the Engendered Minor Mode in Mozart's Operas." In *Musicology and Difference: Gender and Sexuality in Music Scholarship*, ed. Ruth A. Solie. Berkeley and Los Angeles: University of California Press, 1993.

Williams, Bernard. "Mozart's Comedies and the Sense of an Ending." *MT* 122 (1981): 451–54.

"Don Giovanni as an Idea." In Julian Rushton, *W. A. Mozart: "Don Giovanni."*

Whittall, Arnold. "'Forceful Muting' or 'Phatic Dithering'? Some Recent Writing on Opera." *M&L* 71 (1990): 65–71.

Will, Richard James. "Programmatic Symphonies of the Classical Period." PhD diss., Cornell University, 1994.

Witkin, Robert. *Art and Social Structure*. Cambridge: Blackwell, 1995.

Witz, Anne. *Professions and Patriarchy*. London: Routledge, 1991.

Wochnik, Regina. *Die Musiksprache in den opere semiserie Joseph Haydns unter besonderer Berücksichtigung von L'incontro improvviso*. Eisenach-Hamburg: Wagner, 1993.

Zechmeister, Gustav. *Die Wiener Theater nächst der Burg und nächst dem Kärntnerthor von 1747 bis 1776*. Vienna: Böhlaus, 1971.

Zopelli, Luca. *L'opera come racconto: Modi narrativi nel teatro musicale dell'Ottocento*. Venice: Marsilio, 1994.

Index

Page numbers in boldface type refer to illustrations and musical examples.

character as performer, 15, 103–04
compared to similar arias, 248–54
as representation of buffo aria, 19,
103, 257–58
significance, 235
"Canzonetta sull'aria" (letter duet),
70, **71**, 213
"Cosa sento! tosto andate," 324, **331**
"Deh vieni non tardar," 213, 235
as having typical opera buffa
elements, 103, 154–55
"Dove sono," 237
"In quegl'anni," 323
"La vendetta," 247, 257
"Non più andrai," 236, 248, 255, 415
"Porgi amor," 14, 236, 322, 327
"Vo pensando" compared to,
369–74, **371**, 372–74
"Se vuol ballare," 248, 255, 256–57,
414–15
"Susanna, or via sortite," 380
"Vedrò mentri'io sospiro," 237
"Venite, inginocchiatevi," 236, 324,
331
class and gender tensions, 85, 159
ending, 293, 294
Figaro in
as anti-*primo buffo* and complex, 11,
247
arias for, 248–49, 253–58, 413, 416,
416, 418
as misogynist, 235, 249
and role-playing, 247–48
French source, **59**, 60, 70, 73
gardens and flower imagery in,
154–55, 159
libretto, 50, 64–65, 69, 110
new dramatic humanism, 102, 105
opera buffa elements in, 103
reception and commentary on, 195
revival in 1789, 341n

score, French influences, 68–69, 80
singers for, 48–49, 407, **408**, 409

oca del Cairo, L' (Mozart), 99, 106, 257,
386n
Olimpiade, L' (Metastasio / Gassmann),
39
"Gemo in un punto e fremo," 234n
opera, 18th century, modern studies
analysis equated with interpretation,
372, 374–76
analytical research, 312–15, 376–77
concept of multivalence, 16, 17,
338–39, 340
general theses, 340–42
and value-judgments, avoidance of,
12–14, 343, 372–74
opera buffa
background and history, 1, 5–6, 25
characteristics, 5–6, 73, 99, 197, 232
composers, Mozart vs. the "others,"
12–14, 233, 343–44
ending with tutti, 263–64, 266
French models for, 54, 56–57, 58, **59**,
60–65
French musical influences, 66–80
Goldoni on, 37–39, 88, 99
influence and prestige of French
theatre, 57, 80–81
Mozart and, 48, 57, 98–99, 109, 110, 195
and musical styles, 43, 198, 201, 202
and opera seria, 197, 198
plots, criticism of, 57–58, 60, 63
recent study of, 2–5
text vs. music, 195–96
see also ensembles, opera buffa
opera buffa in Vienna
advent, 25, 32, 35
contexts for, 1, 146–47
distintegration of, 46–47
in German translation, 47